ASIA IN THE EUROPEAN AGE
1498–1955

ASIA IN THE
EUROPEAN AGE
1498-1955

MICHAEL EDWARDES

FREDERICK A. PRAEGER
Publisher
New York

BOOKS THAT MATTER

Published in the United States of America in 1962
by Frederick A. Praeger, Inc., Publisher
64 University Place, New York 3, N.Y.

Library of Congress Catalog Card Number: 62–19665

To Reay Edwardes

PRINTED IN HOLLAND BY N.V. DRUKKERIJ THIEME, NIJMEGEN

CONTENTS

PREFACE

THIS WORK supplies a short history of Asia in colonial times, in the form of an outline of the political events that took place under the impact of European expansion. In the wider framework of these happenings, I have also attempted to give some explanation of the motives of colonial aggression, of the impulses that set the conquerors on their way, and the ideas that sustained them in their imperial pretensions.

The nature of enduring conquest – and the four hundred and fifty years which encompassed the rise, fulfilment, and collapse of European dominance in Asia may be said to have at least some of the elements of continuity – is twofold. The sword of the conqueror is inevitably followed, in greater or lesser degree, by the spirit of his institutions. The *pax Romana* spread not only peace but the *mores* of the Romans. The *pax Britannica* and its imitators inevitably exported the political, social and philosophical ideas of the West. As a consequence, Asia was subjected to the impact of European ideas, and the residues of this exposure are now integral to the structure of independent Asia. Because of this, I have given an interpretation of the effect of European ideas upon Asians themselves – for it was out of these that Asians forged the weapons with which they won their freedom. It is in the impact of West on East, and in its consequences, that lies part of the explanation of Asia's 'strangeness' today, of leaders who may at one moment appear just like Europeans and Americans – the inheritors of common institutions – and the next, as inscrutably different, untrustworthy, and misunderstood. I have also tried to explain something of the nature of the Communist challenge to the new nations that have succeeded the old empires, and to show that its roots lie in the four and a half centuries of Asia's 'European Age'. If I have succeeded, the 'lovehate' feelings of the new Asia for the old European colonial powers and for Russia and the United States of America as well will be seen as an inevitable consequence of colonial rule. But these perhaps confusing attitudes are only symptoms of an immense and exciting transformation that is also fraught with the most alarming consequences, not only for Asia but for the world. The 'new' Asia does not yet exist; parturition is still in progress. When it *is* born, it will be the product of mixed parenthood, and an understanding of, and sympathy for, its complex heredity is essential if the West is to appreciate the problems of the new nations of Asia and respond to them in a dynamic and positive manner. This work is intended as a contribution – a very minor one – to that end.

The sources of this book are wide and diverse. Such printed works as have been quoted from and have influenced the formation of my ideas are given in the footnotes. To list the many individuals from whose suggestions and conversation I have benefited would, however indirectly, involve them in at least some quite undeserved share in any errors or misinterpretations which are contained in this work, and for which the only responsibility is mine. It would, however, have been impossible for me to have written as I have, without the understanding and patience of many friends, Asian, European and American, who have willingly submitted over the years to my tedious catechisms of 'how' and 'why'.

But there is one to whom a precise debt must be acknowledged. For typing the manuscript, for translating my almost illegible handwriting into tolerable English prose, and for listening with constructive scepticism to the more arcane arguments, I have to thank the person to whom this book is gratefully dedicated.

INTRODUCTION

The European Age

Europe's colonization of the world was neither a chain of crimes nor a chain of beneficence; it was the birth of the modern world itself.

HERBERT LÜTHY

THIS WORK might well be described as a study in revolution, for, basically, the imperialism of Europe in Asia, with which it is concerned, was an extension of the spiritual, scientific and material revolution that began in the West with the Renaissance. This conception may well be difficult to accept today when the era of European domination over the rest of mankind is too near to us, too reminiscent of blood and anger, oppression, racial discrimination and economic exploitation, for such dispassionate evaluation. Nevertheless, it is not unreasonable to think that this may well be the verdict of history.

Imperialism had a positive as well as a negative side. Today, the residues of both remain to interact with each other in this great time of transition and change in which we live. But memory is, above all things, highly selective; the evil that men do has a better chance of survival than their good. The 'evils' of imperialism still live on in the slogans of Communist and non-Communist alike. All attempt to call in the past to redress the balance of the present. Many of Asia's leaders, finding the day of freedom not quite as rosy as its dawn, still fight the past like club bores reliving the actions of forgotten battles. But with a difference. The battles are not forgotten; they are too near for that. The evils of imperialism are still convenient explanations for current problems. As nowhere else, the burden of the past presses heavily upon Asia, and its weight distorts the patterns of today.

But what is this burden? Much of it still consists of the oversimplified 'facts' that are not history but the propaganda of revolt, convenient but obscure phrases that sound well in manifestos but do not stand up to scrutiny. And yet, as with all slogans of rebellion, they contain a core of truth, though sometimes it is very small and made up of not quite the ingredients we might expect. It is the need to examine the facts behind the slogans that, among other things, this book attempts to satisfy.

*   *   *

Though it is without doubt true that imperialism *was* the diffuser of Western civilisation, this diffusion was not the primary purpose of the imperialists, nor must it be thought that imperialism was the ideal instrument for that diffusion; nor, for that matter, that the civilisation it brought was superior to that of the people it conquered. That a nation is stronger and wealthier is no indication that it has a higher civilisation. Neither do I wish to suggest that more peaceful methods of cultural diffusion could not have been used. This is a matter for speculation. What is incontrovertible is that the European nations, driven outwards by the force of their own revolution, took the ideas of that revolution with them and – in varying degrees according to their temperament – imposed them on those they came to dominate. Europe's *mission civilisatrice* was an essential part of the baggage of imperialism. In some periods it formed a larger part than in others. The rest of the weight was made up of more constant burdens, the desire for profit and power, and the continuing rivalries of nations. But whatever the imperialists' motives – and none expanded their rule out of altruistic love for their worse-off brethren in foreign lands – the impact of Western civilisation could not be deflected. Imperialism was, by its very nature, revolutionary, a destroyer of old orders and imposer of new. So it makes little difference whether or not the empire-builder consciously sought to transform the native society he found. To deny access to European ideas by preventing colonial subjects from acquiring Western languages or education, as the Dutch did in Indonesia, merely delayed the impact.

Whether the actions of the imperialists were 'good' or 'bad' in any absolute sense is a matter for philosophers and moralists. The record of imperialism is not a pleasant one by any standards. But the expansion of Europe in Asia was, to say the least, haphazard; once the momentum began to build up, there was very little to stop it. Though at times statesmen, historians, and philosophers, even poets and novelists, examined with great seriousness the consequences of European rule over alien societies – and they occasionally influenced policy by doing so – the extension of European dominion was in essence the result of an explosive dynamism and power to sustain it, at a time when Asia was to a large extent static and without the will or the strength to resist.

The high peak of the European Age was undoubtedly the nineteenth century. Before that, Europeans had gone to Asia as merchants, as travelling salesmen of an expanding merchant economy. Only the Portuguese took with them a grandiose conception of a universal empire ruled by Christ. It was not until the beginning of the nineteenth century that Great Britain, because of the material consequences of her industrial revolution, could afford to think in similar but less mystical terms. Secure in her overwhelming strength, Britain became the purveyor of a higher material and spiritual civilisation whose boons she did not hesitate to force upon her subjects. To a large extent, however, the forcing was upon willing, even anxious, disciples. The success of power inspires desire, the desire above all to acquire the secrets of that success. But it was not only in the actual possessions of Britain and the other colonial powers that Asians felt such a desire. Basically, even the wish to acquire the secrets of Western material success was the craving for a status symbol, for the re-acquisition of some sense of identity, even if this had to be in the terms of the conqueror. Shrewd observers in Japan, realising that to maintain their independence they must acquire the weapons of Western science, carried out a uniquely successful attempt to drag their country into the modern world before they were forced into it by conquest. Because the indigenous societies of Asia had failed to produce out of themselves a new strength with which to resist the West, only one possible course of action remained – to adopt Western ideas. Traditional culture, and its values, was pushed aside as reactionary and impeding, and Asia's struggle against the West was directed towards achieving the material benefits of the West without its political domination.

Because Britain was the dominant power in Asia in the nineteenth century – the Portuguese empire was in decay and the Dutch, though they came early to Asia, were comparatively late in adopting the rôle of rulers, as were the French – a great deal of the history of Asia in that century, and in the present, is the history of Britain in Asia. Furthermore, it was Britain who, believing in the 'goodness' of her own civilisation, passed on (however sparingly) the main bulk of European ideas. Her colonial policy, ill-formulated as it was, and distorted by the arrogance and bloody-mindedness of some of her empire-builders, was in a profound sense 'progressive'. The reasons for this are complex and by no means altruistic. The expansion of Western-style

education in India was not primarily designed to extend the boons of civilisation to the Indians, but as a long-range instrument of rule. In the nineteenth century, the English were business men, interested first in efficient, and
therefore cheap, administration, and in the production of customers. Education was expanded to supply men for the lower grades of administration, thus
saving money and maintaining the status of the white man by reserving
only the upper echelons of power for his exclusive use. But, having produced
a literate class, the British could not prevent it from reading books or, ultimately, from questioning its inferior rôle. It was those whose acquaintance with
Western ideas was most extensive who threatened the colonial power by
demanding freedom. It will be clear from the following pages that, though
some Englishmen saw this consequence as inevitable, there was no logical
policy other than the entirely pragmatic one behind it. 'No wise man has a
Policy', Kipling makes a viceroy remark in one of his short stories. 'A Policy
is the blackmail levied on the Fool by the Unforeseen. I am not the former,
and I do not believe in the latter.' This might well be the epitaph of nineteenth-century imperialism.

In the twentieth century, the position was to a large extent reversed. The
Unforeseen took its toll. The West, and Britain in particular, had begun to
doubt its own faith; the great dynamic had been eroded by the exercise of almost unquestioned power. The irony of the situation lies in the fact that, just
at the time when doubts assailed the imperialists, Asians were, after a period
of rejection, beginning to accept the civilisation that had been thrust upon
them and were looking forward to changing their own societies by it. In this
can be found the 'progressive' element of imperialism at work. The 'proof'
lies in the fact that it was – and still is – the Asians themselves who identified
it in that way.

But there are other elements in Asia's European Age which are not quite
as abstractly satisfying. From the very beginning, the impact of the West was
destructi It remains so today. Essentially, the impact was not very deep in
intensity; it shook the lower levels of traditional society but did not destroy
them. It imposed a new sector of society upon the old and produced men
who, in reality, belonged neither to East nor West. These men were both the
enemies of imperialism and, paradoxically, its most worthy product. In abstract, this may seem a matter for Western pride, but it might well be premature to indulge it. No real synthesis was accomplished in Asia's European
Age. The peoples who learned from the West learned only sufficient to ensure the end of imperialism itself. They did not necessarily acquire enough

knowledge to save themselves and the nations of which they found themselves rulers. This problem is not part of the structure of the present work. In any case, we are living through it, and its precise nature is only partly revealed.[1] Nevertheless, the principal purpose of the present work is to examine the past and, in doing so, to display the antecedents of today.

The history of Europe in Asia has a wider application than might be thought. Many of its elements were present, later only in time, in colonial Africa. Similar economic, political and cultural forces, once set in motion, have similar consequences despite wide divergences of time and situation, of ethnic and cultural background. Asia's response to the impact of the West has its parallel in the Africa of today. One of the characteristics of imperialism has been that it has forced upon the world stage new social classes who have, in themselves, duplicated Europe's own revolution. It is significant, and worth repeating, that the responses of the old order to the challenge of the West – the Indian Mutiny, the Boxers, or the 1930 rebellion in Burma – were the last upsurge of dying systems, and all fell to superior material strength. The men who beat the West at its own game were Western-style national leaders, who used the West's own weapons against itself. In one sense, the colonial struggle was between two Western-style élites. Between a doubting, weakened, dominant minority and a new dynamic one.

The positive impact of the West was limited; the whole affair a clash of numerically insignificant minorities. The inheritors of Western power in Asia are about as far away from the tradition-orientated majorities as the men they have displaced. This and other factors point to a belief that the revolution begun by the West is by no means over. The consequences of Asia's European Age are still part of the everyday of over half the population of the globe. This alone is surely sufficient reason for a constant reappraisal of the past.

*   *   *

The scope of this book stretches from one reasonable date, that of da Gama's landing at Calicut, to one arbitrary one, 1955. This date is taken because, though enclaves of Europe still remain in Asia, it was the year by which the major presences of Britain, Holland and France had disappeared. The division of the work into two parts is, however, more precise—the war of 1914–18 is one of the great watersheds of history.

[1] For a general appreciation of the consequences of imperial rule upon the Asia of today, see my *The Problems of Asia*. London and New York, 1961.

At the beginning, one can see the tentative exploration of the Portuguese, then the Dutch, and then the British and French, driven outwards by a mixture – varying in its proportions – of avarice, curiosity, missionary zeal, and straightforward bids for power *in Europe*. Soon the spheres of influence become reasonably precise, the claims are staked, and the inexorable logic of expansion – that it is always necessary to occupy a little more territory than one actually needs, in order to defend the piece one already holds – begins to appear. Soon, in turn, this period – one might almost call it the 'romantic era' of colonial adventure, a mixture of trade, politics and individual megalomania – expands into a larger, and perhaps duller, mould. Great Britain, blown outwards by the optimism of the first industrial revolution, begins to impose new ideas of administration and becomes the powerful evangelist of technical and material power, sitting astride the world, a nation of shopkeepers with branches in every bazaar in Asia. Other nations, feeling the new strength and purpose given to them by their own industrial revolutions, set out upon the imperial road. But this is different, for most of the prizes are in Britain's hands and Britain, despite her fears for her empire – threatened to the north, or so she thinks, by Russia's new imperial wave, and to the east in a much lesser degree by France and Holland – is too powerful to push aside. The new imperial powers turn to the vast bulk of China, but because it is too large for any single power to absorb (and as it is certainly not in anyone's interest that this should happen), the imperialists temporarily put aside their rivalries and join forces at the wake. The story of China in the nineteenth century is perhaps the most unpleasant in the whole of Asia's European Age. In the heyday of European power, no one could envisage the end of European domination over mankind. Imperialism was one of the pillars of the world order and nothing, it seemed, could topple it. But the decay had already begun. The war that broke out in 1914 was the beginning of the end.

Apart from the narrative of political events, this book contains short ideological studies of the nature and effects of European ideas, establishing first what they were, and then showing the extent of the transformation which they began. Political events are without meaning unless they are set into this wider context. One of the purposes of this work has been not merely to supply the scaffolding of events but some pertinent interpretation of them. Consequently, this is not a simple work of history in which the dry bones of the past are exhumed for the edification of professional anatomists. All historians have a purpose, a wider view, which in turn colours in varying degree their selection as well as their interpretation of events. From the foregoing pages it should be obvious to the intelligent reader that, to put it at its most crude, my aim has been to search in the past for those clues which help us to understand the present – and even, perhaps, the future. The criteria I have used may not be acceptable to more puritan historians, who allege that the facts always speak for themselves and should not be embroidered with explanations and interpretations. But, as most people know from their own experience, 'facts' often speak with conflicting voices. History is no different from everyday life – for it is the regurgitation of yesterday's life – and there is always the need for guidance. Especially today, when the pressure of events falls equally upon us all, the historian has a valuable function to perform, even if it is only to stimulate curiosity and questioning.

This study is offered with this intent alone. Certain aspects of Asia's European Age are missing altogether – the book has no pretensions to be encyclopaedic – others are dealt with briefly. Among the latter are the economics of empire, which demand a special study to themselves. However, economic factors are dealt with in their specific context of time and place. With all these deficiencies, however, the reader who continues to the end should gain some appreciation of the events, and of the nature, of one of the most significant eras in world history, one that to an unusual extent affects his own future – that of Asia's European Age.

Part One

THE LONG DEFEAT 1498-1914

I

The Gorgeous East

I

THE AUGMENTATION OF THE INDIES

'He does smile his face into more lines than are in the new map with the aug-
mentation of the Indies.'

SHAKESPEARE *Twelfth Night* Act III Scene 2

THE DECLARATION of the West's war against the East was the signing
by Spain and Portugal of the Treaty of Trodesilhas, on 9 June 1494. The
East figured in the treaty only as part of a grander conception – the division of
the world. For, by the terms of the treaty, Spain and Portugal fixed a line
through the Atlantic Ocean running north to south, 370 miles west of the
Cape Verde islands, as the frontier of their zones of activity. The treaty was
confirmed and expanded from a mere piece of sheep's stomach into a mandate from heaven, by the issue of a Bull by the Pope Alexander VI Borgia,
whose vicious face still leers at us from the canvases of Pinturicchio and
whose name has become – with some justification – a synonym for the dark
side of the Renaissance.

This *imprimatur* gave to Portuguese expansion in Asia the tone and vigour
of a crusade, a bursting outwards of passionate fervour for Christ and the
bringing into his fold of the pagan. It was also a great advantage – for God
and Mammon are often the best of allies – that the pagan was not only
pagan, but controller of a monopoly of trade from the East. All Europe's
imports from India and China and the islands of the East Indies came overland through the Persian Gulf, and were subject to tolls levied by the Muslim rulers of the countries through which they passed. Surely the best way to
defeat the heathen was not through costly battles and indecisive wars, but by
breaking his monopoly. This would also be a continuation of the war of liberation; for the peoples of the Iberian peninsula had once been ruled by
Arabian emirs, and had, in fact, fought over three thousand battles against
them between the tenth and the fifteenth centuries. Out of these battles, they
emerged as nations. Much of this history was part of immediate memory, for
the last emirate – of Granada – had not fallen until 1492.

Continuous wars had not exhausted the people of Spain and Portugal. On the contrary, they had been invigorated by them. It was a combination of surplus energy, religious fervour, the need for activity at a moment of strength, and a desire to increase the resources of a tiny country, that urged the Portuguese into their feats of exploration and conquest in Asia.

To destroy the transit trade of the Muslim powers, a route had to be found that bypassed their territories. There could be only one way – the long sea voyage that almost circumnavigated the coast of Africa. This was ventured with great courage and tribulation, and, one day in May 1498, after a journey lasting almost a year, three small ships and 160 men commanded by Vasco da Gama arrived in the waters off the port of Calicut, a town towards the bottom of the west coast of India. Muslim traders were well entrenched there, but the ruler was a Hindu.

A message sent to the king received a reply in the person of the mayor – to conduct da Gama to the city. On his way there, he was invited to enter an imposing building which he took to be a church. Inside, he saw the statue of a woman and, asking what it was, thought they replied: 'Mary! Mary! Mary!' Da Gama knelt down and gave thanks for his safe arrival.

That da Gama accepted the statue as that of the Virgin was by no means unreasonable, as a tradition of the existence of a church in India, founded by the Apostle Thomas, was well known in the West. The goddess in the temple was in all probability Kali, known in that part of India as Mari Amma, 'Mother of Epidemics.' The Portuguese were not to remain so naïve for long.

The little party of oddly-dressed Portuguese, in doublets, hose, and large cloaks, moved on to the palace and an audience with the king. Da Gama presented a letter from the king of Portugal asking for trade between them. The letter was not addressed by name, and had been provided for just such a contingency. The king of Calicut consulted with his ministers and, in a few days, permission was given for the Portuguese to take on cargo.

The Muslim traders, however, were not to take this lying down and sent the mayor – who was in their pay – to the king, with a tale that the Portuguese were criminals and their letter forged. In answer to these charges, da Gama produced a banner with a cross painted on it, and swore that they were not true. Perhaps the banner was viewed as a powerful talisman – fully acceptable in Asia, where magical objects abound even to this day – or the king intended to use da Gama as a threat against the Muslims, but, whatever the reason, permission to load a small cargo was renewed.

The merchants, however, were stronger than the king supposed. As da Gama and his party of twelve were making their way through the town to return to the ship, the mayor had them arrested, and da Gama was ordered to leave Calicut at once, without his cargo. Seven of the party were kept as hostages. An attempt was made to get a message to the king, but without success. The situation of the Portuguese ships was precarious, surrounded as they were by the vessels of the merchants. They had no alternative but to leave. But what of the hostages? Would they be released as promised? To make sure, an armed party of Portuguese was sent up the coast, twenty fisher-men were seized, taken aboard the ships, and sail was hoisted. At this, the seven hostages were taken to the wharf, and as soon as they were safe on board the fishermen were set free – except for a few who were taken back to Portugal as curiosities. All, however, was not over, for sixty small vessels at-tempted to intercept da Gama's little fleet. First-rate gunnery and magnificent seamanship soon scattered the opposition. Sea power and naval expertise had entered the history of Asia and soon would dominate it.

On his return to Portugal, da Gama advised the king that the Muslim traders could be driven from the seas. A series of expeditions was mounted. Portuguese forts spread from Ormuz at the north of the Persian Gulf and Aden at the beginning of the Red Sea, down the west coast of India, through Ceylon, to Malacca in present-day Malaya, and later to Macao in China. Most of this was achieved within a single generation. The fortresses were also ports and places of trade. Before the middle of the sixteenth century, the Por-tuguese controlled sea-borne trade between East and West. No Indian power seriously threatened the strength of their great fortresses, protected by the super-iority of Portuguese military science, and no European power challenged their supremacy at sea.

Great events, we were often told at school, spring from small beginnings, the oak's ancestor is the tiny acorn. In Asia, the heat of European expansion was produced by spices.

It is, perhaps, a little difficult for us to understand the importance of spices to the Elizabethans. It was dictated by a hunger more elemental than that for salvation, or the love of God, or even of gold. From autumn to spring, it was the lot of the Elizabethan nobles and magnates to eat salt meat. Even when fresh meat appeared once again in the summer, it was of poor quality, singu-larly without taste; and in order to protect the fishing industry, fish was eaten on more holy days than was comfortable. Such pallid food demanded pun-gent and exciting flavours. Spices were also part of the superiority of aristocrat over peasant. The rich needed their pepper just because they *were* rich. As they had no tea, they liked heavily spiced drinks. The Dutch, the British and the French were all to be driven by this visceral urge along the trade routes to the Spice Islands.

All had been reasonably well until 1580; English and Dutch merchants bought their spices and other exotics in the markets of Lisbon. But in that year, Spain annexed Portugal. The Dutch, then in revolt against their Spanish overlords, could no longer buy at the Portuguese capital. Neither could the English. Both were to burst out into great activity on the high seas, their Protestant nature giving them added justification in their quest for Eastern trade.

In England, Drake – who, in circumnavigating the globe, had reached the Spice Islands in 1579 – inspired the newly-emerging merchant classes with tales of the wealth of the Indies, a richness which Milton, nearly ninety years later, was to see as the only comparison to be made with that of Satan:

'High on a throne of royal state, which far
Outshone the wealth of Ormuz and of Ind,
Or where the gorgeous East with richest hand
Showers on her kings barbaric pearl and gold.'

But even before Drake's return in 1580, the right to trade with the Levant had been obtained from the Sultan of Turkey, and a company had been founded for the purpose. In 1583, a ship called the *Tyger* set sail with five passengers. Their destination, India. Little was thought of it at the time, but twenty years later the sailing of this little ship had become so much a part of everyday knowledge that Shakespeare, ever ready to use a popular allusion, enshrined it in *Macbeth*:

'"Aroint thee, witch!", the rump-fed ronyon cries.
Her husband's to Aleppo gone, master o' the *Tyger*.'

At Aleppo landed five Englishmen – John Eldred, John Newbery, Ralph Fitch, William Leeds and James Story – who set off on the overland route to India. Eldred was stopped between Basra and Baghdad, the other four were arrested by the Portuguese at Ormuz and reached India as prisoners. There they were fortunate in receiving help from the first Englishman to reach India, Thomas Stevens, a Jesuit missionary who had arrived there in 1579. Leeds, who was a painter, became a monk and stayed in Goa, the capital of Portuguese Asia. The other three escaped. Story, a jeweller, entered the service of the Mughal emperor; Newbery got to Lahore, set off home across Persia, and was never heard of again; Fitch wandered through south India,

Ceylon and Burma, and reappeared in London in 1591. He and Eldred were present when, on 24 September 1599, eighty merchants of the city of London met to establish the East India Company. One of the reasons given for its foundation was that, in the same year, the Dutch had raised the price of pepper from three shillings to eight shillings a pound.

From this we see that the Dutch are now the spice merchants. How did this come about?

*   *   *

Despite lack of access to the Lisbon entrepôt, spices were still available, since the Portuguese had never been more than wholesalers; the distributive trade was in the hands of merchants in northern Europe where the demand was greatest. In fact, the true centre of the spice trade had, by the middle of the sixteenth century, become the port of Antwerp. By 1592, the price demanded for spices had risen so steeply that the Dutch decided to enter the market by trading directly with the producers. In that year, at Amsterdam, a company was founded and in 1595 a Dutch fleet set out for the Indies. Two and a half years later, it returned depleted of ships and men but heavy with profit able merchandise. The Portuguese monopoly had been broken. In 1602, the company received a charter from the States General – the Dutch parliament – vesting in it a monopoly of trade and the right to exercise sovereign powers, conclude treaties, conquer territory and erect forts.

By 1604, the Portuguese had been declared the enemy in a treaty signed with the ruler of Calicut, 'with a view to the expulsion of the Portuguese from the territories of His Highness and the rest of India'. The offensive moved fitfully and irregularly, but always resulted in a defeat for the Portu guese. Amboyna, in the East Indies, fell to the Dutch in 1605, and Jakarta in 1619. In 1641, Malacca was taken; in 1654, Ceylon. By the end of the century, of the great string of forts that linked Portuguese Asia little was left but Goa, Daman, Diu and Macao. The Portuguese had also to contend with the growing power of native states. The Muslim sultanates of the Dec can, after defeating Portugal's ally, the king of Vijayanagar, formed an al liance which included even the ruler of Acheh in Sumatra. The settlements on the Malabar coast and at Malacca were attacked in 1565, but superior discipline and fire power again won out against the rabble of native troops. In 1632, the settlement of Hugli, near present day Calcutta, was captured by the forces of the Mughal emperor, Shah Jahan, and the Portuguese took to the sea that had brought and succoured them, and turned pirate in alliance with the king of Arakan. This alliance has its irony, for the ruler of Arakan, Thiri-thu-dhamma, believed he was a future Buddha and that his mission was to bring the world under the rule of a Universal Emperor. So came to-gether the exponents of two concepts of world government – the Portuguese with their priest-king, the Pope, and the Arakanese with a future Buddha. Both were doomed to failure. In 1683, the Marathas, about to become the most powerful native force in India, plundered up to the gates of Goa, and in 1739 captured Bassein, the northern capital of Portuguese India. From that event onwards, the Portuguese settlements declined in poverty and mis-fortune, a crusade gone sour with pride. The pride remained, and is still dangerous today. For one of the ironies of history is that when the successors to the Portuguese, the British, departed in 1947, the Portuguese enclave of Goa still remained in the flesh of independent India. The first of the Europ-ean conquerors of India has the empty distinction of also being the last.

The Dutch, meanwhile, were not content with merely displacing the Portuguese in the islands of the Indonesian archipelago. In 1652, a colony was established at the Cape of Good Hope as a halfway station on the way East. Between 1661 and 1664, from their base in Ceylon, the Dutch cap-tured all the Portuguese settlements on the pepper-producing coast of Mala-bar. By 1664 they had settlements along the Coromandel coast of eastern In-dia, at Hugli, Kasimbazar, Patna and Dacca in Bengal, and at Surat, Ah-madabad and Agra in northern India.

Three naval wars with England, however, fought between 1652 and 1674, seriously weakened Dutch resources, as did almost continuous fighting with the French between 1672 and 1713. After 1674, an alliance with the grow-ing power of England somewhat restricted Dutch activities, and their bat-tles with the French only assisted the English. The end of the Dutch in India was their defeat by Clive at the battle of Biderra in Bengal in 1759. The Dutch instead returned to the East Indies.

*   *   *

We last saw the English angry at the price of pepper, forming themselves in-to a trading company in London in 1599. This East India Company was established to traffic in the appurtenances of wealth, the adornments of the *luxe privée* of the rich: spices, gems, bezoar stones (an antidote), indigo, camphor and sulphur. But, though the merchants were more than happy to deal in the luxuries of the aristocracy, they were not prepared to have mem-bers of the upper class in their employ. A resolution was passed 'not to employ any gentleman in any place of charge'. It was simply a matter of business, for aristocrats were more likely to desert trade for adventure – with results that might endanger profit.

The first journey of the newly-established company was not to India as we know it, but to Acheh in Sumatra. Captain Lancaster and £30,000 in specie left England in January 1601 and returned in 1603 with over a million pounds of pepper. Unfortunately, sale of the cargo was not permitted until stocks previously captured from a Portuguese ship, and now the property of King James, had been sold. A compromise, however, oiled by bribes to influential persons, was arrived at.

Between 1601 and 1618, nine voyages were made to the East Indies. Business was even extended as far as Japan. In 1609, the Company's charter was renewed, granting it a monopoly of Eastern trade – in perpetuity.

At first, trade consisted in the sale of iron, tin, and lead, and the purchase of spices. Woollen goods which had been exported were, naturally enough in a tropical climate, found unsaleable and rotted away in warehouses. In 1608, the Company's agents in Bantam and the Moluccas wrote that the people there were good customers for Indian calicoes. To acquire these, a trading post in India was necessary, and permission was obtained from the emperor Jahangir to open warehouses at Surat, the main port of western India. The Portuguese, however, were too strong to allow the English to make use of their new-gained permission, until, in 1612, they were defeated in a series of naval engagements at Swally. In 1615, the Portuguese were again defeated in the same waters and when, in 1622, in alliance with a Persian land force, the English captured Ormuz in the Persian Gulf, the Company had little more to fear from the Portuguese. After several treaties, England's right to trade in the East was fully confirmed in the agreement of 1657 between Cromwell and the king of Portugal.

After the naval victories over the Portuguese in 1612 had, at last, permitted the establishment of a 'factory' (i.e. trading post) at Surat, agencies were set up at Ahmadabad, Burhanpur, Ajmer and Agra. These were obtained by a grant from the emperor. In their dealings with this great ruler, the rather down-to-earth merchants were at a distinct disadvantage, and the Company's prejudices against gentlemen were therefore revised. In 1615, Sir Thomas Roe arrived at the court at Agra as ambassador for both the Company and King James. The miserliness of James and the meanness of the merchants made him extremely uncomfortable amidst the luxury of the Mughal court. His employers, having heard of the munificence of Oriental courts, expected

Roe to receive a generous hand-out from the emperor. But the emperor sent him only a female slave ('a grave woman of forty years'), a male criminal and a wild boar. Roe noted in his diary in June 1616 that the emperor's munif-icence to him had amounted to 'hoggs flesh, deare, a theefe and a whore.' Nevertheless, though Roe failed to make explicit agreements, he did at least demonstrate that 'the English were not all obsequious merchants or rough sailors'. Roe was a very shrewd observer and saw through the glittering front of Jahangir's court to the corruption and weakness behind. He also saw the lesson of Portuguese rule in Asia: that possessions need soldiers and cannon to defend them until the protection of territory absorbs all the profits of trade. 'He [Portugal] never profited by the Indies since he defeated them.' For the Dutch, too, Roe saw the same fate. 'It hath also been the error of the Dutch who seek plantation here by the sword. They turn a wonderful stock, they prowl in all places, they possess some of the best; yet their dead pays consume all the gain.' Roe tendered his advice to the Company: 'Let this be perceived as a rule that, if you will profit, seek it at sea, and in quiet trade; for without controversy it is an error to affect garrisons and land wars in India.' The advice was sound, but the pressure of events was soon to push it aside.

Though the English were expanding their trade in India and the Middle East, they were rapidly losing ground in their original place of trade, the Spice Islands. Though allies in Europe, the Dutch and the English were to come to blows in Asia. In the seventeenth and eighteenth centuries, friend-ships and treaties of convenience seldom had much effect. Expediency, when Spain was still powerful, kept the allies together, but on its decline, the Dutch chased the English from the Indies. The Dutch were single-minded and ruthless about their position in the islands, a state of mind which continued until Indonesia finally won freedom. The record of Dutch imperialism is far and away the worst of any European nation in Asia – and the least public-ised. In the seventeenth century, their trading methods were cruelly efficient, armed force being used to make the inhabitants trade with them.

Between 1618 and 1620, the war between the two Protestant powers was open, and Roe warned his employers that something must be done about it in Europe. 'You must speedily look to this maggot,' he wrote, with the refusal to mince words which was his pride, 'else we talk of the Portugal, but these will eat a worm in your sides.' A Treaty of Defence was signed between Holland and England in 1619, which provided for a sharing of trade and mutual protection, but it had no effect on relations in the East. In 1623, the Dutch in Amboyna seized ten Englishmen and nine Japanese,

tortured them into confessing to a conspiracy to assassinate the Dutch gover‑
nor, and executed them with vicious cruelty. The Stuart kings could not af‑
ford to quarrel with Holland in Europe, and it was left to Cromwell to ob‑
tain a small indemnity for the men's heirs by the Treaty of Breda in 1654.

*   *   *

The Massacre at Amboyna ended English activity in the East Indies. They
still held on to one port in Sumatra and another, Bantam, in Java – though
both were lost to the Dutch in 1682. The English turned their face to India
and the stations they had already established there. In India, the Company
remembered Roe's advice and remained for over a century 'in quiet trade',
making no attempt to fortify settlements. The Dutch, on the other hand, ex‑
ercised sovereign power and even enforced a Puritan morality – beheading, for
example, both parties to an irregular union of native and European in their
station at Masulipatam.

For the English, the ten years after Amboyna were years of eclipse. This
was also a time of terrible famine and poverty in the Mughal dominions – a
situation unfavourable to trade. In December 1630, the president – the name
given to the senior merchant – at Surat, wrote to his employers:

> 'an universal dearth over all this continent, of whose like in these parts
> no former age hath records; the country being wholly dismantled by
> drought, and to those that were not formerly provided no grain for either
> man or beast to be purchased for money, though at sevenfold the price of
> former times accustomed; the poor mechaniques, weavers, washers,
> dyers, etc., abandoning their habitacions in multitudes, and instead of
> relief elsewhere have perished in the fields for want of food to sustain
> them... This direful time of dearth and the king's continued wars with
> the Deccans disjoined all trade out of frame; the former calamity having
> filled the ways with desperate multitudes, who, setting their lives at
> naught, care not what they enterprise so they may but purchase means
> for feeding, and will not dispense with the nakedest passenger, not so
> much as our poor pattamars with letters, who, if not murthered on the
> way, do seldom escape unrifled, and thereby our advices often miscarry
> on the other side.'

The English merchants were weak and indecisive, perhaps frightened,
though not unwilling to fight when there was a chance of victory. But things
were unplanned and uncertain. In November 1633, William Methwold
took control of affairs and settled differences with the Portuguese, pending an

official treaty which resulted in the use of Portuguese roadsteads and transit facilities.

This improvement, however, found an enemy back in England. As relations between King Charles I and his Parliament deteriorated, the king became increasingly unfriendly towards the Company, which consisted of the very London merchants who were his opponents. The king authorised two ships to sail east as privateers and prey upon the Company's shipping. Their activities, which included the plundering of Indian merchantmen travelling under passes issued by the Company, considerably embarrassed Methwold in his relations with the Mughal governor of Surat. On hearing of the piracy, Methwold and one companion immediately went to the governor to deny that English ships were involved, but they were shown indisputable evidence that they were. The two men were imprisoned for eight weeks but finally released. One of the privateers was captured by a Company vessel in July 1636.

To add to Methwold's troubles, Charles granted a charter to a rival group of London merchants, in 1635, and their lack of experience caused many problems until these were resolved by a merger of the two companies in 1657.

The great Indian famine of 1630 caused a considerable shortage of cloth, as most of the weavers had died of starvation and disease, though Bengal remained comparatively unravaged. The English attempted to set up agencies in Bengal and Orissa to buy cloth where it was still available, and to profit from the very high price of foodstuffs. This brought the English into coastal trading, as the interior was too disturbed for the safe transit of goods. This meant that their small ships were in continual danger from Arab and Maratha pirates.

Factories were, however, established at Hariharpur in Orissa and Balasore in Bengal in 1633, and these managed to exist despite constant losses and interference from local governors. In 1645, a ship's surgeon, one Gabriel Boughton, became the medical adviser of the Mughal governor of Bengal. The result of his ministrations was prestige for the English name, and trading rights for his fellow-countrymen. By 1647, the Company had twenty-three Indian stations of varying sizes, and employed ninety men on a total salary of £4700 per annum.

The Company was not only active in India but, in the Persian Gulf and the Red Sea, had entered the coffee trade. In 1649, Oxford had the first coffee-shop. London followed three years later. The new drink was quickly successful. In 1659, the Dutch East India Company ordered an experimental consignment of coffee as it was beginning to be in great demand in England. By 1660 another drink was to make its appearance, for Samuel Pepys recorded in his diary in September of that year: 'did send for a cup of tee (a China drink) of which I never had drank before'.

In 1641, the Company had begun to fortify its settlement at Masulipatam on India's eastern coast, an expense which angered the merchants in London. In the same year, a settlement was made at Madraspatam and work begun on Fort St George. It was here that the English first expressed the *de jure* rights of rulers. The murder of 'a common whore for her jewels', by two outcaste men, was the occasion. The local raja 'gave us express command to do justice upon the homicides according to the law of England; but if we would not, then he would according to the custom of Karnatte'. The merchants decided that they were 'unwilling to give away our power to those who are too ready to take it', and 'did justice on them [the murderers] and hung them on a gib-bet'.

The Civil War between king and parliament which had finally broken out in England in 1642, damaged the Company's activities considerably. The king seized its pepper, guns meant for Company's ships were requisi-tioned by parliament. Even in 1655, when arbitration produced £85,000 from the Dutch for the Company's losses at Amboyna in 1623, they were informed that 'His Highness [Cromwell, the Lord Protector] hath great occasion at present for money'. He borrowed £46,000 of the award 'for twelve months'. It was never repaid.

Division at home resulted in division abroad. The Company's agents fought amongst themselves. The Dutch, happy with such dissension, be-came arrogant again. A Company's ship was boarded in 1649 and robbed of its cargo of pepper. On being complained to, the Dutch captain 'fell into high terms and swore all Englishmen were rogues and traitors and that he could not esteem them as he had formerly, they having no king; and withal threatened to do the English all the injuries he could, and for the president and council, he would kick them up and down if they were in his presence'. Even the Portuguese began to raise their heads again. The possibility of the abandonment of the Company's eastern trade was seriously discussed.

In 1651, by the passing of a Navigation Act prohibiting import of goods into British territory except in English ships, an attempt was made to ruin the Dutch carrying trade, and war between England and Holland broke out. News of the war reached the Dutch in the East before the English. Swiftly, English ships were captured and the Company's commerce swept off the seas. The war in Europe ended in 1654, but the tribulations of the English in

India were not yet over. The appointment of Aurangzeb – later to be emperor – as Mughal viceroy of the Deccan in 1653 brought oppression and pillage to the foreign merchants. Levies and customs duties were arbitrarily fixed and extorted. Bribes grew heavier and threats more constant. The English began to look round for a point of safety where men and shipping could lie in some security. The place suggested was Bombay.

During the period of the Commonwealth in England, the Company's monopoly had been pierced by interlopers – private traders who swarmed over Asia destroying the Company's goodwill for a quick profit. These were to be followed by French pirates and later by a French East India Company. By 1657, even the interlopers began to realise that they were ruining everyone's chances of trade, and Cromwell granted a fresh charter when the Company threatened to withdraw from the East. The charter was granted to a new Company formed by an amalgamation of the old with that established by Courteen in 1635. The Restoration, in 1660, resulted in a new charter from Charles II and the right to coin money and exercise jurisdiction over English subjects in the East.

Conflicts at home might be resolved, but a sensible, calm and businesslike attitude did not extend to the Company's factors in India. In 1656, they had antagonised the powerful ruler of Bengal, Mir Jumla, by seizing a junk belonging to him – apparently as security for a claim. Their inept way of handling the consequences led to continued hostility, which was naturally to the Company's disadvantage. A certain madness, a gross unawareness of their precarious position, haunted the Company's servants in those years. In 1660, they provided mortars for an attack by the Mughal ruler of the Deccan on the Maratha leader Sivaji. But the loan rebounded on the lender, and Sivaji raided the Company's agency at Rajapur and captured its factors, took the English prisoner and kept them in dungeons until they were ransomed one year later. Nevertheless, demand for European military science was growing, and native rulers started hiring English gunners for their wars.

In 1662, Charles II married Catherine of Braganza. Part of her dowry was to be the Portuguese settlement at Bombay. Unfortunately, the Portuguese governor refused to accept the transfer, and it was not until 1665 that Bombay became British. To peremptory instructions from Lisbon, the governor replied that he foresaw great troubles for the Portuguese in the secession, and 'that India will be lost the same day in which the English nation is settled in Bombay'. A remarkable prophecy, though the governor was referring only to *Portuguese* India.

From 1662 onwards is a period little known to anyone but specialist histor-ians. It is a period of consolidation for the English, and an exciting, swash-buckling time that deserves a separate work. Here, its unjustified obscurity can only be casually pierced.

In 1662, a new president was appointed at Surat. Sir George Oxinden arrived in time to save the morale of the Company's servants just when Sivaji was challenging the Mughal power and ravaging south India, 'the whole country being a mere field of blood'. In 1664, Sivaji sacked Surat, but was driven off from the Company's property by the English. The Company's prestige shot up almost overnight. The second European war with the Dutch (1665–67) caused far less damage to English interests in Asia than the first one. The Dutch were not so quick to attack the English as they had been be-fore. It was the first symptom of the decline of Dutch power.

Even Sivaji became moderately friendly to the English, but there was still too little security in Surat. The answer was Bombay. This had been held for the king of England since 1665 by a governor, Henry Gary, an irascible man who interfered with the Company and its activities. His administration was arbitrary and cruel and not particularly efficient. Alexander Hamilton recorded in his *New View of the Indies* (1727) that Gary 'condemned a man to be hanged on a Tuesday, and the Man suffered according to Sentence; but on Friday after, the poor dead Fellow was ordered to be called before the Court, but he could not comply with the Orders'. In 1668, in return for a loan, the king handed Bombay over to the Company for an annual rental of £10.

In 1669 Oxinden's successor, Gerald Aungier, began to fortify Bombay as the new headquarters of the Company. This was necessary, as the Dutch were attacking Portuguese stations on the Malabar coast as part of their en-deavour to complete a world monopoly in pepper. In 1668, on the founding of their own Company, the French began to establish factories on the same coast. At the same time, the anti-Hindu policies of the Emperor Aurangzeb were forcing Hindu merchants to look for some place of safety. They sug-gested that if they were offered protection they would move to Bombay with their families – and presumably their businesses. The merchants of Surat, on the other hand, saw not only trade going off to Bombay, but also the security the English factory had given to them. Nevertheless, the move was made.

When, in 1674, Sivaji enthroned himself as an independent king, an Englishman, Henry Oxinden, was officially present at the coronation, and returned with a treaty of peace 'which if punctually observed will be of no small benefit to the Honourable Company's affairs, both on this Island Bombay and their factories which may be settled in Sevagy Rajah's Dominions'.

By 1678 this over-sanguine opinion has changed. Commerce with Bombay was poor, and all due to the depredations of Sivaji and the Mughal admiral, the Sidi, who spent his time looting the mainland. Even Sivaji's death in 1680 brought no relief. His son attacked the Portuguese and plotted to take Bombay. Pirates infested the coast, and the interior was in continuing disorder.

Though the Company obtained injunctions in England against interlopers — Sir Josiah Child buying prohibition from Charles II for £80,000 — little could be done in India. The Company's employees were so badly paid that private trade could hardly be prevented. Bombay grew fast, its military strength and religious tolerance made it a haven not only for Hindus escaping the Mughal terror, but for Christians fleeing from the cruelties of the Inquisition at Goa. From having a population of 10,000 when it was taken over by the English, Bombay had expanded by 1674 to a city of 60,000 inhabitants.

In 1694, the English parliament passed a resolution against the Company's monopoly and gave its opinion that 'all subjects of England have an equal right to trade in the East Indies unless prohibited by an Act of Parliament.' In 1697, the first demonstration of fear at cheap imports from India took place outside parliament, when Spitalfields silk-weavers demonstrated against Indian textiles. Child's 'presents' and bribes had produced a new charter in 1693. His attitude to parliament was to be the continuing one of merchants and empire-builders. Child held 'that the laws of England are a heap of nonsense, compiled by a few ignorant country gentlemen, who hardly know how to make laws for the good government of their own families, much less for the regulating of companies and foreign commerce.'

But enemies of Child found out about the bribes and offered the government a loan of £2,000,000 in return for a charter for a new company which was founded in 1698. Even before this blow fell, the old Company had suffered from the extravagant 'costs' of Child's methods. Where money was lavished in England, in India it was doled out in small coin. Salaries were cut and petty economies enforced. The Mughal emperor, Aurangzeb, again imposed a poll-tax on non-Muslims, and when the Company protested, upped customs dues from two per cent to three-and-a-half per cent. The Hindus responded with action, and war began again in western India. In

Bombay, the new miserliness resulted in protests from the garrison, never happy with its merchant bosses. Further discrimination against the armed forces was followed by a rebellion, and the commander of the garrison, one Richard Keigwin, assumed authority in Bombay in the name of the king (1683). Keigwin tightened up the defence, and when the Mughal admiral arrived in 1684, for his usual wintering in Bombay harbour, he was ordered to leave – and went. No reprisals were made against Surat, a constant threat which had hung over the Company. Keigwin ultimately surrendered, with a complete pardon, to a fleet sent from England.

In 1687, Child made an often quoted remark. It was the duty of the Company, he wrote, so to proceed as to lay 'the foundations of a large well-guarded sure English dominion in India for all time to come', for events were 'forcing us into a sovereign state in India'. This was contained in a dispatch to the Company's settlement at Fort St George in present-day Madras. A year earlier, the Company's representative in Bengal had already assumed one of the powers of a 'sovereign state' by declaring war upon the Mughal Empire – with ten armed ships and 600 men! The Company was apparently no longer interested in 'quiet trade'. Sir Thomas Roe's lesson from the Dutch was to be taken in the opposite way to his intention. Henceforth clerks and merchants were to be conquerors and pro-consuls.

Unfortunately, Child's were brave but empty words. The English were forced to take to their ships and flee to Madras. An attack on Chittagong was a failure. In the end, a humiliating treaty was signed between the English and the Mughals, and in 1690 the Company's ships were once more moored at Calcutta, where Job Charnock founded what was to become the capital of British India.

Interlopers, many of them in league with the Company's servants, still harassed the Company. One was Thomas Pitt, 'a fellow of a haughty, huffing, daring temper' – the great-grandfather of William Pitt the Younger – who later acquired the famous Pitt Diamond, possibly in the way described by Alexander Pope in *Moral Essays*:

> 'Asleep and naked as an Indian lay
> An honest factor stole a gem away.'

However it was got, the proceeds from the sale of the diamond enriched Pitt's descendants, with consequences not only for India, but, in the Napoleonic Wars, for Europe.

Both merchants and interlopers assumed pomp and presence. One, Captain Alley, visiting the Mughal chief of police, moved in 'a splendid

Equipage, habitted in Scarlet richly laced. Ten Englishmen in Blew Capps and Coats edged with Red, all armed with Blunderbusses, went before his pallankeen, eighty Peons before them, and four Musicians playing on the Weights, with two Flaggs before him, like an Agent'. Charnock in Calcutta, according to Alexander Hamilton, 'reigned more absolutely than a *Rajah,* only he wanted much of their Humanity, for when a poor ignorant Native transgressed his Laws, they were sure to undergo a severe whipping for a Penalty, and the Execution was generally done when he was at Dinner, so near his Dining-room that the Groans and Cries of the poor Delinquents served him for Music'. The English, as the Portuguese and Dutch before them, were quick to understand the outward show of power, for as another contemporary, William Hedges, wrote: 'a gaudy show and great noise adds much to a Public Person's credit in this Country'.

In 1696, the English were given leave to fortify Calcutta, and a fort – renamed in 1699 Fort William, after the Dutch king of England – was erected. In the same year, the three villages of Chutanuti, Govindpur and Calcutta were rented from the Nawab of Bengal. The Company had become an Indian land-owner.

The Company's *possessions,* as distinct from agencies or trading stations, were now four in number – Fort St George, Madras; Bombay; Calcutta; and, acquired almost at the same time as Calcutta, Fort St David, opposite the town of Cuddalore on the Coromandel coast. The Marathas, whose free-booting had acquired the latter town, sold the site with all the land 'within ye randome shott of a piece of ordnance' – a method of disposing of real-estate which so appealed to the English that they sent to Madras for the gun with the longest range, and instructed that 'it lyes in the gunner's art to load and fire it to the best advantage'. This demarcation by artillery was made in September 1690, and the villages it enclosed are known to this day as *Gundu Gramam* or 'cannonball villages'.

The Dutch still continued to wage war against native kings in the interest of maximum pepper trade at minimum expense, but the English still preferred to trade even at higher prices, rather than entangle themselves in the mesh of Indian politics. But, as the power of the Mughal Empire waned and powerful nobles began to assert themselves, as the Marathas pressed forward in strength on land and in piracy at sea, it became necessary for the English to become a land power, to fortify their trading possessions. Defence, however, isonly one, inseparable, side of that coin whose reverse is offence.

In the first place, Madras took the initiative. In 1687 it received a charter from England and formed itself into a municipality. Because the local ruler was weak, it made preparations to defend itself – but not only against attack by a native power. In 1674, a little lower down the coast, at Pondicherry, François Martin had founded a French settlement. In 1690, the first clash between English and French was to be a naval battle off the coast, which ended in a draw. The French were now to become the company's enemy, and out of the clash was to emerge the real dominion of the British in India. The Dutch, as we have seen, had expelled the English from the East Indies, but alliance with England against Louis XIV of France had dimmed their antagonism. In its conflict with France, Holland became weaker, and, as it did so, it resorted to bribery in India rather than coercion. The Dutch, declining in Europe, realised that their position in the East Indies was not only unassailable but more profitable economically. By the end of the century, the Dutch had practically abandoned India.

Madras was far in advance of the other posessions in its efficiency and vigour – Elihu Yale, whose name is perpetuated in Yale University, when governor of Madras (1687–92) first applied anti-piracy laws with great severity against Indians and English alike. In 1697, the Company decided to make a deal with one of the principal interlopers, that same Thomas Pitt who had once been described as 'haughty and huffying' and 'not better than a pyrott', and appointed him governor of Madras – where he remained for twelve years to the Company's profit and, in the shape of the Pitt Diamond, his own.

In the meanwhile, the New Company had been faring badly, having first lent almost all its capital to the Crown and, secondly, having employed men dismissed by the Old Company. The New Company, thinking to emulate the embassy of Sir Thomas Roe, had even sent Sir William Norris – an inexperienced and ignorant man – to the Mughal emperor, Aurangzeb, but Norris failed to obtain any agreement. In 1702, the two companies agreed to an armistice, and six years later united into one.

In 1700, the Nawab of the Carnatic, who had just been appointed by the Emperor Aurangzeb, observing the luxury of the merchants in Madras, began to cast a covetous eye upon it. On his appointment, the English had sent the Nawab a present of blunderbusses, fowling-pieces, looking-glasses and other exotic items of European manufacture. The Nawab, however, found the offerings too small and threatened the envoy who presented them. In July 1701, accompanied by ten thousand horse and foot, the Nawab appeared outside Madras. The English offered another present which was refused. Governor Pitt landed marines and made other warlike preparations. This apparently frightened the Nawab, who accepted the present and an invitation to dine with Mr Pitt. A Persian chef was brought in and a light meal of six hundred dishes prepared. 'Dancing wenches' entertained, and so much liquor was drunk that the Nawab passed out. The next year, the Nawab again blockaded the city and was bought off for 25,000 rupees.

Governor Pitt next wrote directly to the central government of the Mughal Empire, and received in 1708 the grant of five villages near Madras. He also received a communication from the emperor's chief minister, graciously reminding him that the Company had not sent the usual presents and enclosing a list for his guidance, which included:

'Birds of the Sorts of Manila Parrots, Newries, Cocatores, etc., or of any sort that can speak, of a good colour and shape. Birds with Copple crowns, and of other fashions...

'Lacker'd Vessels and Porcelane, Scrutores, Targetts and calamdanes, etc., you may send; also Lacker'd Scrutores sett with Mother of Pearle.

'China Ware, what ever is Rare and Fine of any kind or sort, the older the better. The Dishes called Ghoorees, which break when Poyson is put into them, will be very acceptable. You must by all means send some of them.

'Boxes with clock work, China Skreens with clock work, both Painted and with images. Images and Juncks that goe with clock work, etc. Raritys of this kind and fashion will doe.

'Gold and Silver plate, Manilha work (Philigreen); Vessels of Silver, Gold plate enamell'd, Europe work, if to be had, will do.

'Europe fusees; one or two small feild pieces, etc. Gunns will not be amiss...

'A Good Elephant, a Good Horse; Atcheen Horses, the best of the best, and Bengall Horses will also doe.

'Good peices of Ambergrease will do extreamly well, and is the best of all things.

'Clocks and watches that strike or have Chimes you must by all means send.

'Black lead and Red lead pencils of Europe...'

Pitt replied that they were only poor merchants and that they could not send rich presents, but hoped that what they could afford would be acceptable.

The previous year, the last great Mughal emperor, Aurangzeb, had died. The anarchy that followed was to give an opportunity for empire to two European powers, the French and the British. No longer were the nations of the West to wage war among themselves merely for the profits of trade – a series of armed take-over bids between rival corporations. The Portuguese, with their dreams of a Christian world State, had forgotten their crusade when the first vigour died, only to be defeated by the cruel, single-minded, and rational purpose of the Dutch. Now they too had retired from the field to give way to the French and the English. Just as these two began to feel their strength, the great central land power in India, the Mughal Empire, began to fall apart, drawing the European settlements into the vortex of its insecurity. The Europeans were to fight, not only between themselves, but in conscious offensive against the native powers of India. The war against the East was to take on the nature of conquest.

II

CHINA'S EMPERY

'This realm, half-shadowed, China's empery.'
CAMOENS: The Luciad X. 181

The Iron Curtain of Islamic monopoly, first successfully broken by the Portuguese, had at one time almost totally separated the East from Europe. The domination of the Indian Ocean by Arab merchantmen had meant that the products of the East could concentrate at the entrepôts of the Islamic world. The European traders, the great commercial republics of Genoa and Venice, were merely distributors. Attempts to bypass Islamic control of the isthmus of Suez had been made; in 1291, one Ugolino de Vivaldo set out for Genoa in two galleys and was never heard of again. This attempt was not repeated until the navigations of the Portuguese first proved the route around Africa. The reason for this was not fear or timidity, but because the Iron Curtain had been breached for a while from the other side. In 1222, the Mongol Jenghiz Khan defeated an alliance of Russian princes on the river Dnieper. From then onwards, until the fall of the Mongol dynasty (the Yuan) in China in 1368, the empire of Jenghiz and his successors spread across the heartland of Asia to the Black Sea. The *Pax Tartarica*, which provided security within the Mongol possessions, encouraged trade along the old Silk Road from Rome to China.

By the end of the fourteenth century, the curtain had come down again, and the wealth and luxury of China – which had so intrigued the hearers of Marco Polo and other travellers – was no longer accessible to trade. In their drive towards the Spice Islands, the Portuguese occupied Malacca in 1511, whose commercial and strategic importance was then similar to Singapore's today, and three years later they sent a cargo of spices to Canton. The first direct commercial contact between Europe and China had taken place.

The violence, brutality and the bloody struggle for monopolies that are the scaffolding of European activity in the Indian Ocean and the Spice Islands did not extend to the China Seas. Here, violence produced swift and successful retaliation. The land powers of China and Japan were neither the effete monarchies of India nor the semi-barbarous sultanates of the Islands. Prudence and a certain conformity with local customs were found to be safer and more profitable.

The Portuguese discovered that there was almost as much profit in carrying spices to China as there was to Europe, and their first cargo brought handsome return. But they were not allowed to land in China. Convinced of future profit and perhaps impressed by the apparent strength of the Chinese at Canton, the Portuguese sent an ambassador to open negotiations with the Ming emperor in Peking. The envoy left Malacca with eight ships in 1517 and was summoned to Peking two years later. At this time the Ming claimed, and to some extent exercised, suzerainty over Korea, the Ryukyu Islands, Siam, Java, Sumatra and Malaya. By the time instructions had reached Canton to permit the Portuguese envoy to proceed to Peking, a detailed report of Portuguese activities in Malaya and the Islands had reached the emperor – in the form of complaints from his vassals, the Malay sultans. Nevertheless, the envoy proceeded on his journey, until news reached the capital which showed the Portuguese in their true light. One Simon de Andrade sailed to Shang Chuan on the Canton river, landed marines, and began to erect a fort. He was attacked by a Chinese fleet and driven off, and the Portuguese envoy was refused audience when he finally arrived at Peking, was sent back to Canton, and died there, a prisoner, in 1523.

Further attempts to send an embassy failed, and no diplomatic relations were permitted to exist with the central authority in Peking. This did not exclude commercial intercourse on a local basis. At two places, small trading settlements were, unofficially, permitted, but Portuguese arrogance once more led to their being driven away. In 1557, however, after amends had been made in the form of suitable presents for the local viceroy and other officials, a tiny, deserted peninsula in the estuary of the Canton river was leased to the Portuguese as a trading settlement. A wall was built across the narrow neck of land joining the settlement to the mainland, and within the area confined, the Portuguese were permitted to manage their own affairs subject to the authority of the Chinese viceroy in Canton. The peninsula was called Ama-han – Macao. On this scrap of land the Portuguese maintained their exist-ence in complete submission to Chinese authority, reinforced by liberal 'pre-sents' to local officials. This Portuguese ghetto on Chinese soil was to be, in general terms, the pattern of European lodgement in China, from the facto-ries at Canton in the eighteenth and nineteenth centuries to the treaty ports and international settlements of the later nineteenth and twentieth. The first idea of such extra-territorial jurisdictions, actually subject to ultimate Chinese authority, was not imposed by European conquest. From the early years of the Christian era, foreign settlements – mainly of Arabs and Persians engaged in maritime trade – were in existence at Canton, Yangdou and Chu'anchou (the latter known to Marco Polo as Zaytun). A twelfth-century Chinese historian, Chu Yü, described the foreign enclave in Canton:

> 'A foreign headman is appointed over them and he has charge of all public matters connected with them. Where a foreigner commits an of-fence anywhere, he is sent to Canton, and if the charge is proved, he is sent to the foreign quarter. There he is fastened to a ladder and is whip-ped with a rattan from head to foot, three blows of the rattan being reckoned equal to one of bamboo. Offences entailing banishment or more severe punishment are carried out by the department magistrate at Canton.'

Macao was, in fact, a revival of a system suited by tradition to Chinese ad-ministrative ideas.

Spain, which by 1571 had conquered the Philippines and established the capital at Manila, was next to endeavour to do business with the Chinese, and she succeeded in trading at Canton; but she, too, was unsuccessful in opening any form of diplomatic relations with the government in Peking.

The Portuguese, with their enclave in Macao, exercised a virtual monopoly in the China trade, even after their decline in India and the Islands.

The Dutch appeared in Canton in 1604 and 1607, but were not allowed to trade because of Portuguese influence with the local officials. A Dutch at-tack on Macao in 1622 was beaten off, but China's memory of violence kept the Dutch out of the country until the beginning of the seventeenth century. In 1641, because of their forced exclusion from Japan as well as China, the

Dutch looked for compensation elsewhere. They found it in the island of Formosa, and in 1642, after the destruction of a Spanish fortified trading post at Quelong, they gained possession of the whole of this island of 15,000 square miles, an important centre of the sugar trade.

In 1644, the last emperor of the Ming dynasty committed suicide and was succeeded by the new Manchu dynasty, which was not of Chinese, but Mongol origin. This dynasty was to rule China until 1911, for all the period of European expansion in East Asia. For some years, Manchu authority did not extend to southern China, and various supporters of the Ming were active. One, Cheng Ch'eng-kung – called Koxinga by the Dutch and Portuguese, after his Chinese nickname, Kuo Hsing Yeh – is one of the most curious characters in the history of the Far East, for, as René Grousset has put it,[1] he was 'the first representative of that overseas China, then being born, whose expansion on every shore of the Pacific and Indian Ocean represents one of the most important happenings of the nineteenth century' as well as being one of the more potent factors in Asia today.

Koxinga's father spent his youth in Macao and was baptised by the Portuguese. Later, he lived in Spanish Manila and from there went to Japan, where he married. Koxinga was the son of this marriage. His father was a pirate who fought the Manchus along the coast but was betrayed to them in 1646. Determined on revenge, Koxinga for sixteen years raided the southern coast of China in his ships. In 1657, he attempted to capture Nanking, but was repulsed and turned his attention to Formosa as a suitable base for operations. In April 1661, he embarked some thousands of troops in the Pescadores and descended upon the Dutch forts. Koxinga's landings were a complete surprise, as a German mercenary serving in the Dutch forces records:

> 'On the morning of 30 April, 1661, there was a very thick fog, as there had been during the whole night previous, so that one could not see any distance. As soon as the fog had lifted we perceived such a fleet of ships, Chinese junks lying in the sea before Boxamboy, that we could not even estimate their numbers, much less count them. There were so many masts that it was as if a thick wood had appeared. We beheld this sight as if overcome with astonishment, for no one, not even the Governor himself, could have expected this, and no one knew whether they had come as friend or enemy.'[2]

[1] In *The Rise and Splendour of the Chinese Empire*. London, 1952.
[2] Albrecht Herport: *Reise nach Java, Formosa, Vorder-Indien und Ceylon 1659–1668*. The Hague, 1930.

The Dutch, though surprised, were hardly upset. Though a small fort was surrendered to Koxinga, the principal fortifications were at Fort Zeelandia on a little island off the coast. There, over a thousand well-armed men could, they thought, handle anything. This arrogance had firm foundation, for in 1652 two or three hundred Dutch soldiers had defeated an army of some eight thousand Chinese, and 'since that time, the Chinese in Formosa were regarded by the Hollanders as insignificant, and in warfare as cowardly and effeminate. It was reckoned that twenty-five of them put together would barely equal one Dutch soldier, and the whole Chinese race was regarded in the same way, no distinction being made between Chinese peasants and soldiers; if he was but a native of China, then he was cowardly and had no stamina'.[1]

Koxinga, however, was rather a different proposition and after a siege of nine months the fort fell (February 1662). Koxinga had offered the garrison generous terms but they were not accepted. Even on the final capitulation, the Dutch were allowed to leave with flags flying and retire in their own vessels.

Koxinga next planned to capture Manila, but he died in July 1662, aged 39. His conception of a colonial and maritime empire was possibly influenced by European example, and his venture was the beginning of Chinese emigration. His position in history is also unique for his campaign against the Dutch, the first example of the successful use of sea-power – other than as undisguised piracy – by an Asian ruler against the Europeans.

On a diplomatic level, playing upon their assistance to the new Manchu rulers, Holland sent an embassy to Peking in 1655. This resulted only in permission to send a further embassy every eight years; the next embassy, in 1665, produced no political concessions.

The English Company's first contact with China came in 1635, when an expedition was sent from Surat to Macao to bring back gold, pearls, curios, silks, musk, lignum, aloes, camphor, benzoin, and (should there be space) alum, China roots, porcelain, brass, green ginger, sugar and sugar candy. Unfortunately, the Portuguese were not very helpful, and the English commander, Captain Weddell, endeavoured to force his way up river to Canton. He was repulsed, finally apologised, and was allowed to trade, but the expedition made a loss, and Captain Weddell's violence was not forgotten for many years by the Chinese.

By 1685, the Manchus, now stable and rapidly becoming less warlike – and more Chinese in manners and ideas – decided that foreign trade was

[1] William Campbell: *Formosa under the Dutch*. London, 1903.

desirable if properly segregated and controlled. In that year, therefore, the port of Canton was opened to trade and the English opened a 'factory' there and a trading post at Ningpo. In 1699, the Company's vessel, the *Macclesfield*, opened British trade with China, and soon the English were in a leading position amongst the other foreign traders. In 1715, the English erected for themselves a permanent building at Canton. Something of the organisation of trade there will be described in the next chapter.

* * *

European intercourse with Japan began in the middle of the sixteenth century. At that time, Japan was just about to emerge from a welter of civil war and anarchy which had ravaged the country for two hundred years. During the latter part of the century, reconstruction began to take place under the direction of three soldier-statesmen, Nobunaga, Hideyoshi and Ieyasu. On the murder of Nobunaga in 1582, Hideyoshi became master of Japan. He introduced efficient administration and a central authority. He dreamed of a vast empire which would include China, India and the Islands, and – to provide an occupation for the *samurai*, or professional warriors, idle after the end of the civil war – set off on the invasion of Korea in 1591 as a prelude to the conquest of China. In 1598, after seven years campaigning in Korea, Hideyoshi died, and the *samurai* returned to Japan. His successor, Ieyasu of the Tokugawa clan, was appointed Shogun in 1603, and his successors ruled until 1863 as the Tokugawa shogunate, the emperor being merely a symbolic figure.

In 1542 or thereabouts – the exact date is not known – from their base at Macao, the Portuguese discovered Japan by accident. Three Portuguese on a Chinese junk were blown by a typhoon across the East China Sea to Tane-gashima, an island south of Kyushu. Here they were well received, and the arquebuses they carried were so much admired that for years afterwards fire-arms were known in Japan as *tanegashima*. The three Portuguese returned to Macao, bearing gifts and tales to feed the imagination. Before long, a wave of traders and priests inundated Japan, and it was not long before foreigners, Christianity and fire-arms became to the Japanese 'each and equal members in a trinity of terror'. For nine decades after the coming of the Portuguese, through what is known as Japan's Christian Century, missionaries – un-hindered by the people of Japan, but impeded by their own lack of Japanese – propagated their gospel. Converts were numbered by hundreds of thou-sands. Christianity was welcomed, not so much for its religious value but as a vehicle of commerce, military strength and political utility. Nobunaga supported the new religion as a tactical measure. The welcome to mission-aries was more to traders in fire-arms than to distributors of Bibles. Because of the crusading nature of Portuguese trade, it was quite impossible to di-vorce their religion from the products they came to sell. Christianity was not successful only among the lower orders – when the Japanese landed in Korea in 1591, Christian officers and troops formed one of their spear-heads. But Christianity in Asia meant not the love of Christ but the bigotry of his mis-sionaries, with their politico-religious concepts of a world state and its priest-king, the Pope. By its very nature, Christianity was a political movement antagonistic to the totalitarian régime of the shogun. As the priests felt sure of their foothold in Japan, they openly revealed the dark side of seventeenth-century Catholicism: bigoted intolerance, conversion by the sword, the Inquisition, and political subversion.

The central administration, itself an authoritarian military régime, feared association of local princes on the coast with the Europeans and their fire-arms. The Japanese rulers were also disgusted at the gap between the murder-ous brawling of Portuguese sailors and the gospel of the missionaries, as well as flagrant European traffic in Japanese slaves. When a rebellion, replete with Christian banners and slogans, broke out in 1637, it seemed that the only answer was to cut Japan away from contact with the Christian world.

In 1587, Hideyoshi, whose procurer had been refused Christian girls for his employer's harem, had issued five questions to the Jesuit missionaries and on their failing to reply satisfactorily ordered them to leave the country within twenty days. The fathers took no notice, and, after being forcibly deported, returned in disguise determined on martyrdom – which they ulti-mately achieved; though at first Hideyoshi was reluctant to deal with them cruelly. However, both priests and converts were soon indiscriminately tor-tured in the most terrible fashion.

For some years, hostility to foreign missionaries did not extend to foreign traders. Hideyoshi's successor, Ieyasu, wished to encourage merchants other than the Portuguese, but he received little response from the English or from the Dutch who had arrived in the 1580's. The English sent three ships in 1611 but their attempt was timid and unprofitable. After Ieyasu's death in 1616, Japanese xenophobia was extended to traders. A series of decrees re-stricted trade and activity until the last and most comprehensive, the edict of June 1636, finally closed the door on Japanese intercourse with the West.

This edict, addressed to the joint governors of Nagasaki by the four great councillors of the Empire, prohibited the sailing of any Japanese vessel to a foreign country and forbade, upon pain of execution, any Japanese to go abroad, or, if abroad, to return. Foreign children with Japanese foster-parents were to be deported, and Christian missionaries and native converts were to be arrested; a reward of two hundred to three hundred pieces of silver was offered for information leading to the discovery of a Jesuit. In 1624, the English had already left of their own accord. The following year, the Spanish were expelled. Then came the Christian rebellion of 1637 and Portuguese implication in it. In 1638, they too were forced to leave the country.

The Portuguese could not believe that over ninety years of trade would end so abruptly. Despite their decline in India and the Islands, the Portuguese had still been masters of the China and Japan trade. Their expulsion meant economic decline. An attempt to re-open trade in 1639 resulted in the vessels being turned back by the Japanese. A further attempt to send an embassy in 1640 ended with the execution of the four envoys and fifty-seven of their companions, and the burning of their ship. Thirteen men of low rank were sent back to report Japan's determination to keep out the European. Near the place where the Portuguese heads were exposed were erected tablets. One proclaimed:

'So long as the sun warms the earth, let no Christian be so bold as to come to Japan, and let all know that if the King of Spain [and Portugal] or the Christian's God or the great God of all violate this command, he shall pay for it with his head.'

The door was closed. All that a hundred years of contact with the West had given Japan was fire-arms, tobacco, sponge-cake, venereal disease, and some new tortures from the methods of the Inquisition. The memory of the Christian Century was to be a fence against the resumption of relations with the Europeans. Japan had fought her first battle against the West.

Though the door was certainly closed, not all the windows were shuttered. The Dutch, shrewd traders at all times, had deflected the Japanese to their Catholic rivals and had satisfactorily disguised their own brand of Christianity. The Japanese realised the advantages of keeping abreast of events in Europe and those parts of Asia in which the Europeans were expanding, and of having, also, an agent who would supply such foreign goods as they required. The Dutch, therefore, were allowed a precarious foothold on a little fan-shaped artificial island off Nagasaki, which they maintained from 1641 throughout the seclusion period. They were, however, merely made use of, with no respect, importing goods and submitting every year a digest of world events. The island of Deshima measured only two hundred and thirty-six paces in length by eighty-two in width, and the Dutch lived in two-storey cottages. When Dutch vessels arrived, the island was terribly crowded, but during voyages it was occupied only by the factor and a few companions. A high fence topped with spikes surrounded the island and large posts in the water marked the line beyond which no Japanese was allowed to pass. Two strong gates facing the water at the north were not opened except when cargo was being loaded or unloaded, under strict Japanese supervision. A small bridge joined the island with Nagasaki, with a guard-house on the city side. Even the gutters falling into the sea had been made crooked to prevent communication with the outside. A heavy guard of Japanese searched people entering the island. On their yearly visits to the capital, the Dutch were virtually prisoners. The treatment of the Dutch was, however, little different from restrictions operating on the Japanese themselves, as travel within Japan was severely controlled. The Tokugawa shogunate was a police state.

Another European nation was moving outward towards Japan. The importance of this move is in direct proportion to the neglect it has received in Western studies.[1] The Russo-Japanese struggle for mastery in north-east Asia in the present century has its roots in the seventeenth and eighteenth centuries. The eastward migration of the Russians had already begun in the sixteenth century, but the 'Time of Troubles' that followed the death of Boris Godunov in 1605 accelerated the movement away from the anarchy that engulfed European Russia. The main incentive to eastern expansion was the fur-wealth of Siberia. The government was the chief fur-trader, with a monopoly on the sale of sable and black fox to China. In the sixteenth and seventeenth centuries, fur was Russia's most important single item in its domestic and foreign trade.[2]

When the Russians finally reached the Pacific, in the middle of the seventeenth century, they took to the sea in quest of a North-east Passage. Of Japan, the Russians probably received their first information from Dutch teachers in Moscow in the middle and latter parts of the century, though a Dutch atlas showing Japan had been translated into Russian in 1637.

[1] It has at last been given the most extensive and scholarly treatment by G. A. Leisen in his pioneer work *The Russian Push toward Japan 1697–1875* (Princeton, 1959), on which much of the information given here is based.

[2] The expansion of Russia in Eastern Asia is dealt with in some detail in Chapter 5, Parts 1 and 2.

Geographical knowledge about Japan brought from China by the Russian envoy in 1678, or derived from the maps prepared at the beginning of the eighteenth century, put the islands very near to the mouth of the river Amur, and later the Kurile Islands were mistakenly identified with Japan. The first real knowledge emerged by accident. A Japanese coastal vessel was blown by a typhoon onto the coast of Kamchatka, and one of the survivors, Dembei, finally reached Moscow and was received by Peter the Great in January 1702. In 1705, a language school was established in St Petersburg with Dembei as an instructor. In supplying information to the Russians, Dembei failed to mention the xenophobia of the Japanese, and, by mistaking the Russian word for China, Kitai, for Akita – a place in the north-west of the main island of Japan – gave the impression that Japan was joined to the mainland at Korea. Peter the Great, convinced by Dembei of the economic importance of trade with Japan, issued a ukase in 1702 ordering the occupation of Kamchatka and the collection of information about Japan. The Russian quest for Japan had begun in earnest.

2

Outward the Course of Empire: 1710-1858

I

THE CONQUEST OF INDIA[1]

ON THE DEATH of Aurangzeb in 1707, the polity of the Mughal Empire started to disintegrate. With the coming of a weak ruler at the centre, the empire was no longer the sum of its parts but a shadowy cliché contemptuously tolerated – almost a legal fiction.

But the English were tolerably ready to keep afloat in the coming anarchy. Their settlements had been fortified, and a certain degree of friendship, if only the friendship of trade, was between them and the successors in the provinces of the Mughal Empire. The English were beginning to acquire a sense of place. Firstly, there had been trade. The original English settlements were merely emporia, bazaars, places of commerce and no more. Then the element of security entered – the warehouses must be protected. The traders became *armed* traders. The next step was to employ soldiers to defend the settlement; then, to establish 'spheres of influence'. Slowly, the rhythm of empire-building imposed itself on the simplicities of 'trade', and there was nothing that would halt it.

But the English are sticklers for legal niceties. With some difficulty, *firmans* (or signed privileges) were obtained from the Mughal emperor, granting land and other recognitions to the Company, making it, as Edmund Burke was later to point out, legally part of the Mughal dominions, of an empire coming apart at the seams. This legality meant nothing, and brought nothing, for the real enemy was a European one, and the battle would, essentially, be decided on the sea.

The French had originally established a factory or settlement at Pondicherry, near Madras, in 1673, and at Chandernagore, near Calcutta, in 1670. Occasionally hostilities had broken out between the French and the English, but had meant really nothing until the Mughal Empire fell apart.

[1] This section is an expanded version of Chapter One of my book *The Necessary Hell: John and Henry Lawrence and the Indian Empire* (London 1958).

The country was in anarchy; the Mughal Empire, like the British Empire in its early years, was an administrative empire only. It existed in terms of revenue-collecting and the concentration of force at the centre. It imposed no unity on the country, only a discipline – there was no sense of nationhood, only a division of ruler and ruled. When the centre was strong, the parts were weak; when the centre was weak, then the parts revolted, and revolt led to chaos.

Into this chaos came the French, consciously determined on building an empire. Knowing that their success would depend on sea-power, they had occupied the strategic islands of Mauritius and Reunion in the Indian Ocean and all was ready for the great adventure that nearly ended in the French becoming the rulers of India.

In 1735, the governor of Pondicherry began to intrigue in affairs in the Deccan. In 1740, the Marathas, the strongest and most ably led of the Mughals' legatees, invaded the Carnatic, a province which contained both Madras and Pondicherry, and its ruler was given protection by the French. For this the governor of Pondicherry was created a nawab, or prince, and because of it attained a greater measure of respect in Indian eyes than the English had achieved.

The French East India Company was not a trading corporation in the manner of the English. It was primarily an instrument of French foreign policy. It was strictly subordinate to its home governments, and had none of the enterprise or gambling instincts of the searchers after profit.

To it, in 1742, came a man of genius, irascible, imaginative and determined on creating an empire, if only for his own greater glory. To do this, he decided to use Indian forms of government. Surrounding himself with great magnificence, he lived orientally and was recognised by other Indian rulers as one of themselves. The quasi-independent princes aspiring to real independence were in many cases equally matched in strength and resources, and Dupleix, with his intimate knowledge of the country, realised that by throwing even the meagre weight at his disposal on one side or the other, his influence would be decisive. He also established the fact that native troops, trained in European methods, and above all stiffened and led by Europeans, could, in only small numbers, defeat the irregular cavalry of the Indian rulers. This discovery was to be decisive for both the French and the English.

Unfortunately for Dupleix, he was bedevilled by the plans of the French government, and by the great French sailor, La Bourdonnais, who had been sent to harass English ships in the Indian Ocean. Jealousy between the two, it has been said (though without historical foundation), lost France an empire. In 1746, La Bourdonnais captured Madras, only to see it returned by the Treaty of Aix-la-Chapelle in 1749.

Out of this peculiar political rumba, there emerged one of the great names of British India – not a good name, not one to be unreservedly proud of or to emulate, but genuinely great. This name was to appear in a Company Minute on 2nd May 1747:

'Mr Robert Clive, Writer in the Service, being of a Martial Disposition, and having acted as a Volunteer upon Our Late Engagement, we have granted him an Ensign's Commission upon his application for same.'

Indian wars in the eighteenth century were remarkable for their lack of even the expertise of the times. The number of troops engaged were derisive in their smallness, and they were essentially unprofessional, casual and mercenary. To this unmilitary *mélange* came Major Stringer Lawrence, sometimes called the 'Father of the Indian Army', without whom it is unlikely we would ever have heard of Clive. Lawrence began to impose discipline on his tattered forces, and formed them into something militarily effective. The stage was set, and Clive took a leading role.

Clive has become, for the English, one of the few names remembered from the desperate cramming of the schoolroom; he is one of those shadowy beings, an Historical Hero. As a name, he is a convenient tag for a chapter in a not particularly perceptive history: 'The Age of Clive'. It was the age of other names as well, but Clive has caught the desire for symbolic figures, those that symbolise their times, for he dominated them with that peculiar madness which was his substitute for genius.

Clive's seizure, and his defence during the siege, of the fort of Arcot in 1751, was a turning-point in a petty war ostensibly between rival heirs in the Deccan and the Carnatic, but actually between the French and the English. Dupleix' schemes began to crumble and he was recalled to France in 1754. The French were no longer a danger, though they were to remain active in southern India for some years. But in Bengal something took place that shifted attention to Calcutta. Another decisive period for the English was coming.

In Bengal, the English had neglected the fortifications of Fort William, and had not even bothered to organise a regular militia. They had, presumably because of the Company's victories in the south, become rather arrogant and lordly, and acted as if they were an independent and sovereign power. They attempted to operate in a way which foreshadowed the treaty ports and settlements of nineteenth and twentieth-century China, with about as much justification and considerably less success. A contemporary, Captain Rennie, wrote: '... the injustice to the Moors [Indians] consists in that being by their courtesy permitted to live here as merchants, to protect and judge what natives were our servants, and to trade custom-free, we under that pretence protected all the Nabob's [governor of Bengal's] servants that claimed our protection, though they were neither our servants nor our merchants, and gave our *dustucks* or passes to numbers of natives to trade custom-free, to the great prejudice of the Nabob's revenue; nay, more, we levied large duties upon goods brought into our districts from the very people that permitted us to trade custom-free, and by numbers of impositions (framed to raise the Company's revenues, some of which were ruinous to ourselves) – such as taxes on marriages, provisions transferring land property, etc. – caused eternal clamour and complaints against us at Court.' Their arrogance was to lead them into considerable unpleasantness.

Siraj-ud-Daula, a weak youth who has had to bear the animus of the school-book historian, became ruler in Bengal in 1756. He was a 'mean ruffian', wrote one modern historian, 'but we need not seek in original sin his reason for attacking the Company'. He had ample reason to fear the English. The lessons of the south had not been lost on him, and when he saw the English and French starting to fortify their settlements, he ordered them to stop. The French were conciliatory, the English insulting. The Nawab's answer was to march on Calcutta.

The fort was taken by the Nawab after it had been deserted by the governor and many others. Left in command was Josiah Holwell, who survived the notorious 'Black Hole' which is so much a part of the martyrology of British India. The 'Black Hole' was not the result of an act of policy or a display of meaningless cruelty, but of negligence by surbordinates; it was, however, of inestimable value as a portable nightmare until the Mutiny took its place.

When the news reached Madras, an expedition was fitted out under the joint command of Clive and Admiral Watson. Calcutta was captured without any great difficulty in January 1757, and there then followed a period of conspiracy and intrigue out of which few of the principal characters emerge unsullied.

The Nawab was surrounded by a web of deceit and treachery, and at the centre of it were the English. They finally decided to replace the Nawab with his general, Mir Jafar, and, after the French had been neutralised by the capture of their settlement at Chandernagore, fought the renowned but rather paltry battle of Plassey on the 23rd June 1757. This 'battle' consisted of two parts, an artillery display in the morning followed by severe monsoon rain which put most of the Nawab's ammunition out of commission; then an attack by Major Kilpatrick which was foolhardy and precipitate, but extremely successful. Clive's forces consisted of eight hundred Europeans and two thousand native troops, the Nawab's of some fifty thousand men. Casualties were ridiculous – twenty-three killed on the side of the English; about five hundred on the Nawab's.

All the conspirators did rather well out of the revolution in Bengal.

'The Company became *zemindar* [land-owner] of the twenty-four Parganas, 880 square miles, mostly south of Calcutta, with rents estimated at £150,000 [in practice they proved much less]. Clive received £234,000. This was the occasion when, in retrospect, he was astonished by his moderation; but Clive was very easily astonished in this regard. His conviction that whatever personal advantage he collected was somehow different from, and altogether holier than, gain seized by smaller men, was not quite sane in its cold firmness. Watts received £80,000, Walsh £50,000, Scrafton £20,000. Clive thought that altogether the Company and private persons netted three millions sterling. To engineer a revolution had been revealed as the most paying game in the world. A gold-lust unequalled since the hysteria that took hold of the Spaniards of Cortes' and Pizarro's age filled the English mind. Bengal in particular was not to know peace again until it had been bled white.'

In the south, the French had again risen to contest the onward march of the English. Under the generalship of Lally, a brave attempt was made to seize the initiative, but after his defeat at Wandiwash the French finally dropped from the race, though intrigue and conspiracy continued through agents and mercenaries at the courts of Indian princes.

In February 1760, Clive went back to England.

The position of the English after Clive's departure can best be described in the words of P. E. Roberts in his *History of British India*:

'A little body of Englishmen engaged in commercial pursuits had, within a few years, been raised from the control of a single town and some up-country stations, to a real though as yet unacknowledged authority throughout a wide province. Theirs was the power of the sword that upheld the native rulers whose sway was acknowledged throughout Bengal, Bihar, and Orissa. This man, their tool and nominee, was himself in theory the deputy of the Mughal emperor. The divorce of the *de facto* power from the *de jure* sovereignty was at this time the political fashion throughout India. These political shams inevitably had a demoralising effect upon the trend of British policy... For the British in Bengal to have accepted the native political claims at their face-value would have meant that the burden of the administration and of warlike operations would have fallen on their shoulders, while the profits of power would have been paid into the exchequer of worthless and helpless native rulers. The practice generally adopted by the British was to concede the native political claims as far as possible, at the same time taking care that their own services should not go unrewarded.'

In Bengal, profitable 'revolutions' continued, three changes of ruler taking place during Clive's absence in England. During this period, one of the genuinely decisive battles in the history of British India took place at Buxar. In this battle, which was bloody and determined, the Mughal emperor and his prime minister were defeated, and because of it the time was almost ripe for the East India Company to become, as one writer puts it, 'the most formidable commercial republic known in the world since the demolition of Carthage'. The battle at Buxar was the foundation-stone of the British-Indian Empire.

In 1765, Clive returned to Bengal for his second period of administration, and during it the first sovereign act of the Company took place. It 'stood forth as *diwani*', i.e., as the collector and administrator of the revenues of the province. This was an appointment granted by that dim figure, the Mughal emperor, now practically a pensioner of the Company. Though the *diwani* meant that the entire civil administration was in the hands of the Company, Clive did not choose to exercise it directly. This was Clive's 'dual system'. Behind the façade of continuing native forms and administration, the Company exercised genuine authority without appearing to do so, and perhaps frightening others. Clive's political views were contained in a document dated 16th January 1767.

'The first point of Politics which I offer to your consideration is the Form of Government. We are sensible that since the Acquisition of the Dewanni, the Power formerly belonging to the Soubah of these provinces is Totally, in Fact, vested in the East India Company. Nothing remains to him but the Name and Shadow of Authority. This Name, however, this Shadow, it is indispensably necessary we should seem to venerate; every Mark of Distinction and Respect must be shown him, and he himself encouraged to show his Resentment upon the least want of Respect from other Nations. Under the sanction of a Soubah, every encroachment that may be attempted by Foreign Powers can effectively be crushed without any apparent interposition of our own Authority; and all real grievances complained of then can, through the same channel be examined into and redressed. Be it therefore always remembered that there is a Soubah, that we have allotted him a Stipend, which must be regularly paid, in supporting his Dignity, and that though the Revenues belong to the Company, the territorial Jurisdiction must rest with the Chiefs of the Country, acting under him and this Presidency in Conjunction.'

Behind this cloak, Clive rearranged the territory ostensibly ruled by his puppets, and overnight developed, as the product of some immaculate conception, an attitude of high moral indignation. Calcutta became 'one of the most wicked places in the Universe', and the Company's servants, 'beasts of prey'. He tried to put down private trade by establishing a monopoly in salt to the advantage of senior civil and military officers. He was only successful in ensuring that the profits went to the right people. 'My grand object... is that none under the rank of field officers should have money to throw away!' In 1767, he returned to England.

Much has been made of the character of Clive. His administration was rascally and immoral by standards imposed on him by the Victorian coiners of 'improving' proverbs and 'moral' tales. Some of his actions were bad by any standards, even those of his own times. But empires are not constructed with kid gloves, nor made to the measurement of moral laws. When Clive had ended his career, the East India Company found itself with, as Clive himself pointed out, 'an empire more extensive than any kingdom in Europe, France and Russia excepted. They had acquired a revenue of four millions sterling, and trade in proportion.'

He was an empire-builder without scruples, but he did not practise dissimulation and deceit by pretending he was otherwise; and, as Mountstuart Elphinstone wrote: 'In a life spent amid scenes of blood and suffering, he has never been accused of a single act of cruelty'. For this alone a great deal can be forgiven.

In 1773, in England, argument had been flowing about the relationship between the Company and the Crown. Clive had at one stage suggested that the Crown should be the government of Bengal. It was first thought that the Company need only pay a tribute to the Crown, but disclosures made of the administration of Clive showed that the Company was insolvent. Two Acts were passed by parliament, one authorising a loan to the Company; the other being a Regulating Act. This Act established the supremacy of parliament over the Company. It marked the commencement of the decline of the Company as a trading power.

The Act, apart from reorganising the constitution of the Company, called for the appointment of a royal governor-general. The first appointment was Warren Hastings, who was to become, for both his own times and for later historians, as controversial a figure as Robert Clive.

The highlights of Hastings's life are well known. Most people have heard of his impeachment by the House of Commons. He was, undoubtedly, one of the greatest men the English ever sent to the East.

Under his administration, the outlines of British India were formed. He attempted for the first time to establish the concept of a central authority: to introduce a system based not upon the necessity of the moment but on organisation and policy. Above all, he was the first to suggest that India was not merely 'the investment' of shareholders on a remote island off the coast of Europe, but an obligation requiring sympathy and understanding, the essence of good government. In his own age and that of the later Victorians, he was the subject of much criticism, both vicious and puling. In the twentieth century the wheel has turned full circle – to adulation.

His relations with his council, in which he was in a minority, were, to say the least, difficult and were aggravated by the pettiness and personal spite of one member, Sir Philip Francis, the supposed author of *The Letters of Junius*. Hastings's administrative reforms were carried through like a battle at sea, in a continuous running fight, until the death of a member of council put him in a majority of one. The most unpleasant act of his administration, and the one which has excited historians and propagandists to the point of combustion, was the execution of Nandakumar, who was hanged for forgery, while investigations were pending of charges which, encouraged by Francis and others, he had made against the governor-general.

The execution was believed to have been, not for forgery, but for criticism of Hastings. That this was actually a judicial murder cannot be proved. Nandakumar was a casualty in the establishment of Western law and method in India, and the English law making forgery a capital offence was not, in fact, applicable in India until some years after Nandakumar's conviction. It was one of the first examples of the error of trying to impose Western judicial ideas upon an alien consciousness of right and wrong.

Hastings was not free of difficulties outside those of administration. In south India, a French fleet under the command of de Suffren had fought several engagements with the British, and France had found a land ally in the Sultan of Mysore, Haidar Ali. This brilliant monster had enlisted as an officer under the Raja of Mysore in 1749, but had usurped the throne in 1761. In 1769, he found himself strong enough to intimidate the English at Madras into making a very favourable treaty with him. In 1778 the council of Madras drifted into war against him. Haidar Ali descended upon them with an army of ninety thousand men and a hundred guns, burning and pillaging up to the gates of Fort St George. The council appealed to Hastings for help after a force under Colonel Baillie sent out against Haidar had been destroyed.

Hastings responded with men, money and the services of Sir Eyre Coote, who defeated Haidar Ali at Porto Novo. Haidar Ali died in 1782 and was succeeded by his son, Tipu Sultan, who signed a treaty with the British when the French could no longer assist him. Haidar Ali was one of the first to recognise that the essential element in the conquests of the English was that of sea-power. 'The defeats of many Braithwaites and Baillies,' he said, 'will not destroy them. I can ruin their resources by land, but I cannot dry up the sea!'

In central India, the warlike Marathas were again on the march, and after adventurous feats of arms and immense travels across hostile territories by small bands of British troops, a peace was signed in 1782 which was to be preserved for the next twenty years.

On the passage of Pitt's India Bill of 1784, Hastings returned to England, there to become the centre of controversy, and to suffer impeachment. He was finally acquitted on every charge.

So the Indian Empire began. Unformed, casual but hardly accidental. Constructed with mixed motives, vitiated by a passionate preoccupation with personal profit. If there was a logic behind it, it was the hero's logic that action is a one-way street; that there is only one direction and that is forward. It was an immense adventure, played out against a background of incredible bizarrerie, like a thriller at Grand Guignol. Life was lived at an immense speed, a race against disease and circumstance. It was not a 'respectable' period, but it was rich and vigorous. Empires are not made in a steriliser, and the Indian Empire was no exception. From this frequently unpleasant and often dangerous parturition was to emerge an entirely different concept of India which was to remain unbroken until the Mutiny of 1857.

So the disorganised, the almost casual period of British rule in India, the old days of corruption and nepotism were coming to an end. A new India was in the making and the first sound of it was Pitt's India Bill of 1784.

The Bill set up a board of control consisting of allegedly impartial persons of note. A royal governor-general was now to have the authority to over-rule the council and the governors of Madras and Bombay. The directors were left with only one powerful weapon, that of patronage.

Hastings was succeeded by Sir John Macpherson, whose rule was de-scribed by the next governor-general as 'a system of the dirtiest jobbing'. This criticism is just but mild.

In 1786 Lord Cornwallis, whose reputation had apparently not suffered by his surrender to Washington at Yorktown, was appointed governor-gen-eral. He was a new kind of ruler for India: courteous and incorruptible. Quick to smell corruption, he was decisive in suppressing it at every level. He suf-fered from two centres of organised corruption – 'the Augean stables of Benares and Lucknow', as he described them in a letter of 1786. In Benares the Resident, 'although not regularly vested with any power, enjoyed the almost absolute government of the country without control' and his income from dishonest practices was some four hundred times his official income.

Cornwallis soon set himself to the task of cleaning the stables. Under his rule, the civil service was divided into the executive and judicial branches, and salaries were increased, making private trading unnecessary in theory, though in practice various devices were used to perpetuate it. 'I am sorry to say', wrote Cornwallis, 'that I have every reason to believe that at present al-most all the collectors are, under the name of some relation or friend, deeply engaged in commerce, and by their influence as collectors and judges of Ada-lat become the most dangerous enemies of the Company's interest.'

Cornwallis's name will always be associated in the history of British India with what is known as the 'permanent settlement'. This was a revenue Act much needed but misguided. Its intention was to fix the amount of land-tax to be paid. This had previously been arbitrary, assessments being made on the principle of maximum squeeze. It broke up the whole Indian concept of land-rights by guaranteeing freeholds, and has been the subject of much con-troversy, and acres of learned dissertation. The effects (both of the settlement and of the criticism) are still being felt.

Though Pitt's India Act aimed at discouraging the expansion of British India, Cornwallis was forced by the anarchy of the surrounding native states, and by military adventurers as legally respectable as himself, to go to war.

Cornwallis, on his retirement in 1793, was succeeded after an interregnum by Lord Wellesley, who brought with him his brother Arthur, later Duke of Wellington. With the Napoleonic Wars, French agents were active at native courts. Tipu Sultan, who still reigned in Mysore, had been hailed in France as 'Citizen' Tipu, and when the news came of Bonaparte's landing in Egypt, Wellesley declared war on Tipu. In 1798 the fortress of Seringapatam was captured and Tipu killed. The *Pax Britannica* spread a little further.

The Marathas, still a power in central India, were divided amongst themselves. They were defeated in two battles by Arthur Wellesley, and Delhi was occupied by Lake, another competent general whom Wellesley was fortunate to have with him. Wellesley's harsh interpretations of the peace treaty forced another Maratha chief to revolt, and he defeated the British at Bharatpur.

Lord Wellesley was ambitious. He wished, openly, to extend British dominion in India. But his very ambitions were his undoing. The directors of the East India Company deemed annexation bad for trade, and he was recalled in 1805, to be succeeded by Lord Cornwallis, whose second administration was terminated a few months later by death. Cornwallis's second term of office was a failure, but he has his epitaph in the words of that great administrator, Sir John Malcolm:

'However questionable the policy of some of the last acts of this nobleman may be to many, or whatever may be their speculations upon the causes which produced such an apparent deviation from the high and unyielding spirit of his former administration, no man can doubt the exalted purity of the motive that led him to revisit that country. Loaded with years, as he was with honour, he desired that his life should terminate as it had commenced; and he died as he had lived in the active service of his country.'

In 1806, a mutiny broke out amongst the sepoys at a town called Vellore in the Madras presidency.

Regulations had been introduced forbidding caste-marks, and introducing a special type of turban. These were judged by the sepoys to be an attack on their religion. Sir Thomas Munro, writing to the governor of Madras, said: 'However strange it may appear to Europeans, I know that the general opinion of the most intelligent natives in this part of the country is that it was intended to make the sepoys Christians.' These senseless regulations were the shadow of the causes of the great Mutiny of 1857. The mutiny at Vellore followed, on a smaller scale, the pattern of the later and more terrible outbreak. The mutiny was suppressed and followed by executions. The regulations were made without intent, and demonstrate only a criminal lack of under-

standing of native prejudices, which were to become more and more irrel﹥
evant to the rulers as administrative techniques were perfected and the British
became conscious of their 'mission' in India.

Under the governor﹥generalship of Lord Minto (1807–13) a significant
change came over the administration. He found the Company's possessions,
as one writer puts it, ruled by 'a government militarized and still mediaeval'
and left it with the 'amenities of a civilized administration'. During Minto's
period of office, Sir Stamford Raffles occupied Java, and the French were
finally disposed of by the taking of the islands of Bourbon and Mauritius.
Under Minto, the last great native power in India rose in the Punjab under
the leadership of Ranjit Singh.

Minto was not a 'great pro﹥consul'; he was without pretence, and was
very conscious of the humour of the pomp and ceremony which had come
to surround the governor﹥general. He wrote in his 'log kept for the benefit of
the family﹥circle at home':

> 'The first night I went to bed at Calcutta, I was followed by fourteen
> persons in white muslin gowns into the dressing﹥room. One might have
> hoped that some of these were ladies, but on finding there were as many
> turbans and black beards as gowns, I was very desirous that these beard﹥
> ed handmaids should leave me ... which, with some trouble and perse﹥
> verance I accomplished; and in that one room I enjoy a degree of privacy,
> but far from perfect. The doors are open, the partitions are open – or
> transparent – also, and it is the business of a certain number to keep an
> eye upon me, and see if I want the particular service which each is al﹥
> lowed by his caste to render me. It is the same in bed; a set of these black
> men sleep and watch all night on the floor of the passage, and an orderly
> man of the bodyguard mounts guard at the door with sepoys in almost
> all the rooms, and at all the stair﹥cases. These give you a regular military
> salute every time you stir out of your room or go up or down stairs, be﹥
> sides four or five with maces running before you.'

The trappings of empire, the pomp and the splendour were slowly being as﹥
sembled.

In Lord Hastings, who became governor﹥general in 1813, the British
again found a supporter of expansion. His rule saw wars with Nepal, the
real value of which was to enrich the Indian Army with Gurkhas. A vast
campaign was also launched against the Pindaris, marauding bands of rob﹥
bers. This led to the third war with the Marathas, as the Pindaris claimed to
be in alliance with the great Maratha chief, Holkar. After two years (1816–

18), they were defeated and the whole of central India came under the control of the British.

In the meanwhile, the East India Company's charter had come up at home for renewal in 1813. The result was the abolition of the Company's trading monopoly, except that with China, but the Company was to remain the ruler of India for another twenty years until the charter again came up for renewal.

Under Lord Hastings's administration, there flourished some of the greatest men the British had ever exported to India: men who knew, not so much the India which is nothing more than a geographical fiction, but Indians. There were Mountstuart Elphinstone in the Deccan, Colonel Tod in the Rajputana, and Thomas Munro in Madras. These men felt a genuine responsibility for those they governed. Munro, in a letter of 1821, expressed views that were not uncommon at the time, and represent one contribution to the paradox of British imperialism.

'Our present system of government, by excluding all natives from power, and trust, and emolument, is much more efficacious in depressing than all our law and school-books can do in elevating their character. We are working against our own designs and we can expect no progress while we work with a feeble instrument to improve, and a powerful one to deteriorate. The improvement of the character of a people, and the keeping of them, at the same time, in the lowest state of dependence on foreign rulers, to which they can be reduced by conquest, are matters quite incompatible with each other. There can be no hope of any great zeal for improvement when the highest acquirements can lead to nothing beyond some petty office, and can confer neither wealth nor office.'

But these sentiments were commendable rather than immediately practicable, for the many things wrong with Indian manners and morals needed the hand and ruthlessness of an alien autocrat to correct them.

Hastings began many of the reforms that have come to be associated with other and later names. He established the earliest vernacular schools near Calcutta. Canals and other public works were started, and legal measures were enacted to protect the peasant from the landlord.

Hastings was followed by Lord Amherst, the first war against Burma, and another mutiny – this time at Barrackpore, near Calcutta, when native soldiers feared to lose caste by crossing the Bay of Bengal. They also had a sound financial grievance. It was another rehearsal for the great Mutiny of 1857.

On Amherst's resignation in 1828, a new and, fundamentally, the greatest and most unselfish period of British rule was to begin. A contemporary wrote grandiosely, but with truth, that:

> 'This epoch will be referred to as that whence each of the existing States will date the commencement of its peaceable settlement; and the consolidation of its relations with the controlling power. The dark age of trouble and violence, which so long spread its malign influence over the fertile regions of Central India, has thus ceased from this time, and a new era has commenced, we trust, with brighter prospects – an era of peace, prosperity and wealth at least, if not of political liberty, and high moral improvement.'

The name associated with this period is that of Lord William Bentinck, governor-general from 1828 to 1835. The moral effect of his reforms back in England helped to ensure the renewal of the Company's charter in 1833.

Bentinck's administration coincided with, and to a certain extent reflected, the climate of evangelical reform then prevailing in England, which had resulted amongst other things in the abolition of slavery. The evangelicals attempted a revolution in Indian life, but never succeded in rallying the majority of the English to their banners. They did succeed in suppressing some of the more terrible practices of Hinduism, but even this can be described as an administrative measure, concerned primarily with security. *Thugs*, robber bands who strangled their victims, were destroyed. Action was taken against human sacrifice, and against the practice of *sati* (suttee). This latter, the burning of the widow on the pyre of her husband, was well rooted in Hindu life. It was a particularly cruel affair, and, in most cases, not a voluntary one.

But, however praiseworthy these reforms were, they permitted the natural nausea felt at such cruelties to obscure wise judgement. They encouraged feelings of superiority amongst the younger men, and hatred for the older type of administrator who had, it seemed to them, condoned terrible things in the desire to be 'pro-Indian'.

Edward Thompson has admirably summed this up – the commencement of racial estrangement, the beginning of beliefs in the 'white man's burden' and his divinely-ordained 'mission':

> 'The effect of these years of warring against savagery sanctioned by religion seems never to have been noticed. It was summary work, often indistinguishable from the gamekeeper's when he extirpates vermin. It bred an inevitable high-handedness, and scorn for the people whose ethics included such cruelties, and all this ultimately exploded in the

self-righteousness that, at the time, and afterwards, could see nothing in the Mutiny outbreak but villainy. Yet the British conviction of superiority was, perhaps, inevitable. Scorn for the people who expected the woman to serve the man throughout his life and then to burn with his corpse was deserved, if ever scorn was. It is easy to deride Macaulay's Minute in 1833, which decided that education should be on a Western basis, and contemptuously pushed aside Hindu civilisation as of little worth; but – apart from the fact that the system of education adopted has by no means been the failure that it is usually asserted to have been – Macaulay's mind held the scorn of the man who knew at first hand what the fruits of Hindu civilisation had been. It is not reasonable to blame men, who saw constantly what has long disappeared forever, because they did not see the lofty thought that also was a part of Hinduism.'

Bentinck was followed for a short period by Sir Charles Metcalfe, one of the most distinguished men of the Company's civil service. But the rule of not employing a servant of the Company in the highest office in India was rigidly adhered to, and Lord Auckland was appointed in 1836.

At the time, the home government was going through one of its Russophobe periods; and fear of Russian designs on India was the *leitmotif* of Auckland's bumbling rule. He was, admittedly, saddled with instructions by Lord Palmerston, the British prime minister, which encouraged him to believe a Russian attack on India was feasible – which it was not – and gave him the authority to indulge in that most irresponsible and politically disastrous escapade, the first Afghan War. Palmerston's instructions were explicit; Auckland was to

'... judge what steps it may be proper and desirable to take, to watch more closely than has hitherto been attempted the progress of Russian influence in a quarter which from its proximity to our Indian possessions, could not fail, if it were once established, to act injuriously on the system of our alliances, and possibly to interfere with the tranquillity of our own territory.'

The 'proximity to our Indian possessions' can be gauged by the distance between Orenburg, the most advanced Russian base, and the nearest English post at Ludhiana; over two thousand miles! In between was the kingdom of Ranjit Singh, and, unfortunately, Afghanistan.

The war against Afghanistan was disastrous. Out of a force of 16,000 men, most were killed or taken prisoner. Only one, Dr Brydon – who was saved from death by having in his cap, not the Testament so dear to the Victorians, but a copy of *Blackwood's Magazine*, which deflected a sword-cut – reached Jalalabad. Afghanistan was re-occupied after bitter fighting, and the war was ended by an unpleasant and almost irrelevant outburst from the new governor-general, Lord Ellenborough, in 1842:

> 'Disasters, unparalleled in their extent, unless by the errors in which they originated, and by the treachery by which they were completed, have in one short campaign, been avenged upon every scene of past misfortune, and repeated victories in the field and the capture of the cities and citadels of Ghuznee and Caubul, have again attached the opinion of invincibility to the British Arms.
>
> The British Arms in possession of Afghanistan will now be withdrawn to the Sutlej.
>
> The Governor-General will leave it to the Afghans themselves to create a government amidst the anarchy which is the consequence of their crimes.'

The invincibility of British arms was somewhat overshadowed by the fact of their initial defeat by a native power.

The Afghan War led like some chain reaction to another quite indefensible excursion against the Amirs of Sind. This expedition was under the command of an honest eccentric, Sir Charles Napier, who described the campaign as 'a useful piece of rascality'.

In 1839, Ranjit Singh, one of the really outstanding figures in Indian history, died at Lahore. He had astutely recognised the power of the East India Company and had kept his word with them. His death was followed by six years of assassination, palace revolutions and civil war in the Punjab. Finally, in December, 1845, an army crossed the frontier and attacked the British. The first Sikh War had begun.

In less than three months, four great battles were fought at tremendous cost to the British. The commanders on the Company's side were old-fashioned and generally incompetent, only treachery in the Sikh forces saving them, time and again, from rout. At Ferozshah, the British were caught unawares by the resistance of the Sikhs, and the confusion and casualties caused Hardinge, the governor-general who had succeeded Ellenborough in 1844, to exclaim: 'Another such victory, and we are undone!'

The Sikhs were finally defeated, and peace was signed. A regency was set up in Lahore, and Henry Lawrence became the first British Resident. Now began the golden age of the British administrator, the beginning of the 'Punjab system'. It was a system administratively satisfying, but vitiated by evangelical fury. The men were those 'muscular' Christians who, in doing what they suppose to be God's work, ignored man's humanity. But they were very brave men, operating without fear of man or disease, but sometimes on the borders of hysteria with fear of God. One cannot help admiring them, while still feeling distaste for a preocupation which could in the end make them so indifferent to suffering in other people.

It was a great period, the age of the Imperial Hero quarrying with his bare hands the very stuff of empires. It was an age in which everyone contributed to what they supposed to be both God's and England's glory. As Herbert Edwardes, who was one of them, was later to write:

'What days those were! How Henry Lawrence would send us off to great distances; Edwardes to Bunnoo, Nicholson to Peshawar, Abbott to Hazara, Lumsden somewhere else, etc., giving us a tract of country as big as half of England, and giving us no more helpful directions than these: "Settle the country; make the people happy; take care there are no rows!"'

But the peace with the Sikhs had been little more than an armistice, and when Dalhousie took over from Hardinge, in 1848, he was met with another revolt in the Punjab. The signal was the murder of the British agent at Multan. Again bloody battles were fought; again Sir Hugh Gough commanded his troops on the principles he had learned in the Napoleonic War. Again, at Chilianwala, he was almost defeated, but managed to win an overwhelming victory at Gujarat. The Punjab was annexed.

Henry Lawrence, who held the heretical belief that the people of the Punjab would be happier under their own rule than under that of the British, soon gave way to his brother John. The annexation also brought with it that backbone of romance and perennial disturber of India's peace – the Northwest Frontier.

The period when Lord Dalhousie was governor-general was one of the most decisive in the history of British India. Through it rolled the ferments which were to explode in the Indian Mutiny of 1857. It was a period of vast movement and of consolidation, in which justice became stern and friendship between English and Indian an exception. Dalhousie rushed through reforms, developed the 'doctrine of lapse' in which he refused to allow the immemorial right of adoption in the absence of natural heirs, and because of it, added greatly to the Company's dominion.

The greatest annexation of all was that of the kingdom of Oudh. This territory had been grossly misruled for years, and Dalhousie decided finally to take action. Many were against annexation. One, Colonel Sleeman, who had been the leading figure in the anti-*thug* campaign, went so far as to say 'that the annexation of Oudh would cost the British power more than the value of ten such kingdoms, and would inevitably lead to a mutiny of the sepoys'. On annexation, the country was flooded with disbanded troops, and a small fear, soon to fester into a large one, was set in the minds of the 40,000 sepoys in the Company's army whose homes were in Oudh.

In 1851, the last leader of the Marathas, the Peshwa, who for thirty-three years had been a pensioner of the Company, died, and his pension was not renewed to his adopted son, the Nana Sahib. Another of the characters in the tragedy of the Mutiny of 1857 had appeared on the stage.

In 1852, a second war was fought with the Burmese and Lower Burma annexed. In 1853, the first railway was opened; the electric telegraph was introduced. Everything seemed ready for the Victorian pageant of steady and orderly progress.

In 1856, Dalhousie was succeeded as governor-general by Lord Canning, and the drama of the East India Company enters its last decisive act.

This is hardly the place for a detailed examination of the Indian Mutiny of 1857. It has been the cause of much 'explanation', mainly by British historians. Its coming had been forecast by some who had thought the rhythm of reform too quick and indifferent to Indian ideas and prejudices. The evangelical revolutionaries had not hesitated to announce their view that India should become Christian – and thus every gesture, born in many cases of ignorance, that seemed to infringe the frontiers of caste was thought to be part of a deliberate policy of conversion. The country was in a tatter of unrest and needed only a touch to set it aflame. That touch was not long in coming.

As far back as 1843, Henry Lawrence had seen that the trouble would come from the native army of the Company.

'The true basis of British power in India is often lost sight of, namely, a well-paid, well-disciplined army, relying from experience on the good faith, wisdom and energy of its leaders.

We forget that our army is composed of men, like ourselves, quick-sighted and inquisitive on all matters bearing upon their personal interests; who, if they can appreciate our points of superiority, are just as capable of detecting our deficiencies...'

The deficiencies were many. The army had been in the main unemployed since the Sikh wars. Discipline had collapsed, and the best officers attracted away from their regiments by the glitter of civil employment. Those that remained were elderly and incapable of seeing the smoke of danger.

The final touch was the introduction of the new Enfield rifle.

It was necessary to bite a greased cartridge before loading the rifle. The sepoys believed that the grease was made of cow or pig fat, the former a pollution to caste Hindus and the latter to Muslims. The tale was immediately spread that the English intended to break caste by this method. Added to the unrest of the sepoys was the native rulers' fear of annexation. The reforming policies of Lord Dalhousie had resulted in the removal of rulers and the incorporation of their territories into the dominions of the East India Company. The case of the greased cartridges offered the ideal excuse for a rebellion which would bring over the armed forces to the side of the disaffected native rulers.

By the end of 1856, the Bengal Army was murmuring with revolt. 'A consciousness of power' wrote the commissioner of Meerut, 'had grown up in the army which could only be exercised by mutiny and the cry of the cartridge brought the latent spirit of revolt into action'. At Meerut on 9 May 1857, after the sepoys' refusal of the new cartridges, a sentence of ten years' imprisonment had been given to eighty-five men of the 3rd Cavalry. The next day, a Sunday, the three Indian regiments in the station shot their officers, broke open the jail and set off along the road to Delhi some forty miles away. No one attempted to stop them, though there were two British regiments and some artillery in the station. Twenty-four hours later Bahadur Shah, the titular king of Delhi, was proclaimed emperor of Hindustan. The Indian Mutiny had begun.

The Mutiny, or the Great Rebellion, as modern Indian historians prefer to call it, lasted for eighteen months. It was characterised by extreme brutality on both sides. Exaggerations by British historians have elevated the affair into a major epic of British heroism; by Indian nationalists into a War of Independence. It was, in fact, neither. As a rebellion the Mutiny was unorganised, an atavistic reaction rather than a planned revolt; the mutineers had leaders, but no central leadership. As a military operation, it was a small-scale business. Minute armies deployed against each other while disarmed civilians, except in Oudh, were anxious only to be left in peace. As an epic, it is one only of incredible inefficiency on the side of the British. As a 'war of independence' it represented the reaction of a traditional feudal order against administrative and social reform. Its leaders were reactionaries in a changing world, conservative romantics of a type every good nationalist despises.

The Mutiny was, in fact, the meeting of two dying systems; of British India as a 'country' power – an oriental government with European overtones – and of traditional India, unwilling and unable to absorb the militancies of the other. Among the casualties was the East India Company itself, for in 1858 the government of India was assumed by the British Crown. The Company made a graceful exit with a farewell message which is almost poignant in its sentiment. Before this, it had defended itself by pointing out, among other things, that it had laid the foundations of the Indian Empire, at a time when a succession of administrations (under the control of parliament) were losing for Great Britain another great empire on the opposite side of the Atlantic! But petitions, even expertly drafted by John Stuart Mill, were useless. So the Company addressed its servants in India for the last time: 'Let Her Majesty appreciate the gift; let her take the vast country and the teeming millions of India under her direct control; but let her not forget the great corporation from which she has received them, nor the lessons to be learned from its success... The Company has the privilege of transferring to the service of Her Majesty such a body of civil and military officers as the world has never seen before.'

Queen Victoria's proclamation of 1 November 1858 contained within its imperial disclaimers a certain condescension to the heathen, a declaration of amnesty, and the proposition that, with the aid of Providence, a new and happy era was to come.

'When, by the blessing of Providence, internal tranquillity shall be restored, it is our earnest desire to stimulate the peaceful industry of India, to promote works of public utility and improvement, and to administer the government for the benefit of all our subjects resident therein. In their prosperity will be our strength, in their contentment our security, and in their gratitude our best reward...'

India, as the centre of a great Asiatic empire, was to enter upon a new phase – the age of Imperialism.

II

GREATER INDIA

At the beginning of the eighteenth century, the Dutch East India Company was at the zenith of its power. Outwardly, it seemed prosperous, declaring annual dividends of between twenty and forty per cent. Actually, the pressures of expansion, the increase in overheads as dominion widened, and even its own methods of exploitation, were ruining the Company. The Javanese had been reduced to such a state of poverty by the policy of forced sales at low prices imposed upon them by the Dutch, that they no longer had the money for expensive Dutch imports. The Javanese, too, began to grow their own cotton, weave their own cloth, and deal, clandestinely, with Portuguese and English smugglers.

In attempts to stimulate better and more diverse crops, the Dutch began to plant coffee, but a high price encouraged such expansion that production soon outgrew demand. When the directors of the Company cut the price by seventy-five per cent, growers cut down trees; but forced deliveries were made. Dutch policy was to ensure a high price in Europe and a desperately low price in Java. The result was exploitation of a most disastrous kind.

It was in Java that occurred what was possibly the first example of the problem of the Overseas Chinese – which is still a problem in South-east Asia today. By 1700, some ten thousand Chinese were living in or near the city of Batavia, the Dutch capital in Java. Most were craftsmen, tea-traders and cultivators of sugar, and as well as acting as intermediaries for the Dutch they were often intimately concerned in smuggling. But the main danger offered by the Chinese community was the increasing number of indigent Chinese who arrived in the tea-junks from China. Roving bands of these men-aced law and order, and attempts were made to regulate the Chinese by a system of passes. Graft amongst officials made this unworkable. Finally, in 1740, an order was made that any Chinese unable to prove that he was gainfully employed would be deported to the cinnamon gardens of Ceylon. Officials used the threat of deportation as a means to extort money from wealthy Chinese, and a rumour was encouraged that deportees were being thrown overboard when the vessels carrying them reached the open sea. The Chinese, in fear, fled from Batavia and organised themselves in armed resistance. A belief that the Chinese were about to attack Batavia led to the massacre of those Chinese who had remained in the city. The looting and murders lasted a week, the Dutch governor-general making no attempt to end them. Finally, after considerable fighting, an amnesty was declared.

Between 1749 and 1757, the Dutch were involved in a war of succession for the throne of the most important native state, Mataram. The ruler had been returned to his throne by the Dutch, after his own chiefs, in alliance with the Chinese, had revolted. On his deathbed he agreed to cede his kingdom to the Dutch. His brother, however, led the nobles of Mataram in rebellion against the puppet whom the Dutch now placed on the throne. The revolt soon took on the character of a war of liberation from the Dutch. In 1751, the rebels defeated the Dutch force and threatened a deep advance into Company's territory; but the Dutch recovered in time, and peace was fully concluded in 1757. In Bantam, also, a rebellion against the Dutch was put down in 1753; by then, the Dutch were masters of Java, except for some territory in the extreme east which was not subdued until 1772.

Dutch methods, their rigid regulation of spice production and trade, reduced whole areas to dire poverty. Unlicensed growing meant ruthless destruction by inspection teams who made annual voyages of investigation. Peasants were forced to work for tiny wages, and then forced to buy their food from the Dutch at artificially high prices. Not only local poverty resulted from these methods; monopoly and price-fixing encouraged experiments by the English and French in growing spices in their own territories. The harshness of Dutch rule also encouraged piracy, and during the latter half of the eighteenth century great pirate fleets, engaged in slaving, would attack the Company's vessels.

In India, a Dutch attempt to intervene against Clive in 1759 led to the end of their trade in Bengal. In Ceylon, open war with the king of Kandy was, however, settled in favour of the Dutch in 1766. But elsewhere in the Indies, commercial decline was obvious. Efforts that might have averted this were prevented by the quarrel in Holland between the Patriots and the Princely party. In 1780, hearing of an agreement by the Dutch to recognise England's American colonies as independent, the English government declared war on Holland. In the East, Dutch shipping was swept from the seas. Her settlements in India fell to the English, as did the stations on the west coast of Sumatra. Only French naval aid prevented the fall of Ceylon and of the Cape.

The Treaty of Paris, signed in 1784, ended Dutch monopoly in the Eastern seas. Trade was opened to English ships. The challenge to the Dutch in Indonesia went one stage further when, in 1786, Francis Light founded an

English settlement at Penang in Malaya. Attempts to reorganise the Dutch East India Company, by government interference in Holland, were nullified by the occupation of the Netherlands by the French in 1793. The Stadhouder, William V, fled to England, and ordered officers in the Dutch East Indies to put the Company's possessions under the protection of the English, who would, he said, return them when peace was declared. By this arrangement, the Cape of Good Hope, Ceylon, the Dutch ports in India, western Sumatra and Malacca were taken by the English, as were Amboyna and the Bandas. The governor-general in Batavia was, nevertheless, prepared to resist any English attempt to occupy Java. But England was too busy elsewhere even to try. The change of government in Holland, however, resulted in a decision to wind up the Company, and when the Company's charter expired in December 1799, it was not renewed. Its debts amounted to the then immense sum of 134 million guilders.

The egalitarian doctrines of the Batavian Republic, set up in Holland by the French, were not to be allowed to the peoples of Indonesia. The rights of man then – as still in some parts of the world today – meant the rights of the *white* man. Profits still demanded the compulsion of lesser breeds. In Indonesia, affairs were at a critical stage. Though Britain's pre-occupation with Bonaparte's Egyptian campaign prevented her from mounting an attack upon Java, English naval vessels blockaded Batavia and destroyed the remaining Dutch warships. The Peace of Amiens (1802), however, brought relief and a renewed trade in coffee, as the West Indian coffee trade had been ruined by a slave revolt in Haiti. In general, Dutch authority in the islands was unchallenged even from within; the sultan of Bantam had even rallied to the Dutch when the English attacked Batavia in 1800.

With the resumption of war in Europe in 1803, the English reconquered the territories they had given back. The aim of the Dutch in Indonesia was above all to avoid antagonising the English by support of France. The assumption of the throne of Holland by Louis Bonaparte, however, changed everything, and a new governor-general arriving in Batavia in 1808 immediately began to strengthen defences and reorganise the administration. But despite everything, the English captured Amboyna in the Moluccas in 1810. In 1811, an expedition from India was launched against Java. In August, Batavia was occupied without a fight, and by the end of September Java had been surrendered to the English. Lord Minto, then governor-general of India, had been instructed to 'expel the enemy', i.e. the French. There was certainly no intention of *annexing* the Dutch possessions. Stamford Raffles, who was appointed lieutenant-governor, was told by Minto: 'While we are in Java let us do all the good we can'. One of the first steps was to abolish torture. The rulers of Bantam and Cheribon were removed from their thrones and awarded large annuities and the courtesy title of 'Sultan'. In other cases, native States were to continue with the acceptance of English overlordship. Jogjakarta, taking mildness of terms for weakness of power, began to increase its forces. The sultan was deposed and the army cut to a small body-guard.

Forced deliveries were abolished, and the farming of opium was taken over by the government after payment of compensation in cash. Forced de-liveries of coffee and teak continued, however. Unfortunately, the reforms produced neither an increase in revenue nor improvement in the life of the cultivator. Raffles, whose firm intention it was to convince the British govern-ment that Java should be annexed, realised that his only way of doing this was to demonstrate that Java was an economic asset. The introduction of rational tax-assessments and a land-rent system certainly increased revenue, but it also increased expenditure, and every year ended with a deficit. Raffles's land revenue system needed time, and it was the Dutch who were to reap its rewards.

The fall of Napoleon meant the independence, once again, of the Nether-lands. As part of England's policy of making renewed French aggression in Europe impossible, the Netherlands must be strong. With this plan in mind, the Dutch Eastern empire was to be restored. The Convention of London, signed in 1814, confirmed this, and in 1816 the Islands once again became Dutch. Raffles's work, however, was not in vain. The liberal system he at-tempted to erect was, with certain changes, retained. The Dutch, though, continued the forced cultivation of coffee and did all they could to drive European planters out of business. The post-war boom in coffee slumped in 1822, and the monopoly of overseas trade in other hands, mainly English, further disturbed the financial position. An attempt to combat this was made in 1825 with the establishment of a new trading company, with the king of the Netherlands as principal share-holder. In its early years it had little suc-cess in breaking the hold of the English on overseas trade.

In 1825, the discontent of the native states resulted in guerilla wars which lasted until 1830. The financial position was worsened very considerably by the cost of these operations. In 1830, a new governor-general, Van den Bosch, arrived in Java. He began immediately to impose a new economic policy known as the 'culture system'. This, in many ways, was the old system of forced deliveries – with a new look. The peasant was to be forced to devote a portion of his land to the cultivation of specified export-crops. The product would be accepted in lieu of land rent. Dutch merchants would ship it in Dutch ships and sell it in the Netherlands, so making the country once again a world market for tropical produce. Despite opposition on all levels, the system was imposed, as the financial crisis in the Netherlands was acute after a war with the Belgians, which had resulted in the setting up of a new kingdom of Belgium.

The financial returns of the new system were immediate. The prosperity of the Netherlands was a direct result of it. During the operation of the 'System', the population of Java increased from six to nine-and-a-half millions, and in certain areas prosperity even rubbed off onto the peasants. But the stress on cultivation of export crops – indigo, sugar, coffee, tea, tobacco, pepper, cinnamon, cotton and cochineal – implied the neglect of food crops. Serious rice famines occurred in 1843 and 1848. The main criticisms of the system are that the concentration on Java meant that the other settlements were almost completely neglected, and no attempt was made to crush piracy. Recurring famines produced a relaxation in the enforcement of export crop growing, but the abandonment of the system was to be a direct result of the wave of revolutions that swept Europe in 1848.

*   *   *

Indian writers, basing their assumptions mainly upon the work of French and Dutch scholars, have discovered the concept of 'Greater India' in the 'Hindu period' of the history of South-east Asia. This view is slowly being revised as archaeology helps to rewrite the history of the area. But in the period of British expansion in India, the words take on a geo-political meaning – every part of Asia, in some way, became in time a dependency of the British Indian Empire, either by direct annexation, by economic and security influences, or by the impact of other European powers endeavouring to grab a piece of land before the British did.

In Burma, the Portuguese, Dutch and English all, at one time, had trading stations. The English had even established a naval repair station at Syriam, near present-day Rangoon, which, however, they abandoned in 1741. Despite this, the port remained the headquarters of European traders. French influence, which had been growing in the south, was eliminated by the triumph of the Burmese king Alaungpaya over the Mons, then ruling in the south, in 1755. The English, who had established themselves at Bassein and on the island of Negrais, were allowed to remain. A rebellion against Alaung-paya in 1759 produced a rumour that the British had assisted the insurrection, and Burmese troops evicted the English from Negrais but left them at Bassein, from which they finally departed in 1762.

Until the end of the eighteenth century, the coastal strip of Burma on the shores of the Bay of Bengal was independent of Burma proper. This king-dom of the Arakan, as it was called, was annexed by the Burmese king, Bo-dawpaya, in 1785 after a land and naval expedition. The annexation brought the frontiers of Burma up to those of British India, and a new period, fateful, with dire consequences for Burma, began.

Bodawpaya, intoxicated by an easy success against the Arakan, rushed off to attack Siam. The Burmese managed to capture Tenasserim, but were not successful elsewhere and were finally driven off by the Siamese in 1802. The effect of this setback on Bodawpaya was to increase his religious mania. He had already declared himself a future Buddha, and now he turned to the persecution of heretics. He built dozens of pagodas, one of which, if it had been finished, would have been five hundred feet high. Prisoners worked on their construction until, between the demands of slave-labour and military conscription, the whole structure of society began to collapse. Famine killed off thousands, cultivation was abandoned, people fled to the jungle to avoid the corvée. In the Arakan, deportations finally drove the people into revolt, and when strong forces were sent against them from Burma, thousands of re-fugees fled across the frontier into British India.

Realising the dangers, the governor-general of India sent an envoy, Cap-tain Michael Symes, to the Burmese king in 1795. One of the tasks allotted to him was to persuade the Burmese to close their ports to French warships. The envoy was informed, however, that it was below the dignity of the Bur-mese king to negotiate with a mere governor-general, but the envoy carried back with him a royal letter which informed the government in Calcutta that refugees committing crimes on Burmese territory and returning to British India should be surrendered; that permission was granted for the English 'to depute a person to reside in Rangoon, to superintend mercantile affairs, maintain a friendly intercourse, and forward letters to the Presence'; and that the king refused to close his ports to French ships.

The first British Resident arrived in Rangoon in October 1796. Captain Hiram Cox, unfortunately, regarded his appointment, as he put it himself, as 'an attempt to smuggle the wooden horse of Troy' into Burma, and despite his instructions insisted on interpreting his status as that of an ambassador.

His provocative attitude resulted in acute discomfort for the gallant captain, and, fearing that his life was in danger, he sent off an urgent request to Calcutta for an armed vessel to rescue him. The government of India, refusing to be panicked, recalled him. On his return, Cox endeavoured to incite the governor-general to action. But the governor-general would not be persuaded and another Resident was not appointed.

The Arakan frontier still gave trouble, the Burmese viceroy even threatening war on one occasion, and in 1802 Symes was again sent to the Burmese court. A rumour that Bodawpaya comtemplated abdication resulted in Symes being instructed to offer military aid to the heir-apparent, in case of a dispute over the succession. The rumour, however, was without foundation. Symes was kept hanging about for months but his patience paid off when, after the dismissal of a French mission, he was finally received. The threat of war was not mentioned. Symes, on his return, advised that 'a paramount influence in the government and administration of Ava [Burma], obtain it how we may, is now become indispensibly necessary to the interest and security of the British possessions in the East'.

Refugees still fled across the frontiers, and were pursued by the Burmese; an Arakanese revolt broke out, and was again suppressed. The British, occupied elsewhere, had weakened the frontier guards. At the same time, the area was a malarial jungle, deadly to British troops. In 1817, the court of Ava even threatened the British that they would occupy Bengal. If the British did not return the refugees, 'the Lord of the Seas and the Earth [the Burmese king, and not God, as might be supposed] would be obliged to re-assert his authority over such places as Dacca and Murshidabad – undoubted apanages of the Crown of Arakan'. Finally, in 1824, the Burmese general Maha Bandula prepared to attack Chittagong, as the first stage in the conquest of Bengal itself.

War was declared in March 1824. The British plan was to draw the Burmese army away from the Arakan frontier by a sea-borne invasion of Lower Burma, driving up the Irrawaddy to the Burmese capital. While this was in progress, Assam, Manipur, Arakan and the Tenasserim coastal strip would be conquered. In May, the British occupied Rangoon without a fight. Maha Bandula, unaware of this, had crossed the frontier and defeated a detachment of Company's troops at Ramu. Burmese conceit was at its highest – the Burmese even carried a set of golden fetters in which to bring back the governor-general. But the news from the south brought Maha Bandula hurrying towards Rangoon. Sickness decimated both sides, but after Maha Bandula's death in battle the Burmese collapsed and the British occupied Prome. Peace was finally signed at Yandabo in February 1826, with the cession by the Burmese of Assam, Arakan and the Tenasserim strip; the payment of an indemnity of one million pounds sterling; and the conclusion of a commer-cial agreement. Furthermore, a British Resident was to be received at the capital. In contrast to the reality, the official Burmese version of the war and its consequences is worth recording:

'White strangers of the West fastened a quarrel upon the Lord of the Golden Palace. They landed at Rangoon, took that place and Prome, and were permitted to advance as far as Yandabo; for the king, from motives of piety and regard to life, made no preparation whatever to op-pose them. The strangers had spent vast sums of money in their enter-prise, so that by the time they reached Yandabo their resources were ex-hausted, and they were in great distress. They then petitioned the king, who in his clemency and generosity sent them large sums of money to pay their expenses back, and ordered them out of the country.'

It was some considerable time before a Resident was appointed to the court of Ava, though an envoy was sent to negotiate the commercial treaty, which was signed in November 1826. Boundary questions continually occurred, and it was finally decided that such problems must be settled by an envoy at Ava. In 1830, Major Henry Burney, who had had experience at the court of Bangkok, was sent as Resident. Burney was, before long, on good terms with the king but despite this, no proper agreement could be reached with the court, although the indemnity was paid in full by 1832. The situa-tion at court was changed by the insanity of the king, which prevented him from active rule. The chief queen and her brother, a minister, became the real rulers. In 1837, the Tharrawaddy Prince rebelled, in fear of an attempt by the minister and his sister to seize the throne. They hoped for the support of Burney. The Resident's one wish was to get away from the capital and let the protagonists fight it out, but the ministers would not let him go. Burney finally, and reluctantly, acted as mediator and arranged the surrender of the capital to the Tharrawaddy Prince, on the understanding that there would be no bloodshed. Burney's unwillingness to help him turned the prince against the Resident, with whom he had once been friends, and despite his promise to Burney, executions took place and were only ended on the Resident's protest. The prince sneeringly remarked that 'these hat-wearing people cannot bear to see or hear of women being beaten or maltreated'.

The new king now ignored the Resident. It seemed, furthermore, that

Tharrawaddy was seriously considering an attempt to regain the provinces ceded to the British. Burney, pleading ill health, removed to Rangoon and in his report to the governor-general advised a military expedition. This was unacceptable, and a new Resident was appointed. The new envoy was treated in the same way as his predecessor, and soon he was writing rather plaintively to Calcutta, that his treatment was 'such as no English gentleman, or, more extensively, no British subject, ought to be exposed to'. In March, he too on a plea of ill health retired to Rangoon. Early in 1840, the government of India severed diplomatic relations with the court of Ava.

War might now have broken out, but the British were pre-occupied with their disasters in the first Afghan War. Despite rumours and rebellions, an uneasy peace was maintained and the British were soon immersed in the Sikh Wars which left no time for adventure in Burma. Tharrawaddy, by 1845, had like his brother become insane and, in a struggle for power amongst his sons, one, Pagan Min, killed off those of his brothers he felt menaced his pretensions, and became king on Tharrawaddy's death the following year. Pagan Min's two chief ministers instituted a reign of terror. In the two years of their power, six thousand people, or more, are said to have been murdered in order that their possessions might be added to those of the ministers. Public fury finally forced the king to have them executed. Pagan Min exercised little or no control over local officials, and soon reports of the ill-treatment of British subjects were reaching Calcutta. In August 1851, the Burmese governor of Pegu took one step too far, and preferred invented charges of embezzlement and murder against two English sea-captains, collecting from them fines totalling one thousand rupees. The injured parties appealed to the governor-general with a claim for damages. This time India had a powerful governor-general in Lord Dalhousie, and elation over the defeat of the Sikhs was still in the air. The Burmese governor's provocation was trifling compared with earlier ones, but Dalhousie was not the sort of person to be put off by the *size* of the provocation. 'The government of India,' he wrote in an official Minute, 'could never, consistently with its own safety, permit itself to stand for a single day in an attitude of inferiority towards a native power, and least of all towards the court of Ava.'

Dalhousie sent the deputy commander of the Company's navy with two Company's warships and one of the Royal Navy to Rangoon, with a claim for compensation and a demand for the replacement of the governor. The Burmese promised redress and the governor was recalled – but replaced with an official who was even more anti-British. The envoy, Commodore Lam-

bert, a man of somewhat quick temper, responded to the new governor's insulting reception of the delegation by blockading the port. He then exceeded
his instructions by sinking a Burmese ship and when he was, in turn, fired
upon, he silenced the shore batteries and sank every ship he could find. A
strong force was now sent from Calcutta carrying an ultimatum which demanded compensation from the Burmese amounting to what today would be
about £500,000. On 1 April 1852, the ultimatum expired and the British
occupied Rangoon and Martaban.

Unlike the first Burmese War, this one was carried out with efficiency and
despatch; most British casualties, according to one source, were not from
Burmese guns but from Burmese pineapples available at a shilling a dozen!
Dalhousie's greatest obstacle was the British commander-in-chief, General
Godwin, who was over seventy years of age and disapproved of the plan of
campaign. Godwin wanted to press on to the Burmese capital at Amarapura
near present-day Mandalay, but Dalhousie's aims were more limited – the
southern ports and their hinterland, the province of Pegu. The province was
occupied without much fighting and, in December 1852, was declared a
Company possession. No acknowledgement, either offensive or of acceptance, came from the Burmese and Dalhousie began to think seriously of an
advance to Amarapura. In the meanwhile, a revolution was taking place at
the court of Ava. The king's half-brother, Mindon, had been opposed to the
war from the beginning and, after the British advance, he became a popular
hero. An attempt by the king to dispose of him had sent Mindon and his
brother in flight to Shwebo. After a week or two of desultory fighting, the
king's chief minister declared for Mindon. Pagan Min was deposed and
Mindon crowned in February 1853.

The new king, unlike his predecessors, hated bloodshed. Pagan Min was
allowed to live quietly in honourable captivity and, in fact, survived Mindon
by living until 1881. One of Mindon's first acts was to send two Italian
priests, who had been imprisoned with other Europeans in the capital, as
plenipotentiaries to the British. Instead of finding the latter at Prome, the
limit of the annexed territory, the delegation discovered them fifty miles up
the Irrawaddy at Myédé. In the absence of any reaction from the Burmese,
the British had decided to increase their new province by a valuable slice of
teak forest. Mindon did not believe that the British intended to keep Pegu
and refused to sign a treaty ceding the province. The frontier remained at
Myédé. It took the British three years to 'pacify' their new possession. No
treaty was ever signed, but under Mindon good relations subsisted. The en-

voys sent to his court were intelligent and honest men. The king himself was, according to Dalhousie, 'a prince of rare sagacity, humanity and forbearance'. Despite adventurers and others who intrigued to force the king to act against the British when their forces had been depleted by the Mutiny in the Bengal Army in 1857, and despite the damage to his country caused by the loss of its maritime province, Mindon made no move. 'We do not strike a friend when he is in distress', he is reported to have said.

*   *   *

Ever since the English had been driven from Bantam by the Dutch in 1692, attempts had been made to establish repair bases and advance stations for the China trade. Much of the pioneer work in this direction was done not by the East India Company but by private merchants, who, as the Company became more and more involved in its struggle with the French, began to dominate the 'country' trade, i.e. business in indigenous products and manufactures. It was a sea-captain in one such firm of 'country' merchants, Francis Light, who suggested that the Company should acquire Penang, which was close to the Straits of Malacca and only seven days' sail from Madras and the Coromandel coast (see map p. 334). Penang was acquired in 1786. It was not until the British occupation of Java that the idea of using Penang as a dockyard was abandoned.

When Stamford Raffles's hopes for a British Indonesia came to nothing, a suitable site 'inside the gates' – i.e. on the eastern side of the Straits of Malacca – was looked for in earnest. It must be, wrote Raffles, 'a station to command the southern entrance to these straits'. Raffles had in mind the little archipelago of Riau off the tip of Malaya, but the Dutch beat him to it. Various other sites were suggested, but in January 1819 Raffles landed on the island of Singapore and a treaty was signed with the local Malay chief. A slight complication was caused by the necessity of having the treaty confirmed by the Sultan of Johore, in whose territories the island lay. Unfortunately, it was not at all plain who actually was the sultan – a situation arising out of a rather complicated dynastic squabble. Raffles's arrangement was simple. He selected the true heir, then living in poverty in Riau, and installed him as sultan in February 1819. The Treaty of Singapore was, naturally, confirmed by the new Sultan. 'What Malta is to the West', wrote Raffles, 'that may Singapore become in the East.'

The settlement of Penang, no longer under consideration as a naval base, and unstrategically placed 'outside the gate' of the Straits of Malacca, was running at an annual deficit of £80,000 a year. In 1826 some economies were made, and Malacca and Singapore – until then ruled directly as a depend-ency of Bengal – were formed into the Straits Settlements with headquarters at Penang. In 1832, the capital was transferred to Singapore. The strategic situation of Singapore and its position as a free-trade port rendered the chances of a renewal of Dutch monopoly in Far East trade most unlikely. In 1824, a treaty defining spheres of influence was concluded between the British and the Dutch. The trade of Singapore increased at a tremendous rate and, from the beginning, Chinese merchants and their families formed the bulk of the population. Singapore was an entrepôt for the products of East and West and did very little trade with the undeveloped area of the Malay penin-sula behind its back. The port always faced outwards, and it fell to the Japa-nese in 1942 because it was still looking to the sea for its life.

The unwillingness of the Company to get itself involved in the unrest and intrigue of the Malay States could not be maintained. Disturbances and fa-mine at the end of the back garden, and a fire in the house next door cannot be ignored, especially if there is no fire brigade. In 1821, the Siamese, who claimed suzerainty over the Malay sultans, attacked Kedah, the state on which the island of Penang depended for food and other supplies. Refugees poured into British territory, and a company of sepoys frightened the Siamese forces into flight. The British refused to give up the Sultan of Kedah who had fled to them for protection. The difficulties caused by the Siamese oc-cupation of Kedah resulted in a mission being dispatched from Calcutta to Bangkok. The envoy decided that the Siamese army was no threat to the British, and in 1824 the Siamese were even invited to help in the war against Burma – although this was by accident, as the British thought the Raja of Ligor was an independent ruler when in fact he was a Siamese official. From then onwards, treaties were signed with the Malay rajas. Non-inter-vention was sometimes stuck to, at other times ignored, until finally in 1867 responsibility for the Straits Settlements was transferred from the govern-ment of India to the colonial office, and the forward movement in Malaya began.

*   *   *

Siam, in the seventeenth century, had been the scene of many attempts by Europeans to open trade. At one time favour was shown to the English and French, but in 1664 the Dutch, then at the height of their power in the Islands, forced a treaty – by blockading the mouth of the river Menam –

which granted them a monopoly of the trade in hides, the sea-borne trade with China, and certain extra-territorial rights. In 1673, on glowingly exaggerated reports from French missionaries of the imminent conversion of Siam to Christianity, Louis XIV sent a personal letter to the king of Siam. Finally, after a period which would unfortunately take up too much space in the telling,[1] ambassadors were exchanged between France and Siam. By 1687, the French were all-powerful in Siam, in concert with the king's chief minister – a remarkable Greek, Constant Phaulkon. In March 1688, however, the king became ill and unable to carry on the business of state. An anti-foreign conspiracy, headed by the General of the Royal Elephants, succeeded in assuming control and Phaulkon was executed on 5 July. A month later, the king died and the elephant-general took the throne. The French forces, grossly outnumbered, finally retired and, later, France's preoccupations in Europe resulted in the virtual abandonment of her Siamese pretensions. From then onwards, until the middle of the nineteenth century, the Siamese were very reluctant to enter into treaty agreements with European nations, though in 1688 a new treaty was signed with the Dutch.

The closed door remained closed throughout the eighteenth century. Wars with Burma, and dynastic changes (mostly violent) kept Siam out of the orbit of the European. The first crack might be seen in a commercial agreement signed with Portugal in 1818, but it was not until the reign of Mongkut (1851–68) that things began to change. In 1826, Captain Burney concluded a treaty with the Siamese, the clauses of which were remarkably vague but did contain relief for British traders. One of Burney's tasks on his mission to Bangkok was to try and find a member of the old Mon royal family which had once ruled the kingdom of Pegu in Lower Burma. The government of India was seemingly considering the resurrection of the old Mon kingdom. Burney, however, could find no trace of a royal Mon or of any other suitable candidate for the throne. In 1833, an American envoy succeeded in completing a treaty relating to U.S. citizens resident in, or visiting Siam; but an attempt by him and Burney to agree the appointment of consuls was rejected by the king.

In 1850, another attempt by the British and Americans to negotiate better terms for their nations and nationals was unsuccessful. The British envoy was Sir James Brooke of Sarawak. The reasons for his failure may seem odd to those whose concepts of diplomacy are strictly Western, for once again the

---

[1] But see L. Lanier, *Étude Historique sur les Relations de la France et du Royaume de Siam de 1662 à 1703.* Versailles, 1883.

complex and sometimes inscrutable factor of 'face' entered the equation. One of Brooke's vessels went aground and he had to ask for help in refloating it. This, and a rumour of his failures in Borneo, helped to support the view that he was not a person of consequence. To crown it all, his letters were two years old and were not signed by Queeen Victoria in person. All this was taken as a personal affront to the Siamese monarchy. The American envoy, a merchant named Ballestier, was considered of too low a rank even to be received, and he was compelled to leave without even presenting his credentials. During these activities, the king, Rama III, had been too ill to take part in any negotiations. He died in April 1851, and the new king finally unlocked the door; probably just in time, for both Brooke and Ballestier had advised their governments to burst it open.

*   *   *

The area later to be known as Indo-China, comprising Annam, Tongking, Laos and Cambodia, was, in the period covered by this chapter, comparatively free from the European and his grasping fingers, though the foundations for later French aggrandisement were certainly laid.

The Portuguese, with their inevitable ubiquity, had established trading connexions with both Annam and Tongking before the end of the sixteenth century – the raw silk of Tongking becoming one of the chief articles of trade in the Far East. The Portuguese had their headquarters at Fai-fo. The ideological component of Portuguese activity, Christianity, successfully reached Indo-China after the expulsion of the Jesuits from Japan in 1615, and prospered. Their most valuable contribution was the invention of *quoc-ngu*, the romanised script of Vietnamese now in general use.

The Dutch appeared on the scene in 1636 but after nearly twenty years of persecution, and reprisals in return for it, they finally left in 1654. An English attempt to open trade in 1613 was disastrous and, though other efforts were made throughout the century, none was successful.

At the opening of the seventeenth century, the *présence européenne* consisted of French missionaries, and the agents of the Portuguese of Macao. The English had left Tongking in 1697 and the Dutch in 1700. The English, to forestall a possible French move, occupied an island off the western mouth of the Mekong river, a place strategically sited to control trade to the East, in 1702. They abandoned it, however, after a mutiny by native troops three years later. In 1723, the French reconnoitred the island, but found it unsatisfactory. Dupleix sent agents to Cochin China in 1748 and 1752 and the French ministry of marine sent an agent, Pierre Poivre, in 1749. All were unsuccessful. A French plan in 1778 to interfere in the internal affairs of Cochin China came to nothing, as did a similar one suggested to Warren Hastings in 1779. Both failed to develop as the principals had more weighty and preoccupying business elsewhere.

As is the case more frequently than one thinks, when the politician has moved to more pressing affairs and the merchant to easier profit, the missionary establishes more than the kingdom of Christ. The Nguyen dynasty of Hué had been subject to such rebellions and invasions that, by 1777, the sole survivor was a boy of fifteen, Nguyen Phuc-Anh, usually known as Nguyen Anh. His survival was due to the assistance of a French priest, Pigneau de Behaine. Nguyen Anh's fortunes ebbed and flowed, but in 1783 he and the French priest met again and the Frenchman was asked if he could obtain French aid for Nguyen Anh. The real story is obscure, but after the failure of Siamese aid in 1784, Pigneau and Nguyen Anh's four-year-old son, Canh, left on the long journey for Versailles where they finally arrived in 1787. Pigneau's plans to place Nguyen Anh on the throne of Annam were too expensive for a France tottering towards bankruptcy and revolution. Pigneau, however, was able to raise money and volunteers by his own efforts, and they left for Pondicherry at the end of 1787. They arrived in September 1788, just when Nguyen Anh had recaptured Saigon with Siamese help but was without sufficient strength to consolidate his gain. The French volunteers and their arms helped him to accomplish this.

The struggle continued. Pigneau de Behaine, who had been made chief minister, died of dysentery in 1799, but the organisation of Nguyen Anh's army and navy by the French resulted in total victory. In June 1802, Nguyen Anh proclaimed himself emperor of Vietnam and assumed the reign-title of Gia-Long. In 1803, an embassy despatched to Peking received the formal investiture of Gia-Long by the Chinese emperor. The dynasty he founded was to reign until the middle of the twentieth century.

The new state of Vietnam comprised three regions; in the centre were the old lands of the Nguyen with the capital at Hué, which was also the seat of the imperial government; Tongking, with its capital at Bac-thanth, lay in the north; and in the extreme south was Cochin China, with its administrative seat at Gia-dinh. A powerful authority in Vietnam now looked outwards to Cambodia, long coveted by Siam, and in 1812 Vietnam finally imposed a quasi-tributary position upon the state.

After 1802, only four Frenchmen remained in Gia-Long's service. All were given the rank of *mandarin* and special privileges. Napoleon, urged to re-open diplomatic negotiations, was prevented from doing so by the revival of war in Europe. After the Bourbon restoration, French merchantmen were sent in 1817 to trade with the ports of Vietnam. One of the merchants, on his return to France, was appointed consul and went back to Vietnam in 1820 to negotiate a commercial treaty. But in the same year Gia-Long had died and his son and successor, Minh-Mang, hated the Western 'barbarians'. Three unsuccessful attempts, in 1825, 1827 and 1831, were made by the French to open commercial negotiations; but the influence of the 'Great Master', as Pigneau had been called, was dead. The new emperor, a strict Confucian, even issued an edict against Christianity. Minh-Mang died in 1841, and persecution continued under his successor, Thieu-tri. But the Far East had changed almost overnight. A new era of European expansion had dawned on the day when Britain declared war on China in November 1839 (see page 88). The result of this war was Britain's acquisition of a base at Hong Kong and the opening of five Chinese ports to European trade.

The era of the gun-boat and the protection of the flag had begun. In 1843, five French missionaries lay under sentence of death at Hué. A French corvette appeared off Tourane and demanded their release – successfully. Again, in 1845, a threat to bombard the city procured the release of a French bishop, though this adventurous ecclesiastic soon had himself smuggled back in again. The reaction of Thieu-tri was to impose new and stringent regulations upon foreigners. In 1847, another French naval demonstration was made at Tourane in support of a demand for guarantees for the safety of French citizens. The emperor kept the French waiting for a month, and assembled troops on the pretext that they were a guard of honour. He then invited the officers ashore with the intention of killing them. But the invitation was refused, and an attempt by Vietnamese ships to burn the two French vessels resulted only in a large number of junks being sunk before the French sailed away unharmed. Thieu-tri died in 1848. His successor Tu-Duc was even more determined to stamp out Christianity and to keep off the European. Native Christians were branded on their cheek with the characters which meant 'infidel'. Villages were destroyed and many thousands killed. In 1851-1852, two French priests were executed and, after a protest had been rejected, a French warship bombarded Tourane. Tu-Duc's attitude was in imitation of the bellicose Chinese commissioner at Canton, who encouraged violence against Europeans and frustrated negotiations for the revision of treaties.

In 1856 another French missionary was tortured and killed, and in 1857 the Spanish bishop of Tongking was executed. Tu-Duc had this time gone too far. A large French naval force was already in Chinese waters cooperating with the British at Canton, and the Spanish in the Philippines offered help against Vietnam. In 1857, three demands were made to the emperor: he must guarantee religious freedom for Christians, agree to the establishment of a French agency at Hué, and to the appointment of a French consul there. These demands were rejected – precisely as had been expected, for they were merely the excuse to justify French plans which had already been decided upon. After the seizure of Canton by French and British forces there in 1858, a Franco-Spanish force arrived off Tourane. The forts were soon silenced and a force was landed. The beginnings of French dominion had been established.

III

CHINA AND JAPAN

In chapter 1, we left the British sniffing a favourable wind and placing their China trade upon a regular footing with the establishment of a 'factory' at Canton in 1715. Three vessels arrived in the following year, and a convention was signed with the *hoppo* – the Chinese official in charge of trade – which settled such privileges as exemption from customs search of the baggage of supercargoes on the Company's ships, and extra-territorial right of jurisdiction over the Company's own men. Britain's attempts to extend trade to other Chinese ports were unsuccessful, partly because the Chinese preferred to restrict trade to one easily controlled centre, but also because of the attitude of local officials. These officials, in their unwillingness to grant privileges to foreign merchants, reflected two well-established Chinese attitudes: that merchants of any nation (even of China) were of low class, and that foreigners were barbarians. A combination of the two offended all sense of propriety. Even at Canton, where the Chinese were conscious of the value of foreign trade, those very officials who welcomed it, and to some extent came to depend upon it, could not accept that affairs of business were a fit subject for discussions between sovereign states. The 'ghetto-authority' exercised by the supercargoes over their own personnel was fully acceptable to Chinese concepts of responsibility, but any attempt to systematise, by treaty, the organisation of trade, was doomed to failure.

The Chinese solution for the difficulties which were soon to arise – as trade expanded and more and more foreign merchants appeared at Canton – was typically Chinese: that foreigners should have no direct dealings at all with the civil and military officials of the city and province. The traders were there, but officially there was no need to recognise the fact and thereby confer upon them an entirely different status. This attitude, of course, did not mean that the officials and the emperor dissociated themselves from the *profits* of trade. On the contrary, both did rather well – but in a quiet way, like a finan-cier hiding behind nominees. Generally speaking, the foreign merchant paid nothing directly to any official; in between, there was the Co-hong, a group of Chinese merchants who exercised a monopoly in foreign trade. The Co-hong was the whipping-boy of the officials. When 'squeeze' was indulged in, it was the Co-hong that was squeezed. They, in turn, simply raised their prices to foreign merchants.

The trading season began each year in October, when the monsoon winds blew the merchants' sailing ships to the coast of China. Once there, a merchant could conduct his business of buying and selling through one Chinese merchant only, who fixed prices and arranged everything. It might appear that the Chinese Security Merchant, as he was called, was sitting pretty, but this was not so. To get his appointment, the merchant had to pay out large sums in bribes and 'charges'; to keep his appointment, he had to continue to pay. Furthermore, he was held responsible for the foreign mer-chant with whom he dealt, for everything from the purchase of stores to mis-demeanours committed by foreign seamen. Retribution was swift – and ar-bitrary. The Hong merchant lived always in peril of his life.

Despite these conditions, the Chinese merchants were honest men with a sound sense of business. Their relations with foreign merchants were good, often enhanced by warm affection and esteem. Though Chinese officials treated the foreigners with contempt and arrogance, trade expanded and great fortunes were made. To pay interest on large profits in the form of a little hu-miliation once a year is not unbearable.

From October to March, the foreign merchants occupied their little ghetto – a row of buildings on the Canton waterfront, rented from the Co-hong. Within their limitations, the merchants lived well, their buildings being well-proportioned and elegantly furnished. But the area they occupied cover-ed only some eleven hundred by seven hundred feet, and their only place of exercise was a space in front of the buildings, about five hundred by three hundred feet. Except for supervised visits to some flower-gardens, the foreigners were confined to their own little plot. Servants were constantly being withdrawn, as a method of putting pressure on the merchants. They were forbidden to learn Chinese from Chinese teachers.

To the Chinese, this attitude was perfectly proper. The authorities at Peking were not unaware of the pattern of European expansion in Asia – that the flag often followed trade. Do business – but see that it is only business. Accept the foreigner as the instrument of it – but don't invite a tradesman into your house. Operating on this principle, the Chinese kept foreign influence outside their own structure of law and order. Threats and intimidation were necessary to remind the foreigners of their outcaste status; to allow them the protection of the Chinese social and legal order would have been against the whole pattern of their limited tolerance.

This attitude can clearly be seen over the question of homicide committed by a foreigner, where the victim was a Chinese subject. In such a case, the provisions of the Chinese penal code did not operate. A demand was made to the chief merchant of the nation concerned, that a person should be handed over for execution. The Chinese were not concerned with whether it was the guilty person or not, and no attempt to inquire into the circumstances was made, or even considered necessary. In 1784, the accidental death of a Chinese led to the abduction of a supercargo and the blockading of the factories at Canton, until the foreign merchants' governing body, the select committee, handed over the culprit. The man was strangled, apparently without trial, a few weeks later. The position of the select committee was difficult. Large numbers of sailors, rough men anxious for a good time after weeks at sea, were often involved in drunken brawls. The select committee had no legal authority to discipline them, and the Chinese authorities accepted no jurisdiction over them, but merely – in addition to punishing the Hong merchant who had the misfortune to be associated with the foreigner whose seamen were involved – held the president of the select committee *personally* responsible for the sailors' behaviour. Naturally, the foreign merchants appealed for help to their home government. An attempt was now made to open diplomatic contact with the court of Peking, in order to negotiate a treaty which would define, in some way, the rights and responsibilities of the foreign merchants.

An embassy, under the leadership of Lord Macartney, visited Peking in 1793, but was treated as a tribute-bearing mission, and no negotiations were permitted to take place – in fact, its only result was the tightening up of the methods by which foreign trade was carried on.

While the central authority in China was strong under the great Emperor Ch'ien Lung, the attitude to foreign merchants was primarily one of distaste – a distaste born out of a sense of superior civilisation and strength, and rein-forced by a purely empirical awareness of the danger that ordinary merchants might become armed merchants if they were not continually overawed. When Ch'ien Lung died in 1799 – he had abdicated in 1796, but still dominated his successor – the central executive gradually grew weak under licentious and incompetent emperors. Corruption and misgovernment at the centre spread very soon to all levels of the administration. Piracy off the coasts, and rebellion on land, disturbed the peace of the Celestial Empire. In a climate of anarchy, distaste was soon to sharpen into fear.

China's belief that all Europeans were violent and aggressive was continu-ally being reinforced. Those she actually saw in the flesh, the sailors, were al-ways riotous and belligerent, and nations are all too often judged by their loudest citizens. The expansion of Britain – despite Lord Macartney's at-tempt to explain it away as an accident – was there for all to see, whatever sophistry might do to hide it. In 1802, as part of the war on all fronts against the French, it was recommended that British troops should occupy Macao, ostensibly to help the Portuguese defend the place. Apart from the fact that Macao was on Chinese territory, it was useless as a harbour – trade would still have to continue at Canton. The reaction of the select committee at Canton was to send an urgent memorandum pointing out the dangers of the proposal. But their advice arrived too late; the expedition had already left Bengal. Fortunately, the commander of the force was persuaded to keep his ships out of sight while negotiations were opened with the viceroy of Kwangtung, under whose jurisdiction Macao lay. Before the negotiations could fail – which they undoubtedly would have done – peace was signed in Europe and the expedition abandoned.

In 1808, however, war against the French having been resumed, a British naval force was landed at Macao to the accompaniment of strong protests from both Portuguese and Chinese. The governor-general of India had been led to expect – by the new president of the select committee at Canton, a Mr Roberts – a rather different welcome. The reaction of the Chinese was characteristic. They simply ignored the admiral in command of the force, stopped trade at Canton, and made preparations to attack the merchant ships which were anchored down river at Whampoa. Mr Roberts had gone too far, the British were not yet ready to fight, and the naval force was withdrawn. Al-though Mr Roberts was dismissed, the damage had been done. The viceroy had found that, by threatening the merchants, he could overawe foreign naval forces. A dangerous precedent had been established.

While the British East India Company still operated a monopoly on the China trade, the excitability of its servants remained fundamentally outside the responsibility of the British government. But in 1834, the Company lost its monopoly and the China trade was opened to the competitive vigour of private merchants, their heads filled with the enervating optimism of industrial Britain and a consciousness of her greatness overseas. The East India Company's monopoly had already been breached, in the early years of the century, by American merchants who had the support of British merchants wishing to break the Company's hold on the China trade. To the Chinese, this mattered little. To them, there could be no change in the mechanics of commerce and no difference between a senior official appointed by a trading company and one appointed by the British government. Here they were sadly mistaken. Humiliations inflicted on the manager of a business were merely part of the price of profit. Similar treatment of the official representative of a foreign power is an insult to the nation. Britain, in its messianic period, was unlikely to tolerate such treatment. Ignorance on both sides led inevitably to conflict. The British were unwilling to understand the Chinese attitude – a second embassy in 1816, though courteously received, produced no results – and the Chinese by no means understood the nature of the change from merchant monopoly to government protection for individual traders.

In 1834, the British government appointed Lord Napier as chief superintendent of British trade in China. Napier's attempts to negotiate with Chinese officials resulted in the stoppage of trade, the withdrawal of servants, and the blockade of the factories at Canton. The Chinese viceroy was deprived of office for permitting Napier to enter Canton without full authorisation, and the Hong merchants were thrown into prison. Three months later, Napier died at Macao. The position of the foreign merchants at Canton now worsened. Insulting proclamations were issued by the viceroy, mobs in the city were incited to demonstrate against the foreigners. The situation was explosive.

In March 1839, a new official with very wide powers arrived from Peking. This was Commissioner Lin, and his instructions were to put an end to trade in opium. His first act, characteristically, was to threaten to execute one or two of the Hong merchants if the opium in the foreigner's warehouses was not surrendered. Foreigners were to surrender their opium stocks and sign a bond guaranteeing to turn over for execution any person bringing in opium for sale. To ensure that they understood, Lin imprisoned the merchants in the factory area by surrounding it with troops and armed boats, withdrew servants, and cut off supplies of food and water. Ten days later, the new chief superintendent, Captain Elliot, partially gave in by agreeing to surrender 20,000 chests of opium. The restrictions were relaxed and permission was given for trading to resume. Although Elliot now imposed an embargo on all British trading, merchants of other nations resumed their trade. Finally, in defiance of Elliot, one British captain signed a bond on his own responsibility and made off up river. What Elliot would have done next is difficult to say. He was of indecisive character and completely out of his rather shallow depth. The deadlock was resolved for him by the murder of a Chinese in a brawl with some English sailors. A demand to surrender the murderer was refused. Again the Chinese withdrew servants and supplies. The Portuguese governor of Macao was ordered to expel the British from that territory. Proclamations were issued instructing the inhabitants of coastal villages to arm themselves and attack any Englishmen who attempted to land on the coast. Finally, on 3 November 1839, two British warships anchored at the mouth of the Canton river were – on their commander's refusal to give up someone to be executed for the murder of the Chinese – attacked by a fleet of twenty-nine armed junks. The Opium War had begun.

The Opium War is a landmark in the expansion of the colonial powers. It is, in fact, the first *imperialist* war in Asia, i.e. it was a war fought in the name of the sovereign power of Britain, and not in that of the East India Company. It was a war fought in the interests of a European moral code, in support of the essential Western concept of *individual* responsibility as against the Chinese concept of *collective* responsibility. It was also fought to impose the strictly European idea of the equality of nations *by right*, rather than the Chinese concept of the superiority of China and the organic inferiority of everybody else. These are the reasons, the only reasons, why a reluctant British government went to war with China – reasons as bad, or as good, as any other. Unfortunately, the actions of nations, however they may be rationalised by politicians, are usually compounded from individual self-interest. Nations, particularly those entering upon a period of power and prestige, proliferate moral issues with which to clothe less reputable motives. An aggressive mercantilism was quick to understand the weapon at its disposal (identification of the prestige of an individual with that of his nation as a whole) and quick to use it, with varying success, right through to that high noon of imperialism in Africa which ended in 1914. However high-minded the excuses for Britain's actions, however reluctant she might be (in the tawdry rhetoric of the statesman) 'to draw her sword from the scabbard', the war that began in 1839 was actually fought to protect and support the smuggling of a deleterious drug into China, in direct contravention of the laws of that country.

The background to the opium trade is important and must be examined, however briefly. Trade with China since the time of the Roman Empire had been commerce in luxury, in fine silks and porcelain, the outward show of civilised living. Rome could offer nothing in exchange except money, and the drain of coin from Europe to China was one of the great economic problems of the ancient world. European trade in the eighteenth and nineteenth centuries was to suffer from the same problem. To silk and porcelain had been added tea and rhubarb, the demand for which grew every year. But China's demand for European products and manufactures did not. More often than not, the East India Company's ships arrived at Canton without cargo. Europe's trade with China was in cash. The drain on bullion in Europe was the primary cause of the opium trade; for the drug was the one commodity that could actually be *sold* in the East for cash. Apart from the moral and physical ill-effects of opium, against which edicts were constantly being issued, commerce in opium began to reverse the East's favourable trade balance and led to the export of silver from China.

Trade in opium being illegal, smuggling – with or without the assistance of local officials who received a handsome cut of the profits – was essential. The East India Company prohibited the transport of opium in its ships, but, as the largest producer of opium in the world, saw nothing wrong in selling it by auction in Calcutta to anyone prepared to carry it in his own vessels. By the end of the eighteenth century, the trade, which was mainly conducted through Macao, had risen to over four thousand chests of opium a year.

In 1799, a quarrel over the division of profits led to the issuing of another edict against the trade by the viceroy of Kwangtung. As the official who was to enforce the order was accustomed to implement his income from this lucrative source, no one had anything to fear. In order, however, to cut the Portuguese out of their share, the opium ships now moved closer up the Canton river to the island of Whampoa, and sold their cargo over the side of the ship to Chinese dealers. For the next twenty years, Whampoa was the centre of the opium trade. Then, in 1821, a middle-man who collected the 'fees' – for payment to officials who overlooked the existence of the illegal dealings in opium – was arrested for some other offence and, to save himself from the consequences of one crime, turned informer on another. The opium traders moved down to the mouth of the river and the trade settled itself into depot ships – floating warehouses – at Lintin. From these, fast boats driven by thirty or forty oars would carry the opium to the Chinese mainland.

This development changed the nature of the trade; the actual smuggling was now carried on by Europeans. Anxious only for quick and substantial profits, these men no longer considered the etiquette of bribery through middle-men as a suitable instrument for their trade. The foreigners now dealt directly with Chinese officials. Their well-armed vessels were quick to attack government junks. To opium other articles of a less pernicious quality were added in the smugglers' catalogue. The merchants who operated from Lintin were mainly American and 'free' English, the latter being those who defied the still continuing China trade monopoly held by the English East India Company. It was the aggressive nature of the smugglers' methods which was to lead to conflict.

It is, perhaps, difficult for us to understand the attitude of the British, and to some extent the American, governments in permitting – or, rather, over-looking – the moral consequences of the trade in opium. But, in practice, morality is not an absolute thing: the 'hanging judges' of eighteenth-century England, the unenlightened magnates of the Industrial Revolution, would recoil in horror at the callous indifference to human suffering which has its monument at Hiroshima. There are always, within any society, those who with logic and statistics are able to balance good and evil. The opium trade was purely a matter of book-keeping, of commercial solvency. In the nine-teenth century, nothing washed whiter than the detergent of profit. This atti-tude operated on two levels. Basically, the British government was concerned with the opium trade only in the way in which it affected the stability of In-dian finances. Putting aside any question of principle, it would have been better to abandon trade in opium in favour of the export of British manufac-tures. But, as we have seen, China did not want the products of European factories, while Europe did demand the luxuries that China had for export. Opium was the means of paying for these. In 1797, the East India Company – which had already, in 1773, taken over a monopoly in the sale of opium – assumed also the monopoly of its manufacture. The Company, as we have seen, while prohibiting the carriage of opium in its own ships, encouraged it in others, and wiped its hands of the trade once the opium had been sold by auction in Calcutta. At first, the Company had restricted production and inflated prices, but by 1830 it had increased output and reduced prices in order to attract maximum sales. The quantities steadily increased until, after 1865, opium grown in China itself reduced imports. Revenue from opium at the beginning of the nineteenth century averaged about a million pounds sterling a year; at the end of the century, it was over seven million. The export of opium from India was not prohibited until 1926.

The Opium War, then, had three causes – the need for stability in Indian finances, the aggressive individualism of British merchants (so essential a part of the explosion of expansion that followed the Industrial Revolution), and the administrative structure of China which inhibited control of trade by treaty with barbarian nations. The details of the war need not concern us. It was almost entirely a series of naval operations against Chinese ports, from Canton to the Yangtze. The war was interrupted by negotiations, but after the capture of Chinkiang (July 1842) had cut communications between Peking and the south, and when preparations were being made to attack Nanking, the Chinese came to terms.

The result was the Treaty of Nanking (August 1842). The main provi-sions of the treaty were as follows: (1) that five ports, Canton, Amoy, Foo-chow, Ningpo and Shanghai, should be opened to the British for residence and trade; (2) that the island of Hong Kong should be ceded to the British as a naval and commercial base; (3) that intercourse between British and Chinese officials should be on a basis of equality; (4) that a 'fair and regular' tariff on exports and imports should be published, in order to avoid the arbitrary fixing of dues by local officials; (5) that the Co-hong should be abolished; and (6) that China should pay an indemnity to cover the costs of the opium seized from Captain Elliot, the debts of the Co-hong to British merchants, and the expenses of the war. In 1843, a supplementary treaty was signed fixing a schedule of tariffs and containing a clause which guaranteed most-favoured-nation treatment for Britain and the beginning of extra-terri-torial rights.

Other Western nations profited from the British action. In 1844 the Ame-ricans signed a treaty opening the same five ports to them, and extending extra-territoriality. In the same year, the French signed a similar treaty, and also obtained an imperial edict permitting them to erect Roman Catholic churches in the 'treaty ports' and allowing Chinese to become Roman Catholics. In 1846, the French were granted an edict confirming tolerance of Roman Catholicism and promising restoration of churches confiscated in the persecutions of the past. The edict of 1844 was extended in 1845 to cover Protestants, and the Belgians were given the right to trade. In 1847, Sweden and Norway received the same privileges, and in 1851 a trade convention was signed with Russia.

These treaties, and the edicts that emerged from them, were the basis – the legal basis – of foreign penetration of China over the next ninety years. The most sinister of their results was the extension of extra-territoriality. Under this system, foreigners were not subject to Chinese law in any way. As de-fendants in a criminal action concerning Chinese, foreigners were to be tried under their own laws and in their own courts; in civil cases, they could call on their consuls for aid, which meant in practice that they won their case. The seeds of the xenophobia of later years, and all the consequences of that hatred today, had been well and truly planted.

In the interregnum between the signature of the Treaty of Nanking and the second wave of Western aggression in 1856, the pressure of the West upon China increased. Hong Kong developed into a thriving port and city. Foreign merchants settled there and at the five treaty ports. With them came that other arm of foreign penetration, the missionary. The extension of steam navigation expanded trade, and the development of the Pacific littoral of the United States in the 'forties and 'fifties increased commerce across the ocean. An important development, pregnant with the most far-reaching of conse-quences, was the emigration of Chinese labour to the mines of California and Peru and the plantations of Cuba and British Guiana. These men were to return with ideas fundamentally alien to the norms of Chinese society. The city of Shanghai rapidly grew into a centre of foreign trade, and the French, British and Americans established settlements – later, in 1863, to combine as the 'International Settlement'. Even Portugal assumed the sovereignty of Macao, though this was not formally ratified by the Chinese until 1887.

The treaties, however, though they established enclaves and regulated trade, did not solve the problems which had caused the war in the first place. In Canton, which still maintained its position as a leading centre of trade, the foreign settlement – now filled almost to bursting-point with merchants and their staffs – remained unaltered in size. Negotiations to enlarge it always failed, and friction increased. The smuggling of opium continued unabated. The emigration of Chinese labour was often encouraged by violence and fraud, men being, in some cases, press-ganged into the ships. Great Britain, still dissatisfied, demanded revision of her treaty – there was a clause making provision for such a request after twelve years – in 1854. The new demands were for more privileges, access to more Chinese cities, legalisation of the opium trade, and the right for Western envoys to reside at Peking. In these demands, Britain was supported by America and France. In 1856, the American envoy attempted, on his own, to secure revision of the Sino-U.S. treaty. All attempts ended in failure.

In such situations of tension, with memory of a successful war still fresh, trivial incidents are often the cause of conflict. In October 1856, a Chinese vessel owned and crewed by Chinese but flying the British flag, having a British captain, and trading out of Hong Kong (its port of registry), was boarded by Chinese officials at Canton. On the grounds that the vessel, the *Arrow*, was a pirate, most of the crew was arrested and the British flag hauled down. British demands for satisfaction for the 'insult' to the flag were of no avail. Unfortunately, the British governor of Hong Kong was determined on a showdown. Despite the quite reasonable reluctance of the viceroy to climb down, all the arrested crew were released. The governor, however, wanted not justice but submission.

Next day, British naval forces sailed up the Canton river, captured the forts commanding the approaches to Canton, and began bombarding the viceroy's palace. The Chinese replied with what, despite its ambiguity, was certainly a declaration of war. In Britain, the government supported the action of its consul but was defeated in the House of Commons. Parliament was dissolved and in the election that followed the country demonstrated its approval of the government's China policy.

France and Britain, allies in the Crimean War which was just coming to a close, prepared for a full-scale war in China. The United States, which in late 1856 had disabled a Chinese fort on the Canton river in reprisal for another flag insult, declined an invitation to join in, but nevertheless saw to it that an envoy was on hand to reap any profit that might accrue. Action was delayed until late in 1857 by British operations against Persia and the outbreak of the Mutiny in India, but then a Franco-British naval expedition captured Canton and deported the viceroy to Calcutta. Britain, France, America and Russia now despatched their demands to Peking. The reply was unsatisfactory and the French and British, moving their fleets northwards, captured the Tahu forts which protected Tienstin and thus threatened the imperial capital. The emperor gave in and treaties were signed with the two belligerents and their associates.

The exchange of treaties, after their ratification by the home governments of the Western nations, was to take place at Peking. The Russian envoy accomplished this, which one might have thought a simple task, without difficulty, but when, in 1859, the British, French and American ministers arrived at Tientsin for the same purpose, trouble resulted. The American envoy went to Peking and exchanged treaties, though with some inconvenience and humiliation, but the French and British – who had at least fought and won their treaty for themselves – insisted on journeying to Peking by their own route instead of that stipulated by the Chinese. They were opposed and, in attempting to force their way through, were driven back by Chinese troops. In 1860, the French and British returned with military support, recaptured the Tahu forts, took Tienstin and moved on Peking. China's arrest of a party sent forward under a flag of truce, and the death of some of its members, led to an act which has never been forgotten to this day by the Chinese – the deliberate looting and then the destruction of the Summer Palace at Peking. The British commander was Lord Elgin, in whose family there seemed to exist a tradition of looting the beautiful, for his father had some forty years before removed portions of the frieze, pediments and metopes of the Parthenon in Athens and sold them to the British Museum for £35,000.

*   *   *

As we have seen (p. 42 ff), the door of Japan had, at the end of the seventeenth century, been closed in the face of the European, except for the peephole left to the Dutch at Deshima – which also served the Japanese as a window on the outside world. The Russians, however, had continued their search for Japan across the Siberian plains. Geographers made their journeys, and spies moved into Japan itself, often in the guise of castaways. Russia herself had no designs on Japan – whatever some of her explorers and cartographers might have felt – for Russia's hold on her Siberian territories and in particular upon its Pacific coast was tenuous, subject to local uprisings which were commemorated in the very place-names, such as that of Massacre Bay. Towards the end of the eighteenth century, an attempt was made to open trade with the Kurile Islands and Hokkaido, but the immense losses incurred in Russia's first attempt warned off private capital from any repetition. Official interest in Japan, however, was revived by contact between some Japanese castaways who were brought to Russian territory and the Professor of Natural Science at St Petersburg, Adam Laxman. Laxman suggested an expedition to Japan, ostensibly to escort the castaways who wished to return home, and in 1791 the professor's plan was accepted by Catherine the Great. A year later the expedition set off for Irkutsk, on the way to Japan.

Laxman was well received, and after some negotiations the Russians met envoys of the Shogun at Matsumae. Here, they were given gifts, and handed a paper which they could not read. It turned out to be a reiteration of Japanese policy towards foreigners and a demand for their immediate departure – a friendly gesture, in fact, as they ought really to have been arrested and dealt with according to Japanese law. However, if the Russians wished to return, bringing with them the two castaways – who had, apparently, been too ill to travel – they might proceed in one *unarmed* vessel to Nagasaki, the capital. For this journey Laxman was given a permit.

> 'Permission for entrance into Nagasaki harbour is granted to one vessel of the great Russian empire; as explained already, foreign vessels are forbidden to come to places other than Nagasaki, and we repeat that the Christian faith is not tolerated in our country, so that upon arrival there be no sign of it, either in act of worship or oblation; should any agreement be reached, nothing must be done contrary to our laws as laid down in the prescript handed to you by us; it is for this reason that we give the paper to Adam Laxman.'

The permit had been cut in half, one piece retained by the Japanese. After the exchange of further presents, the expedition returned to Russian territory.

The Nagasaki permit was taken by the Russians to mean permission to trade, and it might well have been turned into this if it had been used energetically. The Laxman expedition had been received with courtesy and kindness. Japan seemed more tolerant and ready than at any time during the century. But the Russian government was sceptical, and pre-occupied with the spread of revolutionary ideas in America and France. In 1796 Professor Laxman, and later in the year, Catherine the Great, died. The Russians turned away from the Far East and left the initiative in the hands of a private body, the Russian-America Company. In 1803, this Company sent Nikolai Rezanov to Nagasaki, carrying the Russian half of the permit and with orders to negotiate a commercial treaty. After a courteous reception, he was told to leave and the real nature of the permit was explained to him. Rezanov lost his temper and threatened the Japanese with retribution – but he left quietly, and, apparently, with good humour on both sides. Rezanov, however, took his revenge soon after by obliterating a Japanese settlement on Etoforu Island. One of the results of this action – apart from the suffering of the inhabitants – was to make the Japanese change their name for the Russians, from *aka-hito* or 'red men' (presumably because of their hair), to *aka-oni* or 'red devils', equating them with the red devils that haunt representations of the Buddhist hell. The Russian aggression had a decisive effect on the policy of the Shogun. Fantastic rumours of a Russian invasion spread throughout Japan, and the Shogun took immediate and decisive measures for defence. The Dutch were ordered to translate books about Russia, and the Japanese themselves began to explore the northern islands. In 1809, a Japanese explorer entered Manchuria and penetrated to the lower Amur, returning with much information on the territories he had travelled through.

Discussion continued in Japan on how the menace of Russia should be met – concessions, or defence of the closed door. Some thought that trade should be opened, others, with the lessons of the past as their allies, warned that trade was merely a stepping-stone to dominion. The latter opinion, hallowed by the expediency of tradition, seems to have won.

Various private expeditions were made by Russians over the next fifty years. One, in 1807, resulted in much information about the Japanese to expand and titillate growing Russian interest. Russia's outward expansion in Asia (see p. 164 ff) included an attempt to annex the island of Sakhalin, but the pressure of the Crimean War and the threatened approach of Japanese military reinforcements resulted in Russian evacuation of the island. A treaty signed in 1855 left Sakhalin a joint Russo-Japanese possession. Russian *official* interest in Japan was still weak, mainly for financial reasons. The Emperor Nicholas I had almost sent an official mission under Putiatin to Japan in 1843, but was persuaded not to by the minister of finance. A private expedition substituted for it was, like its predecessors, a failure.

The situation in the Far East, after the foreign treaties that resulted from the Opium War, was one of continuous change. Established patterns of strength and security – all of which protected, and to a large extent, permitted the seclusion of Japan – were being broken. In 1844, William II of the Netherlands, in a remarkable letter to the Shogun – 'our Friend, the very noble, most serene and all-powerful sovereign of the great empire of Japan' – had tried to explain the superiority of European science and military power. The Shogun rejected the king's request for changes in the laws relating to foreigners, but he did not overlook the warning.

The real threat to Japanese seclusion was not the European powers but the growing strength of the United States, caught in the messianism of its 'manifest destiny'. As early as 1797, Americans had attempted to open a trade in furs with Japan. In 1837, an unarmed American vessel which hoped – under the guise of repatriating Japanese castaways – to open Japan to trade, had been driven away by cannon fire. A renewed effort in 1846 was also unsuccessful. But by 1848 the United States had established her western seaboard, and the American push across the Pacific Ocean was begun. American interest in the Pacific had emerged at the time of the Revolutionary War and the severing of English trade monopolies with the East. America's drive across country to the Pacific littoral was organically connected with the desire for Asian markets. The idealists of this young nation were just as prone to shibboleths as the older imperialist powers and were caught in the same grandiose visions of 'civilising missions'. Its pioneers saw, as they moved westward, that the fertile open spaces of the mid/West could become the granary of East Asia and its salesmen purveyors of science, liberal govern/ ment and the true religion.

The European nations were well aware of approaching American ex/ pansion in the Far East. None more so than Russia, who for so long had painfully attempted to open Japan to trade. American activities were a very real threat to Russian prestige and position in Asia. The news of an immi/ nent American expedition to Japan persuaded the Russian emperor to au/ thorise an official expedition, under the command of Vice/Admiral Putiatin. Putiatin's ships were to go round the world to their destination. A frigate, the *Pallada*, sailed from Kronstadt in October 1852, and was joined at Ports/ mouth in England by a newly/built, iron/screw schooner, the *Vostok*. Both left England in January 1853 and arrived off Nagasaki in August of the same year. The American fleet under Commodore Perry had arrived the month before.

Japan, as we have seen, conscious of its isolation in the new patterns of power in the Far East, was groping towards a foreign policy. Perry and Putiatin certainly opened the door, but it had already been unbarred and the decision taken not to defend it. In response to the threat of Western military strength, an 'agonising re/appraisal' of Japanese policy had been going on for some years, and some Japanese leaders were turning again to the expan/ sionist ideas of Hideyoshi, who in the sixteenth century had dreamed of a Japanese overseas empire and had even attempted to establish it with his disastrous campaign in Korea. Pressure from the Western powers was to open the door of Japan not only to let foreigners in, but to let the Japanese out. Hideyoshi's dream of empire was to drive the Japanese into mainland Asia and the Greater East Asia Co/Prosperity Sphere. To acquire the military strength for this, it was necessary to let in Western science.

After much debate, treaties were signed with the United States in March 1854 and with Great Britain in October of the same year. Putiatin's nego/ tiations had not been successful and Russia's pre/occupation with the Crim/ ean War had led to his withdrawal. Russia's position, however, was eased by Perry's success – not because Perry wanted it so, but because the Japanese realised that it might be possible to play off the foreigners against each other to Japan's advantage. Putiatin returned in October 1854, determined to get better terms than those granted to Perry, which were, in fact, little more than a shipwreck convention and the opening of ports which were placed most unsuitably for trade with the heart of Japan.

Putiatin was, paradoxically, aided by a disaster. An earthquake and a tidal wave in Japan deprived him, despite Japanse help, of all his vessels. The Russians thus shared in a Japanese tragedy. Reciprocal aid replaced official isolation, kindness replaced protocol, and hospitality, suspicion. The new spirit was carried over into the negotiations. In the treaty signed in February 1855, Russia gained a third port, Nagasaki, to add to America's two, a delineation of the Russo-Japanese frontier, reciprocal territoriality, and a most-favoured-nation clause.

Putiatin was now faced with the difficulty of returning to Russia with the treaty. British warships were active off Japan and no help could be expected from them, as Britain and Russia were at war in the Crimea. The Americans, however, were more helpful, and it was through them that Putiatin was able to send copies of the treaty to St Petersburg; but they could not send a vessel to repatriate the Russians.

Meanwhile, the crew of one of the sunken Russian ships had, with Japanese help, begun to construct a schooner. Every step in the building of the ship was recorded by Japanese artists and engineers, and the Japanese who worked on this ship later became the fathers of Japanese shipbuilding. Putiatin travelled home in the new schooner and the remainder of the expedition in an American clipper and a German brig. The latter was seized by a British warship and the Russians aboard taken prisoner. They were not repatriated until after the war in 1856.

Neither Perry nor Putiatin really opened Japan. This was left to the American consul-general, Townsend Harris, who, virtually without the assistance of his government, in July 1858 negotiated a commercial treaty. Hearing of this, Putiatin returned to Japan and signed a similar treaty in August, considerably extending the provisions of the original agreement.

The result of foreign penetration, however shallow it might be, was to have formidable consequences for noth the Japanese and the West. In Japan, the ripples moved outward into a wave that was to engulf the shogunate, restore the position of the emperor, and turn Japan into a powerful modern state.

3

The Meeting of East and West: The First Impact

I

SOLDIERS OF CHRIST

AS WE HAVE SEEN (p. 19 ff), the Portuguese entered Asia as paladins of Christ with crusading zeal, intent upon drying up the great sea of paganism and uniting the Indies, and the world, in a spiritual empire at whose head would reign the Pope as priest-emperor and vice-gerent of God on earth. The Portuguese exported the sword rather than the spirit of their faith – for them to attempt to come to terms with spiritual Asia could only be heretical. The number of conversions within the Portuguese dominions, and there were many, was achieved by threats and by the desire of those outside the rigid system of the Hindu social order to find a place in the new dispensation. Just as the majority of Christians in the former British Indian Empire were from outcaste or low-caste groups – seeing in the religion of their rulers a new status within society as well as a possibility of preferential treatment – so it was with the 'pagans' in the Portuguese possessions. But, there, such sensible adaptability was reinforced by the stake and the fire of the Inquisition.

The belief of the Portuguese was simple: the heathen lay under the surety of eternal damnation, on the very edge of the pit. It was the duty of the Portuguese to snatch them – however much they might resist – into the arms of Christ and the certainty of His salvation. Only then could the kingdom of Christ extend its love and happiness over all its subjects. Sometimes the great crusade was forgotten in the enervating luxuries of conquest. Pride, idleness, wealth and vice often obscured the grand design, but sudden revivals born out of a fear for their souls would force the Portuguese once again into a great surge of missionary endeavour. The greatest of these revivals followed the mission of St Francis Xavier, the Apostle of the Indies, who arrived in Goa in 1542 to begin the conversion of the whole of Asia.

Xavier made many converts among the lower classes, identifying their suffering with their separation from the love of the true God. His ten-year mission was carried out quite unknowingly, for Xavier's interest was in souls and nothing else, in terms which the Asian peasant readily understood. Barefoot and in a ragged habit, black of beard and eye, Xavier radiated that passionate certainty of communion with God which is the hallmark of the holy man throughout the East. His mission, however, was more successful in its example than in what it achieved.

Those who were to follow Xavier continued his work of conversion among the lower levels of society. But the Society of Jesus, of which, with Loyola, he was the founder, was moved to try rather different methods. The work of conversion among the common people was moving only slowly. Surely, the later Jesuits thought, it would be simpler to convert the rulers and the intellectuals. If they could be brought into the fold, the rest would follow. Naturally, the approach must be different, an appeal must be made to the mind by scholars, not mystics, by diplomats rather than saints. At the time of Akbar, the emperor who succeeded to the Mughal throne four years after the death of Xavier, the government of Goa was usually represented at native courts by Jesuit diplomatists. Two, the Fathers Aquaviva and Monserrate, reached Akbar's court in 1580 and sought, in the time they could spare from their ordinary business, to convert the emperor to Christianity. The emperor's tolerance and the apparent consideration he gave to their sermons and discourses tempted them into announcing to Rome that his conversion was imminent. Unfortunately, neither understood the nature of Akbar's mind or his insatiable desire for the meat of philosophical controversy. But, as a man does not become a cow by eating beef, neither did Akbar become a Christian by listening to the learned exegesis of the Jesuits. Nor did he become a Jain, a Hindu, a Zoroastrian (or even a Muslim, though he ostensibly was one), yet he invited the learned of all these religions to propound their views before him. Akbar was an intellectual to whom the dispute and the argument were more important than conviction. The Jesuit Fathers were not clever enough, or clear-sighted enough, to realise it.

Far more interesting were the two attempts made to accommodate Christian beliefs to the patterns of Asian thought. Both are exciting because, for the first time, Christianity no longer consigned Asian religions into the general sea of 'paganism'. Instead, it faced up to the challenge of modes of thought and philosophic ideas of great maturity. The recognition of their existence and their right to be challenged was a step forward of immense significance, though an abortive one. Both attempts were abandoned, not because of their failure but because of their success.

During the hundred years or so that followed da Gama's identification of the goddess Kali with the Virgin Mary, the Portuguese learned a good deal about popular Hinduism. They knew nothing of the inner core of Hindu metaphysics. By the end of the sixteenth century, however, the knowledge that there existed philosophical ideas of considerable depth and complexity was reasonably widespread, but these ideas were thought to be either an offshoot of Greek transcendentalism or, as one late seventeenth century scholar decided, 'it might be inferred that in former times the Indians heard of Christianity, and that their religion is an imperfect imitation or corruption of ours'.

Acceptance of the possibility of a common root of ideas led the Jesuits, now convinced that conversion from the top was the surest method of spreading Christianity, to begin an investigation into Brahminical beliefs. Their aim was, firstly, to demonstrate the inferiority of these to Christian beliefs, and then to devise a syncretism, some reconciliation between Christianity and Brahminism – just as Aquinas, in the *Summa Theologica*, employed Aristotle's logical method to establish a transition from Greek to Christian ideas. Today we have access to the Sanskrit classics, which the Jesuits did not. From them, we can see that any attempt at a reconciliation on a dialectical level was doomed to failure. Nevertheless, an attempt *was* made, and it remains one of the most interesting efforts at compromise – and understanding – ever made between East and West.

The person selected for this enterprise was Robert de Nobili, an Italian aristocrat who had become a Jesuit. He arrived in Goa in 1605 with instructions to make his way to Madura, then the most important centre of Hindu learning. The choice of an Italian was as much a part of the Jesuit plan as the decision to send him to Madura. The Portuguese had, since 1567, been actively hostile to Hinduism in their territories. Temples had been destroyed and their revenues diverted for the upkeep of Christian churches; Brahmins were, on Sundays, forced to listen to sermons. De Nobili, as an Italian, could honestly dissociate himself from the Portuguese and their deeds. This he did, and claimed he had given up all for the life of an ascetic. On his journey, he dressed as a Brahmin.

Once at Madura, de Nobili learned Tamil, one of the most difficult of Indian languages. But he found that the holy texts were available only in Sanskrit and that no one but a true Brahmin could learn that language.

Nevertheless, through a Brahmin friend, de Nobili succeeded in obtaining copies of the secret texts and studied them until finally he felt that his knowledge of them permitted him to advance his syncretic system. This he did in 1609, by publishing a book in Sanskrit, exquisitely phrased and brilliant in argument. How de Nobili managed to affix Christianity – with its essential concept of the duality of man and God, and the nature of revelation – to the Brahminic vision of the non-dual nature of reality in which all things are part of the Atman, the World Soul, indivisible, unknowable, yet real, and awareness of whose existence comes through meditation when subject and object disappear... how de Nobili managed this we do not know, for his book no longer exists. Yet his ideas *did* appeal, possibly to some Hindu thinkers who were moving away from belief in absolute non-duality.

De Nobili now took the next, and most dangerous step, of moving from philosophy to ritual. He built a church. For de Nobili to establish himself as a *guru*, or teacher, was all very well. The precedent was firmly established, a place existed for him within the structure of society, his actions sat comfortably within the Hindu tradition. But to establish a place of worship, to indulge in alien rituals, removed him from it and placed him in opposition to the outward expression of Hindu beliefs. To argue and speculate is one thing, but to deny, by the exercise of ritual, the existence of the manifestation of the absolute – the Trinity of Brahma, Vishnu and Siva – was atheism. De Nobili was charged with just that. He survived the accusation, only to be crushed by the unwillingness of the leaders of his own church to accept the concessions he made to caste prejudices in allowing converts to wear the Brahminical cord and other forms of social identification. De Nobili realised that these were outward appearances which could readily be accepted, just as pagan festivals had been absorbed by the early church. In this belief he was confirmed in 1623 by a decree of Pope Gregory XV:

> 'Brahmins are kept from the confession of Christ by difficulties about the cord and the Kudumi [the tuft of long hair worn by South Indians]. Desiring to procure the conversion of these nations, after suitable discussion we accord to the Brahmins and other Gentiles the cord and the Kudumi, sandal paste and the purification of the body. These should not be received in idol temples but only from priests after they have blessed them.'

But de Nobili's victory came too late. The sounds of controversy had reached the Brahmins. The role of *guru* no longer sat comfortably on de Nobili's shoulders. The isolation of the recluse and the respect that came with it were broken. Though de Nobili continued to teach and convert, it was outside the intellectual circles of Madura that his mission was successful. The great experiment, de Nonili's dream of converting the Brahmin hierarchy, dissolved into an argument over caste-marks and cords – in themselves, important, but in no way comparable with the grand vision of the Italian Jesuit.

The other confrontation of the spiritualities of East and West took place in China. Here, contact with the Christian world had once been extensive. In the time of the T'ang, the eighth century, Nestorian Christianity received the protection of the emperor, though its converts were mainly among the Persian and Turkish residents. Christianity's first really significant contact took place with the Mongols, and the Pope began to consider them as active allies against Islam. The Mongols at one time appeared to be on the verge of conversion, for, as they moved towards a more settled dominion, they were in search of a faith. Kublai Khan asked in 1269 for a hundred learned Christians to attend a great conference of many faiths convened at Peking, but the men who were sent took with them an unshakable belief that they were to deal with uneducated barbarians. Confronted by the subtle arguments of Buddhist, Taoist and Confucian scholars, the crusading enthusiasm of the Christians could not compete with the sophistication of highly civilised Asians. But they did make one thing clear, that the missionary effort of the West had deep political implications. The Mongols soon saw the difference between the aggressiveness of Western Christianity and the teachings of Christ. Because of this, the Nestorians, without political aims, continued to have influence. Western missionaries continued to enter the Mongol dominions, but their converts were mainly among Chinese-born foreigners. With the collapse of the Mongol dynasty in 1368, their work was destroyed by a violent anti-foreign reaction that spread throughout China. For two centuries China remained outside the range of missionary expansion, until the incursion of the European into Asia once again brought a dynamic and aggressive Christian effort.

Again, it was the Society of Jesus that was to launch the boldest enterprise in the history of Christianity in Asia. In 1601, Matteo Ricci reached Peking – in the garb of a Buddhist monk and with the Chinese name of Li Ma-tou. Noticing the contempt with which the Confucian *literati* looked upon the now decadent Buddhism, he swiftly changed his robe for the customary dress of a scholar. Ricci's first object was to gain the protection of the emperor. He did this by presenting the emperor with a harpsichord, a map of the world, and two chiming clocks. His petition was clearly expressed; the wise man from the West brought with him the science of the West: 'Your humble subject', he wrote, 'is perfectly acquainted with the celestial sphere, geography and calculations. With the aid of instruments he observes the stars, and he understands the use of the gnomon.' Ricci received an imperial pension, and was allowed to reside in the city. He attained the highest favour of giving les/sons in science to one of the emperor's sons. To Ricci, it seemed that Western science would open the door to Christianity. Ricci and his successors be/came, as far as was possible, indentified with China. Ricci even produced a map of the world in which the two hemispheres centred upon China and not upon Europe. The Jesuits wore the outward appearance of mandarins, ate Chinese food, spoke Chinese well. They also observed that Confucian/ism and ancestor/worship, the beliefs of the rulers, were not so much a reli/gion as a moral code which might be reconciled with Christianity. Ricci produced several works of Christian apologetics – and a Chinese translation of Euclid's *Elements*. He also observed the fundamental importance of the calendar in Chinese life, its occult significance in the ordering of festivals which ensured the stability of the throne as well as the prosperity of the nation. The action of a Jesuit astronomer in reforming the calendar, and re/volutionising Chinese astronomy, also discredited the Muslim astronomers whose errors had endangered the throne.

Secure in their scientific superiority, the Jesuits believed that the time was ripe for a fusion of Christian and Confucian ethics. They drew up a plan for what was, in fact, the establishment of an autonomous Chinese church, complete with its own rites. The first ruling, of Pope Innocent X in 1645, was unfavourable to the Jesuits. The controversy, famous in the history of the church, continued with great bitterness until 1742, when the Bull *Ex Illa Die* wrecked the work and the hopes of the Jesuits completely. Ironically enough, nearly two hundred years too late, in December 1939, the Vatican announced that ancestor/worship and Confucian rites were not incompatible with the Catholic faith.

Until the final blow fell, the Jesuits continued their work. In the middle of the seventeenth century both the son and the empress of the Ming ruler, Yung/li, were baptised, the former with the name of Constantine. Unfortu/nately, the hope implicit in such a name was not fulfilled, as the days of the Ming were already numbered and the reign of the Manchu was beginning. The Jesuits, however, found the new regime still anxious for their scientific expertise; but in 1665 an edict was promulgated which banned Christian proselytising, though this did not remove the influence of the Jesuits. The emperor, K'ang Hsi, stated his viewpoint:

> 'As to the Western doctrine which exalts the Lord of Heaven, it is opposed to our traditional teaching. It is solely because its apostles have a thorough knowledge of mathematical sciences that they are employed by the state. Be careful to keep this in mind.'

The services to the state of two Jesuits changed K'ang Hsi's attitude. The first, Father Verbiest, cast the cannon which ensured an imperial victory over rebels in 1674. The second, Father Gerbilian, as a member of a Chinese delegation to the Russians, helped to negotiate the Treaty of Nerchinsk in 1689 (see p. 166 ff). In 1692, K'ang Hsi issued two edicts of toleration. The first declared:

> 'The men of the West have rectified the calculation of the calendar. In times of war they have repaired old cannon and constructed new ones. They have devoted their energies to the good of the empire and have taken much trouble to this end. Moreover, since the Catholic religion contains nothing evil or irregular, its adherents should be able to continue to practise it freely. We order that the former memorials and resolutions against the said religion be withdrawn.'

The 'Rites' controversy, however, destroyed all the advantages of the re-opening of China to Christianity. When, in 1715, the 'Rites' were condemned, the emperor himself supported the Jesuits; but the intervention of a heathen in theological matters only assisted their enemies. In 1717, the emperor, angered by the disregard paid to his explanations, forbade the preaching of Christianity. The great experiment was over.

The Jesuits in India and China had both attempted a compromise. One with the metaphysic of Brahminism, the other with the ethical system of Confucius. Both had failed despite the success of their creators. The Jesuits saw the universality of Christ's teaching in terms of adaptation and compromise. Unfortunately, they saw it at the time of Europe's expansion, when Western traders and pirates called themselves 'Christian' and supported themselves with the uniqueness of their faith. Henceforth, the missionary effort was to impose not Christianity, as such, but a Westernised version of the teachings of Christ, an expression not of the brotherhood of man but of superior civilisation.

*   *   *

Unlike the Catholic Portuguese, the Protestant nations in their first move into Asia did not carry with them any concept of a Christian world state. Their aim was trade, not conversion. Primarily, this was due to activity in the newly formed Protestant churches being concentrated on reformation at home, and quarrels with Catholics. The heathen would, in fact, have to wait. As late as the end of the eighteenth century, when the great missionary William Carey was on the eve of his departure to India, and anxious to discuss 'the duty of Christians to attempt the spread of the Gospel among the heathen nations', he was told at a gathering of clergymen: 'Young man, sit down. When God pleases to convert the heathen, He will do it without your aid or mine.'

The English East India Company, sensible to the dangers both of proselytism and noble birth, had a clause in its Charter forbidding the sending out to India of 'missionaries and gentlemen'. The prohibition of missionaries continued until the Charter Act of 1813. The European community in India feared the missionary would endanger the security of the British presence by attempting to interfere with the delicate balance of caste. The violence of missionary enthusiasm was a genuine menace to British rule in India, as the Mutiny of 1857 was to prove. Lord Minto (governor-general, 1807–13) summed up the dangers of Christian propaganda in a letter to the chairman of the court of directors of the Company:

> 'Pray read especially the miserable stuff addressed to the Gentooes [Hindus], in which, without one word to convince or to satisfy the mind of the heathen reader, without proof or argument of any kind, the pages are filled with hell fire, and hell fire, and still hotter fire, denounced against a whole race of men for believing in the religion which they were taught by their fathers and mothers, and the truth of which it is simply impossible it should ever have entered into their minds to doubt. Is this the doctrine of our faith?... If there are two opinions among Christians on this point, I can only say that I am of the sect which believes that a just God will condemn no being without individual guilt.... The remainder of this tract seems to aim principally at a general massacre of the Brahmins of this country. A total abolition of caste is openly preached.

But the pressure of such people as Wilberforce and Charles Grant was to result in the opening of the Company's territories to the reforming zeal of Christian missionaries. Wilberforce, whose name lives on for his work in the abolition of the slave trade, described this as 'that greatest of all causes, for I really place it before Abolition' – a surprising but characteristic outburst, reflecting as it did the class-consciousness of this new Protestant crusade. For it was to be a campaign, not to save the ignorant heathen, but to save Englishmen who had fallen into the hands of the Devil. Not only were the English living in sinful luxury, they were also protecting the pagan and his gods, administering temples, organising festivals, and, in general, serving as a 'wet-nurse to Vishnu'.

Both sides armed themselves with tracts and pamphlets, and the battle began. Suttee, infanticide, idolatry, religious suicide, all were brought forward to discredit the protagonists of 'hands off Hinduism'. They, in turn, pointed out the glories of Sanskrit poetry, of architecture, and the general proposition that the religious prejudices of fifty million people should be left alone in the interests of security and good business. But the crusaders won – as might have been expected. One contemporary wrote:

> 'The ban was removed from the missionaries; the lock was struck off the church doors; the Scriptures were permitted to be circulated through the length and breadth of the land, with any comments or arguments that were deemed necessary, and for the first time our Christian government ceased to oppose the diffusion of Christianity in the East.'

But it did not assist it! The furthest it was prepared to go was to appoint a Bishop with his headquarters at Calcutta and his See the whole of the British dominions. The opening of India to the missionaries was more than just the opening of a door to the propagation of an alien religion. It resulted in considerable reforms in certain aspects of Hindu life, and produced an aura of rigid respectability in the rulers. Both were, in abstract, good things, but they emerged out of an arrogance as uncompromising as that of the Portuguese who had sailed for Asia to conquer it for Christ.

The Protestant missions, however, gave greater importance to the dissemination of Christian knowledge than to formal conversion. They became not so much the agents of the Christian God as the propagandists of a superior civilisation. The logic is difficult to analyse, but the belief grew out of a necessity for moral justification. The English, because of their political and scientific superiority, needed a non-material explanation for it, as well as a moral principle to control it. They also sought a moral justification for their rule in India. This they found in the Christian 'duty' to make India Christian, but not superficially by the mere act of conversion. The evangelicals believed in the sudden transformation of society, with the penetration of reform into the lowest reaches of the social organisation. This new crusade was to have strange results, for though it did not convert the heathen to any significant extent, it began a revolution that is still in progress. The social and political impact of Christianity, allied with the new technology, was to set Asia upon a new road, the end of which is not yet in sight.

II

'MISSION CIVILISATRICE'

The beginning of a new conception of power in Asia grew out of the change in relationship between India and Britain. The Industrial Revolution in Britain converted Asia from a supplier of luxury goods into a vast potential market for the new products of the machine. This change in the economic purpose of overseas expansion brought with it a change in political and moral attitudes, an entirely new concept of responsibility, and a belief that the 'benefits' of a higher civilisation must be made available to those unfortunate enough to stand outside it. Belief in the superiority of Western ideas was not entirely empirical. The great outsurge of the Industrial Revolution brought a new element to the class structure – an aggressive, eager and self-conscious body inflamed by the new horizons of technology. The new middle class which was emerging in England saw in the products of their looms and iron-works the materials for a new Jerusalem. Only an acceptance of Divine Purpose could permit the mind to encompass the possibilities of the new world which was opened by the Industrial Revolution. As the results of the emerging economic patterns were essentially material, they reflected a new role for Christianity, a concern for the welfare of man on earth as well as in heaven. Wilberforce made this quite clear in a speech in the House of Commons in June 1813:

> 'Christianity, independently of its effects on a future state of existence, has been acknowledged even by avowed sceptics, to be, beyond all other institutions that ever existed, favourable to the temporal interests and happiness of man...'

The Portuguese had found, in Islam's association with the monopoly of trade in the Indies, an opportunity to give to commerce the sanction of religion and a right to use commerce as a part of their crusade against the pagan. Their view of a Christian world state was on two levels. As agents of the spiritual empire of the Pope, their rights to the commerce of its material parallel were inalienable. In our own times, the Japanese – with their grandiose concept of a Greater East Asia Co-Prosperity Sphere – propounded a similar parallel between the sacerdotal nature of the emperor of Japan and the economic and political domination of the world.

The evangelicals in England also envisaged an interplay of spiritual and material, the alliance of their religion and commerce.

Charles Grant, a director of the East India Company, wrote in 1797:

> 'In considering the affairs of the world as under the control of the Su-
> preme Disposer, and those distant territories... providentially put into
> our hands... is it not necessary to conclude that they were given to us,
> not merely that we might draw an annual profit from them, but that we
> might diffuse among their inhabitants, long sunk in darkness, vice and
> misery, the light and benign influence of the truth, the blessings of well-
> regulated society, the improvements and comforts of active industry?...
> In every progressive step of this work, we shall also serve the original
> design with which we visited India, that design still so important to this
> country – the extension of our commerce.'

The extension of the evangelicals' belief to the organisation of society rested upon one basic conception, that the character of man was a product not of his physical, but of his moral environment. This emerged from the essential Protestant belief that Europe's progress was a direct result of the liberation of the individual, the legacy of the Reformation. Therefore India must have its counterpart, an assimilation on the deepest level. Above all, an anglicisation of the whole fabric of Indian society.

The first purveyors of these revolutionary ideas were, ironically enough, staunch supporters of the East India Company's monopoly of trade. Most possessed a vested interest in its maintenance. They thought they could re-verse the pattern of government in India without interfering with the mer-cantilist concept that political dominion existed for the sake of the drawing-off of tribute. The rational extension of Grant's views was free trade, colon-isation and capital investment – not the drawing away of wealth, but the creation of prosperity. Though the original evangelicals did not see the economic consequences of their beliefs, the new middle class did. The fusion of evangelical ideas with those of the free traders resulted in the colonial policy of nineteenth-century liberalism.

Belief in a civilising mission allied with expansion of trade completely atomised the old order of colonial aggrandisement. The new manufacturer was interested neither in frontiers nor political dominion, and, in fact, saw the latter as an impediment to Britain's new role of supplier to the world, ruler of an empire of trade. To civilise a native was to create a customer, to oppress him merely cost money. In such dominions as Britain already possessed, and was to possess, she must educate the natives to buy British goods. Macaulay gave expression to this view in a speech on the new Charter Act in 1833:

> 'It would be, on the most selfish view of the case, far better for us that the people of India were well-governed and independent of us, than ill-governed and subject to us; that they were ruled by their own kings, but wearing our broadcloth, and working with our cutlery, than that they were performing their salaams to English collectors and English magistrates, but were too ignorant to value, or too poor to buy, English manufactures. To trade with civilised men is infinitely more profitable than to govern savages. That would indeed be a doting wisdom, which, in order that India might remain a dependency, would make it a useless and costly dependency; which would keep an hundred millions of men from being our customers in order that they might continue to be our slaves.'

At last the ideas of Grant and Wilberforce, that the most profitable conquest was that over the mind, were to be put into practice. English education, from which all blessings would undoubtedly flow, was to be let loose on India. Its results were to have a profound effect not only on Asia, but also on the West. Above all, whatever the changes in attitude and the vacillations of political parties, it prepared the way logically for Indian independence – not so much as a right but as a natural consequence of Britain's civilising mission.

Belief in the efficacy of English education as a panacea for all the ills of India was, to the early liberals, as essential as their belief in God. To the Methodists and evangelicals in England, the relation of God and man was entirely personal and access to this relationship could only be achieved through His revealed word. A minimum standard of literacy was the key to conversion – ability to read and understand the Bible were revolutionary instruments. Education, they were convinced, would raise the Indians from their slough of superstition and idolatry. Macaulay maintained, in a letter to his father in 1836, that if his plans for education in India were carried out there would be no need to proselytise. The operation of knowledge among the 'respectable classes' would convince them of the superiority of Christianity and the necessity of conversion.

Though essentially arrogant, the reformers were genuinely convinced that a transformation of India was for the good of the Indians as well as themselves. Because the results achieved by reform coincided with European self-interest, the moral aspect has often been dismissed as hypocrisy of the most unpleasant kind – exploitation disguised by humbug. But this is not true. The nature of the continuing liberal attitude to India was a combination of real altruism and a desire for commercial profit. There was no question in the minds of the early liberals that India would one day be independent – but it would be a new India transformed by Western institutions and moral values, and fit to become a partner in the new prosperity that commerce would release to all.

The evangelicals, as we have seen, believed implicitly in the regenerative effects of Western education. Knowledge was the key to heaven, and to heaven on earth as well, to individual happiness and dignity. Through knowledge of Divine Law, man would purify man's law. The order of evolution was precise; the evangelicals did not believe that human laws could transform character or liberate the individual – the law-giver was God, not man. In this, the evangelicals were only the theorists of the *mission civilisatrice*. It was to be left to the Utilitarians to show how to organise its application. This they did by substituting human for divine law, by re-moving God from the equation. They were revolutionaries who believed that the regeneration of man could be achieved by legislation, by transform-ing the mechanics of social living. To them, sin was a product not so much of the unawareness of God as of poverty; the moral condition of a people was dependent upon their material life. This was a question of politics, not edu-cation. 'Ignorance', wrote James Mill in his *History of British India* (1819), 'is the natural concomitant of poverty; a people wretchedly poor are always ignorant; but poverty is the effect of bad laws and bad government; and is never characteristic of any people who are governed well.' The essential split between evangelical optimism and the doctrines of utility lay in the pessi-mism of Mill. He did not accept the superiority of English civilisation or the boons of commerce. The application of *English* justice was, for him, no key to happiness. Mill was a social mechanic. Efficient government, and the pre-sence of experts to run the machinery, were to him all that mattered. But the spare, cold logic of the Utilitarians was too drab to withstand the warm, enervating messianism of the new industrial classes. In practice, the result was a compromise between the long-term regenerative power of education and the immediate consequences of reformist legislation. Basically, both the evangelical and Utilitarian approaches were abstractionist. The renovation of society was subject to some universal theory – for the former, it was the moral pre-occupations of Christianity, for the latter, a sort of theology of institutions. The early reformers, believing in the superiority of Western civilisation, were not prepared to wait for it to be proved; the proof was already clear to them. The more obvious examples of the inferiority of Indian practices were legislated away – widow-burning, infanticide, and so on. The imposition of Western administrative methods by judicial reform continued, but with the conviction that these were the tools of a superior civilisation rather than the mechanics of efficient government.

It is in Thomas Babington Macaulay that we see the new image of reform. His belief in education was undimmed when he became Law Member of the government of India in 1834, but it was to be not only the instrument of Christian conversion, but the means of producing a class of Indians who would be interpreters and partners in Britain's civilising mission. The political consequences were clear to him and those who thought like him – along the line, somewhere, was Indian self-government. This did not worry Macaulay, for not only did such a thing lie deep in the future, but it would also result in a new and beneficial relationship between Britain and India. In the meanwhile, however, the tasks of government remained. Macaulay's concept of reform – and it is indicative of the slowing down of reformist momentum in England – was away from the great sweeping gestures of transformation, towards the less speculative and more specific areas of change. To him, reform was the remedying of defects in the machinery of government rather than a total transformation of society. The essence of Macaulay's influence was the acknowledgement of expediency. The principles of government were established, but their practice was subject to the logic of each situation, and not to unyielding theories. Macaulay was, in effect, the last of the reformers. By establishing that the criterion of good government was that it should be rational and efficient, it was ensured that direct interference in the life of the people, in their religion and social practices, came to an end. By the time Macaulay left India in 1838, the age of reform was over. Furthermore, British India was about to enter a period of war and expansion that was to last for two decades. The government, as a writer lamented in the *Edinburgh Review* in 1841, 'had no adequate leisure for civil concerns of the utmost importance to the happiness of millions'. In fact, the early Victorians were no longer quite so sure of themselves, nor so convinced of the imminence of the Golden Age.

The pragmatic line established by Macaulay was to continue, and, before the Mutiny, it found its most energetic exponent in Lord Dalhousie, governor-general from 1848–56. To Dalhousie, efficient government meant centralised government, a strong executive and no romantic nonsense. Within

his system of administrative efficiency, there was even a place for the evangelical enthusiast. The Dalhousie method, as exemplified in the 'Punjab System', safely canalised the Old Testament impulses of such men as Henry
Lawrence by uniting the judicial and executive functions in one man, and
then holding him rigidly to account for what he did with them.[1] Dalhousie,
in effect, represented a new climate of optimism in England, where the industrial troubles of the hungry 'forties were over and a new prosperity hit the
manufacturing classes. Again, the ideals and hopes of the first reformers
produced a heady vision of an anglicised India. Again, too, education was
to be the key to happiness and greater markets for English goods. Added to
this was the greatest single tool of material progress – for India was about to
enter the Railway Age. That same Charles Trevelyan who had written in
1838 of the regenerating quality of English schooling, in his *The Education
of the People of India* – a classic statement of the permanent liberal attitude to
India – hailed the railway as the means by which 'the whole machinery of
society will be stimulated' and 'every other improvement whatever, both
physical and moral' intensified. This belief in the *mission civilisatrice* of commerce and education was to survive the shock of the Mutiny and, in increasing dilution, to remain as a partial justification of British rule until the end of
the empire.

Such was the ideological nature of the reform of British administration in
India. What was its effect upon the Indians themselves? For the peasant, the
nature of the impact lay essentially in the spread of poverty. Good government demanded that there be efforts at amelioration – but these could succeed
only superficially, for the causes of poverty were endemic in the British connection.[2] Upon the 'educated' classes, the effect of Britain's self-appointed
civilising mission was profound. Before the Mutiny, though to take this
event as a dividing line is quite arbitrary and is used here only for convenience,
the full blast of English education had not been released – for it was only in
1857 that the first Western-style universities were established at Calcutta,
Bombay and Madras, and, soon after, that grants-in-aid to private schools
began. Even before Macaulay's emphasis on English education, the English
language had already been taught, and substituted for Persian (the legacy of
the Mughals) in official documents. To obtain any public office, English was

---

[1] For Henry Lawrence and the 'Punjab System' see my *The Necessary Hell: John and Henry
Lawrence and the Indian Empire*. London 1958.
[2] The impact of evangelical and Utilitarian ideas on the life of the peasant, as well as of the
educated classes, is dealt with in some detail in my *History of India*. London and New York, 1961.

essential. For Indian businessmen, English was an indispensable require-ment of trade. It was in this group of middle-men that the effect of Western ideas was to be seen first.

The externals of Western civilisation had already become a part of the life of the Indian aristocrat. His armies carried European arms, were drilled, and often led, by Europeans. Architectural forms had been borrowed – as the city of Lucknow remains to this day a witness. European-style carriages, pictures and wines had all become a part of the world of wealth. But intel-lectual influences were few. The Indian aristocrat accepted European objects as exotic playthings, and had no interest whatsoever in European ideas and philosophies. The new middle classes, however, were often men of culture and taste. Aware of the apparent superiority of Western civilisation, they quite naturally wished to know the secret of it. At the same time, there were on the British side officials and missionaries who were also scholars, and – acquiring Indian languages – these managed to penetrate some of the thought-patterns of Indian culture. The first reaction of the middle classes was epito-mised by Ram Mohun Roy (1774–1833), who added to his knowledge of Sanskrit, Persian and Arabic, the English, Greek and Hebrew languages – so that he could read the Christians' Bible. The result of his researches was not a wholesale acceptance of Western beliefs, but an attempt to reform Hin-duism. With Dwarkanath Tagore – grandfather of the poet Rabindranath Tagore – Ram Mohun in 1828 founded the Brahmo Samaj, the aim of which was to purge Hinduism of its idolatry and evil practices. For nearly seventy years, the Brahmos stimulated Bengali intellectual life, awakened the Hindu conscience, and prepared it for the struggle with Western ideas by refusing to accept the inferiority of Indian thought. Ram Mohun also founded the first Indian newspaper.

The second reaction was short-lived as a movement but continuing in its inspiration. Founded under the influence of the half-caste poet Henry Louis Vivian Derozio, its roots lay oddly in the ideas of Rousseau and the works of Shelley and Byron. It despised all religion and espoused reform, and staged attacks upon superstition and orthodoxy – by recklessly hurling beef-bones into Hindu houses and shouting 'We have eaten Mussulman bread'! The main effect of the movement was in its radical belief in intellectual freedom. The twining of this strand with that of the Brahmos gave to Bengal a period of immense and fertile intellectual activity, and made the Bengali renaissance a milestone on the road to freedom.

Until the Mutiny, the impact of Western ideas produced results only amongst a few intellectuals. There was a period of examination, rejection, imitation, and adaptation, when intellectuals began to compare their own traditions with those of the conquerors. The ferment was in no way halted by the Mutiny, for this was a rebellion of the old governing classes, happy to accept the military science and the domestic novelties of the conqueror, but wanting no part in the new world created by the ideas of the West. Their answer was to rebel with the weapons the West had given them. But to the others it became increasingly obvious that the British could best be defeated by turning against them, not their science, but their own beliefs in justice and freedom. The growth of the movement for freedom was slow but sure – and a direct consequence of Britain's 'civilising mission'.

Elsewhere in Asia, the European powers cared little about ideas – not because they recognised how dangerous such things can be, but because they had not reached the stage of reform within their own countries. The Dutch in Indonesia insulated their territories from Western ideas, preserving, in a sort of administrative amber, the traditional culture-patterns of the Javanese. The French were busy acquiring their empire and therefore had little time to spare for the export of French civilisation. This was to come later. But the *missions civilisatrices* of the Dutch and French were, when they took place, of different nature from that of the British. The French aim was to make the Vietnamese intellectual into a French intellectual, and to a large extent they succeeded. The Dutch, until the present century, did not even attempt to make their Asian subjects learn the Dutch language. Dutch liberals were humanitarian employers who believed in giving their employees security and welfare services, but only in the interests of good business – the sort of conscience that can only be reflected in the balance-sheet. The British aim was to create better customers, the Dutch better workers, and the French good Frenchmen. In the long run, it was only the British who came near to success.

4

Imperialism at its Zenith: 1858-1914

I

THE BRIGHTEST JEWEL

WITH THE ASSUMPTION of power in India by the Crown, British rule in the sub-continent reached its final patterns. The Mutiny was the last attempt to throw the British into the sea. Thereafter, a well-disciplined police force and an incorruptible administration, backed by white troops, were all that was necessary for the maintenance of peace within the frontiers. The rulers of India could settle back into the pleasant exercise of efficient and, therefore, by Utilitarian standards, good government. The civil service could retire into the remote paternalism of Platonic Guardians, withdrawn from the people yet jerking the strings of their lives.[1] The white man's burden was a collection of files. India became a show-piece, the exotic appurtenance of great power – the brightest jewel in the British Crown. But a jewel must be guarded and must glitter in a setting worthy of its beauty – and value. The expansion of Britain in Asia after 1858 (though this second movement outwards did not actually start until 1876) was concerned with the security of India, the provision of coaling stations for her fleets, and spheres of influence against her European rivals.[2] The British Empire in Asia was a British-*Indian* Empire, whose capital was in Calcutta. The third British Empire that appeared in Africa from 1870–1914 was of an entirely different nature from that of her second, in Asia, and its acquisition had little or nothing to do with the problems of her Asian possessions. The annexation of Egypt and the Sudan is a special case, for the existence of the Suez Canal, the life-line in India, had to be protected – though this could have been achieved without annexation. The *de facto* cause of the assumption of power in Egypt was the inability of

---

[1] For the effect of the 'new order' upon the lives of the people, see chapter 6, p. 199 ff.
[2] British acquisitions in Asia after the assumption of power in India by the Crown were as follows:
Fiji Islands 1874, Baluchistan 1876–89, Malay Protected States 1883–95, Socotra 1886, Upper Burma 1886, North Borneo Protectorate 1888, Sarawak 1888, British New Guinea 1888, Sikkim 1890, Kowloon 1898, Wei-hai-wei 1898.

Britain and France to collect interest on loans made, not by those countries' governments, but by private individuals.

By 1850, the British had reached the frontiers of Afghanistan. Fear of a possible advance by the Russians into India had led to the disastrous first Afghan War in 1839, when British India's frontier lay on the river Sutlej and the independent kingdom of the Punjab lay between the Sutlej and the frontier passes. Now, the threat of Russian expansion was no longer quite so irrational, for Russia, turning away from the failures of the Crimean War, was determined upon the subjugation of Central Asia right to the northern frontiers of Afghanistan. Both countries had their theorists of a 'forward policy', and their truculent sabre-rattling could be used as a weapon of diplomacy in *Europe*. Fear of Russia, which seems to us now – looking down the corridor of time – a dangerous illusion without foundation in fact, was to the rulers of India a very real thing. They, however, took the consequences of their fear to the most excessive lengths. One British statesman, Lord Salisbury, was even driven to remind the 'wild men' of his own party that excessive dread of Russia might be mitigated by the use of large-scale maps. Ignorance of elementary geography was often the most outstanding characteristic of supporters of the 'forward' school. Above all, the advocates of the 'forward policy' were on both sides drawn from the ranks of soldiers who, more often than not, disguised a passionate desire for glory under the sober cloak of strategic necessity. The classic statement that sums up their policy has all the deceptive logic of simplicity:

> 'You wish the red line of England to advance no further. But to enable this red line to retain its present position... it is absolutely necessary to occupy *parts in advance of it*.'[1]

This logic was to be put to the test.

The Crimean War ended any possibility of agreement between Britain and Russia on the subject of Central Asia. The Russian Empire was expanding in this political vacuum for almost the same reasons as the Indian Empire, which now reached the North-west Frontier, had done. But now the chances of a clash between the two empires in the wastes of Afghanistan had substance, and the motivating power of policy changed from a straight-forward desire for strict security to a concern with the wider field of European rivalries. The frontiers of India were no longer in Asia, but in Westminster.

The problems of the North-west Frontier were not only those in which

[1] *Views and Opinions of General John Jacob*. Bombay, 1858.

British imperial policy was involved. There was also the local question of the trans-frontier tribes. Both, however, were inextricably linked. Attitudes and policies which were appropriate to one were inflicted on the other. General principles were evolved with great diligence out of a purely border policy. Straightforward administrative measures were vitiated by confused imperial thinking.

Under the Sikhs, the Pathans and Baluchs – who occupied the fantastic conglomeration of hills and valleys between the Indus and Afghanistan – had scarcely been administered at all, and the area was in a perpetual state of guerilla war. When the British arrived to administer these frontier areas, the need to control the tribes was accentuated – or perhaps one should say bur-dened – by that chronic pre-occupation of the Victorian empire-builder, the duty to civilise. The fact that the tribes were, at least nominally, subjects of the Amir of Afghanistan, lent colour to the views of the 'forward' school who hoped to intervene in Afghanistan. Those subscribing to its doctrines dreamed of a 'scientific' frontier, well inside Afghanistan territory, which would enclose refractory tribes within the confines of the Indian Empire. Another consensus of opinion was that the barren, rocky land of Afghanis-tan and a turbulent collection of independent tribesmen were the best defence against an expanding Russia. Strategically, the latter were probably right, but they overlooked the fact that an empire which is autocratically ruled by an alien minority cannot tolerate anarchy on its frontiers: chaos is no respecter of boundaries and cannot be stopped at a customs post.

Initially, the old Sikh frontier was maintained and trans-frontier trade en-couraged. Lord Lawrence (John Lawrence), fresh from the lessons of the Mutiny, sought to consolidate India during his term as viceroy. His policy was one of peaceful progress at home and non-interference in the internal affairs of India's neighbours. He conceived that his duty in India was to centralise and unify, and that these responsibilities formed the sum total of British aims and endeavours. He saw the Afghan problem as a will-o'-the-wisp, leading to dangerous swamps, and failed to understand why – as his biographer put it – he should 'make the imperial policy of India depend upon the flight of a random bullet or the dagger of a paradise-seeking Ghazi'. Or, indeed, why he should 'employ our Indian army on a service which they hate, and so to increase the difficulties of the recruiting officer, which are already formidable enough'; or why 'throw away crores of rupees on barren mountain ridges and ever-vanishing frontier lines, while every rupee is sorely needed by a government which can hardly pay its way, and by a vast population which, living on little more than starvation rates, cries aloud to be saved from the tax-gatherer on the one hand and from actual starvation on the other'.

Lawrence's conception of a 'close border' was typical of the man. He was an administrator, not a dreamer; phlegmatic, rather than a visionary. He took his views of strict neutrality, as he did most things, to their logical conclusion. He would support any faction in Afghanistan that appeared stable, but would help no one to achieve the throne. In a letter to Afzal Khan, one of the many contenders for power in Afghanistan, Lawrence blandly wrote:

> 'My friend, the relations of this government are with the actual rulers of Afghanistan. If your Highness is able to consolidate your Highness's power, and is sincerely desirous of being the friend and ally of the British government, I shall be ready to accept your Highness as such...'

No attempt at a settled administration of the frontier tribes was made. It would have been too expensive for John Lawrence, who practically lived within the bars of the Indian budget. Instead, refractory tribes were subjected to punitive expeditions, the so-called 'butcher-and-bolt' tactics which, by destroying the tribes' crops, added to their incentive for plunder and unrest.

But the end of non-intervention was at hand. Superficially, it might seem that such a policy was based on ordinary common sense and a memory of the first Afghan War, or perhaps even on moral grounds, but this was not, in fact, the case. Lawrence never forgot the lesson of the Mutiny – that British government in India was maintained by a combination of power and consent and that a wave of popular feeling, properly led, and supported from outside, could in all probability drive the British into the sea. Lawrence's aim, an aim to which all imperial policy must be subordinate, was simply to prevent the possibility of another – and perhaps more successful – mutiny. This was given explicit expression in his covering despatch to Minutes in reply to Sir Henry Rawlinson's Memorandum – which had proposed measures 'to counteract the advance of Russia in Central Asia, and to strengthen the influence and power of England in Afghanistan and Persia',

> 'Should a foreign power, such as Russia, ever seriously think of invading India from without, or, *what is more probable*, of stirring up the elements of disaffection or anarchy within it, our true policy, our strongest security, would be found to lie in previous abstinence from entanglements at either Kabul, Kandahar, or any similar outpost... in the contentment, if not in the attachment of the masses; in the sense of security of title and

possession... in the construction of material works within British India, which enhance the comfort of the people while they add to our political and military strength... coupled with the avoidance of all sources of complaint, which either invite foreign aggression, or stir up restless spir, its to domestic revolt.'

This was one of the last state papers of Lord Lawrence's administration. In 1869, he was replaced by Lord Mayo. The policy of non-intervention was maintained until, during the administration of Lord Northbrook (1872–6), a Conservative government took office in England. In 1874, Disraeli – still flamboyant in manner – brought to English politics a brilliant, if irrelevant, sense of colour. Pro-Turkish and anti-Russian, he seemed, like a great actor, to dominate the stage with the most expansive and romantic gestures. He was fascinated by the fireworks of diplomacy, the rattling of sabres, the chartering of special trains. Instead of putting diplomatic pressure on St Petersburg, Disraeli chose to make a show of force in Afghanistan. The 'forward policy' and its supporters were to have their chance. Northbrook was instructed to suggest to the Amir that a British Resident should be accred, ited to Kabul. Northbrook protested, and later resigned, maintaining with prophetic insight that the imposition of a Resident on the unwilling Amir would, in all probability, 'subject us to the risk of another unnecessary and costly war in Afghanistan before many years are over'.

To succeed him came Lord Lytton, armed with instructions for 'a more definite, equilateral and practical alliance' with Afghanistan, and blinded with imperial delusions. His political concepts emerged from a poet's world; he was seduced by the grandeur of an imperial mission, but he set about giving it reality with the most rational single-mindedness. As a preparation for the war which would inevitably come, Quetta was occupied in 1877.

In 1878, tension between England and Russia had been increased by England's refusal to acknowledge the treaty of San Stefano, which settled Russia's dispute with Turkey. In order to bring pressure to bear on Russia, Disraeli occupied Cyprus and rushed Indian troops to Malta. Russia's ob, vious reply was to rumble in the vastnesses of Central Asia in the hopes of forcing the government of India to the logical conclusion of its frontier tactics – an expedition against Afghanistan.

On June 13, a Russian agent left for Kabul to attempt to involve the Amir in a treaty very little different from the one which Lord Lytton had pro, posed. But, on July 13, during the Russian agent's absence from Europe, a treaty was signed in Berlin, and he was recalled from Kabul.

Disraeli at this stage realised what a strong position Britain was in, and was ready to open negotiations with St Petersburg, but Lytton and Lord Cranbrooke – then Secretary of State for India – were of a different mind. Lytton saw Russia's apparent withdrawal as the last chance to prove the ideas of the 'forward school' and the first step on the road to a fulfilment of his imperial concepts. The *casus belli* was carefully manufactured. An Afghan frontier official's courteous refusal to allow a mission under Neville Chamberlain to proceed to Kabul was inflated by Lytton into a 'forcible repulse'. Lord Cranbrooke bullied the English cabinet into permitting Lytton to demand an apology and the immediate reception of a mission. On November 21, three Indian armies crossed the Afghan frontier. On the 30th, a letter from the Amir – dated November 19 – was received, accepting the mission. This, however, made no difference to Lytton.

After a number of rather desultory engagements and the occupation of Kandahar and Jalalabad, the Amir, Sher Ali, fled to Russia, where he died in February 1879, and his son, Yakub Khan, signed the treaty of Gandamak in May 1879. The new Amir received various subsidies, in return for which his foreign policy was to be controlled by the government of India.

The Resident appointed to Kabul was one of the leading exponents of the 'forward' movement: Louis Cavagnari, who was described by a contemporary as 'a man of rash and restless disposition, and overbearing temper', consumed by a 'thirst for personal distinction'. In fact, he was just the man to precipitate a repetition of the murder of Alexander Burnes in the Kabul Residency in 1841. Cavagnari and his staff and escort were massacred on September 3, 1879, for the simple reason – as Abdur Rahman wrote in his autobiography – that 'the British envoy looked upon himself as ruler of Afghanistan, and dictated to Yakub what he should do. This boasting was disliked by the Afghan people, and they attacked him'.

Retribution was again the rallying cry. Barbarities were commonplace. General Roberts, taking to heart the government's order that 'punishment should be swift, stern and impressive', permitted indiscriminate hangings, and the burning of villages. An administrative scandal came to light in India with the breakdown of the military accounts department: Indian agriculture had been seriously damaged by the army's requisition of draft animals. The vast structure of threats and deceit crumbled about the viceroy. The government in England fell, and Lord Lytton resigned.

The new Liberal administration appointed Lord Ripon as viceroy, and Abdur Rahman – for long a pensioner of the Russian government – succeeded to the throne of Afghanistan. The 'forward' policy was totally dis-credited.[1]

Though the problems of Afghanistan and the Russian threat to India temporarily receded, they remained the axis on which much of the govern-ment of India's policy revolved. Frontier affairs, both in their imperial aspect and in the local problem of the tribes, offered a continuing excuse for drastic administrative actions, as well as a valid argument for retaining large ele-ments of well-armed British troops in the country – ostensibly for the defence of the frontier. Frontier methods of repression, swift, efficient and brutal, offered an unfortunate example to other parts of the country. Apart from the drain on Indian finances, pre-occupation with the North-west Frontier led to neglect of other frontiers, and to a specialisation of training which was found to be useless in 1942, when India was really threatened with invasion. But the possibility of an attack on India's eastern frontiers was quite beyond the bounds of reason in the last two decades of the nineteenth century, espe-cially as, in 1886, Upper Burma had been annexed.

This last major aggression by Britain in Asia has certain similarities to events in Afghanistan, with France instead of Russia as the rival power. After the war of 1852 (p. 76), Upper Burma had been ruled from 1853 by Mindon, king of Ava, and for twenty-five years his relations with British Lower Burma had been correct if not cordial. In 1862, the formation of the province of British Burma out of the divisions of the Arakan and Tenasse-rim (acquired in the war of 1826), and Pegu (annexed in 1852), convinced Mindon that his relations with the British needed to be established on a firm-er footing than heretofore. That year a British mission was despatched to Mandalay, under the pressure of the Manchester chamber of commerce – who, in the belief that there was a large Chinese market for British cottons, had persuaded the government of India to investigate a route through Upper Burma to Yunnan – and concluded a commercial treaty with Mindon. Un-fortunately, Mindon's wise plan for a new relationship with his former en-emies was frustrated by insurrections and attempts to depose him.

Mindon was particularly disappointed by British unwillingness to supply him with arms, though they were fully aware of the internal threats to his rule. Because of this short-sightedness, he endeavoured to open relations with other European states, notably France and Italy. In 1872, Mindon's chief

[1] The foregoing is an edited version of the author's study of frontier policy before and after the second Afghan War, published under the title 'An Earthen Pipkin and Two Iron Pots' in *United Asia* Vol. 7 No. 1. Bombay 1955.

minister visited England, but he was introduced to Queen Victoria by the secretary of state for India – as if he were a vassal – instead of by the foreign secretary, as the representative of a sovereign state. The minister, on his way to London, had negotiated treaties in Paris and Rome. The French were already active in Mandalay, the new capital built by Mindon, having helped in the construction of the city, as well as supervising the Royal Mint and arms factory. They at once sent an envoy to Mandalay to obtain ratification of the treaty, but without success, for while Burma wanted a full alliance providing for supply of arms, France hoped for the concession of the ruby mines of Mogok – a royal monopoly. A secret agreement, however, was concluded on three clauses: French good offices would be provided in the settlement of disputes between Burma and another party; French officers would be supplied to train the Burmese army; and French citizens would be subject to Burmese courts of law. The agreement was disavowed by the French government on the grounds that the French envoy had exceeded his instructions.

The British completely failed to understand Mindon's position. Their contemptuous relegation of the kingdom of Ava to the same status as an Indian state offended Mindon deeply. The British business community in Rangoon had, as commercial interests always have, complaints about Mindon's trade practices. Also, this was a period of great national arrogance, of the empire on which the sun never set, and of a pride ridiculously sensitive to the most puerile of slights. Burmese court etiquette required, among other things, the removal of shoes, and though the ceremonial had been considerably modified so as not to embarrass Europeans, it still gave offence to the representatives of Great Britain. In 1875, the British Resident at Mandalay was instructed to keep his boots on in the royal presence. The result was that the king would no longer consent to receive him.

Mindon died in 1878, leaving forty-eight sons and a disputed succession. While he lay dying, the king summoned the most popular candidate – there was no right of primogeniture – the Nyaungyan Prince, to the palace. But he, fearing a plot against his life by the supporters of another candidate, the Thibaw Prince, fled to the protection of the British Resident – who unwisely sent him and his younger brother to Calcutta as pensioners of the Indian government. Mindon now suggested the joint succession of three of the princes. This, his ministers maintained, would lead to anarchy, and on Mindon's death Thibaw was placed on the throne. The ministers believed that with a weak king they could introduce a form of cabinet government in the European style – in fact, a constitutional monarchy. They reckoned, how-ever, without Thibaw's principal wife, Supayalat, who in 1879 prevailed upon the new king to murder about eighty members of the royal family – on the pretext that they were planning rebellion. The British Resident now threatened to break off all relations with the court, and in a panic, fearing a British march on Mandalay, the Burmese mobilised their troops. But Britain was occupied elsewhere, in Afghanistan, and against the Zulu in Africa. Burma would have to wait. When the British Resident in Kabul, Sir Louis Cavagnari, was murdered in September 1879, however, the British govern-ment feared that the same thing might happen in Mandalay, and with-drew the assistant Resident (the Resident himself had left in August) and his staff.

The court of Ava, realising for the first time the seriousness of the situation, sent an ambassador with presents to the viceroy of India. At the frontier of British Burma, the envoy was detained, and told that unless he was empow-ered to negotiate a new treaty, the viceroy would not receive him. After six months of futile negotiation on his status, he returned to Mandalay. Possibil-ity of a rapprochement between the two countries presented itself in 1882 over the question of the demarcation of the Burmese frontier with Manipur. A Burmese envoy sent to Calcutta was given a friendly reception, but provo-cative actions by the Burmese on the frontier destroyed the possibility of im-provement in relations between Burma and British India.

Meanwhile, Upper Burma was dissolving into chaos and anarchy. Ban-dits roamed the countryside, the Kachins were in rebellion, Chinese guerillas burnt the town of Bhamo, and the feudatory princes of the Shan States threw off their allegiance. A conspiracy to depose Thibaw and to replace him with the Myingun Prince, then in exile at Pondicherry, came to nothing when the French interned him. In 1884, Mandalay was once again a scene of butchery, when suspected conspirators were murdered. British and Chi-nese commercial interests again demanded that something should be done – a change of government, or outright annexation. The chief commissioner of British Burma favoured the replacement of Thibaw by the Nyaungyan Prince, but the government of India – suddenly respectable under the memory of a similar attempt to replace rulers in Afghanistan – argued that internal mis-government was not an excuse for outside intervention. In 1885, the prince died, and with him the possibility of anything other than annexation.

It now turned out that Thibaw's intransigence over the Manipur frontier question was dictated by an attempt to play France off against Britain.

French activities in Annam and Tongking (see p. 132) were making the British uneasy, and Thibaw thought the time was ripe for a repetition of Mindon's tactics of 1872. A Burmese mission sent to Europe in 1883, super-ficially to collect information about Western industrial and scientific tech-niques, once again raised the vexed question of the import of arms when they reached Paris. A protest by Britain resulted in the French government's guarantee that no facilities would be granted for the purchase of arms. The mission, however, remained in Paris.

Under pressure, the French finally admitted that the Burmese were at-tempting to negotiate a full treaty of alliance which would include the right to purchase arms. France's prime minister, Jules Ferry, assured the British government that no such treaty had been, or would be, concluded. Never-theless, the Burmese still hung on in Paris. Under further pressure, the French admitted to signing a 'harmless' commercial treaty, with no political or military agreements. A French consul would be stationed at Mandalay. He arrived to take up his post in May 1885.

It soon turned out that Ferry's harmless treaty included the establishment of a bank at Mandalay, and the construction of a railway from there to Toun-goo in British Burma. The consul advised Thibaw to improve relations with the British and again receive the Resident. Then he could negotiate treaties with France, Germany and Italy, and establish his neutrality. This advice was rejected. Meanwhile, rumours of French plans continued to circulate. The French were, rumour said, about to take over the management of the royal monopolies, to control the postal system, to run a fleet of river steamers in opposition to the British-owned Irrawaddy Flotilla Company, and organise overland trade with Tongking.

While this was going on in Burma, the government of Jules Ferry had fall-en, and a copy of a secret letter from him to the Burmese envoy in Paris fell into the hands of the British. The letter contained a carefully guarded promise that on the pacification of Tongking by the French, arms would be delivered to Burma through that country. On disclosure of the letter's contents, the French government – embarrassed by difficulties in Tongking and wars in China and Madagascar – repudiated their consul's actions and recalled him.

The revelation of the secret promises of the French government caught Thibaw at an awkward moment. Safe, he thought, under the protection of his agreements with France, and urged on by French commercial interests, he had decided to attack the major British trading organisation in Upper Burma. This, the Bombay Burmah Trading Corporation, held the concession for extraction of teak from the forests north of Toungoo, part of which were in Upper Burma. The corporation was accused of extracting more teak than it had paid for, of bribing Burmese officials and failing to pay Burmese foresters the amounts due to them. Without delay and without examination of evidence, the corporation was found guilty of defrauding the king of the equivalent of £73,333, and the foresters of £33,333. The corporation was ordered to pay twice the first sum to the king, and the second to the foresters. In default, its timber and property would be seized. The decision was published in August 1885.

An appeal to the court of Ava for arbitration was rejected in October. As the war department in Calcutta had had a plan for the invasion of Upper Burma ready for some years, the viceroy felt able to issue an ultimatum on 30 October, to expire on 10 November. This caught Thibaw unawares. He replied, refusing to re-open the case, but stating that a British envoy would be received at Mandalay 'as in former times'. To another paragraph in the ultimatum, demanding that he place the conduct of external affairs under the control of the government of India, he replied that 'friendly relations with France, Italy and other States have been, are being, and will be maintained'.

From the British point of view, threatened, as she believed, by French expansion in Indo-China, there was no alternative but to act. On 14 November, British troops crossed the frontier, and a fortnight later, after an almost bloodless campaign, occupied Mandalay and took Thibaw prisoner. The British would have preferred to set up a protectorate, but the only suitable candidates were dead – either murdered by Thibaw, or having died in exile. On 1 January 1886, Upper Burma was finally annexed, and in the following month became a province of British India.

The abolition of the monarchy produced a reaction throughout Burma, even in those portions previously administered by the British. The pacification of the country took five years of heavy fighting and the employment of 32,000 troops and 8,500 military police. When settled government was finally established, the customs of the country were ignored and the Indian system of direct administration imposed. This caused considerable difficulties. The treatment of Burma as just another Indian province led directly to the withdrawal of Burma from the Commonwealth when the country achieved independence in 1948.

With the annexation of Upper Burma, the British Empire reached the limits of its territorial expansion. The great conflicts for dominion amongst the European powers was at an end. This did not mean that friction between them was also over, but the major partition of Asia was now established. The nature of conflict was to change from aggression to a search for internal security, for the maintenance of power rather than its expansion. The weapons of conflict were no longer to be arms, but ideas.

II

MALAYA, INDO-CHINA AND SIAM

Between 1867, when responsibility for the Straits Settlements passed from the secretary of state for India to the colonial office, and 1873, the policy of non-intervention in the affairs of native Malay States was rigidly maintained, despite the insecurity and disorder that reigned. Once again, the logic of empire that cannot permit anarchy on its frontiers was assisted by the pressure of commercial interests. Exploitation of the natural resources of the peninsula was considerably hampered by the disintegration of order in the states. Apart from the petty wars of the sultans, an explosive charge existed in the vast concentration of Chinese labourers at the mining camps in Perak, Selangor and Negri Sembilan, where allegiance was divided between two hostile secret societies. Clan fights were commonplace and piracy was an occupation of some profit. This disturbed state of the peninsula occurred at a time when the European powers were refreshed by a new imperialist spirit. When, in fact, the old patterns of trade and dominion were reinforced by the scramble for world power, above all for world markets. Britain had reached her overriding position on the wave of her industrial revolution. But now other European countries were in competition with her. The Dutch once again were on the move in Indonesia, and a bargain was struck in 1871 between them and the British over the former's activities in Sumatra. There, the Dutch were bringing under their control certain east coast ports which were, by treaty, open to British trade. The Dutch confirmed the right to trade in return for a free hand against the Sultan of Acheh, whose piracies caused trouble to both countries. In 1869, the sultan had been unsuccessful in obtaining the assistance of Turkey against both the Dutch and the British. The position of Acheh on the northern tip of Sumatra (map p. 334) was of great strategic importance, especially since the opening of the Suez Canal (1869) and the increased amount of shipping in the East. The bargain consisted in the cession by the Dutch of settlements on the Gold Coast of West Africa, and a guarantee of equal opportunity for the British to trade in the Indonesian archipelago, in return for which the Dutch were to have a free hand in Sumatra.

The new order in Malaya began with the famous Pangkor Engagement of 1874, when the governor of the Straits Settlements placed his own nominee – who was also the legitimate claimant – on the throne of Perak. This engage/ment provided that the British would help to maintain order and protect the sultan. Clause 6, the most important and far/reaching in its consequences, laid down that 'the sultan receive, and provide a suitable residence for, a British official, to be called a Resident, who shall be accredited to his court and whose advice must be asked and acted upon in all questions other than those touching Malay religion and custom'. Clause 10 completed the Resi/dent's position in the state – 'the collection and control of all revenues and the general administration of the country to be regulated under the advice of these Residents'.

By 1895, all the principal Malay States were operating under the Residency system. Problems there had been; one Resident had even been assassinated. The difficulties of communication with Singapore left Residents very much to themselves, and though, from 1876 to 1882, the governor of the Straits Settlements had a Secretary for Malay Affairs, the appointment was discon/tinued because no one with sufficient knowledge of the states and their prob/lems could be found to fill it. This was all very well while the economic de/velopment of the peninsula was in the hands of Chinese capitalists, but on the influx of European capital it became necessary for some central au/thority to co/ordinate the administration of the states. The result was the in/auguration of the Federated Malay States in July 1896.

The Federation Agreement protected the sultans and increased their in/come, while giving the British complete administrative control. At the same time, the appearance of sovereignty left to the Malay rulers supplied a con/venient device by which the British could ignore the peculiar position of the Chinese both as capitalists and labourers. As a result of the new order, the population increased, and revenue grew from eight and a half million dol/lars in 1895 to twenty/four millions in 1905. Railways and roads were built, and post offices and banks spread over the country. The rate of progress was formidable and without parallel in the history of British overseas administration.

In 1909, a Federal Council was formed at the desire of the sultans, so that they might have some representation in their own government. The council, however, merely functioned as an agency of the British high commissioner, and the sultans had no legislative functions whatsoever. The reasons for this were simple. The first ten years of the twentieth century saw an economic revolution in Malaya which hurled her into the industrial maelstrom. The concomitants of this new position – health, education, techniques – could not be dealt with by the sultans, bogged down in their mediaeval conceptions and lack of expertise. Vast amounts of foreign capital flooded into the tin mines and rubber estates of Malaya. By 1900, Malaya produced half the world's total output of tin. Rubber, which was first planted in 1877, was slow to compete with the Brazilian product. But the rubber boom of 1910-12 resulted in such an expansion in both acreage and technical efficiency that by 1914 Malayan rubber could be delivered in New York at a lower price than that from South America.

In 1909, the four northern States of Kedah, Perlis, Kelantan and Trengganu came under British control, under the terms of the Anglo-Siamese treaty of that year, but all refused to join the Federation. Johore was also outside and it was not until 1914 that a British adviser was accepted.

By the outbreak of the first World War, the political structure that was to last until the Japanese invasion twenty-nine years later had been established. It consisted of three distinct systems: the Straits Settlements, a British colony directly controlled; the Federated Malay States, administered under the front of sovereign native rulers; and the Unfederated States, in which the British Adviser (not Resident) interfered as little as possible.

*   *   *

The capture of Tourane in Vietnam in 1858, by the Franco-Spanish fleet (see p. 83), brought troubles in its wake. The inhabitants had completely stripped the town before their departure, and supplies were unobtainable. The admiral therefore decided to evacuate the town and attempt to capture Saigon. This he achieved in February 1859. In November of the same year, an attempt was made to re-open negotiations with the Emperor Tu-Duc. French demands had been increased – French consuls in the three ports of the empire, and a chargé d'affaires at the capital, Hué. As Tu-Duc attempted delaying tactics, a naval force destroyed more forts near Tourane. On resumption of hostilities in China in 1860, however, French forces in Indo-China were withdrawn, leaving only a Franco-Spanish garrison of 1,000 men at Saigon. From March 1860 to February 1861 this small force held out against a besieging army of 12,000 Vietnamese.

The China war ended in January 1861 and a strong French naval force and 3,000 troops left for Saigon to raise the siege. This campaign was successful, as were those that followed, until by November of that year the French were masters of the whole of Lower Cochin China. In May of 1862, Tu-Duc asked for terms. He was involved with a serious rebellion in Tongking and wished to make peace in the south. The result was a draft treaty signed at Saigon, which ceded to France the three eastern provinces of Cochin China, agreed the payment of a heavy indemnity, freedom for the Catholic religion in all Tu-Duc's territories, and the opening of the ports of Tourane, Balat and Kuang-an to French trade.

The delivery of this draft treaty to Paris was delayed by storms, and when it was finally received back at Saigon, Tu-Duc refused to ratify it. Only when the French threatened to aid the rebels in Tongking did he agree to its ratification. In the meantime, the new French commander, Admiral Bonard, had foolishly replaced the French Residents, appointed by his predecessor to supervise the administration of the provinces, with Vietnamese mandarins. The result was a spate of rebellions. By 1863, the situation was serious. Back in Europe, Napoleon III was almost convinced of the advisability of abandoning French interests in Indo-China but was persuaded not to do so by his minister of marine. The French then proceeded to bring order to their newly acquired provinces.

In 1863, King Norodom of Cambodia, a vassal of Siam, was persuaded to sign a treaty placing his kingdom under French protection. Siam, with British support, protested, and her Resident at the Cambodian capital forced the weak king to sign a document acknowledging that he was a vassal of Siam and his true rank only 'Viceroy of Cambodia'. The king of Siam further stated that he would supervise Norodom's coronation and receive his homage. It was now the turn of the French to protest. As the Cambodian regalia had been left at Bangkok for safe keeping, the king of Siam insisted that Norodom should be crowned there. Norodom decided to set off for Bangkok in March 1864. The French commander thereupon threatened to occupy the Cambodian capital, and when Norodom left for Siam French marines took over the royal palace and raised the tricolour flag. Hearing of this, Norodom returned and ratified the treaty establishing a French protectorate over his country in April 1864. Siamese claims on Cambodia were finally settled in 1867, when Siam agreed to surrender her rights of suzerainty in return for the provinces of Battambang and Siemreap. Norodom was not consulted.

Resistance to French rule still continued throughout the French provinces of Cochin China from armed bands based in the three provinces of western Cochin China. In June 1866, the French occupied these provinces against very little opposition. With the occupation of the delta of the Mekong river, the French began to look to the possibilities of trade with western China, just as Britain, controlling the delta of the Irrawaddy, was looking in the same direction. French exploration of the Mekong, however, proved it to be utterly useless as a trade route between Saigon and Yunnan. The expedition that made its way up the river nevertheless returned with information about the waterways linking Yunnan with the Red River of Tongking. This was to have a profound effect upon French expansion after the Franco-Prussian War of 1870-1.

In 1873, Francis Garnier, who had been a leader of the expedition exploring the Mekong, was sent to Hanoi to arbitrate between a French merchant, Dupuis – who had occupied part of the city by force – and the local mandarins. Garnier was an impulsive man, determined to rescue French prestige in Asia from the deflation it had received through its defeat in Europe, and, finding the mandarins unwilling to negotiate, he seized the citadel and, later, control of Lower Tongking. The court at Hué was ready to negotiate with the French, but the local mandarins bought the assistance of robber bands of Chinese, known as the Black Flags, and Garnier was killed in a sortie against them.

The French governor of Cochin China had, in fact, sent an envoy to order Garnier to refrain from his aggressive acts, but the envoy arrived in Hanoi after Garnier's death. The French were withdrawn from their captured forts, despite the loss of face, and a treaty was concluded with Tu-Duc which granted considerable concessions to the French in return for arms and instructors to help in the pacification of the country. The whole affair was treated as a display of weakness by the French and, as soon as French forces left Tongking, Tu-Duc rejected the treaty, persecuted Christians, and subjected French officials to considerable indignity. He also renewed his allegiance to the emperor of China as an insurance against French aggression.

Anarchy in Tongking increased. Tu-Duc, playing a double game, encouraged bandits as a weapon against the French and asked Chinese aid in suppressing them. He hoped that any French attempt to occupy Tongking would involve the French with both parties.

By 1880, France had recovered from her defeat by Prussia and was determined to revive her power in the East. On the excuse of protecting French

lives, an expedition entered Tongking in 1882. The aim of the French government was to bring not only Tongking but Annam under a French protectorate. The French campaign was carried out with considerable brutality
and resulted in conflict with China. This undeclared war was concluded in
March 1885, by China's crushing defeat of a French force. News of this
disaster brought down the government of Jules Ferry, and the new administration signed a peace agreement with China.

The Emperor Tu-Duc had died in August 1883, and his successor Hiep-
Hoa signed an agreement with France in the same year making Vietnam a
French protectorate. In November, the emperor was assassinated by patriots
and succeeded by Kien-Phuc – who was, in turn, deposed in July 1884 and
replaced by Ham-Nghi. In July of the following year, Ham-Nghi fled to
Laos. The French now intervened and placed their own candidate, Dong-
Khanh, on the throne. It was not until 1895 that Tongking was completely
pacified, and rebellion and unrest continued for many years.

In 1887, the protectorates of Annam, Tongking and Cambodia were,
with Cochin China, formed into the *Union Indochinoise*. The French occupation of Indo-China was the result of a long and protracted struggle. Internal security was continually threatened by rebellion, and French methods of
repression can only be compared with those of the Dutch in Indonesia. It is
no coincidence that it was these two nations that hung on to their possessions
in Asia until the very last, or that they accepted the independence of their dominions unwillingly, and in the same bloody way as they had originally
captured and held them.

*   *   *

Mongkut, who succeeded Rama III as king of Siam in 1851, had, in fact,
been the rightful heir to the throne on the death of Rama II in 1824. At that
time, Mongkut was a Buddhist monk, and after his elder brother's seizure of
the throne he remained in the order until his accession. This freedom from
the concentration-camp seclusion of an oriental court combined with
Mongkut's immensely enquiring mind had a profound effect upon his administration. As a monk, his constant pilgrimages had brought him in contact with all sorts of people from the highest to the lowest. He studied Latin,
mathematics and astronomy with a French soldier-missionary, and learned
to read and write English from American missionaries. His reading was
wide and his knowledge of international affairs unprecedented, and unequalled, in an Asian ruler. The personality of Mongkut, and his recognition that

Siam must come to terms with the outside world, were the largest single factors in the preservation of Siamese independence in the nineteenth century. Because of him, Siam was the only state in South-east Asia not to come under European control.

As Rama III lay dying, the chief members of the royal family and the highest officials of the realm decided to ignore the claims of his sons, and invited Mongkut to succeed. This he did reluctantly, and on the condition that his brother, Itsarate Rangsan, be appointed Second King. This prince, who spoke fluent English and lived in European style, though never prominent in public affairs had great influence in his brother's government. His political opinions were well in advance of Mongkut's, whose mind was a mass of contradictions brought about by the clash of Western ideas and Eastern conservatism. In the West, these contradictions are known only through the unfair portrait of the king published by Mrs Anna Leonowens, the English governess engaged by him in 1862 as tutor for the royal children, a picture further distorted by the musical *The King and I*.

In 1855, Mongkut concluded a Treaty of Friendship and Commerce with Britain. The negotiations were assisted by the appointment of Sir John Bowring, who was a personal friend of the king, and was liked and respected by the Siamese. Also, the documents he carried were not issued by the governor-general of India but by Queen Victoria herself, under her sign manual – an important factor in prestige. The terms of the treaty were the most favourable ever granted by Siam to a foreign power. Duty on British goods was limited to three per cent, the import of opium – subject to certain restrictions – was permitted, and a scale of import duties was agreed. British subjects were permitted to buy or rent land near the capital, and a consul resident at Bangkok was permitted to exercise civil and criminal jurisdiction over British citizens. The signing of the treaty (it took only a month to negotiate) started a chain reaction, and agreements followed with France and the United States in 1856, Denmark and the Hanseatic cities in 1858, Portugal in 1859, Holland in 1860, and Prussia in 1862. In 1868, Sir John Bowring negotiated treaties on behalf of Belgium, Italy, Norway and Sweden. Britain, however, reaped the main profit. Singapore and Hong Kong engaged in trade with Siamese ports, the Bombay Burmah Trading Corporation acquired most of the teak concessions in northern Siam, and soon Britain had the largest investment in the country. The real effect of this new contact with the West lay in the employment of Europeans in the government services. Mongkut, and his successor Chulalongkorn, appointed many Europeans as heads of departments.

The British dominated, but a former Belgian minister of the interior became Chulalongkorn's general adviser, a Dane was head of the provincial gen-darmerie, and an Italian head of the military cadet school.

Mongkut's relations with France were initially cordial, but when France began her expansion in Cochin China the situation deteriorated and, after the treaty of 1867, in which Siam surrendered her rights in Cambodia, he moved even closer to Britain. Mongkut's death was caused by his immense interest in scientific affairs. An eclipse of the sun was visible in Siam in August 1868, and Mongkut, wishing to demonstrate the importance of science to his country, set up an expedition to witness it. Unfortunately, the spot chosen was malarial, and the king was struck by fever. He died a month later.

Mongkut had built roads and dug canals and, in 1861, minted flat coins. His reforms in administration had only just begun. Their effect upon the traditional patterns of Siamese life had not yet been felt. His successor, Chu-lalongkorn, then sixteen years old, was left with a country still without a fixed legal code, with no proper financial system, no modern army, no railways, and very few roads. As he was a minor, a regency ruled until 1873, and Chu-lalongkorn travelled abroad and studied administrative methods in Java and India. He returned to Siam determined upon sweeping reforms. His first act was to announce that the practice of prostration in the royal presence was abolished. His father had removed the ancient tabu against looking upon the king directly. In the reign of Mongkut's predecessor, Rama III, the king left the palace only once a year, and his route was cleared of people, who had to shut themselves in their houses. While Chulalongkorn often drove about in public, he still made no attempt to cut himself away from the pattern of ha-rem life or the hot-house jealousies of the palace.

Reforms continued in every sphere of activity until, at Chulalongkorn's death in 1910, Siam was at least as well administered as the European do-minions in Asia. Above all, she had maintained her independence.

Internationally, Siam found herself in the centre of the conflicting interests of France and Britain. The former, ruthlessly carving an empire in Indo-Chi-na, found Siamese claims of suzerainty irksome and her attempts to establish them, provocative. After the annexation of Upper Burma, Britain and France agreed on the necessity of having Siam as a buffer state between their posses-sions. The question then arose of the area of Siamese territory and the need for a demarcation of her frontiers, particularly in the north, where Britain had inherited the tributary relationship of certain of the Shan States with the former kingdom of Ava. French exploration of the Mekong and her obvious intention of making it her frontier with Siam, meant that the two empires would have a contiguous frontier. In 1893, a French ultimatum was delivered in Bangkok, which demanded that Siamese troops in conflict with the French should be withdrawn from the Mekong. This was accepted by the Siamese, but did not satisfy the French government in Paris, which instructed its envoy to demand the cession of the whole of the territory on the left bank of the Mekong (see map p. 333), including Luang Prabang, and an indemnity of three million francs (then about £120,000) for the damage caused by the Siamese fort at Pahnam to French warships making their way up to Bangkok in order to threaten the city! The envoy also demanded the punishment of those responsible. The Siamese accepted the last two proposals but offered a compromise on the first. The French envoy then threatened to leave the capital if his demands were not met in full.

Britain now began to be alarmed. If France annexed the Mekong territory, her frontier *would* touch that of Burma, Siamese independence would be seriously threatened and Britain's interests menaced. Britain protested, then accepted a French assurance of her willingness to create a buffer state and to guarantee Siamese integrity. Despite previous experience of French duplicity, the British government even went so far as to advise Siam to agree to the French demands. Britain's position seemed, to Chulalongkorn, a denial of her friendship and interests in Siam. But Britain feared that the 'fiery Chauvinism of the Colonial Jingoes of Tongking and Saigon' – as Lord Curzon described it – would have resulted in the occupation of Siam if the demands had not been met. Britain also feared that the influence of the colonists upon the government in Paris might have widened any Anglo-French conflict in the area into a European war.

This possibility was very real, as can be seen from the results of a petty affair in the state of Keng Cheng in 1893. A Buffer State Commission established that year ran into difficulties over the question of sovereignty. Britain proposed to transfer the little state of Keng Cheng to Siam, but France claimed that, by the Franco-Siamese treaty, the state belonged to her since it lay on the left bank of the Mekong. The ruler of the state, in understandable confusion over his status, decided that his best course was to raise the French flag. On the arrival of J. G. Scott, the British member of the commission, in December 1894, the ruler took fright and fled. Scott hauled down the French flag and raised the Union Jack. When the French envoy turned up in January 1895, this flag was still flying. A major international incident seemed to be in the making. The Buffer State Commission was dissolved and an hysterical outburst in France nearly led to war. Negotiations, however, concluded with Britain renouncing her claims to territory east of the Mekong in return for a joint guarantee of the independence of the Menam valley. The agreement was signed in January 1896.

For Britain, this was a good bargain. She had never had any intention of annexing land across the Mekong, anyway, and Siam retained four-fifths of her population and remained the richest country (economically) in the whole of the Indo-Chinese peninsula. France, on the other hand, acquired a great deal of territory in terms of acreage, but it was of no value whatsoever economically. When France realised this in later years, constant quarrels with Siam kept a dangerous situation in existence. The drain on French finances in the occupation of its newly acquired territory was heavy and unrewarding.

Anglo-French rivalry over trade with Yunnan died when it was discovered that the possibilities were not as golden as everyone had thought. The French built a railway linking Tongking with Kunming and it was intended that this should link up with the Burma railways. The cost, however, and the difficulties of construction in northern Burma, as well as the very dubious chance of any reasonable return, led Lord Curzon – then viceroy of India – to veto the proposal in 1900.

The Entente Cordiale of 1904 between France and Britain ended controversy over Siam. The French concluded new agreements with Siam, involving an exchange of territory. In 1909, Britain surrendered her extra-territorial rights in Siam in return for sovereignty over the Malay States of Kelantan, Trengganu, Kedah and Perlis. Siam was also granted a loan of £4,000,000 for railway construction. On the whole, Siam was the gainer, and the settlement with France was to introduce a new period of reforms.

III

INDONESIA

Constitutional changes in Holland in 1848 placed her colonies under the supreme control of the king, and made colonial legislation the responsibility of the Dutch parliament. Initially, this had very little effect in the Dutch East Indies, but a regulation of 1854, which came into force two years later, provided that power be exercised by a governor-general and council. The regulation also envisaged the abandonment of the 'culture system' and the forced cultivation of crops. Reforms, however, in the hands of a Conservative government in Holland, moved desperately slowly. In 1860, the publication of a novel, *Max Havelaar* – written pseudonymously by E. D. Dekker – once again exposed the oppression of the Javanese under the culture system. The success of the book, a work of very considerable literary merit, created wide support for the Liberal opposition. A former planter, I. F. van der Putte, published a number of pamphlets which also helped the struggle against the system. In 1863, van der Putte, who obviously knew by intimate experience the vicious effects of the system, was appointed by a Liberal prime minister to the ministry of colonies. Free enterprise, the Liberal panacea for all economic ills, resulted in the abolition of forced cultivation of pepper in 1862, cloves and nutmeg in 1863, indigo, tea, cinnamon and cochineal in 1865, and tobacco in 1866. All, strangely enough, no longer profitable. Sugar and coffee, continuing and expanding sources of profit, continued to be forcibly cultivated. A number of abuses were also removed. Compulsory labour in the forests was abolished in 1865 and, from 1867, the budget of the Indies was subject to the control of the home parliament. By the Sugar Law of 1870, the government was to cease the cultivation of sugar in twelve years from 1878. Coffee continued a state monopoly until 1917, and opium, salt, and pawnshops (an extremely profitable line of business), continued as state monopolies until the end of Dutch rule. Liberalism in its Dutch form considered the colonies as a purely business venture, and its desire to save the inhabitants from oppression was subordinate to making Dutch possessions safe for private capital. From 1870 onwards, private investment in agricultural production in Java was considerable, and the value of state exports declined from 46.5m. guilders in 1870 to 16.3m. in 1885, while that of private enterprise increased from 61.2m. in 1870 to 168.7m. in 1885.

Most of the investment was in Java, and the outer settlements were neglected not only economically but administratively. Outside Java, Dutch rule virtually did not exist. The activities of James Brooke, the 'white Raja' of Sarawak, in Borneo, and the annexation by Britain of the island of Labuan, pushed the Dutch into action and a more energetic policy of exploration, intervention and annexation was carried out in Borneo, Bali and the Celebes. The Dutch, however, paid most attention to the island of Sumatra, and slowly began to establish control. But it was the treaty of 1871 between Britain and Holland (see p. 127) that gave the signal for a new era of Dutch expansion.

The independent sultanate of Acheh on the north-western tip of Sumatra had as its chief source of revenue the occupation of piracy. By the Treaty of London (1824), it had been made the responsibility of the Dutch to keep the seas around Acheh free from pirates. The Dutch maintained that this was impossible so long as Acheh not only gave port facilities to pirate vessels but was, in fact, encouraging their activities. To stamp out piracy, Achinese ports must be occupied. The treaty, however, prevented this, because one of its provisions was a guarantee of Achinese sovereignty. Dutch expansion in Sumatra led the Sultan to ask Turkey for aid – an appeal from a Muslim ruler to the only Muslim state of world stature. Turkey, threatened as she then was by Russia, was unable to help. After the treaty of 1871, the Dutch opened negotiations with the Sultan on the island of Riau. On their way home, the Achinese embassy stopped at Singapore and began secret discus-sions with the American and Italian consuls there. The Achinese proposals were turned down by the Italian consul, but the American drafted the terms of a commercial treaty between the two countries. A false report that the American consul had asked for warships to be sent to Sumatra to protect American interests resulted in a strongly-worded protest from the Dutch to the American secretary of state, and an equally sharp rebuttal. The Dutch made one more attempt to negotiate with Acheh. The Sultan, however, was unyielding, and the Dutch began the longest and hardest-fought campaign in their colonial history.

In April 1873, a weak Dutch force was sent against Acheh, and had to be withdrawn. A larger one, sent in December of the same year, captured the Sultan's chief minister who died shortly afterwards. Operations were then suspended in the hope that his successor would accept Dutch sovereignty. But Dutch hopes were blasted by a widespread revolt and bitter guerilla fighting. Between 1878 and 1881, a large number of chiefs were forced to submit. The Dutch, believing resistance to be broken, began to set up civil government. The result was another outbreak of revolt strengthened by a declaration of a holy war against the infidel. Dutch policy fluctuated with each new governor, leniency led to a further rising, and in turn to coercion. A new campaign of all-out military attack began in 1898. By the next year, the Dutch dominated Acheh proper, and the rebels were being chased into the outer territories. By 1904, most of the important chiefs had submitted to the Dutch forces but disturbances continued until the exile of the claimant to the sultanate in 1908. Military government continued, however, for an-other ten years.

The campaign against Acheh had considerable effect outside the narrow limits of Indonesia. It was the first major outbreak of Muslim fanaticism in the late nineteenth century. It undoubtedly had its effect upon the actions of the Mahdi in the Sudan, and stimulated a new wave of anti-European hatred in the countries of Islam. Realising this, the Dutch cultivated good relations with Mecca by encouraging the pilgrim traffic between Indonesia and the holy city, and by appointing a Muslim Indonesian as Dutch vice-consul there.

The forward movement in Indonesia was not confined to the bitter and lengthy campaign against Acheh. Between 1875 and 1881, the Moluccas and Lesser Sunda islands were brought under control, and much was done to consolidate Dutch power in the rest of Sumatra outside Acheh. In Bali, where Dutch interference had been unsuccessful and explosive, a rebellion by the Sasaks of Lombok against oppression by the native rulers of Bali broke out in 1891. Attempts at negotiation having failed, a Dutch expedition occupied Lombok in 1894. In 1898, a new system was introduced into Acheh. This was the so-called 'Short Declaration' by which any chief agreeing to recognise the authority of the Dutch was confirmed in his rule. By 1911, some three hundred self-governing states, including the remainder of Bali, came under Dutch control.

The forward movement was a product of the great wave of European scientific and industrial arrogance which surged over the world and partitioned it into a Greater Europe. In Indonesia, economic development was impressive. Between 1870 and 1900, exports almost doubled in value and the import trade quadrupled. A few great financial complexes dominated Indonesian economy. We have seen how Dutch Liberalism overflowed with noble sentiments about colonial responsibility but was very slow to do much about it. The culture system *was* abandoned, but as reluctantly as a reforming drug addict gives up morphia. In 1901, the Liberal government in Holland launched a new 'ethical policy' of decentralisation and native welfare. The same fumbling hesitations were once again in evidence. Though a decentralisation law had been passed in 1903, envisaging the delegation of power from the home government to the governor-general – and so on, down to Indonesian officials – nothing had been done to implement it by the time of the outbreak of the first World War.

IV

THE RAPE OF CHINA

The treaties of Tientsin (1858) and Peking (1860) opened China to extensive penetration by the West. New ports put vast new areas at the feet of
foreign traders (see map p. 335), and in turn these entrepôts became the agencies of disintegration, radiating new values and ideas into the heart of Chinese
society and institutions. The Yangtze river was also opened to foreign navigation and, in Peking, in order to demonstrate the new era, ambassadors of
the Western powers were to live not as the representatives of barbarian tributaries but as those of independent nations on a footing of equality with
China itself. No more could the illusion of Chinese superiority be sustained,
nor the conviction that the world was divided into Chinese and barbarians.
Furthermore, foreigners carrying with them the explosive charge of Western
ideas could, if armed with the proper papers, go wherever they pleased.
Again, Christianity and the Christians, Chinese as well as foreigners, were
given protection from persecution. This added another factor to extra-territoriality, for it permitted *Chinese* citizens who were also Christian to obtain
the assistance of a foreign consul against Chinese officials. The treaties also
ceded land opposite Hong Kong to Britain and legalised the opium traffic.

The penetration of China by the European powers reflects a new stage in
the evolution of the Western empires. Superficially, it might seem a repetition
of the beginnings of dominion in India and elsewhere – the flag following
trade. But this was not so. Territorial aggression did take place but, significantly, only upon the inner Asian frontiers of China. Russia apart, the
Western powers preferred 'spheres of influence' to annexation, and a cooperative pillaging of China to the risks entailed in dominion. No single
European nation was really capable of absorbing China into its imperial
scheme. None could afford to fight the others for it. Above all, the principal
power, Great Britain, was concerned only with the peaceable conduct of
trade. Russia could continue to nibble at the north, and France at China's
tributaries in the Indo-Chinese peninsula. Britain's interest was in supporting a regime in Peking which was stable without being too powerful, and in
helping it to maintain a united China under orderly rule. This attitude lasted
roughly from 1861 to 1895. The opportunity it gave to China was immense.
If Chinese leaders had realised the virtue of Western ideas as weapons against
the West itself, as the Japanese had done, they would have grasped the chance

to reorganise the empire and to learn from the West. Unfortunately, the very success of the Western invaders and of internal rebellions such as that of T'ai P'ing – which appeared to be motivated by Western ideas – turned the ruling scholar-class against any possibility of reform. All the West represented was the downfall of the cultural heritage of the Chinese, a threat to the traditional patterns of society. The answer – and the reasoning was perfectly sound from the Chinese point of view – was a return to the old ways. The road to disaster could not have been more firmly trodden.

During this period, the penetration of foreign influence and ideas contin-ued. In 1863, following the indemnities charged against the customs revenue in the Treaty of Peking, a foreign inspector-general was appointed. This was an Irishman, Robert Hart, and under him the Imperial Maritime Customs, as it was called, became the most efficient service in the empire. All its chief appointments were held by foreigners, most of whom were British. It was controlled directly from Peking and represented a complete departure from the traditional Chinese method of decentralising authority. Christian mis-sionaries spread education of a Western type, introduced Western medicine, and circulated literature containing Western ideas that were not only religious in character. They were also very convenient as a means of bringing pressure on the Chinese government – for persecution, riots and disturbances caused by, or directed against, missionaries were commonplace. Attempts by the Chinese to conclude new agreements to regulate missionary activity were al-ways turned down by the Western powers.

In spite of the presence of the foreigner, as trader or missionary, throughout the empire, the effect upon Chinese society was almost nil. Foreign trade was mainly confined to the treaty ports, and inland trade existed on the traditional patterns. Foreign capital investment was discouraged, for the Chinese feared the extension of foreign economic interests outside the ports. Because of this, the use of Western appliances, the railroad, the telegraph, and such things as mining machinery were slow to find their way into China. Some attempts were made to reorganise the armed forces upon European lines, but these were neither extensive nor particularly successful. There were, however, minor adaptations of policy. During this period, a time without foreign wars or serious internal rebellion, it appeared that by keeping the Westerners at arm's length China would be untouched by the destructive influences they brought with them. But every Christian convert, every building raised in the Western style, every contact between a Chinese and a foreign merchant, was a hole in the rotting structure of Chinese conservatism. The irony of the situation would soon be clear. The blow would come, not from the West but from an Asian country that had learned the secret of Western success and intended to use it to ensure its own.

Sino-Japanese relations and the war of 1894-5 are dealt with in some detail in the next section. The effect of Japan's victory was two-fold. Firstly, there was the emergence of Japan as an active factor in Far Eastern politics; secondly, it acted as a signal for the renewal of foreign aggression against China.

*   *   *

The success of the Japanese and the territorial concession made to Japan in the peace treaty ended the period of trade without dominion. Throughout the world, the scramble for colonies continued. The have-nots of Europe partitioned Africa with the haves. In Asia very little was left. In this heyday of Europe, hurled along in the mad search for outlets for surplus capital, investment was more important than trade. 'Backward peoples' must be given the boons of Western rule, and no self-respecting imperialist could allow a country like Japan to pick the plums. Germany, France and Russia brought pressure on Japan to renounce its claims on Chinese territory and to take a larger indemnity instead. This rapped Japan over the knuckles and forced China into a foreign debt. To pay the indemnity, she must borrow. The first portion of the loan was made by France and Russia on the security of the maritime customs. To offset this, Britain and Germany insisted that China should also borrow from a British and a German bank. This she did, giving as security the customs revenue and the salt tax.

In 1895, France gained a modification of the Sino-Annamese frontier and the opening of three new treaty ports there. French engineers and manufacturers were also to have prior rights in the event of exploitation of the mines in the Chinese provinces of Yunnan, Kwangsi and Kwangtung. In turn, this led to a Sino-British agreement (1897) on the China-Burma frontier, a promise not to cede territory without British consent, and an assurance that railway construction in Yunnan would connect with lines in Burma. Additional trading facilities were also obtained.

In 1896, Germany, not to be outdone, asked for a coaling station on the China coast, but was refused. She then decided that Kiaochow on the southern coast of Shantung was the most suitable place. Two German missionaries supplied a convenient pretext for action by being murdered in Shantung in November 1897. Kiaochow was seized by German naval forces and an indemnity was exacted. In March 1898, Germany obtained a ninety-nine-year lease of Kiaochow bay, as well as about two hundred miles of hinterland, the right to build fortifications, a concession to build two rail- ways in the province, and a promise that, should China require financial, technical or material aid in Shantung, she would ask Germany first. A few days after the conclusion of this agreement, Russia obtained rather similar concessions at Dairen and Port Arthur (see p. 174 ff.). Great Britain, whose chief interest was still in unrestricted trade rather than the acquisition of ter- ritory, fearing the expanse of Germany and Russia, acquired the lease of the port of Wei-hai-wei 'for as long a period as Port Arthur shall remain in the possession of Russia'. At the same time, she promised Germany that she would not build a railway into the interior in competition with German in- terests. Britain also obtained a ninety-nine year lease on further territory in the Kowloon peninsula opposite Hong Kong (1898). In the same year, not to be outdone, France was given a ninety-nine-year lease to the bay of Kwang- chow in south-western Kwangtung. It seemed as if the partition of China would be only a question of time.

Other moves seemed to support this. In 1897, France obtained a promise from China that she would never cede the island of Hainan to any third power. In 1898, a similar assurance was given for the Chinese provinces which bordered French possessions in Indo-China, and Britain received similar guarantees for the provinces adjoining the Yangtze.

The most interesting development of this period, with some of the same overtones and dangers as beset foreign bases today, is what might be called 'aggression by railroad'. The process is fairly simple; in the first place, a demand is made for the concession to build a railway; when this is built, it forms an ideal basis for a claim to the territory it traverses. In China, the rails themselves formed a stake in the country, and a good bargaining point when partition finally came. Late in 1896, China, in return for a promise of aid against any repetition of Japanese aggression, signed a secret pact with Russia which included a concession to build a railway across Manchuria. This, known as the Chinese Eastern Railway, was to be a continuation of the projected Trans-Siberian track (see p. 173). China also undertook to ac- cept loans only from Russian banks for her own proposed tracks north of the Great Wall. Apart from the German concession in Shantung, Britain's was the predominant financial interest in the Peking-Mukden line; the Belgians contracted to finance the Peking-Hankow road in 1898; and British and German interests were concerned in the proposed railway between Tientsin

and the Yangtze which the Americans thought they had acquired the year
before. France obtained concessions in the south, including one for the track
between Tongking and Yunnan, in 1896 and 1898. The Hankow-Canton
concession given to the Americans in 1898 was later repurchased by the
Chinese from a Belgian group who had bought a controlling interest in
the American company. The British signed agreements in 1898 for roads
from Shanghai to Nanking and from Shanghai to Hangchow. Britain also
made reciprocal agreements with Germany and Russia, defining their
spheres of concessionary rights. If partition was to come, the looters had already staked their claims: Manchuria and Mongolia to Russia; Shantung to
Germany; much of the south and south-west to France. Presumably, Britain
would not stand aside if the knife fell, and to her would probably go the
valley of the Yangtze.

Three attempts, however, were to be made to save the Chinese Empire from
disintegration. The first came from outside and is usually known as the 'open
door policy'. Its aim was to keep all of China accessible to foreigners without
distinction or restriction. Britain, the first of the aggressors, had conditioned
her aims with the liberal conceptions of free trade. She had made no attempt
in 1842 to keep to herself the privileges she had won. It was only with great reluctance that she had entered the struggle for special privileges when the new
imperial powers determined upon the leasing of territory and the creation of
spheres of influence. Britain's attitude was by no means altruistic; the 'open
door' allowed her to enter with all the advantages of a long-established imperial
system. The acquisition of further territory in Asia was no longer a part of her
policy. Anyway, she was much more concerned in the scramble for Africa.

Action, however, did not originate with Britain. The United States,
whose interests in China had been small, in 1898 acquired Hawaii and the
Philippines. In 1899, the secretary of state John Hay proposed in notes to
Britain, France, Germany, Italy, Japan and Russia that there should be no
interference in the 'sphere of influence' of one nation by other nations, and
that the Chinese customs tariff and other dues in those areas should be the
same for all. A favourable reply was received from all these countries though
the Russian note was evasive. The Hay proposals conditioned the right of
equal trade-opportunity for all with the recognition of 'spheres of influence'.
Nevertheless, there is no doubt that the acceptance of these proposals helped
to avert partition of the Chinese Empire by producing an area of agreement
within the conflicting interests of the major powers, and reducing fear of unilateral action by any one of them.

It must not be thought that, while the foreigners were arguing over her body, China was doing nothing but accept the demands of the Western powers. Not being in a position to defend herself, she was permitted only the stratagem of delay. Occasionally, China scored a victory, as in 1899 when she successfully refused to grant a concession for a naval base on the coast of Chekiang to Italy. But these tactics could not save her. She could only be saved by a resurgence of national feeling or a reorganisation of the state. Though the Manchu administration had decided to seek strength in a return to the old ways, the lessons of Western success were not entirely lost upon certain officials and intellectuals. The turning point was undoubtedly the defeat of China by Japan, when many Chinese realised that to save their country they must adopt some of those Western methods that had raised Japan to victory.

The reformers varied in their radicalism. One society, sponsored by the great viceroy Chang Chih-tung, still stressed loyalty to the dynasty and to Confucian principles, whilst advocating the adoption of Western technical and scientific devices. Another and more significant reformer was Sun Yat-sen, the startling results of whose activities we shall see later. Sun, born in 1866 in a village some forty miles from Canton, was educated in Honolulu, became a Christian, and later took a medical degree. Beginning practice in Macao, he organised a reform society there. Ordered to leave by the Portuguese, he went to Canton, and after Peking's refusal to take action on a petition to start agricultural schools, Sun joined in organising a revolt against the Manchus. The plot was discovered and some of the conspirators executed, but Sun escaped to Hong Kong (1895) and then to Japan. He then spent his time agitating amongst the overseas Chinese for the overthrow of the dynasty and the establishment of a republic. In 1906, the Chinese legation in London attempted to send him back to China, but he was protected by the British government.

More immediately prominent inside China was K'ang Yu-wei, who sought Confucian sanction for his radical ideas, maintaining that the sage was not a conservative but a creative ethical leader. K'ang outlined a programme of popular elections, and the abolition of the family unit, with both children and old people becoming the responsibility of the state. Between the end of the Sino-Japanese war and the summer of 1898, a number of reforms took place or were proposed on both a national and provincial level. Schools teaching Western subjects were established, and the Chinese themselves began to plan railways.

The reformers found an unexpected ally in the Emperor Kuang Hsü, who had ascended the throne as a minor in 1875. During his minority, the real power was exercised by Tz'u Hsi, known as the empress dowager. After the emperor had taken over the reins of administration, she still dominated the government of the country though, at the beginning, Kuang Hsü was permitted to go his own way. The emperor, brought up in the seclusion of the Forbidden City, was neither physically nor mentally tough enough to save the empire by reforms. Despite his ignorance of the outside world, he was aware of the necessity for changes and had read the reformist literature of the time, including the works of K'ang Yu-wei. In the summer of 1898, the emperor appointed K'ang as his adviser and began the so-called hundred days of reform.

Contrasted with the changes of a few years later, the innovations of June-September 1898 do not appear particularly radical. Against the background of the reactionary conservatism of Chinese officials of the time, however, they were almost revolutionary. Reforms included the reorganisation of civil service and military examinations, and the establishment of an education system which would include an imperial university, in whose curriculum there would be Western as well as traditional learning. An official bureau of translations was to be established so that Western books and, in particular, technical treatises could be made available in Chinese. Railway building was to be extended and the army and navy re-formed upon Western lines.

This flood of imperial decrees naturally caused opposition, not only in the conservative ranks but amongst those who believed that reforms should be introduced slowly. The division of the court into two rival factions, conservative and reformist – but both mainly concerned with destroying the other with whatever weapons came to hand – also complicated the situation. The reactionary elements looked to the empress dowager, Tz'u Hsi, as their leader. In September 1898, this remarkable woman took control of the government. Before this actually took place, the emperor attempted to remove Tz'u Hsi's powerful supporter, Jung-lu, by having him secretly executed. But Yüan Shih-k'ai to whom the emperor entrusted the execution, betrayed the plot to the empress dowager. Tz'u Hsi acted immediately and, on 22 September 1898, had the emperor seized; though he was allowed to live and retain the title of emperor, he was kept a prisoner in part of the palace while the empress dowager assumed the regency. Many of the reformers were caught and executed, but K'ang escaped and fled the country. Many of the reforms of the hundred days were abandoned and a new attempt to save the country from disintegration began. This time it was to be an attempt to throw the foreigner out, not to accept his ideas and expertise. The appeal was immediate. The defeat by Japan, the arrogance of the foreigners in the treaty ports, the scramble for railway concessions, and the continuous irritant of missionary activity, inspired bitter feeling on practically all levels. To add further to the unrest, famine began its ravages. Outbursts against foreigners became commonplace.

In the north, the reactionary rule of the empress dowager brought the appointment of anti-foreign officials. A local militia, originally intended for the protection of railway stock and installations, was now called upon by the empress dowager to prepare itself for defence of the country. The militia was known as the 'Righteous Harmony Fists' (I Ho Ch'üan), and it is from this name and the physical exercises that they practised that came their Western title of 'Boxers'. Equipped with slogans such as 'Protect the country, destroy the foreigner', the Boxers were also associated with some of the secret societies, and recruited into their ranks the toughs and criminals of the cities. Like their predecessors, they believed in occult protection and possessed charms to make them invulnerable to the swords and bullets of their enemies.

From 1899 onwards, the Boxers began to indulge in overt anti-foreign activity. In Shantung, they persecuted Christians and killed an English missionary. The governor, under pressure from the European powers, was replaced, but at court he was hailed as a hero and appointed governor of Shansi. In June 1900, in Chihli (Hopei), Christians were massacred, and all foreigners stood in danger. To protect the latter, and also the legations in Peking, an international force was sent from Tientsin on 10 June. This was heavily attacked and only just managed to fight its way back. To protect the foreign residents of Tientsin, the Tahu forts commanding the river approach to the city were occupied on 17 June.

This act was greeted by the Boxers, understandably, as a declaration of war. The Tientsin concessions were attacked and the ministers of the foreign powers in Peking ordered to leave the city within twenty-four hours. On 20 June, the German envoy was murdered on his way to the foreign affairs department, and that afternoon, foreigners and Chinese Christians were besieged in the Roman Catholic cathedral and the legation quarter. An allied expedition fought its way to Peking and relieved the legations in the middle of August. Throughout the country, foreigners were in grave danger, but, except in the north-west, little loss of life occured. In Hopei, Shansi, Mongolia and Manchuria, however, more than two hundred foreign missionaries and several thousand Chinese Christians were killed. At court, however, there were those who realised the dangers of war with the foreign powers and successfully restrained the more hot-headed officials. They were also success-ful in dissociating the government from the actions of the Boxers, and this was recognised by the foreign admirals off Tientsin, who declared that they were merely defending their nationals against the Boxers.

By the autumn of 1900, the situation from the Chinese point of view was nothing short of disastrous. Peking was occupied by the allies, and was be-ing plundered of its treasures by their troops. The court had fled to Hsianfu, and foreign troops roamed Hopei rescuing foreigners and inflicting arbitrary vengeance. The Russians had taken advantage of the troubles to occupy most of Manchuria.

The settlement finally agreed to in 1901, though harsh, nevertheless pro-tected China's territorial integrity and fixed an indemnity within her capa-city to pay. An Anglo-German agreement designed to prevent the acquisi-tion of land or the closing of the 'open door', was accepted in whole or in part by France, the United States, Italy, Austria and Japan.

The terms of the protocol between the allies and the Chinese included the erection of a memorial to the murdered German minister; the prohibition of arms imports for two years; the payment of an enormous indemnity of more than £ 67,000,000 at the then sterling value, plus interest at four per cent, in thirty-nine annual instalments to end in 1940. This sum was secured upon the maritime customs and the salt-tax, and was divided in varying propor-tions – the largest going to Russia – among thirteen of the powers. Other provisions included extra-territorial and defensive rights for the legation quarter in Peking, and the occupation of strong points between Peking and the sea to ensure communications.

Instead of saving the Chinese Empire, all the empress dowager and the reactionary elements clustered around her had succeeded in doing was to in-crease China's foreign indebtedness and humiliation. She had also ensured the end of the dynasty. At the same time, however, the possibility of partition had receded. If the Boxer insurrection had occurred only a few years before it did, it would have supplied the excuse for annexations. Yet from the troubles, China emerged with her independence guaranteed, if restricted. This was due to a number of factors ranging from the unwillingness of the great powers to involve themselves in the possibility of large-scale conflict in *Europe* over the division of China, to a recognition that there was more to be gained from 'spheres of influence'.

One power, however, did not agree. Russia, the only country with a major land frontier with China, was reluctant to leave Manchuria. Great Britain, the United States and Japan were opposed to Russia's occupation, and it was left to Japan, reinforced by an alliance with Britain, to fight (see p. 157 f.). Japan's victory over Russia led to the annexation of Korea in 1910, and the inheriting of Russia's position in Manchuria. There, the principle of the 'open door' policy was continually flouted. The British government did little, bound as it was by a treaty with Japan, which had been renewed in 1905 and 1911, and it was left to the United States to attempt to moderate Japanese plans in Manchuria (see p. 158 f.). Manchuria was to remain a storm centre until its final occupation by Japan in 1932.

The failure of the Boxers and of the reactionary policy of which they were the spearhead, hastened the crumbling of the old order and resulted in a progressive collapse of authority which was to last until 1926. The Manchu dynasty, which had been in decline since the close of the eighteenth century, was still unable to offer dynamic leadership but it did attempt, after 1900, to reorganise the government on new and more realistic lines. Reforms in the civil service were begun, and a constitution was promised. Army reorganisation was partly carried out by Yüan Shih-k'ai. Provincial and national assemblies were called, the former in 1909 and the latter in 1910. It is possible that, given leadership, the dynasty might have adapted itself to new demands, but in 1908 Tz'u Hsi died, apparently only a few hours after the imprisoned emperor, Kuang Hsü. The new emperor was an infant, and the regent a weakling.

The overthrow of the dynasty was accomplished by a revolution that broke out in Hankow and Wuchang in October 1911. The success of the rebels was unexpected even by their supporters, and Wuchang, Hanyang and Hankow were quickly occupied and a republic declared. The government in Peking recalled Yüan Shih-k'ai, whom it had dismissed in 1908, but he was willing to come only on his own terms. If he had acted immediately the revolt might have been suppressed, but he did not, and though he recaptured Hankow at the end of October, city after city declared itself against Peking. In December, a national council assembled in Nanking and elected Sun Yat-sen, who had returned from Europe, as president of the Chinese Republic.

Before Sun's arrival, negotiations had been opened between the rebels and Yüan. On 12 February 1912, the young emperor issued an edict announcing his abdication and instructing Yüan to set up a republic. In order to unite the nation, Sun withdrew from the presidency and Yüan was elected in his place. The old order, centred upon the emperor and drawing its strength from a Confucian bureaucracy, was swept away. Institutions of very considerable antiquity were to give place to Western forms of government. Unfortunately, there was to be no transition period when the old could slowly be replaced by the new. Furthermore, the personality of Yüan Shih-k'ai was more that of the founder of a dynasty than of a republican and constitutional president. The provisional constitution adopted at Nanking in 1912 placed the president under the control of parliament. When elected, this was to be dominated by radicals, who now formed a political party – the Kuomintang.

The clash came in 1913, when Yüan negotiated a large loan with bankers in Britain, France, Russia, Germany and Japan. Assured of the money to buy arms and the support of his foreign investors, Yüan replaced the military commanders in the Yangtze valley and the south with his own men. When his critics, with the support of Sun Yat-sen, broke into rebellion, he easily defeated them and forced Sun to flee to Japan. Yüan's next act was to unseat the Kuomintang majority in parliament, in November 1913. In January of the following year, parliament was dissolved.

In 1915, after a carefully rigged referendum, Yüan declared the restoration of the monarchy with himself as emperor. His foreign friends advised delay, and in December a rebellion broke out in Yunnan and began to spread. Yüan postponed his enthronement and, as the rebellion grew more and more widespread, abandoned the restoration. But the rebels were not prepared to leave him in power. Yüan died in June 1916 before he could be removed from office. The Chinese monarchy, an institution going back to pre-historic times, could no longer be revived. The tribulations of the republic were now to take its place.

v

THE RISE OF MODERN JAPAN

The conclusion of the treaty of 1858 by the American Townsend Harris was followed by similar agreements with Great Britain, France and Russia, and later with twelve more Western powers. The terms of the treaties included extra-territorial jurisdiction by foreign consuls, and a fixed scale of customs dues. Both were a diminution of Japan's sovereign rights and formed, as usual, a continuing source of irritation especially as the acceptance of the treaties had not been supported by all influential Japanese. The penetration of Japan by the foreigner, though in itself superficial, divided the country into three camps. The struggle between them was to change the structure of Japan and to launch her on the road to Pearl Harbour.

The first of these groups believed that the success of the West proved the superiority of her ideas, and that if Japan was to escape becoming a part of one or more of the Western empires she must learn as quickly as possible the techniques and expertise to match the foreigner at his own game. The hopes of this group were reinforced by the nature of Japanese culture. There existed a precedent for the adaptation of foreign ideas in Japan's acceptance of Chinese civilisation in the seventh and eighth centuries A.D. This acceptance was neither uncritical nor mechanical. Though the Japanese took their religion and their philosophy, their costume, sports, writing, cooking, music, art forms, gardens, and administrative organisation from China, they did so only superficially. The Japanese are, by nature, essentially exploiters and adapters, and as Chinese culture offered the highest state of civilisation then known to them the Japanese took it over as a tool of living, to be used until a better one came along. The Japanese wore Chinese culture like a man who always orders a new suit in the colour, cut and pattern of the old. However much the dress remained the same, the body inside it was continually changing. Within this garment of an alien culture, Japan, despite her isolation from the West, was going through changes very similar in nature to those which had brought the West from a feudal to a capitalist structure. Behind the decaying feudalism of the Tokugawa shogunate, a strong middle class had developed and, as merchants and bankers owning a large share of the national wealth, represented the beginnings of a capitalist society. The next stage, of industrial capitalism, was therefore a natural progression in the evolving economic structure.

This group which believed in the necessity of learning from the West was at first very small, but within fifteen years its members were to rule Japan. They soon realised that the dual government of the Tokugawa, ruling in the name of a powerless emperor-figure, was a handicap in relations with the West, and some of the group began to work for the restoration of the emperor to executive power.

At the court of the Shogun, a second group believed in opening the door only wide enough to satisfy the foreigners and no more. The third group believed in keeping the door shut, breaking the treaties with Western nations, and throwing the foreigners out of the country. For some time, these opinions dominated the shadowy imperial court at Kyoto. Here the emperor was believed to favour them, especially as the court was under the control, not of the Shogun, but of the rulers of the Western fiefs who – since the decline in the power of the Shogun – had acted independently, owing him only nominal obedience. These rulers decided that the treaties negotiated with the Shogun were treasonable and sought to influence the emperor to re-assert his authority and force the Shogun to cancel the treaties. Under the influence of this clique, the emperor ordered the Shogun to expel the foreigners. This the Shogun could not do, in view of the superior arms of the Western nations. At the same time, his precarious position against a growing tide of national sentiment would not permit him to refuse the order of the legal head of state. He therefore asked Kyoto for time, while delaying as much as possible the granting of concessions to foreigners. These, not understanding, and possibly not caring about the Shogun's problems, now accused him of duplicity.

The Shogun's position rapidly deteriorated. The number of foreigners in the treaty ports increased and even Christian missionaries, protected by the foreign settlements, were once again actually proselytising. Clashes between Japanese feudal lords and foreigners became widespread. In 1862, a party of Englishmen, ignorant of Japanese etiquette, unwittingly insulted some retainers of the Daimyo (literally 'great name', a feudal baron) of Satsuma, and one of them was killed when the Japanese attacked them. The Shogun apologised and paid an indemnity, but the Daimyo refused to surrender the guilty men and the Shogun was not strong enough to force him to do so. The British therefore sent a naval force and bombarded the Daimyo's capital.

In the same year, the ruler of Choshu – an area commanding the narrow straits of Shimonoseki (see map p. 337) – in response to the emperor's edict ordering expulsion of the foreigners, opened fire on American, Dutch and French vessels passing through the straits. A protest by the three powers, together with Britain, demanded that the Shogun punish the Daimyo of Choshu. This the Shogun was unable to do. The four powers then sent a squadron to the straits, demolished the forts, and destroyed the Daimyo's fleet. The ruler promised not to re-erect the forts, and to pay an indemnity. A force sent by the Shogun to make Choshu pay up was repulsed, and finally the indemnity was paid by the Shogun himself.

About this time it became plain to the foreign envoys at Yedo, the capital of the shogunate, that the relative positions of the Shogun and the emperor were rather different from what they had at first supposed. In their ignorance, the Europeans had believed that the emperor was merely a sort of chief priest, and the Shogun the legitimate ruler. In 1863, after the affair at Shimonoseki, a demand was made for the emperor to renew the treaties. To reinforce their demand, the powers sent the request not to Yedo, but to the port of Hiogo near the imperial seat of Kyoto, suitably embellished with a show of naval force. The powers also 'requested' the opening of Kyoto and its port Osaka to foreigners, and a reduction in customs duties. Overawed, the emperor agreed.

It was now apparent to all that the Shogun was unable to protect the country against the foreigner who even threatened the imperial capital. The emperor, under pressure from the rulers of the Western fiefs, disgraced the Shogun, who resigned. The emperor, however, was not yet ready to assume power. The new Shogun, in an attempt to restore the fortunes of the Toku-gawa, began to reform his forces on Western lines, but the tide was against him. To reinstate the authority of the shogunate would lead inevitably to a disastrous civil war. This the new Shogun recognised and, in October 1867, he resigned. An imperial edict abolishing the office and the principle of dual government followed, and brought to an end a system which had been in operation for seven hundred years.

Eight months before the resignation of the last Shogun, the Emperor Ko-mei had died. Though young, he was reactionary and anti-foreign. His suc-cessor, Mutsuhito, was only fourteen and, naturally, under the influence of his advisers. The period of Mutsuhito's reign (January 1868–July 1912) is known as the Meiji ('enlightened government') era. The adaptation and use of Western political modes during the period resemble the adaptation of Chi-nese civilisation in the seventh and eighth centuries and later, though resistance to the former produced wider conflict. After the fall of the Tokugawa, rapid industrialisation of the country produced significant changes in the pattern of life, particularly in the growth of vast urban centres. At the same time as the pressure of Western-style capitalist structures demanded new outlets, the population increased immensely and Japan began to look for places not only to trade with but to colonise. Added to this was a new sense of national pride and arrogance (see chapter 6, p. 194), which demanded equality with the Western powers. The combination of demographic, economic and patriotic pressures drove Japan outwards into a further imitation of the West – as an aggressor. The first expression of this was the claim that all territories in-habited by Japanese, or belonging geographically to the group of islands which make up Japan, were by right Japanese. These claims covered the Ryukyu islands (which include Okinawa), the Bonin islands, the Kuriles,

Sakhalin, Hokkaido, and Korea! (See map p. 337). Hokkaido was without doubt Japanese, having paid allegiance to the Shogun, though its population was the non-Japanese Ainu. A vigorous programme of colonisation and development was set in motion. Sakhalin and the Kuriles were also claimed by Russia, but an agreement resulted in the acknowledgement of Japanese sovereignty over the Kuriles in return for her abandonment of claims to Sakhalin (1875). In 1878, the Bonin islands were annexed without opposition.

The problem of the Ryukyus was somewhat complex. Ethnically, the inhabitants were related to the Japanese, and in feudal times the islands had been considered part of the domain of the ruler of Satsuma. In 1868, Japan finally claimed the islands as part of her territory and when, in 1871, an attack on the islands by Formosans led to the killing of some of the inhabitants, the Japanese demanded redress from Peking. The Chinese rejected Japanese rights in the Ryukyus (the king of the Ryukyus had sent tribute embassies to Peking), and disclaimed responsibility for the savages of Formosa. In reply, Japan occupied southern Formosa (1874). When Peking protested, the Japanese demanded an indemnity. On the edge of war, the Chinese gave in and paid the indemnity, and the Japanese withdrew. The king of the Ryukyus, who had entered into treaty relations with the Western powers as an independent sovereign, was persuaded to accept Japanese rule, and in 1879 the islands became part of Japan.

In Korea, the situation was similar but even more difficult, for the country had, in the past, accepted (often simultaneously) a tributary relationship with both China and Japan. Since the withdrawal of the Japanese after the death of Hideyoshi in 1598, Korea's resentment at the cruelties of the Japanese invasion had kept her in the orbit of China. In 1868 and 1869, unaware – like practically everyone else – of the coming changes in Japan, Korea had refused to receive envoys from that country.

Japan feared that in her search for an ice-free Pacific port Russia might have designs upon Korea. Russia's presence in Korea would be a serious hindrance to Japanese expansion and would restrict the possibilities of her gaining from the disintegration of China, now brought about by the aggression of the Western powers. Nevertheless, Japan did not yet feel herself strong enough to indulge in responsibilities on the Chinese mainland. In 1875, however, when a Japanese gun-boat was fired upon by a Korean fort, an armed expedition was despatched and succeeded in forcing a treaty. China on this occasion made no objection to Korea negotiating as an independent power.

Japan's opening of Korea was followed by treaties with the Western powers, as well as bringing about the activity of a reform party in Korea itself. China, a bulwark of conservatism, now lent her support against the reformers in Korea and, in 1882, the conservatives attacked the Japanese legation in Seoul as a reply to Japan's overt support of radical elements opposed to the government. Japan demanded, and received, an indemnity and the right to guard her legation with her own troops. In 1884, another outburst of conflict between conservatives and reformers led to appeals for help, addressed both to China and Japan. Both sent assistance and, in 1885, an agreement was signed between the two countries by which each undertook to warn the other of any intention to send troops into Korea, 'in case of any disturbance of a grave nature'.

Japan's desire to end extra-territoriality on her own soil was slow to be satisfied. The treaty powers were unwilling to allow their nationals to submit to the jurisdiction of Japanese courts. Negotiations to end this humiliating restriction upon Japanese sovereignty took place in 1871, 1882 and 1886 – but all failed. Meanwhile, however, a new civil and military code was being formulated along Western lines, and soon the reason for extra-territorial jurisdiction would no longer be valid. It is possible that one of the reasons for the adoption of Western modes of justice *was* this vexed question of extra-territoriality. It finally ended in 1899, though complete control of the fixing of customs dues was not in Japanese hands until 1911.

Internally, Japan was, by 1894, ready to march out in strength upon the stage of world politics. Her army and navy were fully Westernised, and behind them lay an industrial pattern to serve them and profit by their successes. The opportunity was to come in Korea. In that country, conflict continued between the government and the partisans of reform, and the menace of Russian designs grew stronger. In 1894, a rebellion broke out, and China – maintaining, rather belatedly, that Korea was a tributary and not an independent power – sent in troops to suppress it. According to the terms of the 1885 agreement, China informed Japan of her action; but not until after the troops had been sent. Japan responded by also sending a force to Korea. Though the rebellion quickly ended, neither China nor Japan removed their troops from Korea – and when the Japanese proposed that China should co-operate with her in reorganising the administration and suppressing disorder, China claimed exclusive authority in Korea and the right to decide both the number of Japanese troops in the country and the use to which they were to be put. The Chinese government thought that Japan was not in a position to

go to war, as a bitter struggle between the lower house of the Japanese parliament and the government was then dividing the land. In China, the old
contempt for the country that had once copied her civilisation blinded her to
the changes in Japan. Though they had been warned by Tokyo of the
danger of war, the Chinese began to increase their troops in Korea. In July
1894, a clash between Chinese troops and a Japanese naval force was followed by a declaration of war.

Some historians have seen, in the speed and enthusiasm of the Japanese
response, the desire of the government to unite the nation by a policy of expansion, which would at the same time divert demands for a cabinet responsible to an elected parliament. Whatever the reason, internal dissensions
ceased. The Chinese were soundly defeated and, by the Treaty of Shimonoseki (April 1895), gave up considerable territory and agreed to pay a large
indemnity. Japan gained, or thought she had gained, the Liaotang peninsula
in southern Manchuria, Formosa, and the Pescadores, and the opening of
certain ports.

The German emperor, with remarkable foresight, saw the Yellow Peril
that would shake the foundations of European power in the world. The
Russians merely saw an immediate threat to their influence in northern
China. This combination, plus the French, forced Japan to give up the
Liaotang peninsula (see p. 174f.). This was a severe blow to Japanese national
pride. Its effect was to convince Japan of three things – that Russia was the
block to her status as a major power on a basis of equality with the West;
that she must expand the strength of her armed forces for an eventual conflict
with Russia; and that she must acquire an ally in the Western camp. For the
time being, Japanese ambitions in Korea, whose independent status had now
been recognised, and in Manchuria, were halted. The profit was to go to the
Western powers who, seeing in Japan's victory over China proof of the
fundamental weakness of that country, now began the 'rape of China'.

The Boxer insurrection of 1900 was to lead Japan once again into the
affairs of China, for Japanese troops formed part of the allied force that was
sent to the relief of the legations in Peking. But again, the troubles in China
had permitted Russia to advance her interests in China by the occupation of
further provinces in Manchuria. There is no doubt that, if Russia had been
prepared to co-operate with Japan in a fair division of influence in the Far
East, an alliance between the two countries could have been concluded; but
Russia had no intention of dividing the profits of expansion with any other
party. Japan, realising that a war with Russia was inevitable, strengthened her

armed forces and looked around for a friend – someone who would prevent a repetition of the aftermath of her war with China. She found the most powerful of allies in Great Britain.

The expansion of Russia in Asia (see chapter 5) almost always threat, ened the interests of Britain, yet, apart from the Crimean War, no *direct* con, flict had taken place between the two powers. Britain had fought wars in Persia and Afghanistan to prevent the expansion of Russian influence and had encouraged others to resist her, but on the inner Asian frontiers of China, Britain had no means of resisting Russia's advance. The only place it could be stopped was in Europe, and through a European war. The rise of Japan, and the hostility of Russo, Japanese interests in northern China, supplied the answer – why should not Britain fight to the last Japanese?

In 1902, a pact was signed between Japan and Britain. It recognised the special interests of the two countries in China and Korea and provided that, should one of the contracting parties go to war with another power to defend those interests, the other would remain neutral and use its influence to pre, vent other powers from attacking its ally. If another power joined in the fight against one of the parties, the other would come to its assistance. The real ad, vantages of the treaty went to Japan, for it gave to an independent Asian na, tion, only half a century before at the mercy of the West, the prestige of an al, liance with the greatest naval, financial and commercial power in the world. Russia would find it difficult to acquire allies willing to fight Britain as well. Nevertheless, Japan hesitated by negotiation. Russia was still a major power. The Japanese offered to consider Manchuria a Russian sphere of influence if, in turn, Russia would recognise Korea as within Japan's sphere. Russia re, fused, and her activities on the northern frontier and off the coast of Korea convinced the Japanese government that Russia intended to move into the peninsula. Without a declaration of war, Japan attacked in February 1904. The war was bitterly fought, but Japan had the advantage of easy communi, cations and a well, organised military and naval machine. Despite crushing defeats, Russia was in fact not so much beaten by the Japanese in the field as by a combination of factors which included revolutionary activity in Russia itself. It is possible that the Tsar and his advisers considered that a war with Japan would divert attention from the reform movements at home, on the time, honoured principle that a successful adventure abroad unites a nation as nothing else. The war, however, was unpopular from the beginning and, as defeat followed defeat, demonstrations, strikes and disorders developed in, to actual revolution. The Tsar was therefore quite ready to negotiate. The

Japanese, too, found their finances crumbling under the threat of a long and costly war. Consequently, when Theodore Roosevelt, president of the United States, offered to mediate, both powers welcomed the intervention.

The terms of the Treaty of Portsmouth (USA) were not as harsh as any-one, least of all the Japanese, had expected. By it (1) Japan's 'paramount political, military and economic interests' in Korea were confirmed; (2) Manchuria was to be evacuated by both parties; (3) the Russian possessions in the Liaotang peninsula, leased from China, and her mining and railway privileges in south Manchuria were transfered to Japan; (4) Russia would hand over the southern part of Sakhalin; (5) the seas to the north and west of Japan were to be opened to Japanese fishermen; (6) each power was to re-imburse the other for the cost of maintaining prisoners of war (there was a considerable balance in favour of Japan); (7) each country was allowed to keep a fixed maximum of railway guards in Manchuria; (8) neither was to use the Manchurian railways for strategic purposes, nor to erect fortifications in Sakhalin; and (8) both were to assist in the restoration of Chinese sover-eignty in Manchuria, except in the leased areas, and to maintain the 'open door' policy towards all nations on a basis of equality.

In Japan, the treaty was received by most of the nation as a betrayal of the decisive victory of Japanese arms. But the gains made by the war and by the subsequent settlement were very considerable. The Russian advance had been stopped, and Japan was now finally established upon the Chinese mainland. Furthermore, there could now be no question that Japan was anything but a world power – the only non-European nation since the Turks to defeat a first-class Western power. She had also, by defeating one Western empire, planted the seeds of disintegration in the others. For her victory show-ed that the West was not invincible. To the nationalists and reformers of India, the East Indies, and China, emerging slowly from the dark night of colonial supremacy, Japan's victory was a prophecy of independence, just as in her defeat forty years later was to be the reality.

Britain's investment seemed at that time to have paid off; her aims, peace in the Far East and the open door to her commerce in China guaranteed, had been fully realised. In 1905, as the Treaty of Portsmouth was under negoti-ation, Britain and Japan renewed their alliance, but this time its scope was extended to India where Britain still feared Russian designs, and to the Far East in general. This time, the pact was one of mutual assistance in the case of attack by only one other power upon the interests of either. The treaty was again renewed in 1911, but by this time the Russian threat to British interests had been removed by the conclusion of the Triple Alliance between Britain, France and Russia. Another enemy, Germany, was now in sight. In 1907, an agreement on China had been signed between Japan and France and Russia. In 1908, a treaty with the United States guaranteed the maintenance of the *status quo*. Japan's position in the Far East, and in the world, was assured.

Confirmed in her success, Japan extended her control in Korea. Within a few weeks of the signature of the Treaty of Portsmouth, she forced the king of Korea to sign a treaty handing over the control of her foreign affairs to Japan, and accepting a resident-general to supervise the administration. This move, though severely impairing the principle of Korean independence repeatedly recognised by Japan, was accepted by the Western powers and the United States. The dual government of Japanese advisers and native court could not continue without serious friction and, in 1910, Japan annexed Korea as part of the Japanese Empire.

In Manchuria, the imperialist desires of the Japanese could not be pandered to so simply. Japan had gone to war with Russia ostensibly to preserve the integrity of China. Manchuria was undoubtedly part of the Chinese Empire. Nevertheless, and in spite of treaty agreements to the contrary, Japan felt that Manchuria was a legitimate area for economic expansion, if nothing more. The ambitions of Japan were not entirely obscured from the view of the other nations with interests in the Far East. The key to Manchuria was, quite obviously, the existing railway system and the possibilities of its expansion. No sooner had the treaty of Portsmouth been signed than the American railway tycoon, E. H. Harriman, offered to buy the tracks acquired from the Russians by the Japanese. His plan was to girdle the earth with a transport system controlled by himself, by acquiring control of the Siberian railway, and steamship services across the Atlantic and the Pacific. Harriman's offer was not accepted by the Japanese, but he went on to negotiate for those lines still held by the Russians, while British and American financiers sought railway concessions from the Chinese government in what had been accepted as Russian and Japanese spheres of influence. The United States government now entered the arena with a proposal to neutralise the Manchurian railways. By this plan, the powers would jointly lend China the money to buy the existing Russian and Japanese lines and to construct additional ones. Their administration would be, at least for a period, in the care of an international commission. The proposal, if it had been accepted, would have dealt a severe blow to the existence of special interests and spheres

of influence, and, because of this, could hardly be acceptable to the imperialists in power in St Petersburg and Tokyo. Instead of leading to a protection
of Chinese interests, it threw the one-time enemies into an agreement (1910) to
act together to protect and coordinate their respective interests in Manchuria.

Japan was also immensely active in China proper. Well did she realise
that her industrial manufacturers, with their guarantee of low-wage, low-
selling-price production, would find a ready outlet amongst the teeming millions on the mainland. Furthermore, the mineral wealth of China remained
virtually untapped. Vast deposits of coal and iron ore were on Japan's door-
step. Both industry and the government rose to the occasion. Japanese merchants descended on China. Japanese steamers, heavily subsidised, worked
the great rivers. In education, Japanese teachers were to be found in Chinese
schools and Chinese students, anxious for the boons of Western civilisation,
found it nearer and cheaper in the university of Tokyo. The Chinese reform movement began to look to the Japanese model as their example.

The Chinese revolution of 1911, by the disorder that followed it, weakened the central authority and further opened China to the risk of foreign
demands. Japan was quick to claim satisfaction for offences against individual Japanese. She too, with Russia, demanded the right for her bankers to
join with those of Britain, France, Germany and the United States in funding
an enormous loan to the republican government, secured upon taxes and the
salt monopoly. The United States withdrew when their new president, Wilson, declared that the terms of the loan were an infringement of China's independence. Japan and the four other countries now had control of Chinese
finances. The first World War was to strengthen Japan's position in the Far
East as the Western powers fought to the death in faraway Europe.

VI

THE UNITED STATES AND THE PHILIPPINES

Though American merchant ships had done business with China since
1785, and her sea-captains had explored the South Pacific,[1] the beginnings

[1] An expedition commanded by Charles Wilkes, which set out in 1838, included Samoa,
New South Wales, Wilkes Land in the Antarctic, the Fiji and Hawaiian islands, the Philippines, Borneo and Polynesia. His mission included surveying, commercial negotiations, and
the establishment of consular representation. The value of his work was not appreciated until
the present century, when naval and air bases on tiny dots in rhe Pacific became part of the
ring fence of American security.

of a more organised interest in the Far East had to wait until the 'manifest destiny' of the United States had been satisfied by the nation's expansion to the shores of the Pacific.

Apart from an insistence, in 1843, that the US government would never consent to the annexation of Hawaii by either Britain or France, American official interest in those islands was slow to mature. In 1854, a treaty of annexation signed between the American consul and the Hawaiian king was not even submitted to Congress, and it was only the expansion of missionary and commercial activity which produced a treaty in 1875. By this time, America had begun to see the Pacific as merely a frontier area to be crossed in pursuit of a growing commerce with the Far East. With this recognition came the colonial concepts of 'spheres of influence', 'most favoured nation', and the appurtenances of imperialism. Secretary of State Blaine, shortly after the 1875 treaty, declared:

> 'The Hawaiian islands cannot be joined to the Asiatic system. If they drift from their independent station, it must be towards assimilation and identification with the American system to which they belong by the operation of natural laws and must belong by the operation of political necessity.'

In order to prove this – after a further treaty had been signed in 1884, leasing Pearl Harbour as a naval base – the United States refused to join Britain and France in guaranteeing Hawaiian independence.

In 1893, a revolution by American nationals deposed the queen of Hawaii, and, despite the refusal of President Cleveland to put a treaty of annexation before the Senate, the pressures of American involvement in the affairs of the Far East led to annexation by the unilateral action of the US Congress. In July 1898, Hawaii became part of the United States.

Further extensions of American interests in the Pacific assisted the expansion of her commercial interests. By 1900, Alaska and the Aleutian islands had been purchased, Midway and Wake islands had been acquired, Hawaii annexed, part of Samoa was under American protection, and Guam and the Philippines were occupied. It was with the latter that the United States became a Far Eastern power.

The Philippines, as we have seen, had been conquered by Spain in the sixteenth century. The penetration of Spanish culture was extensive and deep – no other body of colonial peoples conformed so closely to Western patterns. This was due to the success of Roman Catholic missions. The overwhelming majority of the population was converted to Christianity. Until the middle of the nineteenth century, the Philippines remained a closed theo-cracy ruled by religious orders who dominated the life of the islands. The opening of the country to foreign trade brought closer contacts with the West as a whole. The abolition of the state monopoly in overseas trade saw the beginnings of a merchant middle class, and out of it grew the desire for national expression. Revolutionary activity amongst the Filipinos resulted in some relaxation of clerical rule. It was at this stage that the United States came upon the scene.

In May 1898, in the course of the Spanish-American war, Commodore Dewey defeated a Spanish fleet in Manila Bay. Annexation followed, though only after considerable opposition in the US Congress. The government of President McKinley denied any colonial mission in the Philippines, but however much America disliked it, however much they criticised the im-perialism of other nations (and continued to criticise it) the logic of expansion was inalienable. If the United States wanted to continue with her commercial interests in the Far East, occupation of the Philippines would permit her to guarantee and expand them. The president salved his conscience by declaring that 'there was nothing else for us to do but to take them all, and to educate the Filipinos, and uplift and civilise and Christianise [*sic*] them, and by God's grace do the very best we could by them, as our fellow men for whom Christ also died.' The reply of the Filipinos was to substitute America for Spain as the enemy of their freedom, and it was not until 1902 that the last armed resistance to American rule was finally suppressed.

Despite the pressures of anti-imperialism, the United States had little or no intention of granting independence to the Philippines. Until 1901, the ad-ministration of the country was left to the army, but in that year a civil gov-ernment under William Howard Taft, later president of the United States, was inaugurated. His instructions from President McKinley are a classic statement of imperialism in its paternal, 'welfare-of-the-nation' period. The government of the Philippines was not to be an exercise in the application of theories, but was designed for

> 'the happiness, peace and prosperity of the people... and the measures adopted should be made to conform to their customs, their habits and even to their prejudices, to the fullest extent consistent with the accom-plishment of the indispensible requirements of just and efficient govern-ment.'

In 1907 was taken what is often hailed by American historians as a striking step towards self-government, and consequently an example of the essential

progressiveness of American colonial rule. In that year, a Philippine assembly was elected and convened, and the Philippine Commission, the administrative body appointed by the US president, became the upper house of a
bicameral legislature. That the granting of even this much representation was
not entirely an act of altruism can be seen in America's fear of conflict with
Japan in the Far East. Theodore Roosevelt wrote to Taft in August 1907.

> 'The Philippines form our heel of Achilles. They are all that makes the
> present situation with Japan dangerous. I think that in some way... you
> should state to them that if they handle themselves wisely in their legis-
> lative assembly, we shall at the earliest possible moment give them a
> nearly complete independence... I think that to have some pretty clear
> avowal of our intention not to permanently keep them and to give them
> independence would remove a temptation from Japan's way and would
> render our task easier.'

It is not too difficult to see American policy in the Philippines as a parallel to
that of the British in India – prevention of the upsurge of a revolutionary
nationalism by the slow granting of representative institutions, coupled with
continual promises of independence. The 1907 system remained in force until 1913. In 1909, the clause in the Spanish-American treaty of cession,
which forbade discriminating tariff legislation against non-American commerce for a period of ten years, ceased to operate. The Philippines were
brought inside the American tariff wall, and a free trade policy between the
two countries resulted in almost complete American monopoly of the import
and export of the islands.[1] The first World War diverted American attention from the Far East. The new world that was to follow its end was to
involve the United States more and more in the problems and dangers of
Asia.

[1] For US domination of the islands' financial structure, see Part Two, chapter 3, section IV.

5

Russia in Asia: 1558-1914

THE ABSORPTION OF SIBERIA

THE EXPANSION of imperialist Russia has certain parallels with that of the British Empire. The expansion of the latter falls into two distinct parts: dominion by colonisation, as in America and Australia, and dominion by administration without colonisation, in those tropical areas unsuitable for white settlement. The Russian Empire similarly expanded into the empty spaces of Siberia, having its dominion in the form of pioneer settlements. But in Central Asia, the first moves were of subsidiary alliances with the khan-ates, followed by direct administrative control. Russian expansion, however, was much slower than that of the British, for the pressures were of a different kind. The English, Dutch, French and Portuguese empire-builders were propelled, at first, by an urgent quest for trade. The empires of these powers, and their rise and fall, were the product of competitive aggression. The final victory, as it then appeared, went to Great Britain because she was the first major industrial power and moved irresistibly forward on the wave of eco-nomic and financial supremacy. The Russian Empire, on the other hand, though tied as inextricably as the others to the pressures of merchant aggres-siveness, was fundamentally a direct heir to the legacy of yet another, and Asiatic, dominion, and expanded – however slowly and hesitantly – to fill the vacuum left by its collapse. Russia, as the Grand Duchy of Muscovy, was, during the later Middle Ages, a tributary of the empire of the Mongols. Russia's eyes had always been turned towards Asia where its real enemies lay. When the Mongols collapsed, the Russians surged outwards and be-came their successors. The patterns of Russian expansion are very like those of the United States in the nineteenth century – a movement towards the sea as the natural frontier. In Siberia, empty spaces drew the Russians towards the Pacific. In the south, the lure was the warm-water ports of the Black Sea and the Persian Gulf.

Russia's first outward move might be equated with the grant in 1558, by Ivan the Terrible, of a piece of land on the bank of the river Kama, which traverses the European base of the Urals. Gregory Strogonoff, to whom the grant was made, surveyed the mountains, crossed the range, and entered Asia. His reception by the Muslim inhabitants was rough, and Strogonoff appealed to Ivan for help. The Tsar granted him authority to raise a force and, if necessary, to take the offensive against the Tartars.

In the Ural district were a number of Don Cossacks banded together under the leadership of one Yermak Timofevitch. Yermak and his rabble were little more than bandits – the true nature, whatever the disguise, of most of the early empire-builders. A pardon from the Tsar brought Yermak – and eight hundred Cossacks, Germans, Poles, and escaped criminals – under the leadership of Strogonoff. In 1569, this force crossed the Urals and captured Sibir and the lands to the banks of the Irtysh and the Ob (see map p. 338). Yermak's success brought others, and whole tribes of Cossacks moved into the new country. In 1587, the city of Tobolsk was established upon the river Irtysh.

Success, especially if it pays off in prosperity, breeds success. Adventurers moved further afield, and as a result Tomsk was established in 1604, Yeniseisk in 1619, Yakutsk in 1632, and Okhotsk in 1638. There was little opposition to overcome. Western and central Siberia were soon annexed. In little more than half a century from the founding of Tobolsk, the empire of the Tsars had increased by over four million square miles of river and forest.

The expansion of Russia into Siberia, though carried on with government approval, was the result of private enterprise. But though the pioneer led the way, the government controlled the incentive, for the state held the monopoly of trade in furs. The pioneers exacted furs as tribute from the natives, and the government took them from the traders as tax. Again, a parallel with the United States and Canada emerges, for one of the incentives that drew Americans to the Pacific coast was the search for fur.

Russian administration in Siberia centred upon the organisation of the fur trade – the wealth it represented fostered graft and corruption, and the cruellest of oppression. In all other branches of trade the government took its ten per cent, even upon the sales of women. The government in Moscow enjoyed the revenue with little interest in the honesty of the administration. That its officials were corrupt, the government was well aware, and it took steps to prevent them from enjoying the product of their oppressions; but it was not concerned in stopping the oppressions themselves. When the chief officer of the province (*voevoda*) was due to return to Moscow at the end of his period of office, the customs officers on the Siberian frontier were instructed to fall upon the officer's party without warning, and to search for smuggled furs 'in the waggons, trunks, baskets, clothes, beds, pillows, wine-barrels, boxes, in the baked bread... to search men and women without fear of any one... examine their persons, their trousers, and note especially whether the women have skins sewn into their petticoats... look sharp that they do not get away with any furs.'

By 1649, the Russians had reached the Pacific coast at the sea of Okhotsk. From the drive to the east, the new adventurers began to look south. In 1644, one Vasilii Polarkov had penetrated to the Amur river. His report of the riches he had found incited further exploration. In 1650 and 1651, Erofei Khabarov followed his trail, but the tribute and plunder he exacted from the weak tribes of the region resulted in the intervention of the Manchus, now rulers of China. The clashes that resulted postponed Russian expansion in the Amur region for two centuries.

The government in Moscow now woke up to the danger of allowing men like Khabarov to indulge in irresponsible banditry. Khabarov was recalled to Moscow. In 1655, the Manchus attacked the main Russian position in the region and, though repelled with heavy losses, devastated the land. Attempts to turn Cossacks into farmers failed and the region was sunk in anarchy. By 1661, the Russians had abandoned the whole of the Amur, but twenty years later they had moved back and were firmly established, or so it seemed, with a provincial capital and stronghold in the city of Albazin. The reply of the Manchus was swift and decisive. A powerful army razed Albazin to the ground. The inhabitants, including the Russian commander and his men, were allowed to retire to Nerchinsk. This act of clemency had little effect upon the Russians who, as soon as the Manchu forces had withdrawn, reestablished Albazin and other settlements on the Amur. The Manchus despatched a formidable army to settle the matter once and for all, but the Russians, before they could be decisively defeated, despatched emissaries to negotiate peace. The result was the Treaty of Nerchinsk, concluded in 1689, which demarcated the Russo-Chinese frontier and left the Amur region in Manchu control. This was the first treaty concluded between China and the West. The terms of the treaty were short and to the point, and it is interesting to compare the Chinese and Russian versions. Both agree on the six points of the treaty, but differ widely on their respective preambles. The Chinese version reads:

'In order to suppress the insolence of certain scoundrels who cross the frontier to hunt, plunder and kill, and who give rise to much trouble and disturbance; to determine clearly and distinctly the boundaries between the empires of China and Russia; and lastly to re-establish peace and good understanding for the future, the following articles are by mutual consent agreed upon...'

The Russian version blandly ignores the 'insolence of scoundrels':

'The plenipotentiaries in order to remove all cause of discontent between the two empires, to conclude a permanent peace, and to settle frontiers, agree in their conference at Nerchinsk to the following articles...'

Face was, no doubt, saved on both sides – in their own language.

On the completion of negotiations, the Chinese left Nerchinsk and the Russians demolished their fort at Albazin – but began to fortify Nerchinsk it-self. Russo-Chinese relations were now friendly and, three years after signing the treaty, a Russian diplomatic mission was despatched to Peking and established itself there in 1693.

Despite the slight change in the line of expansion, the outward move of the Russians continued. In 1707, the peninsula of Kamchatka was declared Russian territory and, two years later, the first prisoners were sent to Siberia. Some 14,000 persons, mainly prisoners of war, were banished to the steppe country of the Tsar's newly acquired empire. Asiatic Russia became a place of administrative exile.

The Chinese, having ousted the Russians from the Amur territory, pro-ceeded to insure themselves against a repetition by forbidding communi-cation across the frontier, and rigidly controlling trading rights. In spite of this, trade increased, though much of it was smuggling behind the benevo-lently turned back of the local mandarin; his benevolence, while command-ing a high price, still permitted substantial profit. The Russians now began to realise just what had been lost to them by the Treaty of Nerchinsk, and Tsar Peter sent an embassy to Peking in an attempt to re-open trade without restriction.

The ambassador arrived in Peking in 1721 and was received with a res-pect totally unlike that given to the emissaries of other European nations. An audience with the emperor produced the most flattering expressions of good-will which, on his return to St Petersburg, the envoy magnified into a pledge of wider relations between the two countries. On the strength of this, a caravan was sent to Peking, but it arrived when the emperor was dying. The caravan was turned back to the frontier, and the Russian diplomatic agent left behind by the ambassador was ordered to leave the city.

The failure of the attempt to open direct trade with China resulted in a further drive towards the Pacific and the annexation of territory to the extreme north-east. The problem of the Amur river still remained. If Russian vessels were allowed to use the river, supplies for Kamchatka could be taken by that route, then across the sea of Okhotsk. Despite pressures from historians, geographers and generals, no attempt was made to revise the Treaty of Nerchinsk either by force or diplomatic means, until 1806. In that year a mission was sent to Peking in an attempt to negotiate free navigation of the Amur. The Chinese refused to make any concession whatsoever. Still nothing was done to force China's hand.

In 1847, a new governor was appointed to Eastern Siberia, Count Nicholas Muravieff. His first step was to send a party of Cossacks to explore the river in 1848. The expedition was never heard of again. Muravieff next sent exploring parties and surveyors to find the mouth of the Amur. In 1850, a Lieutenant Orloff did discover it, and in the following year, two towns were established some distance up river. In 1852, Urup, one of the Kurile islands, was occupied. In 1853, Alexandrovsk was founded on Castries Bay and a port was established on the western coast of Sakhalin (see map p. 338).

In 1854, Muravieff decided upon the seizure of the Amur. That he did so at this particular time was probably a result of the outbreak of the Crimean War and the presence of French and English naval forces in the Black Sea, which prevented the despatch of stores to Siberia by the long sea route. The terms of the Treaty of Nerchinsk were held by Muravieff to be subordinate to the necessity of victualling the Russian outposts on the sea of Okhotsk and the sea of Tartary, despite the fact that these settlements were on Chinese territory. Muravieff did, however, communicate with the mandarin at Kiakhta, who stated that he was unable to do anything without reference to Peking. This, Muravieff decided, was a waste of time, and an expedition consisting of a steamer, fifty barges, and many rafts, set off down the Amur for Shilinsk. The force included scientists and topographers, several big guns, and a thousand soldiers.

No opposition was met with by the Russians and, having safely navigated the river to its mouth, Muravieff returned to Irkutsk. In the meanwhile, a small Anglo-French naval force had appeared off Petropavlovsk in Kamchatka, in August 1854. An attempt to take the place failed, and the ships retired. Three months later, a larger force returned with instructions to take Petropavlovsk at all costs, but they arrived only to find that the Russians had abandoned it.

No attempt was made by the Ango-French naval forces to enter the Amur river and destroy the Russian settlements on its banks. They preferred to sail about the sea of Okhotsk looking for prizes, though they captured the island of Urup in 1855. The end of the Crimean War in 1856 resulted in the re-occupation by the Russians of the lost settlements. New towns and military stations were built, colonists established, vessels built. Muravieff, who had gone to St Petersburg in 1855, returned with a free hand, in the middle of 1857. During the next few months, troops, emigrants and supplies were sent down the river. One of the travellers who used the Amur was Count Putiatin, on his way to Japan (see p. 96 f.). On his journey, Putiatin transmitted a letter from the Tsar to the dowager empress of China offering to assist her against the T'ai P'ing (see p. 141 f.), in return for the cession of Manchuria to Russia. The offer, naturally enough, was unacceptable to the Chinese, and resulted only in a series of protests about Russian encroachments on Chinese territory. Muravieff hurriedly left for St Petersburg to confer on the next steps to be taken. As we have seen (p. 140 ff.), China was in no position to resist demands made upon her – she lay prostrate before the European aggressors. Muravieff forced upon China the Treaty of Aigun (May 1858), which gave Russia the whole of Siberia without the loss of a single man, or payment of money.

When the Chinese signed the treaty, they were at war with France and England. In June 1859, the Chinese managed to repel the allied envoys on their way to Peking and, thinking that this success was a major victory, began to harass the Russians in their newly acquired possessions. The Russian envoy sent to Peking to protest against violations of the Treaty of Aigun arrived just as Anglo-French forces occupied the city. The result was a new treaty, ceding the whole of the maritime province of Manchuria to the Russians. The empire of the Tsars now occupied all the sea coast of Asia north of Korea. Later in 1859, the town of Vladivostok was founded, and plans were laid for the construction of a railway from there to St Petersburg. It was to be more than thirty years before it was finally completed.

II

RELATIONS WITH CHINA AND JAPAN

The occupation of the maritime province of Manchuria, and the secure establishment of Russian power along the Amur, was the beginning of a new period in the history of the Far East. The final patterns of Russian expansion towards the Pacific roughly coincided with the re-entry of Japan in-

to the affairs of East Asia, and the complete subjection of China to the interests of the Western powers.

Though Russia's position upon the Pacific shores of Siberia was now assured, she still did not possess an ice-free port, and it was in search of such a
place that Russian policy turned its face from the east to the south. It did so
at precisely the time when Japan was both willing and able to initiate an
active policy towards China and its coastal possessions, Formosa and Korea.
This new direction of Russian expansion can also be seen in the sale of
Alaska to the United States of America in 1867. The renewed vigour of
Russian activity in the Far East has a lesson for us today. The policy of the
Tsars might seem, from a superficial view, to be compartmentalised – as does
that of the Soviet Union today. But this view is the product of the short-
sightedness of the specialist, who tends to contain activity within the limitations of his own specialisation. In the middle of the nineteenth century,
as today, Russian policy had an overall unity which is obvious if the 'explanations' of the pundits, historians, and political commentators alike are
ignored. A quotation from a French contemporary of the activity we
are at present concerned with has as much pertinence today as when it was
written.

> 'Russian policy, more than any other, is remarkable for its manifold and
> intricate effort, which embraces so many countries at the same time, in
> Europe and in Asia. At the moment when it seems stopped and de-
> feated on one side, it rises up again and extends on the other; under the
> blow of a defeat it ties anew all the threads of its vast and persevering
> designs. The immensity of its sphere of action, the diversity of its terri-
> tories, readily give it a mystery favourable to its intentions...'[1]

Russia's Balkan pretensions had been, at least temporarily, shattered at the
conclusion of the Crimean War. As a reflex from this defeat, activity increased in Central Asia and on the inner Asian frontiers of China.

The Treaty of Aigun and the much more valuable treaty of 1860 proved
to the Russians the superiority of their armies over those of China, a China
which had become the plaything of foreign powers. But one thing, and one
thing alone, prevented Russia from making a vigorous attack on China,
with the inevitable inclusion of the northern portion of that country in the
empire of the Tsars – the distances involved from the main centres of Russian
activity. Large-scale Russian expansion, expansion, that is, not into empty

[1] V. de Mars. 'La Diplomatie russe dans l'extrême orient', *Revue des Deux Mondes*, vol. LXI.
Paris, 1866.

spaces but into the populated dominions of another country, was hamstrung by the difficulties of communication. At this period, Russian intercourse with China was almost entirely conducted across the caravan route from Kiakhta along the Gobi desert to Peking. British influence was almost entirely centred in the region around the Canton river. The north was open. Again, Russian relations with China over the previous two centuries had on the whole been characterised by moderation. Contact was respectful and, on occasion, in marked contrast to that with the Western powers, even cordial. This very calmness, however, reflected yet another drag on Russian expansion. The topographical and commercial information about China available to Russian policy-makers was meagre. It does not appear that any Russian explorer had penetrated into China south of Peking. Estimates of the material wealth of China were probably based upon the barren wastes and intemperate climate of Mongolia and Manchuria. If adequate intelligence about the real wealth of China had been available to the Russians, attempts would certainly have been made, probably with success, to absorb her into the Russian Empire.

This tolerance and friendliness born out of ignorance still persisted for a short time after the treaty of 1860, even though one of the clauses permitted Russians to travel throughout the Chinese Empire without restriction of any sort. But these pleasant relations were shattered by events in Chinese Turkestan in 1863, when the Muslim population rose, under one Yakub Beg. The defeat of the Manchu generals sent to restore order led to internal dissensions amongst the rebels, and anarchy throughout the province. The Russians, on whose borders a reign of terror now subsisted for nearly eight years, at last decided to take affairs into their own hands. The situation in Chinese Turkestan seriously affected Russian trade in that area, and, furthermore, unrest is no respecter of frontiers. Russian forces entered the district of Ili and defeated the rebels in 1871. After pacifying the area, Russia told China what she had done and that she was willing to restore to China the territory she had occupied, as soon as the Chinese were capable of maintaining their authority there. By 1879, the Chinese – assisted by the death of Yakub in 1877 – had restored order in Kashgar and, marching on Ili, requested its return. The Russians ignored the request. The Chinese envoy sent to St Petersburg negotiated a treaty by which Russia returned a portion of Ili in exchange for five million roubles and commercial privileges. The envoy, on his return to Peking, was repudiated and clapped in gaol under sentence of death. This upset the Russians so much that they sent a naval force to the China coast, and war was only averted by the intervention of the British ambassador in Peking. Despite the efforts of a war party at the court of Peking, a treaty was negotiated and the envoy released.

The treaty of 1881 called for the restoration of most of Ili to Chinese sovereignty, the payment by China of a rather larger indemnity (nine million roubles), and navigation rights on the rivers of Manchuria – the first step to the Russification of that country. Other provisions protected the rights of Russian farmers in the area retroceded, and gave new rights to Russian consuls and traders. Furthermore, Russian scientists and cartographers had surveyed the area fully, making any future occupation of Ili a much simpler task. The treaty, on the whole, was a most profitable transaction for Russia.

The occupation of Ili had demonstrated the overwhelming difficulties any attempt to reach the fertile plains of China would have to contend with. Mountain ranges, snowcovered table lands, and sandy deserts, easy to annex but impossible to hold as bases, acted as a barbed wire entanglement against the possibilities of expansion. Only two practicable routes lay before the Russians should they decide to attack China: the caravan trail from Kiakhta, which was quite impossible for military traffic; and through Manchuria. Russian attention now turned towards the construction of military highways, the building up of lines of communication, the exploration of river systems, and the establishment of bases.

The routine was simple. One or two Russian traders would arrive in a small town. If they were not well received – their rights were guaranteed by treaty – a *sotnia* of Cossacks would appear to 'protect' them, and then a military post was established. The same process then continued southwards. All this, it must be remembered, was in Chinese territory. As in the case of the Europeans in southern Asia, the flag followed trade.

From 1881 to 1895, Russian ignorance of China was dispersed. Geographers, military surveyors, scientists, protected by Cossacks, were at work all over China until Russian geographers knew more about the physical features, and Russian military experts more about the strategic possibilities, than the Chinese themselves. The Russians also had an eye on the coastline of Korea, then an independent kingdom under the suzerainty of China, and the possibilities of an icefree port. But Russia had decided that patience was the best policy.

Until the last quarter of the nineteenth century, Korea had remained cut off from the outside world. An attempt by the United States in 1871 to open the door, as had been done with Japan, resulted in bloodshed but no nego tiations. An astute observer, Sir Robert Hart, remarked 'if America goes no further in this matter, Korea will ripen like a pear and then drop into the jaw of Russia'. But it was Japan, not Russia, who made the next move. In 1876, Japan forced a treaty upon Korea which accepted her as an independent state and not as a Chinese vassal. China's reply was to encourgage the king to make treaties with the US and the European powers, just as if he *were* in-dependent. Then, too late, the Chinese tried to revoke this policy by sending Yüan Shih-k'ai, later first president of the Republic of China, to restore Chi-nese authority. But Korea was in the throes of a civil war. Realising that this was their opportunity, the Japanese strengthened their position – aided by the sentimentality of the United States, who thought the Japanese were helping Korea to throw off the yoke of Chinese rule. In 1884, during a pal-ace upheaval, the king sought protection from the Japanese who occupied the palace; they were attacked in turn by both Koreans and Chinese. A convention, however, followed the next year, when China and Japan agreed to withdraw troops from Korea and not to send them again without noti-fying the other. In the same year, in an attempt to save Korea from the Japan-ese, the king concluded a convention with Russia, as he realised that Korea's only chance of independence lay in having the protection of a foreign power. This convention allowed Russia to occupy Port Lazareff, and requested the loan of Russian officers to train the Korean army. There was such an outcry that Russia allowed the agreement to be repudiated.

The Russians were meanwhile planning to make their next conquests by railway. The first sod of the Trans-Siberian railway was cut by the heir to the Russian throne (fated to be the last of the Tsars), in 1891. Construction began at both ends of what was to be over four thousand miles of railway track linking European Russia with Vladivostok. It was finally completed in 1905. By 1894, however, the line had been carried from the Urals to the western shore of Lake Baikal. To the Japanese, flushed with their diplomatic successes and their quickly acquired facility with the European expertise of modern war, this seemed a major setback to Japan's 'historic role' in East Asia. The expansion of Russia into such territory, which Japan considered as her rightful zone of influence, would be considerably facilitated by the new railway system of the Russians. Japan therefore must act first.

The Sino-Japanese war of 1894-5, fought ostensibly over the independ-ence of Korea, is recorded in another chapter (see p. 142 ff.). The results were the renunciation of China's traditional suzerainty over Korea, and the cession to Japan of Formosa, the Pescadores, and the Liaotang peninsula (on

which stands Port Arthur), as well as other concessions. The further consequences were even more serious for China – the great European powers renewed their aggressions against her (see p. 142 ff.). Allied, as always, in
the interests of plunder, aggression in imperialist times made strange associates. Great Britain, France and Russia brought pressure to bear on Japan,
which was hardly in a position to resist them, to give up the Liaotang peninsula on the specious excuses that the occupation of the peninsula was a
direct threat to the Chinese capital, rendered Korean independence illusory,
and menaced peace. Japan renounced her claim in return for a larger indemnity.

To pay the indemnity, China had to borrow from foreign financiers. Russia, in association with French bankers, won the privilege of making the first
payment – on the security of the maritime customs and the salt monopoly,
and, of course, the possibility of further concessions. Among other advantages, Russia obtained the lease for twenty-five years of Talienwan (more
commonly known in the West as Dairen), and Port Arthur on the tip of the
Liaotang peninsula, with the right to erect fortifications and naval installations, and a railroad to connect the area with Manchuria. Russia's success
resulted in further encroachments upon Chinese territory by the other powers.
This period in the history of Western colonial exploitation – a period in
which the nations of Europe descended on China like predatory animals – is
now paying off in the xenophobia and intransigence of Communist China,
and in the terrible, and possibly final, threat to world peace.

One of the results of the scramble for concessions was that Japanese aims in
China suffered a setback. Russia once again, posing in her now traditional
role of China's friend, reaped the profits – and, it seemed likely, would continue to do so. The Boxer uprising of 1900 (see p. 147 f.) was to bring substantial returns to all the European powers involved in its suppression. Russia,
who had quietly occupied the three eastern provinces of Manchuria, again
and again delayed the evacuation agreed under the terms of the 1901 agreements between China and the Europeans. The Chinese were also persuaded
to hand over to Russia the control of the Chinese Eastern Railway, the
theory being that, should Japan renew her aggression on Manchuria, troops
could be moved quickly to its defence. This was part of a Franco-Russian
plan to achieve domination of the whole of China by construction of railways throughout the country. Furthermore, both countries planned to obtain
control of Chinese finances through the loans advanced to her to pay indemnities to Japan.

These plans, and the imminent possibility of their success, represented a real threat to the interests of Great Britain, the United States and Japan. To Great Britain, then at the zenith of her power, it was fundamental that China should remain weak but independent, subject to spheres of influence but under the domination of no one power or group of powers. This attitude was dictated not only by the precepts of free trade but by the very nature of Britain's influence in the Far East. As the greatest sea power (her navy was stronger than all other European navies put together), Britain exercised her influence from the sea. She had no land frontier with China except in northern India and Burma, and even these were militarily impracticable. The main centres of Chinese authority were accessible from the sea, and a weak China could quickly be brought to reason by an expedition inland. But Britain had no contact with those areas where the frontiers of China met those of Russia.

Britain's attitude to China had always been concerned with the maintenance of an open door to trade. Territorial expansion was not part of her policy. Privileges and trading posts were her primary requirements. This was also the view of the United States, who in 1898 had acquired the Philippines and Hawaii – convenient stages on the way to trade with China. To these two countries, FrancoRussian influence would mean tariff discrimination.

Japan's interests were apparently the same, but in fact they were reinforced by a desire to repair the *diplomatic* defeat of her recent war with China and to increase her influence over what she considered her legitimate field of activity. The United States was unwilling to go to war in support of its open door policy. Great Britain was involved in the Boer War and its aftermath. It was left to Japan to act. She did so with the full approval of Great Britain, an approval which was reinforced by a licence in the form of the AngloJapanese treaty of 1902. The end of the road was to be the attack on Pearl Harbour forty years later. The main provision of the treaty enjoined upon the contracting parties an obligation to come to each other's aid should the interests of either be threatened in the Far East. Here lay Japan's opportunity – *carte blanche* to act on behalf of the greatest power in the world.

Russia generously supplied the opportunity. In 1901, she had attempted to have her illegal occupation of the whole of Manchuria recognised by China. This was opposed by Great Britain and Japan, and in 1902 Russia agreed to withdraw her troops from Mukden and part of south Manchuria, to return the Eastern Railway to China within six months, to evacuate Mukden and Kirin altogether within the following six months, and to withdraw from Chinese territory within a third period of six months. These promises were not kept, and Russian troops and military installations were reinforced. In June 1903, the Japanese government proposed to Russia an agreement by which the contracting parties would respect the integrity of China and Korea, while recognising Japan's interests in Korea and Russia's in Manchuria. These proposals were rejected by Russia. In February 1904, Japan recalled her minister at St Petersburg and, three days later, attacked the Russian fleets at Chemulpo and Port Arthur, and landed troops at Chemulpo. Details of the war are of little interest to us here. Russia was defeated on land through a combination of Japan's command of sea communications and the total destruction of a Russian fleet which was intended to destroy these communications. This fleet had sailed almost round the world from the Baltic, and had very nearly caused a European war in the process, by sinking some British fishing boats off the Dogger Bank – under the impression that they were Japanese torpedo boats! The action in which the Russian fleet was destroyed by Admiral Togo was the first sea battle fought with modern battleships.

A peace treaty was signed between Japan and Russia at Portsmouth (USA) in September 1905. The terms were remarkably mild. No indemnity was claimed from Russia, and both sides agreed to withdraw their troops from Manchuria. Russia, however, gave up to Japan her rights in the Liaotang peninsula and in the railways of south Manchuria, and recognised Japanese interests in Korea. The Russian drive towards domination of China was halted, and the rise of Japan confirmed.

III

THE ROAD TO INDIA

The title of this section is perhaps misleading, but it reflects Russian expansion in Central Asia as seen by the British in the nineteenth century. The British looked to the North-west frontier of India with the uncritical awareness of historical precedent. All the invasions of the sub-continent before those of the Europeans had been nurtured in the power-house of Central Asia, and the armies of the Muslim invaders had poured through the passes of the north-west. The British forgot that these invasions had been by comparatively small numbers of troops, well-disciplined and well-led, against unorganised opposition. The lessons of history can be learned indiscriminately. Fear and facts together are often the enemies of sound judgement. But it is easy to be pompous long after the event, and that fear of Russian designs

and ignorance of Russian motives which historians find so difficult to understand within the context of the nineteenth century are, unfortunately, the
commonplaces of our own times.

In the last century, Russian soldiers no doubt dreamed of an attack upon
the British Empire in India. Empires always have their theorists of expansion.
No doubt, too, Russian statesmen encouraged the more outspoken of their
'forward school' to rattle their sabres at the doors of the European enemy, as
a means of putting political pressure upon the government in London. But it
is doubtful whether the rulers of Russia seriously considered an invasion of
India, whatever the activities of its wild men in Central Asia. 'The statesman', as Edward Thompson wrote, 'does not discourage the dreams of his
soldiers, but he need not believe in them'.[1] The Russian advance to the gates
of Afghanistan was the occupation of a power vacuum, an occupation as
imperative as Britain's own expansion to India's North-west Frontier. Land
empires, of necessity, expand to fill the area contained by settled government
or impassable natural features. Russian domination of Central Asia was
subject to the same logic. The political impact upon the administration of
India has already been discussed (p. 119 f.). Here, we must follow the
history of the imposition of Russian rule upon the khanates of Central Asia.

The precise date of the first Russian relations with the independent rulers of
Central Asia is not known. There is no doubt that, as early as the beginning
of the seventeenth century, the Cossacks of the Ural indulged in raids on the
territory of the Khan of Khiva without much success and, on some occasions,
with downright defeat. In 1703, however, the Khan – perhaps impressed by
reports of Russian expansion into Siberia – despatched an envoy to Moscow
with a request for Russian protection. Nothing came of this for nearly ten
years, until reports of the wealth of the Amu river basin reached the Russian
capital. These reports were believed and were reinforced by trustworthy information that large deposits of gold were to be found in Bokhara, at that
time a virtually unknown country.

These reports coincided with the end of Tsar Peter's wars against Sweden
and Turkey. With the possibilities of westward expansion seriously limited,
Peter turned to Turkestan as the answer to his restless demand for a greater
Russia. In 1717, an expedition left St Petersburg. It consisted of some 3,000
infantry, Cossacks and dragoons. The way had been mapped by a survey
party which had made a secret reconnaissance of the country around Khiva.

---

[1] *Rise and Fulfilment of British Rule in India.* London, 1934.

By treachery, or rather, superior cunning, the Khan persuaded the commander of the Russian forces to visit him, and then got him to divide his
forces into small groups so that they could be more conveniently accommo-
dated as the Khan's guests. This being done, the Khan's troops fell upon
them and massacred them and their commander. An expedition of vengeance sent by Tsar Peter was dispersed by a storm in the Caspian Sea. Khiva
remained undisturbed for nearly eight years.

In 1725, Peter again sent an envoy to the Khan of Khiva without any
marked result. Six years later, Peter's successor, the Empress Anna, also sent
a mission to discuss a treaty between the two countries. The Khan refused to
let its members enter the city, and they returned even more empty-handed
than when they had set off, as bandits attacked them on their journey home
and stole their baggage. In 1734, the leaders of the Kirghiz hordes, fearing a
Russian expedition against them, offered allegiance to the Russian empress,
and in 1740 their example was followed by the Khan of Khiva. His offer of
allegiance resulted in his removal from the throne – and assassination – by
his suzerain, Nadir Shah, the ruler of Persia. The new Khan was leader of
the lesser horde of Kirghiz; and unknown to Nadir Shah, apparently, he
had already made his submission to Russia. On being ordered to wait upon
the Shah, to explain his actions, the Khan – perhaps wisely, knowing the
temper of his overlord – fled from Khiva with the Russian officers who had
– perhaps unwisely – assisted him at his accession.

Relations with Khiva continued only in terms of a tax upon Russian
travellers and the kidnapping of Russian subjects for the slave market, but
still the Russians did little more than protest. In 1834, and this very date de-
monstrates the essential slowness of Russian expansion into Central Asia, a
fortress was constructed at Kultuk bay on the Caspian as a possible advance
base against Khiva. Five years later, an expedition under General Peroffski
left Orenburg (see map p. 339) to attack Khiva – which was some eight
hundred miles away across an almost waterless desert. The expedition was a
complete failure. Extreme heat and lack of water had seriously reduced Peroffski's forces when he arrived at Abu Bulak in July 1839. In order to ensure a supply of drinking water for the rest of the march, Peroffski decided
to wait until November before moving on to Khiva. Snow would then supply all the water he needed. Conditions, however, were almost Arctic, and,
having reached a point only halfway between Orenburg and Khiva in May
1840, Peroffski was compelled to turn back. He did so with only a third of
his original force still alive and only a thousand camels left out of the 10,000

he started with. To add to Peroffski's burden, shortly after his return to Oren-burg he learned that one of the aims of the expedition – the liberation of the Russian prisoners held as slaves – had already been achieved by diplomacy. To make it worse, this triumph was the work of an Englishman, Captain James Abbott.

Despite this, or possibly because of it, a second expedition was ordered by the Tsar in 1841. But the Khan of Khiva, hearing of it, sent declarations of friendship to St Petersburg, and issued proclamations guaranteeing protection to Russian subjects. In the following year, a non-aggression treaty was signed. Russia appeared to have no further designs upon Khiva. In order to reinforce this appearance, Tsar Nicholas – then on a visit to England – agreed 'to leave the khanates of Central Asia to serve as a neutral zone interposed be-tween Russia and India, so as to preserve them from dangerous contact'. This promise, even though Khiva did not keep hers in respect of Russian subjects, was easy to make, for Russia was expanding elsewhere into areas more easily subdued.

In northern Turkestan, Russian forts spread along the Jaxartes, until in 1848 they reached the Aral Sea. By 1853, Fort Peroffski – founded upon the ruins of Ak Musjid – dominated the Sir Darya, and it was an open secret that Russia's next move was to be across the desert of Kyzyl Kum to Tash-kent, if not further still, to Samarkand and Bokhara. The outbreak of the Crimean War in 1854, however, halted activity in Turkestan. Russian ex-ploration and survey work nevertheless continued, and though in 1857 both the Khan of Khiva and the Amir of Bokhara sent envoys to congratulate the new Tsar, Alexander II, on his succession – Nicholas had died in 1855 – this produced no closer contact. It only served to remind the new Tsar's advisers of the humiliations of the past and the continued robbery, murder, and kidnapping of Russian subjects.

The Khan of Khokand, whose territories the Russian advance down the Sir Darya directly threatened, attempted, in 1860, to stop the Russians by force. The Khokandis were utterly defeated and, by the middle of the year, a Russian campaign against Tashkent had resulted in the capture of that city. The Russians now prepared for the final occupation of Khokand. At this stage, news of Russian activity in Central Asia once more reached the out-side world. It did so because, during the campaign for Tashkent, a famous place of Muslim pilgrimage had come into Russian possession when the town of Turkestan was captured, about a hundred miles north of Tashkent. Because of the interest in Russia's plans aroused in the countries of Europe, and particularly in England, the Russian chancellor, Prince Gortchakoff, decided to issue a Circular Note to the powers explaining Russian policy in Central Asia. It was, he maintained, the consequence of dire necessity. Alexis Krausse, a nineteenth-century commentator on Russian expansion, summarised the contents of the Note as follows:

'... the Russian statesmen pointed out that Russia had found herself brought into contact with a number of semi-savage tribes, who proved a constant menace to the security and the well-being of the empire. Under these circumstances, the only possible means of maintaining order on the Russian frontier was to bring these tribes into subjection, but as soon as this had been accomplished it was found that the new converts to civil-isation had in turn become exposed to the attacks of more distant tribes. And so it became necessary to establish fortified posts among the out-lying peoples, and by a display of force to bring them into submission. The chancellor pointed out that this position was in no way peculiar to Russia in Central Asia. The United States in America, France in Al-geria, and England in India had all been compelled by absolute neces-sity to push their frontiers out so as to absorb people who formed a con-stant menace to their security, and the chief difficulty with which a states-man had to deal was the question as to when the expansion was to end. In conclusion, Prince Gortchakoff proceeded to define the mission of Russia in Central Asia. The great aim which the servants of the Tsars kept in view was the civilisation of the wild countries which formed the district known as Turkestan. No agent had been found more efficacious in this respect than the establishment of commercial relations. The people were ignorant and quarrelsome, and they had to be taught that more was to be gained by favouring and protecting trade than by rob-bery.'[1]

The reasoning of the Note was impeccable. As an analysis of the nature of colonial expansion, it is difficult to fault. The *romance* of empire is only the face of propaganda, the incitement to sacrifice among the young men who must die for it. The mythology is only there to distract attention from the re-morseless logic Prince Gortchakoff exposed. Empires expand, not out of desire but of necessity, and when the necessity is no longer there, they decay.

Whatever the overtones, the Russian Note struck true to the country most likely to know. Great Britain, instead of protesting, kept silent. The Rus-

---

[1] *Russia in Asia: a record and a study*. London, 1899

sians continued their 'work of necessity' in Khokand. In December 1864, an attempt was made by the people of Turkestan to recapture their holy city. The Amir of Bokhara entered Khokand with a large army, issuing as he went an instruction to the Russians that they should immediately become Muslims. A Russian envoy was seized and imprisoned, but when the Amir's forces met the Russians at Irdjar, the Bokhariots fled, leaving the road to Samarkand open. The new governor of Turkestan, General Kaufmann, in an endeavour to achieve his aims without bloodshed, offered a treaty to the Amir. By its terms, Samarkand would be formally ceded to Russia. The Amir found the treaty unacceptable, and once again attacked the Russians, only, for the second time, to be put to flight. Kaufmann then occupied Samarkand and, leaving a small force in the citadel, moved on in a final attempt to dispose of the Amir once and for all. After his departure, the Russian garrison found itself besieged by over twenty thousand men, but it managed to hold out until Kaufmann's victorious return. A treaty with Bokhara was finally signed in June 1868. The terms included an indemnity payable in gold; the cession of the valley of the Zerafshan, and the city of Samarkand, to Russia; free passage through Bokhara and protection whilst there for Russian subjects; and the right to trade. Kaufmann, in return, undertook not to 'occupy or molest' the city of Bokhara

Success along the line of the Jaxartes turned Kaufmann's attention to the Russification of the whole of east Turkestan. In 1851, a treaty had been signed with China, the Treaty of Kulja, which legalised trade between the two countries, but, apart from caravan traffic between Jungaria and Semirachensk and the construction of factories at Tchugutchak and Kulja, the agreement had not been particularly productive. The existence of the treaty was kept a secret until 1861, in an attempt to conceal from England the objects of Russian expansion in Asia. The actual terms of the treaty were not disclosed until 1871. But the rising in Kashgar in 1865 (see p. 171), though it created the possibility of acquiring additional territory, demonstrated the difficulties of administering the turbulent tribes. Chinese Turkestan could wait. Kaufmann, therefore, turned to the west, where Khiva remained unsubdued and the upper Oxus still unoccupied. Geography and climate were still the real enemies. In the way of the Russian advance were the arid wastes of the Kara Kum and the frozen region of the Ust Urt plateau. In 1869, a strong fort was established at Krasnovodsk on the eastern shore of the Caspian Sea, and preparations were begun for another expedition against Khiva. But a rebellion of Kirghiz and Cossacks of the Don threatened Uralsk and

Orenburg, and was not suppressed until the autumn of 1870. Kashgar, also, again burst into rebellion. Yakub Beg was rumoured to be conspiring with the rulers of Bokhara and Khiva to raise a holy war against the Russians. The order was given to march upon Khiva when news came of the abandonment of Ili by the Chinese (see p. 172). Under Russian pressure, the Muslim rebels evacuated Chinese territory as the Russians occupied it. The danger in eastern Turkestan was now over.

There still remained, however, the problems of Khiva and Bokhara. Rus- sian agents incited the Turkomans to revolt against the Khan of Khiva and, while he was occupied with the rebellion, a Russian force – moving across the steppe from Krasnovodsk – was to attack the Khivan army. Again, climate, topography, and the guerilla tactics of the Khivans combined to repulse the Russian expedition, and it was compelled to retreat with the loss of its baggage. This last defeat was the point of no return. Kaufmann deter- mined on the reduction of Khiva. His plan was an attack with large and well-armed forces, divided into two prongs, one starting from the Caspian and the other from Tashkent.

In order to plan the operation, Kaufmann returned to St Petersburg. The situation once again demanded diplomacy, for Khiva was on the road to India. Great Britain must once again be soothed. The news of the Russian defeat and the intended attack upon Khiva had caused a sensation in London, and a special envoy was sent by the Tsar to 'explain' Russian intentions. The sole object of the new expedition was, according to the envoy, 'to punish acts of brigandage, to recover fifty Russian prisoners, and to teach the Khan that such conduct on his part could not be continued with impunity.' As to the *occupation* of Khiva,' not only was it far from the intention of the emperor to take possession... but positive orders had been prepared to prevent it, and directions given that the conditions imposed should be such as would not in any way lead to the prolonged occupation of Khiva.'[1] A soft answer which turned away protest.

In March 1873, a column commanded by General Kaufmann in person, and comprising some 5,500 men and eighteen guns, left Tashkent. Another of under 3,000 men commanded by Colonel Markossoff advanced from the Caspian, and a third, under General Vereffkin, of 2,000 infantry and six guns, moved down from Orenburg. The Khan sent out emissaries to India and Persia, seeking aid, but without success. He then declared he would fight

---

[1] *Parliamentary Papers, Central Asia* No. 1, 1873

to the bitter end. The three columns, moving at between twenty-seven and thirty miles a day, pressed on despite intense cold. Kaufmann had given instructions to the other commanders that, should they reach the oasis of Khiva before him, they must wait before they attacked the city – the glory of its capture was reserved for the governor of Turkestan.

Despite the Khan's declared intention to fight every inch of the way, the advancing forces continued their march across the sandy deserts without interference, apart from an occasional encounter with marauding Kirghiz or Turkomans; and on 26 May, General Vereffkin reached the Oxus. There he found a fort of considerable size, occupied by the Khivans. The next day, a party of the enemy was discovered lower down the river, who on seeing the Russians, sent an envoy with an offer of surrender! While discussions were in progress, the main body of the Khivan forces made off. These tactics were repeated later in the day. In the evening, the town of Khodjeili was found to be deserted. After occupying it, the Russians received delegations from various Kirghiz tribes offering their submission. Attacks by bodies of Yomud Turkomans continued, but all were unsuccessful.

On 2 June, a number of Khivans came to the Russian camp pleading for protection, and from them Vereffkin learned that the Khan's forces numbered as few as 7,000 men. On the same day news came that General Kaufmann would probably reach Khiva in three or four days. On 6 June, the Khan sent an invitation to the Russian commander suggesting that he should come to Khiva and arrange peace terms, and asked for an immediate armistice. Vereffkin, remembering the Khan's previous treacheries, refused. Later, he heard that Kaufmann had fought and dispersed a considerable Khivan force that had attempted to oppose his crossing of the Oxus. Apart from this information, Vereffkin had no news of Kaufmann's actual whereabouts. The former had now reached Khiva and was considerably harassed by constant attacks by small bands of Khivans as well as by gunfire from the city walls. Vereffkin decided to attack. On 9 June, he advanced, pushing back the enemy and silencing many of their guns, to within fifty yards of the city gate.

At this point, when the city could easily have been captured, and when his officers were ordering the final assault, Vereffkin remembered his instructions to wait for Kaufmann. Vereffkin consequently ordered a retreat and was himself wounded in it. As soon as the bombardment of the city ceased, an envoy came out asking for an armistice, which was agreed to; but it was broken by the Khivans, and the Russian bombardment was renewed. That same night, news arrived that Kaufmann was barely seven miles away, and was engaged in negotiations with the Khan's uncle. The terms of peace agreed upon were severe and entirely contrary to Russia's declared intentions. They included the cession of the entire territory of Khiva from the right bank of the Oxus, together with the river delta, an indemnity of 2,200,000 roubles, customs exemption for Russian traders, and the relegation of the Khan into a vassal of the Tsar. After the signing of the treaty, Kaufmann entered Khiva on 10 June 1873.

The force under Kaufmann, apart from a minor engagement, had seen little fighting, yet it was to have the privilege of occupying the city. Those officers on Kaufmann's staff who had hoped for honours and awards for their efforts in battle were naturally angry at having no opportunity to win them, so Kaufmann's response was to create a campaign for his own force to distinguish itself in. At hand was an easy enemy, the comparatively peaceful tribe of Yomud Turkomans. The elders of the tribe had been amongst the first to send in their submission to the Russian conquerors, but this was not allowed to influence the course Kaufmann had ruthlessly decided upon. Calling the elders, he demanded of them an indemnity of 300,000 roubles, to be paid within fifteen days, and detained hostages as security; and in order to ensure his men's 'glory hunt', he insisted on payment in money and not in kind. The demand was made on 17 July 1873. The next day, Kaufmann ordered General Golovatchef to attack the Turkomans forthwith and exterminate them. The result was the butchering of a whole tribe, men, women and children, without provocation in the interest of medals and promotions.

The next stage in Kaufmann's plans was a treaty with Bokhara. This was signed in October 1873, and established the right of free navigation of the Oxus and the establishment of trade between Russia and Bokhara. The Russians now began to establish the rudiments of administration, as distinct from butchery, in their newly acquired dominions. The new province of Transcaspia was formed in the winter of 1873, with its headquarters at Krasnovodsk. The pacification of the area was, however, difficult, and plans for the building of new towns were temporarily suspended because of a rising in Khokand. The Khan appealed to Kaufmann for assistance, claiming that the rebels were Kirghiz from Russian territory. The request was refused. The trouble in Khokand continued well into 1875, in which year Kaufmann sent an envoy to the Khan asking permission for a Russian expedition to pass through Khokand on its way to Kashgar. On his arrival, the envoy found that the Khan's brother had joined the rebels and so had the

state army. The Khan decided, under the circumstances, to put himself under Russian protection and fled to Tashkent. His successor sent an envoy to
Kaufmann blaming the insurrection on the oppressions of his predecessor,
and expressing his desire to live in peace with the Russians. Unfortunately
for him, the people of Khokand were being incited to a holy war. Kaufmann now acted. The Russian campaign was successful and the city of
Khokand was captured. The task of pacification was not so easy. In March
1876, the khanate of Khokand was annexed and formed into a province of
the Russian Empire, under the name of Ferghana.

Historical parallels are always worth searching for, especially as they so
rarely exist, but it would be true to say that the battle of Irdjar was the Plassey of the Russian Empire – a derisory engagement which nevertheless marked
the beginning of a new era. The Russification of Central Asia proceeded
with speed and decision, though not without opposition. The Turkoman
country was conquered by General Skobelev between 1881 and 1884; this
included the occupation of the Merv oasis (1884). The land between Merv
and Pendjeh was similarly taken in 1884-5, and a war with Britain narrow-
ly avoided. The Russo-Persian and Russo-Afghan frontiers from the Caspian Sea to the Chinese border were finally delimited between 1885 and
1895. In March 1895, a treaty was signed with Afghanistan by which all
the Pamir north of the branch of the Oxus flowing from Sari-kul and a line
drawn eastward to the Chinese frontier passed into the hands of Russia. An
empire had been built in thirty years.

IV

THE STRUGGLE FOR PERSIA

The failure of Peter the Great's excursion to the east of the Caspian inspired
him to try his luck to the west. In 1722, the Tsar sent an embassy to the Shah
of Persia, replete with imaginary complaints and very real claims in compensation for them. On their being refused, Russian troops entered Daghestan
and took Derbend on the coast of the Caspian Sea. Peter's next move was to
stir up rebellion in the independent principality of Georgia, but he died before he could complete his plans for annexation. In the years that followed,
the menace to Georgia came not from Russia, but from Persia, and in 1783
the then ruling prince signed a treaty of allegiance with the Empress Catherine in return for protection against attack by Persia. Twelve years later, the

Shah invaded Georgia, and without much difficulty took the capital, Tiflis. The Persians devastated the countryside, giving, as one of them described it, 'the Georgian unbelievers a specimen of what they were to expect on the Day of Judgement'. In response to the terms of the treaty, a Russian army entered Georgia in 1796, captured Derbend and Baku, and pursued the retreating Persians almost to the gates of Teheran. It seemed likely that the Russian invaders would conquer the whole of Persia without much difficulty, but the death of Catherine resulted in the army being recalled by her successor, Paul. It was only on his death in 1800 that Russian interest in Persia revived. The new Tsar, Alexander, ordered an expedition to the south – the first result of which was the annexation of Georgia in 1801. The Russians continued their triumphal march into Persia, the Persians refusing battle until, at Erivan (1804), they stood and their army was defeated. Great Britain, who had been appealed to by the Shah for aid, sent officers to command Persian troops, but, when friendly relations were established between Russia and Great Britain in 1812, withdrew them, and acting as negotiators promoted the Treaty of Gulistan between the two belligerents in 1813. The terms of the treaty were particularly favourable to Russia. All the territories she had captured in her campaign were awarded to her. Russian naval forces were permitted to navigate the Caspian, but the Persians were forbidden to do so, even off their own seaboard. The duty on Russian exports to Persia, and imports from her, was restricted to five per cent. Unfortunately, the language in which these terms were couched was so confused that continuous squabbling resulted over their interpretation. The frontier between the two countries was perpetually under armed dispute, until in 1826 Russia forcibly occupied a district claimed by the Persians. At this, the Persians, under the command of the heir to the throne, invaded Russia.

The campaign, which lasted for two years, was a series of defeats for the Persians, who finally capitulated and signed the Treaty of Turcomanchai in 1828. As well as recapitulating all the clauses of the Treaty of Gulistan, it included an indemnity of thirty million roubles and gave to Russia sovereignty over the whole of the Caucasus, excepting a small corner in the south-east bordering on the Black Sea. At the same time, Russia had been engaged in a successful war against Turkey, resulting in the occupation of the port of Poti on the Black Sea and the fort of Akhaltsikh, between Tiflis and the sea.

Relations between Russia and Persia became almost friendly. The Shah realised he could not fight his northern neighbour with any chance of success. Russia henceforth was able to dominate Persia by intrigue rather than costly occupation, and the country became in every sense a satellite, a front for Russian sorties against the growing power of the British in India, who were already looking at the Persian Gulf as a bay on the British Indian ocean. The decline of English influence over Persia was a direct result of Britain's unwillingness to help Persia in her war with Russia, despite the obvious advantages to her in doing so. When Persia asked for financial aid to pay her indemnity to Russia, Britain bought her way out of her treaty with Persia (which contained a guarantee to aid her against any other European nation) for the sum of £300,000. The whole of the Anglo-Persian treaty, however, was not abrogated. In particular, a clause remained to the effect that, in case of war between the Afghans and Persia, the British should not interfere except if requested to mediate.

Russia's next move was to jerk her puppet into an attack upon Herat, ostensibly to rescue the city from Afghan rule. On this occasion, the Persian army was directly commanded by Russian officers. Protests by the British envoy had no effect. Neither did an appeal to the Tsar, who returned an evasive reply. The governor-general of India therefore sent a British officer to Herat to organise its defence. He did so, so well that the city defied the Persians for nine and a half months. Further British protests at St Petersburg and Teheran having no effect, an expedition was despatched to the Persian Gulf and occupied the island of Kharak. But the raising of the siege of Herat which soon followed did not reduce Russian influence in Persia. The British expedition only fostered ill-will against England in Teheran, and contributed to Russia's hold upon the country.

From the Russian point of view, intrigue was not to be indulged in for the fun of the game or for profits in the mists of the future. Tangible results in the form of exclusive rights in the waters of the Caspian led to the establishment of a naval arsenal on the island of Ashurada, as a forward base for activity in the area. Russia's open support of Persia in a border dispute between her and Turkey again increased Russian prestige and influence, but the death of the Shah in 1848 brought the accession of a new ruler and the appointment of a chief minister determined upon a policy which would keep Persia clear of both Russian and British influences. The minister's success in this aim led to his downfall. The Shah, jealous of the reputation of his employee, had him executed in 1852.

The problem of Herat again raised its head when the new ruler of that place offered his allegiance to Persia. The status of the city had been defined by a convention between Britain and Persia, signed in 1853, which required the latter not to make any attempt against it. The Shah waited nearly three years to make up his mind and, in December 1855, sent an army to occupy Herat. An attempt by the inhabitants to throw out both their own ruler and the Persians received no support either from the Afghans or the British, and in November 1856 the city surrendered to the Shah. Britain immediately sent troops to the Persian Gulf and occupied Bushire. A new treaty called for the evacuation of Herat by the Persians; this was completed in July 1857, and the city restored to Afghan rule.

The Russians, though disappointed by the outcome, were advancing into Central Asia, a more profitable and less internationally explosive area of expansion. They nevertheless continued the appropriation of Persian territory around the Caspian Sea. Persian protests against these seizures continued throughout Russia's expansion in Transcaspia until, finally, a frontier agreement was negotiated in 1881. Russian influence, however, continued to grow in the frontier areas until Persia was in fact virtually partitioned between the Russians, who dominated the north, and the British, who controlled the south.

In 1896, the Shah was assassinated and, under his successor, the deterioration of the country was rapid. Loans from both Russia and Britain were corruptly squandered, and with the decrease in Russian influence after her defeat by Japan in 1905 a revolutionary movement began in northern Persia. In the face of a growing anarchy, those two old enemies, Russia and Great Britain, concluded an agreement in 1907, which formally guaranteed the integrity of Persia whilst dividing the country into zones of economic interest. Further rebellions caused the Shah to take refuge in the Russian embassy at Teheran in 1909, and, from there, he abdicated in favour of his son. Two years later, with Russian connivance, he made an abortive attempt to reoccupy Teheran. An American financial adviser, appointed by the Persian government in the same year, challenged the position of both Britain and Russia. The consequence was a Russian ultimatum demanding his dismissal. Persian nationalists thereupon attacked a weak Russian force at Tabriz, killing a hundred soldiers. Russian troops took reprisals and forced Persia to accept the terms of the ultimatum and dismiss the American adviser. Anti-Russian incidents, however, continued until the outbreak of the first World War overwhelmed Russia's long-term plans. The Tsars had left it too late.

6

The Meeting of East and West:
The Second Impact

I

THE TROJAN HORSE

TO THE PORTUGUESE, the trade of their eastern possessions was an instrument, one of many, of the greater victory of Christ. For the Dutch, the
French, and the British, trade was trade as well as a weapon in the narrow
field of European rivalries. It was only as the British became the dominant
European power in Asia, and searched for a moral justification for this, that
they found in the alliance of industrial progress and evangelical Christianity
a supernatural explanation for the superiority of their civilisation. For them,
the tablets of their law had come down from another Sinai, and their arrogance was that of a chosen people. The atavistic reaction of the Indian Mutiny was a battle of the gods as well as a revolt, for the God of the British was
feared as much as – if not more than – the efficiency of their military science.
After the Mutiny, the British God was still associated with the regime, but
as a silent partner referred to often, but officially confined to the civil station
and the swearing-in of viceroys. Missionaries continued their activity, but
mainly in the field of social service, in education and medicine. Christianity
seemed no longer to threaten the Indians, for in their reaction to it, and the
discovery of the vitality of their own religious tradition, the superiority of the
British could be seen as a matter of organisation and technology, the keys to
which could be obtained without taking their religion as well. Furthermore,
the demands of administration left the British little place for the pioneer spirit;
the moral pattern of their government was quite sufficient, and officials no
longer needed the shot of benzedrine that the God of Battles supplied. The
British concepts of duty and responsibility were Platonic rather than Christian. Members of the Indian Civil Service now began to think of themselves as
philosopher-kings and princes.

But elsewhere, the wild men of God, the religious enthusiasts, could still
play a part – not so much as partners of a Western imperialism, as K. S.

Latourette has said, but as unconscious allies in the new aggressions. It must not be thought that the way these men were used was the product of some carefully thought out Machiavellian plan. Napoleon, in the early nineteenth century, had declared that 'the religious missions may be very useful to me in Asia, Africa and America, and I shall make them reconnoitre all the lands they visit. The sanctity of their dress will not only protect them but serve to conceal their political and commercial investigations.' No other Western statesman actually said anything as blunt as this, but it became their policy just the same. Yet the involvement of Christian missionaries in politics emerged only from the reasonable belief that a nation should always give protection to its own nationals. The politicians of the nineteenth century saw nothing immoral in guaranteeing to missionaries the same right of unrestricted entry into Asian countries as they demanded for the products of their mills and factories. They were quite incapable of realising that the religion of the missionaries would not be viewed as an article of trade but as the Trojan horse of Western domination. To the peoples of China and elsewhere, it appeared that trade not only followed the flag, but guns and gun-boats followed the missionary who had been forced upon them by treaty.

As we have seen (p. 81 f.), in Indo-China the French missionary bishop, Pigneau de Behaine, raised an army to place his own candidate upon the throne of Annam, and had a French military expedition to help him do so. When missionaries were forced upon Asians by treaty, they were considered as part of the package of aggression. When they were attacked, as when Tu-Duc massacred Christian bishops and priests, this view was bloodily confirmed by the retaliation such actions provoked. In China, the terms of the Treaty of Nanking – which closed the Opium War in 1842 – classed, in the Chinese view, the forced importation of the drug with the opening of the country to Christian missionaries. The Chinese saw no difference in the nature of the two things. The new treaties that followed the sack of Peking in 1860 inextricably associated Christian missions with extra-territorial rights. As 'protected persons', missionaries frequently became involved in local politics. Some Chinese found it advantageous to become Christian so that they could call upon the protection of a foreign power against their own government. The missionaries were seen as a fifth column, an advance guard of the West and its subjugation of the whole of China.

The results of Christian missionary effort in China were comparatively small. Those who were converted were more often than not assured by the missionaries of the worldly advantages of being known as Christians, under the protection of the missionary and the guns of those who protected *him*, rather than the spiritual gifts of Christ's teaching. Until well into the present century, most of the clergy were European and American. Their churches, in pseudo-Gothic style, were obviously non-Chinese and were known as Yang-tang, 'European temples', as blatantly representative of extra-territoriality as any gun-boat or consul's flag. Furthermore, the fundamental difference between the peaceable message of Christ and the aggressive actions of the 'Christian' powers was obvious to everyone. On another level, the confused doctrines of Christianity, stemming as they did from alien traditions, had no direct meaning for the Chinese, for there seemed to be no connection between the teaching and action. The West, then, was hypocritical, and the religion of its missionaries only a disguise for darker things.

The missions, in spite of this, had a profound impact upon the civilisation of China, disintegrating as it was under the blows of Western aggression. Christianity, too, was to emerge for a moment in an Asian guise. After the Opium War, missionaries – mainly Protestant – spread throughout China. One, a Baptist, passed on his message to a certain Hung Hsiu-ch'uan. Hung, a visionary, proclaimed himself 'the younger brother of Christ', and his mission to create the kingdom of God upon earth. This kingdom Hung called T'ai P'ing, 'Supreme Peace'. Hung's dynamic leadership brought to his banner all the anti-Manchu sentiment latent amongst the Chinese, and the progress of his rebellion was startling. Hankow fell in 1852, Nanking in the following year, and in 1854 Tientsin and the imperial capital of Peking were seriously threatened. Hung never ceased to insist upon the Christian nature of his kingdom, and foreign missionaries were welcomed in its territories. Western Christians at first approved of the T'ai P'ing, until they recognised that Hung had drawn his inspiration direct from the Bible and not through the intermediary of Western missionaries. Unlike them, Hung saw Christianity as a universal faith, but in a particularly Chinese form. Hung had made an adaptation, a new compromise, by a wedding of Christian fundamentals with the Chinese conceptions of kingship. Hung was just as much the 'son of Heaven' as the Manchu emperor, but the son of a Christian heaven, and also the son of God. This bizarre interpretation antagonised the parochial minds of the missionaries. Hung's temporal successes frightened the Western powers. The divorce between the Christian front and the actual *realpolitik* of the imperialist nations is here most obvious. Hung represented an effect, however odd, of the spiritual message they so prided themselves on bringing as a part of their *mission civilisatrice*, but political and economic interests were at stake, and to the West the choice was never in doubt. The T'ai P'ing offered the possibility of a strong and united China, though in fact the lessons of Chinese history leave little doubt that the movement would ultimately have collapsed. A weak and pliable Manchu emperor was necessary to the West's plans for the exploitation of the Celestial Empire. So the T'ai P'ings were defeated in the bloodiest of civil wars by the Manchus supported by the West. The only mass movement in the whole of Asia directly inspired by the teachings of Christianity received the dustiest answer from the Christian powers of the West.

Christian missions continued their work amongst the crumbling ruins of Chinese civilisation. On the lowest level, conversions were made; for famine and the relief organisation of the missions made it possible to buy faith for a bowl of rice, until many of the converted came to be known derisively as 'rice Christians'. In many parts of the country, the missionary was the sole representative of the imperial powers. It mattered nothing that he did not see himself as one. The xenophobia of the Chinese has its real meaning in this reaction to the ubiquitous missionary as the occult front of the superiority of the West. Surrounded by collapsing values, and unnerved by the bitter realisation that the insulating fabric of Confucianism had been irretrievably rent, the Chinese turned against the missionaries and their places of worship. As the old props of the regime, the emperor and the mandarins, seemed unable to act, the mob itself rose and destroyed the symbols of its unease. The Boxer rebellion was basically anti-missionary and anti Chinese convert, and its first acts were to be the massacre of Christians and the destruction of their churches.

The failure of Christianity in Asia was inevitable, for its guilt was established by association. The universality of Christian teachings was never apparent, for the religion of the foreigners was always tagged as a foreign religion, a symbol of exploitation and aggression. Such good works as its missionaries did was outside the context of proselytism – humanitarian acts rather than religious ones. It is unlikely that Christianity in Asia will ever recover from the smear of Western imperialism though it is always possible that a new Hung may attempt once again to spread the 'Supreme Peace'.

*　　*　　*

India was fortunate in having its atavistic reaction to the spiritual impact of the West crystallised into the Mutiny of 1857. The failure of the revolt brought a new dimension of peace and security, and the opportunity to examine the apparent failure of Indian traditional values. At the same time, expansion of Western-style education in schools and universities revealed to Indians that the West had philosophical and ethical sources that were neither Christian in origin nor in belief. Though Indian philosophy had no place in the curricula of higher education, the emphasis on Greek ethical systems later led the curious to the examination of Indian systems. A realisation of the impact of Indian ideas upon Western philosophers also resulted in the exploration of these ideas by Indians themselves, and a growing reassurance in the value of their own traditions. When the Indians realised that the Eastern ideas that had most influenced the West came from Buddhism, Vedanta and Yoga, a new sense of pride in the past became a support for a growing sense of national maturity. Having despised their standards for failure to stand up to the impact of the West, Indians could only recover them once they had recognised the true source of the superiority of their conquerors.

This they did in the latter part of the nineteenth century through the Western-style education forced upon them by their rulers. In China, intellectuals were compelled to go abroad in order to acquire the palladia of the West; but in Japan, Western philosophy and science could be ingested at home. Many Chinese received their knowledge of Western ideas in Japanese universities. The great discovery made by Asian intellectuals in the late nineteenth century was that the success of the West, its domination of the forces of nature, and its political domination of the world, were not as esoteric as the first shattering impact had made it seem. The machine by which the West propelled iron ships and railroads, dug great pits, and flung iron bridges across rivers, appeared at first to be the result of some occult power, to lie in the possession of a fabulous secret. That very machine, or one of its brood, clanking away in a building in Lancashire – a place as remote as paradise – could shatter the whole rural industry of Asia and destroy a thousand years of craftsmanship with its cheap manufactures. But the secrets could be learned and used. The first stage was to acquire the foreigner's language, to imitate his institutions as well as his science, for technical superiority could only exist within the framework of general culture. No Asian could accept that the wonders of Western technology could be separated from the West's political institutions, for these were the West's own criteria of value. The constant insistence by colonial rulers on the superiority of Western institutions forced Asia to accept the West at its own valuation. When Indians, for example, looked into their past, they looked not for the weapons with which to defeat the West – for they already knew what these weapons were. They looked instead for racial justification and for traditional dignity, in order to assert their *equal* right to the purely mechanical instruments of material and political freedom. They were searching, in fact, for a sense of nationhood, for the West taught them that the importance of the nation-state lay in its sense of folk, community, and history.

In this search, the West once again assisted, for the proliferations of scientific discovery were not confined to mastery over the forces of nature alone. Scientific criteria must be applied to all branches of culture. The dilettante approach to the past was to be abandoned in favour of organised curiosity, above all to standards of accuracy that paralleled those of the applied sciences. From European historians, philologists, anthropologists, and archaeologists, Asia was to receive a new and dangerous sense of the past. Amaury de Rien-court, though writing of China, might well be speaking for the whole of colonial Asia when he says:

'Digging, reassembling, collecting, cataloguing the innumerable ele-ments of forgotten worlds and of civilisations which have been blotted out of men's memory by pitiless sands and jungles, cleaning away the cobwebs of myths and legends which have become inextricably mixed with factual data, Western scientists began to extract fragments of a for-gotten past which slowly added an entirely new dimension to Chinese consciousness. Although sketchy and patchy, the past of China was slowly emerging under the cold glare of scientific research in good, chronological, historical, geographical, and ethnical order, a new gleam-ing monument of frozen history. China's *subjective*, two-dimensional appreciation of a mythical past which was to be nothing more than an ethical model for those who were living in the everlasting present gra-dually collapsed before a three-dimensional view based on incontro-vertible scientific data and a coolly *objective* understanding... Historical perspective, which was deemed to throw light on a past that had no intrinsic reality because it lived only in the memory of the living, now began to detach itself from the human observer and stand outside of him, encased in the objective rigidity of scientific research.'[1]

Before the work of the 'cultural scientists', Asia was history-less, its people unable to observe the historical process, because they were unaware of its existence. But as soon as the educated classes became conscious of the move-

[1] *The Soul of China.* New York, 1958. London, 1959. This brilliant, though sometimes prolix book is one of the most revealing works on China written by a European.

ments of fluctuation and decay within their own civilisation, they were able to view the overwhelming and apparently unshakable superiority of the West as just another 'time of troubles'. They also learned from the new objectivity that history provided that the future must be fought for, that far from being the result of providence or divine order it was the construction of man himself. This discovery was of tremendous importance, for it coincided with the realisation that the secrets of Western economic success were, at least in theory, available to everyone. But, above all, in discovering their own history, Asians learned that the West was also subject to the rise and fall of rulers, that the historical process was universal.

Armed with new criteria of historical comparison, the insistence of the colonial powers on the superiority of their institutions now seemed to Asians to be supported by laws of historical growth. For, having accepted the West's discovery of history, Asians, lacking a philosophy of history of their own, accepted the universal application of these laws. Consequently, it appeared that Asia lagged behind the West only in time, that the West was only a little further along the road which the East would inevitably follow in the working out of the process of history. From this premise, it was natural that Asians should demand the tools of the future, and a speeding up of the journey along the road to freedom. Here were the seeds of nationalism. The road was marked upon the map, the destination was clear. History demonstrated Asia's right to make the journey. It also showed that she would have to fight for it, as the West had done. But again, the weapons were also there, and the outcome was inevitable. The real Trojan horse was not Western Christianity, which completely failed in its attempt to capture the soul of Asia, but the West's discovery of Asia's past, and the revelation of its own. Furthermore, the horse was inside the West's own citadel.

That there was another road, and another destination more in keeping with the essential nature of Asian thinking, was not yet known, though Lenin – following Marx – was already signposting the way.

II

THE BEGINNINGS OF NATIONALISM

In the practical sphere of political life, the trends that were appearing in Asian thought (outlined in the preceding section) were slow to take form. In India after the Mutiny, the expansion of administration, its growing efficiency, and the feeling of security from armed rebellion was viewed by all classes as an indication of the permanency of the British connection. The beginnings of nationalism can only be seen in the consideration given by the educated classes to methods by which they could *influence* the government on their behalf. The basis of such influence lies in a consensus of opinion, and one of the principal instruments for moulding that opinion and bringing together those who think upon similar lines, is a free press. In Bengal, at the centre of British rule, the *Hindoo Patriot*, the *Amrita Bazar Patrika*, and the *Bengalee*, were, by the seventies of the last century, important organs of opinion. In Madras, the *Hindu*, and in the west the *Mahratta* and the *Kesari*, polarised anti-government feeling. All were influential enough to occasionally embarrass the administration. The British-owned papers, representing as they did special-interest groups, were often as anti-government as the vernacular press – sometimes even more so. In 1878, a Vernacular Press Act was passed in an attempt to muzzle the native-language newspapers, but it merely ensured the greater authority and prestige of the Indian-owned papers published in English. The Act itself was received by Indians as a piece of racial discrimination.

Nevertheless, the daily and periodical press became a sort of passport to the new ideas of democracy and political freedom. Through them, a man of the south could, *for the first time in India's history*, feel that he had something in common with the men of the north, the east, and the west. Cheap and efficient postal services cemented this belief by helping the interchange of ideas and, finally, the railway could bring men physically together from the furthest points of India.

At the same time, the classic elements of middle-class discontent – lack of employment in the rank they felt due to their education and position, and the indifference of the ruling class to their interests – emerged in India. An educated class with a sense of grievance is often more dangerous than a peasant with a sword. The educated turned to their natural allies, to the middle-class business man, anxious for support in their struggle for fiscal change. Few, if any, thought of independence, of freedom from British rule. All sought a slice of the cake.

Most of the Indian 'moderate' leaders were reformers, legatees of the beliefs of the Brahmo Samaj. They sought to clean up their religion so that it could add a strictly Indian counter-weight to their acceptance of the material institutions of the British. Their ultimate aim was self-government within the British Empire, and they saw themselves as the inheritors of the prophecies of

Macaulay and others. In the words of one of them (Gopal Krishna Gokhale), they saw India 'industrialised, socially emancipated, and self-governing'.
To the British they owed 'the blessings of peace, the establishment of law and
order, the introduction of Western education, and the freedom of speech and
appreciation of liberal institutions that have followed in its wake', and recognised that 'the continuance of British rule means the continuance of that
peace and order which it alone can maintain'. They envisaged themselves as
initially in the same role as that typically British institution, a 'loyal opposition', to press for reforms and, one day, when their turn came, to change
the government from within.

The first meeting of the Indian National Congress in 1885 was, and was
intended as, an expression of moderate opinion. The later role of Congress in
the struggle for freedom has tended to inflate the importance of its beginnings. Its early programmes were cautious and evolutionary, and had strong
European connections. One of its founders was a retired civil servant, Alan
Octavian Hume, who, on a visit to England, obtained the support of the
radical politicians John Bright and Charles Bradlaugh. Later, a propaganda
sheet, *India*, was published in London, and an Indian, Dadabhai Naoroji,
was actually returned to the British House of Commons.

In the beginning, Muslims did not participate in Congress, as their principal spokesman, Sir Syed Ahmad Khan, maintained that as democracy
meant the rule of the majority it therefore meant government by Hindus. Later, Muslims did join Congress, and by 1890 nearly a quarter of the delegates
(totalling almost 1,000 in number) were Muslims.

By 1892, the first 'loyal' period of the Congress was over and criticism of
the government and, in particular, of the new Councils Act, was loud and
unfriendly. The government of India, which had looked upon Congress as
a suitable safety valve for the loquacity of the Indian intellectual, now became definitely hostile. The moderates found themselves between the Scylla
of an unsympathetic government and the Charybdis of a growing extremism.

The partition of Bengal in 1905 brought with it Hindu-Muslim conflict,
and for some years the Muslim elements withdrew from Congress. The main
threat to Congress, however, was to come from the extremists. Their philosophy, such as it was, had as its mainstay a belief in Hindu nationalism. This
appealed to two apparently irreconcilable elements in India – the orthodox
Hindus, reacting against Western civilisation by a solidification of their
religious beliefs, and the younger men, partly educated in the Western manner yet finding themselves without status in a new system while the traditional

order of society seemed to be disintegrating around them. The result was a strange blending of Western ideas of nationalism with enthusiasm for the old religion. In the extremists can be found the epicentre of the impact of East and West.

The most characteristic figure of extremism was Bal Gangadhar Tilak (1856–1920), for he represents the improbable combination of atavism and modern revolutionary ideas. He first came into the limelight with his attack upon the Age of Consent Bill (passed 1891), which sought to prevent the evils of child marriage. His actions were carried out with such vigour as to endear him to the aggressive nationalists, and his reactionary conservatism brought him the strong support of Hindu orthodoxy. Hinduism itself had been undergoing a reaction to the eclecticism of the Brahmo Samaj. In Bengal, Ramakrishna and his disciple Vivekananda led a 'back to the *Vedas*' movement, based on the belief in a golden age assisted by an uncritical approach to Hindu sacred texts. Swami Dayananda, who had been a founder of the Arya Samaj, though accepting to some extent the idea of reform in the practices of Hinduism, still maintained, as Max Müller recorded, that 'everything worth knowing, even the most recent inventions of modern science, were alluded to in the *Vedas*. Steam engines, railways, and steamboats – all were shown to have been known, at least in their germs, to the poets of the *Vedas*', thousands of years before. This belief was reinforced by the lavish and unscholarly praise bestowed on ancient Hindu civilisation by Theosophists such as Annie Besant, Madame Blavatsky, and the American, Colonel Olcott. For the first time, Hinduism was given support and reassurance in Western terms, and for a while Theosophy appeared to offer the possibility of a synthesis of East and West upon a religious level. Mrs Besant became a public figure and helped to found the Benares Hindu university and, in 1915, the Indian Home Rule League.

At first, the Hindu revival was more religious than political, and consequently, anti-Muslim. In 1882, Swami Dayananda founded the Cow Protection Society as an overt attack on the beef-eating Muslims. Tilak, searching for a popular hero, found him in the Maratha chieftain, Sivaji, who had successfully fought against the Muhammadans at the time of the Mughal emperor, Aurangzeb. It is in this attitude of the early Hindu extremists that lies the seed of Pakistan, for Congress continued to have an extremist element inside it, vocal in its support of anti-Muslim religious attitudes.

In western India, the transformation of the Hindu revival into a political weapon was the work of Tilak in the Deccan, and Lajpat Rai in the Pun jab. To them, Congress owed its 'war mentality'. In Bombay, Tilak founded the vernacular newspaper *Kesari*, revived the annual festivals of Ganesha, the elephant-headed god who was, and is, the most popular deity in western India, and formed the cult of Sivaji as a symbol of the agitation and physical force which, he maintained, was the only way to fight the British. In 1896, a government attempt to enforce plague restrictions in Poona was fomented by the *Kesari* into a religious war. Two British officers on special plague duty were murdered. Those responsible were executed, and Tilak was sentenced to eighteen months in prison for incitement to murder.

Tilak's successes proved to other parts of India that a vernacular press combined with an appeal to religious prejudices could be used as a revolutionary instrument. Tilak himself was not in any real sense a national leader, but a parochial one, representing not Indians but Hindus and Marathas; his method was to use local pride and a local hero to stimulate the masses. Though Gandhi was later to refer to him as the 'maker of modern India', it was less a statement of fact than a prophecy which might well have come true. But one thing Tilak achieved, and it was fundamental to the freedom movement. He proved not only that it was possible to attack the myth of British superiority on an intellectual level and in Western terms, but to arouse a whole people in the struggle for freedom. His discovery was to give to Congress that ambivalence which was its strength when fighting the British and its weakness when it succeeded to power.

The arrest and imprisonment of Tilak closed the first period of political extremism. Bengal once again became the centre of agitation. There, the newspaper *Yugantar* – edited by a brother of Vivekananda – played the same role as the *Kesari*, with the goddess Kali replacing Ganesha. The movement in Bengal differed from that in the west. It looked not to ancient heroes but to local patriotism, to the myth of a wealthy and flourishing Bengal despoiled by foreigners. The opportunity came with the partition of 1905. Basically, the partition was a reasonable administrative measure. Calcutta, the capital of Bengal, was also (until 1912) the imperial capital, and this concentration of powers in Bengal did not lend itself to efficient organisation. It was proposed that a new province of Eastern Bengal, with its capital at Dacca, should be created. Logically, this proposition was supported by the existing religious division of Bengal, for west Bengal was predominantly Hindu, and the east, Muslim. But partition struck at the belief in the Bengali 'nation'. The nationalists were thus supplied with a ready-made target, for on no occasion were the people most involved in the consequences of partition ever consulted by the government. For the first time, the nationalists had a single, specific issue over which to fight, rather than vague general beliefs in 'freedom' and 'rights'. If partition could be reversed by agitation, a real victory would be achieved, and – on a much smaller scale – Russia's defeat by Japan would be paralleled upon Indian soil. Furthermore, partition supplied a rallying point for both moderates and extremists. In the struggle, the opposition would have the strength of unity.

Two new weapons were to be used in the campaign, terrorism, and the economic boycott. The boycott began in August 1904. It was widely supported, especially by Indian mill-owners, and the wearing of homespun cloth became one of the manifestations of the struggle for freedom. Secret societies were formed amongst students; bomb-throwers and political assassins became popular heroes, and their funerals scenes of hysterical emotion. A number of murders occurred, the first in Muzaffapur in 1908. For his comments in the *Kesari*, Tilak – who had been active again after his release from jail – was sentenced to six years' imprisonment on the same charge as before, incitement to murder. Terrorist activity was not confined to India and, in 1909, Sir Curzon Wyllie was murdered by a Punjabi at the Imperial Institute in London. This outrage at least brought home to the British public the existence of a nationalist movement in India. The partition of Bengal was revoked in 1911, and the last important attempt at political assassination was made, the following year, on the life of the viceroy, Lord Hardinge, as he made his state entry into Delhi.

The rise of Japan, and her victory over a 'European' imperialist power in her war with Russia (1904–5), formed a startling contrast with the state of India, the backwardness of her economic life, and the subordinate status of her people under foreign domination. Nationalists began consciously to associate their country's poverty with British 'exploitation'. Until the end of the nineteenth century, very few Indians had travelled abroad; this was partly because of the Hindu prohibition against crossing the 'black water' of the sea. When they did travel, Indians found in Europe the same attitudes of superiority and colour prejudice as they had suffered in India. Britain's view of her own importance, these travellers found, was part of a wider Western belief. When this was realised, the nature of Japan's victory over Russia became clear, and the Russo-Japanese war could be seen as the first battle between East and West, a heartening victory in the struggle of Asia for freedom from foreign domination. Furthermore, Japan's success was the product of an adaptation of Western technology and institutions to Asian requirements. 'We once thought', wrote Sun Yat-sen, 'that we could not do what the Europeans could do; and we now see that Japan has learned from Europe, and that, if we follow Japan, we too will be learning from the West as Japan did.'[1] Nationalists in India and other parts of Asia began to see the signs of victory, however long that victory might take to achieve. Events were reinforcing the lessons of history.

In Britain, despite a growing reaction against the aggressive imperialism of the late nineteenth century, Indian nationalism was not taken seriously; but by 1907, reforms in the administration were under active consideration. These took time, partly because of the organic delays of the British parlia-mentary process, but also because London had a well-founded tradition of never hurrying over matters affecting India. Meanwhile, terrorist activities continued, and the viceroy, Lord Minto, employed the weapon of depor-tation against political leaders. The so-called 'Morley-Minto Reforms' were embodied in the Indian Councils Act of 1909. This increased the right of criticism in the provincial and central legislatures which had been set up by the Act of 1892, and provided for indirect election to them. Morley (the secretary of state for India) had no intention of making the legislatures any more than purely advisory bodies. 'If I was attempting', he said in a speech in the House of Lords, 'to set up a parliamentary system in India, or if it could be said that this chapter of reforms led directly or necessarily to the establish-ment of a parliamentary system in India, I, for one, would have nothing at all to do with it.' As two historians of British India, writing in 1934, so ac-curately put it: 'The government had thus organised for itself a parliamentary opposition, with no function except to criticise, no chance of taking office, and no real responsibility to the rather vague electorate which they were sup-posed to represent.'[2]

The reforms, however, introduced a tragic element into the struggle for Indian freedom. The Muslims, who had begun to take a new interest in politics, had been driven away from Congress by the religious prejudices of the Hindu extremists and, in self-defence, formed the Muslim League in 1906. They also began to look outside India to the rest of the Islamic world. There they saw the West absorbing Muslim countries into its colonial sys-tems. The Muslims began for the first time to see themselves not so much as Indians, but as part of the greater world of Islam. Fear of the Hindu majority drove them to demand that the principle of communal representation – i.e.

[1] *San Min Chu I.* Shanghai, 1927
[2] Thompson and Garratt: *Rise and Fulfilment of British Rule in India.* London, 1934

the reservation of seats in the legislatures for racial and religious minorities – should be incorporated in the Act of 1909. The myth of the 'two Indias' was henceforth to be given official sanction, however indirect the sanction might be.

A further involvement in the world outside India can be seen in the position of Indians overseas. Large numbers of Indians had emigrated to various parts of the empire as indentured labour, and by 1901 there were over two and a half million Indians outside India. About half this number was in Ceylon and Malaya, and the remainder was divided between such countries as British Guiana, Mauritius, Fiji, Natal and East Africa. Because of caste restrictions, most of these emigrants were of the lowest social groups, and were employed as labourers. Their treatment was by no means of the best and it was not until 1917 that the indenture system (by which a manual worker contracted to serve for a fixed term of years, and was then entitled to choose between a free passage home or remaining in the colony as a free labourer) was finally abolished. In most cases, Indian labourers had taken the place of freed slaves, and their servile position was almost identical with that of their predecessors. In the African territories, free Indian labourers added yet another element to the racial mixture, and they were often discriminated against. In 1895, the Natal government placed a tax of £3 on those who refused to re-indenture or leave the country. In the Transvaal, the Boer government's treatment of Indians was one of the minor causes of the South African war. It was in South Africa, too, that M. K. Gandhi first organised passive resistance against authority, and from that country he returned to India to begin a new phase in the struggle for freedom, after the first world war had shaken the foundations of the Western empires.

*   *   *

Elsewhere in colonial Asia before 1914, nationalist movements were slow to emerge. In the Dutch East Indies, an increasing awareness of their cultural past led a small group of Javanese intellectuals to make demands for popular education. The Dutch had made little or no attempt to establish any form of educational system in their possessions. In 1900, a woman, Raden Adjeng Kartini, daughter of the regent of the state of Japara, became the vocal champion of education for women. Like Waidin Sudara Usada, a retired medical officer who in 1906 began to campaign for schools, she believed in the rejuvenating power of Western-style education. In 1906, Usada founded the first nationalist association, Budi Utomo ('High Endeavour'), with the establishment of schools as its aim. This was followed in 1911 by the foundation of the Sarekat Islam. This organisation was a byproduct of an Islamic revival amongst the Javanese and Sumatrans in response to a new wave of Christian proselytism. Originally, Sarekat Islam was an organisation of Javanese batik traders who were endeavouring to resist the stranglehold of Chinese merchants on the rural economy, and its aims were (1) promotion of Indonesian commercial undertakings, (2) mutual economic support for its members, (3) raising of the intellectual and material standards of Indonesians, and (4) protection of the Islamic religion. The first congress of the new movement was held in Surabaya in 1913, when its leader, Omar Said Tjohro Aminoto, declared that the organisation was not antiDutch and would pursue its aims in a constitutional manner. At its first nationwide congress in 1916, delegates representing a membership of 360,000 attended, and a resolution was passed demanding that Indonesia should be granted selfgovernment in association with the Netherlands. Indonesian nationalism, like other anticolonial reactions, was to receive a special impetus from the Russian Revolution of 1917, and it was really that year which saw the beginning of organised opposition to Dutch rule.

In France's possessions in IndoChina, the façade of native administration served to obscure the true sources of power and was used by the French as a convenient form of camouflage. In Annam, Cambodia and Laos, the kings and nobility existed alongside the French administration. The actual work was carried out by native officials under French supervision but without interference except under the most drastic circumstances. In Cochin China, a direct French colony, schools were established from 1879 onwards where the French language was taught in conjunction with the vernacular. These schools, however, were of a very low standard, being primarily concerned with the manufacture of interpreters. Similar schools were established in the French protectorates, but on a very limited scale. In 1906, public instruction was reorganised and the education system was based upon the village elementary school with the possibility that a good student could move on to schools where French was taught. Such Westernstyle education as there was helped to produce Vietnamese nationalism, though there already existed a strong antiFrench sentiment amongst the Vietnamese, whose defeat by the French had been both bloody and recent. At no time was the country free from unrest. Conspiracies were constantly being discovered, and suppressed with considerable ferocity. The Japanese victory over Russia in 1905 had its effect in IndoChina, too, and gave extra impetus to nationalist unrest. The

Vietnamese, even after their independence from China in 939, had remained culturally Chinese in character. The influence of such modern Chinese reformers as K'ang Yu-wei (see p. 145) turned them to the study of Rousseau and other French writers. When, in response to demands for higher education on Western lines, a university was opened at Hanoi, the Vietnamese intelligentsia rushed at the opportunity it offered. But student rioting in the following year led to the closing of the new university. After the end of the first World War, it was reopened. Only then did political parties begin to appear in Indo-China.

Part Two

THE GREAT AWAKENING 1914-1955

The 'European Civil War' and its Consequences

'THE GREAT WAR of 1914–18 was, from the Asian point of view, a civil war within the European community of nations.'[1] This simple conclusion is one of the clues to that outsurge of nationalist activity in Asia which, with the aid of another war, was to end in her freedom from colonial rule.

The war that broke out in 1914 was the result of conflict between two semi-feudal empires with common frontiers, Tsarist Russia and Austro-Hungary. Imperialist rivalries were not directly involved nor, initially, were the highly developed maritime empires. Though a few years before, conflict between France and Germany over possessions in North Africa had nearly developed into war, it appeared to many at the turn of the century that an accommodation between the new and the old imperial powers might well lead to amicable division of the world between the major capitalist powers of Europe, France, Great Britain and Germany. This fear of a 'super-imperialism' lies at the heart of J. A. Hobson's pioneer study, *Imperialism*, published in 1902. The significance of Hobson's work does not lie in its brilliant analysis of the 'new' imperialism of the fully-developed capitalist powers, but in the ignorance it shows both of the probability of inter-imperial rivalry and of the seeds of anti-imperialism which were already fructifying within the old colonial possessions. If discerning intellectuals like Hobson were so over-awed by the structure of imperialism as to believe not only in its permanency but in its expansion, it is easy to understand why politicians believed so too. It is easy to see, too, why nationalist leaders in colonial Asia demanded not complete independence but a position within the imperial world order. The war of 1914–18 was a great watershed of history, a shaker of standards and beliefs. Some writers have believed it to be the cause of the decline of the Western empires, but as we shall see in the following chapter, the explanation is not quite so simple.

The principal effect in Asia of the imperial powers' involvement in the conflict between Russia and Austro-Hungary was felt in China. The conflagration in Europe drew attention away from China and, without doubt,

[1] K. M. Panikkar: *Asia and Western Dominance*. London, 1953.

finally removed the possibility of its partition among the Western powers. The new Chinese republic, barely three years old, immediately realised how dangerous the consequences would be should European rivalries spread to the foreign enclaves on her territory. At the outbreak of war, the Chinese government asked the powers involved that conflict should be kept away from the settlements, and declared her neutrality. The good offices of the United States were requested and given, though without effect, as only Germany – with everything to gain from the preservation of the *status quo* – assented to the exercise of them.

Japan, however, saw in the powers' preoccupation in Europe a chance to expand her influence in China. On the outbreak of war in August 1914, Japan suggested to Germany that she should withdraw her naval vessels from Chinese waters and hand over to Japan the leased territory at Kiaochow; adding, with deadly irony, that she should do so 'with a view to eventual restoration of the same to China'. Germany did not respond to this heavily weighted advice and – using her treaty obligations under the Anglo-Japanese alliance as an excuse – Japan declared war. The Japanese then attacked Kiaochow which was legally Chinese territory, after warning the Chinese not to accept retrocession by Germany. In November 1914, with the moral approval of Great Britain and the assistance of a small British military contingent, the Japanese army captured Tsingtao, the port of Kiaochow.

Though in August 1914 the Japanese prime minister had hastened to declare that Japan had 'no desire to secure more territory in China', in January of the following year she made twenty-one demands upon the Chinese government, which, if they had been wholly accepted, would have reduced China to the status of a tributary of the Japanese Empire. An attempt was made by the Japanese to preserve secrecy as to the content of these demands, but it leaked out and resulted in a protest by the United States' government. The United States maintained that it could not 'recognise any agreement entered into between the governments of China and Japan impairing the treaty rights of the United States and its citizens in China, the political or territorial integrity of the republic of China, or the international policy relative to China known as the 'open door' policy'.

In China, President Yüan Shih-k'ai – unable to resist Japan by force or to hope for assistance from the Western powers – accepted most of the demands, keeping in mind the possibility of later calling upon the treaty powers for help against their implementation. The republicans of Canton, headed by

Sun Yat-sen, violently opposed acceptance. In 1916, using a clash between Chinese and Japanese troops on the Manchuria-Mongolia border as an excuse, Japan further extended her influence in northern China, and in 1917, in return for the sending of a naval force to assist the allies in their anti-submarine operations in the Mediterranean, Japan received secret assurances from Great Britain, France and Russia, that they would support Japan at the peace conference in her claims on former German possessions in China. It would seem from this that the partition of China into spheres of influence was to continue after the war, and that Japan's assistance was being cynically bought with pieces of China's territory.

In 1917, under pressure from the American minister in Peking, the Chinese government broke off diplomatic relations with Germany, and in August of that year followed the United States in declaring war on Germany. Internally, the authority of the central government, which had succeeded Yüan Shih-k'ai's administration, collapsed under the pressure of warring factions. An unsuccessful attempt was made to restore the imperial dynasty, and China found itself divided, with one clique established at Peking coming more and more under Japanese influence, and another, forward-looking and dynamic, at Canton. The Peking government received large loans from Japan on the usual security of the public services. This forced the European allies to reconsider their position in China, and ultimately led to the setting up of a financial consortium, of Great Britain, France, Japan and the United States, through which all loans to China were to be channelled. In 1917, an arrangement (the Lansing-Ishii agreement) was concluded between Japan and the United States, which, after a declaration of 'equal opportunity in the commerce and industry of China' for all countries, contained a statement by the United States recognising 'that Japan has special interests in China, particularly in that part to which her possessions are contiguous'.

At the Peace Conference at Versailles in 1919, a Chinese delegation representing both the Peking and Canton governments demanded the return to China of German possessions, and the abrogation of the Sino-Japanesse treaties of 1915 which embodied the twenty-one demands. The European allies, mindful of their secret agreements with Japan, awarded the Shantung concessions to that country. The result was that China refused to sign the Treaty of Versailles, making a separate treaty with Germany, in which the latter surrendered all her privileges in China. Treaties were also signed with the new nations that had emerged in Europe after the peace settlement. Un-

like former treaties between China and the European nations, these contained no provision for extra-territorial rights. The first breach, albeit a not
very productive one, had been made in the wall of the 'unequal treaties'.

For Japan, the European civil war had brought nothing but gain. Her
industry, and shipbuilding in particular, had expanded to meet the ever-
growing demands of the allies. Financially, her gold reserves made her a
creditor nation in a world of falling currencies. She also acquired, legally, as
a mandate from the newly-established League of Nations, all the former
German-owned islands in the Pacific north of the equator. Economically,
their value was small, but strategically they were to be of paramount importance in the war against the United States, Britain and Holland in the early
1940's. Over the larger issues, however, Japan was frustrated by the fears of
the European allies and the United States. At the Washington Conference of
1921–2, she was persuaded into returning to China, as she had promised, the
former German possessions at Kiaochow – a promise which she had had no
intention of fulfilling. Japan's attempts to take advantage of the collapse of
Russia by acquiring territory in Siberia were also frustrated. Though Japan
tried to profit from the confused situation in the Far East after the Russian
Revolution, and landed some 70,000 men at Vladivostok – ostensibly as
part of an allied force, though actually outnumbering the other contingents –
diplomatic pressure by the United States, and the establishment of order in
Siberia by the Bolsheviks, forced her to withdraw finally in 1922.

At Versailles, the Japanese sought a resolution recognising the principle
of racial equality. Though accepted as allies, Japanese nationals were still
discriminated against. President Wilson of the United States helped to draft
the resolution, which was to be incorporated in the covenant of the new
League of Nations, but was himself subjected to isolationist pressures from
home. A compromise amendment, endorsing 'the principle of the equality
of nations and just treatment of their nationals', was passed by a small majority. Wilson, as chairman, ruled that as the vote was not unanimous the
amendment could not be accepted. Japan, frustrated in what to her were the
just spoils of war, was now humiliated by the white nations. This added a
fine propaganda note to future Japanese action, for she could pose as the
champion of the non-white peoples against the continuing arrogance of the
West.

*   *   *

A long period of external peace had kept India, the principal colonial possession of the greatest Western empire, virtually outside the web of European politics. The outbreak of war in 1914 produced what seems to us today an incomprehensible outbreak of loyal enthusiasm. Some modern Indian writers, misunderstanding the nature of their own nationalist movement at this time, attempt to pass this genuine expression of loyalty off as a reaction only of those princes, soldiers and officials whose sole interest lay in the support of an alien government. But in fact, moderate national opinion, expecting a British victory within a few months, assumed that India's help in assuring that victory would result in immediate rewards. Furthermore, no national leaders, apart from the extremists, believed that India could establish an independent national government. The limit of their aim was ultimate self-government within the British Empire, on the precedent of the old dominions of Canada and Australia. Consequently, over most of India a truce from politics followed the declaration of war. Recruiting for the army produced over 800,000 combatants and 400,000 non-combatant men. Large contributions to the Red Cross and support for war loans poured in. The security of the country was such that the British garrison was reduced to 15,000 men, and many of the administrators handed over their jobs to Indians. In this way, two of the nationalists' demands – reduction in the 'army of occupation', and more of the higher posts for Indians – were almost unintentionally granted.

As the war dragged on, popular enthusiasm decreased. The government, unused to mass support, was unable to channel it into productive endeavour. By 1916, recruiting under pressure had begun, and the middle classes found themselves virtually forced to contribute to war loans. Prices began to rise, and the collapse of the Indian Army's commissariat and medical departments in Mesopotamia spread uneasy rumours of administrative inefficiency and indifference. The war against the sultan of Turkey – still the Caliph of Islam – was naturally unpopular with Muslims. Indians rightly became weary of a war that not only persisted interminably on faraway battle-fields but meant greater pressures upon themselves without any corresponding responsibility for its conduct. Rebellion in Ireland encouraged the extremists in their belief in violence as a solution for India's problems. Moderate opinion, which had suffered a loss in the death of Gokhale in 1915, no longer seemed in touch with an ever-changing reality. The commercial classes, which had formerly been luke-warm backers of the moderates, chafed under wartime restrictions and began to involve themselves more and more in the nationalist movement, with funds and support.

Tilak, who had been released from jail in 1914, emerged two years later once again the leader of revolt. Cooperating with Mrs Besant's Home Rule League, he persuaded the Muslim League to support him in the famous Lucknow Pact with Congress, and in 1916 captured Congress from the nerveless hand of the moderates. Tilak's views had grown less provincial, and his religious prejudices had been sufficiently modified to make him ac-ceptable to the Muslim leaders. The moderates were never again to have in-fluence in Congress. Their leaders, lacking an army behind them, became elder statesmen and mediators in the no man's land between the government and the nationalists.

Congress now demanded *immediate* home rule. The government began to think in the old moderate terms of *ultimate* self-government. In the British House of Commons on 20 August 1917, the new secretary of state for India, E. S. Montagu, made a declaration that the object of British policy was to be 'not only the increasing association of Indians in every branch of the ad-ministration but also the granting of self-governing institutions with the view to a progressive realisation of responsible government in India as an integral part of the British Empire'. At the same time, an announcement was made that Indians could be appointed to full commissions in the Indian Army. The secretary of state left for India in October of the same year for discus-sions with the viceroy; and these later became the basis of the Montagu-Chelmsford report, details of which must be left to a later chapter (see p. 241 ff). The publication of the report was received with hostility in India and indifference in Britain. That its publication coincided with a new and dan-gerous German offensive on the Western front may explain part of the latter, but not all. The general principles laid down in the report were accepted by the British government and were embodied in the Government of India Act of December 1919.

Unfortunately, the period between Montagu's visit and the passing of the Act had witnessed events in India which have a parallel only in the after-effects of the Mutiny of 1857. The government of India had begun to feel it-self menaced by revolutionary activity, though in fact this illusion was only the product of efficient nationalist propaganda. Nevertheless, the government felt itself handicapped by the existing security regulations, and set up a com-mittee under Mr Justice Rowlatt to enquire into what it called 'criminal conspiracies', i.e. terrorist activities. The Rowlatt report was published shortly after the appearance of the Montagu-Chelmsford report, and, together, they made rather odd reading. On the one hand, the British at Westminster were envisaging some delegation of powers, while on the other, the British in Delhi were reinforcing themselves with the apparatus of the police state – the trial of political cases without jury, and the weapon of summary internment. Naturally, Indians saw this as giving with one hand and slapping them down with the other.

The end of the war brought back the old administrators – sullen with the frustration of slow promotion after the excitement of the war, and determined to treat that war as an interlude in the happy superiority of British life in India. To Indians, no longer convinced of their inferior position, it seemed that the worst features of the British occupation came back with the old administrators, and that the Sedition Acts which followed the Rowlatt report indicated a new period of repression. To the apprehensions of the educated classes was added a new dimension of unrest, this time amongst those classes previously unaffected by the nationalist struggle. Two English historians writing in 1934 saw clearly, when others still did not, one of the sources of the involvement of the masses in the struggle for freedom.

'A number of factors, more or less connected with the war, carried nationalist sentiment into classes which had been previously almost immune from political influence. The influenza epidemic, which affected so many parts of the world in 1918, swept across India, attacking about a third of the population, and resulting in some twelve or thirteen million deaths. It caused more havoc in a few months than bubonic plague during the previous twenty years. The disease ran its course unchecked, leaving a feeling of depression and uncertainty which was intensified by the poor harvest of 1918, and the rapid rise in price of the villagers' small requirements. A partial break-down of the railway system added to the difficulties of the villagers and to the opportunities for rapacity on the part of dealers and middle-men. Soldiers and men from labour corps returned with grievances of their own due to the hasty demobilisation and unfulfilled promises. They formed a critical and discordant element in the villages. Factories were making enormous profits, but owners, British as well as Indian, kept wages low, and did not attempt to use the surplus wealth to effect permanent improvements in housing and settling the mill population.'[1]

The feeling of unease produced a semblance of a united front against the government. Among the peasants, no real sense of the national struggle, as such,

[1] Thompson and Garratt *op.cit.*

ever appeared. To this day, they form an inert mass, shifted sometimes into activity by those capable of giving direction to inchoate feelings of oppression. Such a man was Mohandas Karamchand Gandhi, who had returned to India from South Africa in 1915. As late as July 1918, he was still a moderate, believing freedom to be the achievement of equal partnership within the empire. He even took part in recruiting campaigns for the Indian Army, but the end of the war and the return of old, familiar faces to the administration convinced him that India had been tricked into giving her support to Britain's war by specious and empty promises. Furthermore, like many other Indians, he thought that President Wilson really believed in self-determination for all, and that the only great non-imperial power in the world would look with sympathy upon India's aspirations. Unfortunately, the allies never intended self-determination to refer to anyone outside Europe, where the splitting-up of Austro-Hungary demanded some high-flown justification.

Under Gandhi's leadership, Congress now began a campaign against the so-called Rowlatt Acts. Their straightforward provisions were distorted by extensive propaganda throughout the countryside into the most ogre-ish of interferences in the life of the people. The rumour was spread that the Acts required inspection of a man and woman before marriage, and restricted the number of plough-bullocks a peasant could own to two. Once again, Tilak's belief that any lie was justified if it helped the national struggle was to become a political weapon. Gandhi added to the movement two unique elements, both essentially part of the Hindu tradition. These were the conceptions of *satyagraha*, the vow to hold to the truth, and *ahimsa*, the doing of no harm. From these he produced the idea of passive resistance and its instrument, the *hartal*, a day of fast and suspension of business which was the equivalent of a strike in an industrial society and, at the same time, a traditional Hindu method of protest. The use of these ancient weapons for modern ends was the prime contribution of Gandhi to the technique of revolution.

In March and April 1919, the pressures of unemployment, high prices, the return of soldiers to the insecurity of their former lives, and the renewed arrogance of returning officials, precipitated outbursts of popular indignation, very few of which were the products of extremist organisation. Rioting was almost entirely confined to the Punjab and western India, and the mobs who attacked isolated Europeans and government buildings did not appear to have either leaders or specific objectives. Most of the rioting in Delhi, Lahore,

Amritsar, and elsewhere, was characterised by racial hatred. Gandhi was arrested on his way to the Punjab in April, an act which provoked a riot in the mill town of Ahmadabad, where he was well known and loved. He was released and helped to restore order.

On 15 April, martial law was declared in the Punjab, in consequence of an act which became one of the great rallying cries of Indian nationalism. Amritsar, a city of some 300,000 inhabitants, and the chief religious centre of the Sikhs, stands about 250 miles north-west of Delhi. There, on 10 April, two nationalist leaders were arrested and deported. A large crowd attempted to enter the European cantonment and, on being turned back, began rioting in the city. Two banks were attacked, the railway station set on fire, four Europeans were murdered and others attacked, including a woman missionary who was left for dead. The military, under General Dyer, restored order and all public meetings and assemblies were declared illegal. On 13 April, a meeting gathered in a large enclosed space known as the Jallianwalla Bagh. On hearing of this, General Dyer went personally to the spot with ninety Gurkha and Baluchi soldiers and two armoured cars, with which he blocked the only exit. Then, without warning, he ordered his men to open fire on the densely packed crowd and, on his own admission, fired 1605 rounds before he withdrew, leaving the armoured cars to prevent anyone from leaving or entering the Bagh. Official figures of dead and wounded were given as 379 and 1200 respectively. Dyer's action was approved by the provincial government. The following day, a mob rioting and burning at another spot was bombed and machine-gunned from aircraft. On 15 April, martial law was declared and not lifted until 9 June. During this period, Indians were forced to walk on all fours past the spot where the woman missionary had been attacked and, according to the report of the Hunter Commission, which enquired into the disturbances, public floggings were given for such minor offences as 'the contravention of the curfew order, failure to salaam to a commissioned officer, for disrespect to a European, for taking a commandeered car without leave, or refusal to sell milk, and for similar contraventions'.

The commission of enquiry from whose report the quotation is taken was set up in October 1919 with four British and four Indian members. Three of the British were members of the civil service, the Indians men of moderate opinions. All severely criticised the actions of General Dyer. But the Indian belief that the old repressive ways were again to be imposed was reinforced by the testimony of General Dyer, who made it clear in his evidence that he

had gone down to the Jallianwalla Bagh with the intention of making a fe-
rocious example for the rest of India.

> 'I fired and continued to fire until the crowd dispersed, and I consider
> this is the least amount of firing which would produce the necessary
> moral and widespread effect it was my duty to produce if I was to justify
> my action. If more troops had been at hand the casualties would have
> been greater in proportion. It was no longer a question of merely dis-
> persing the crowd, but one of producing a sufficient moral effect from a
> military point of view not only on those who were present, but more es-
> pecially throughout the Punjab.'

Though the government of India vehemently dissociated itself from any such
policy of intimidation, Dyer was expressing the general opinion of most of the
civil and military in India. Dyer was removed from his command, but his
actions, and presumably his motives, were supported by a large section of the
British press, by members of parliament, and others, and a sum of £26,000
was subscribed as a testimonial for this fine example of a gallant British soldier. It is not too difficult to understand the very special position that the
massacre of Amritsar holds in the minds of Indians. In British-Indian relations it was a turning point, more decisive even than that of the Mutiny.
Henceforth, the struggle would permit of little compromise, and the good
faith of British concessions would always be in doubt. It is in the light of this
that we must see Indian reaction to the Montagu-Chelmsford reforms and
the others that followed. Elsewhere, the whole of Asia could see that the
hopes Indians had placed in the coming of a new era had been crushed by
the most progressive of the colonial powers. What hope then could there be
for those ruled by the Dutch and the French?

In 1917, a new political structure had appeared in the world as a result of
the Bolshevik revolution in Russia. In that same year, Lenin, one of the
architects of the new system, published a small book which he called
Imperialism. From it, and from the success of Soviet Russia was to be derived
a new factor in the emerging Asian nationalism – one which was a direct
consequence of the war from which the old imperial powers seemed to have
won greater strength and sureness of purpose. The next chapter will show
whether that purpose was as sure as it seemed.

2

Europe in Retreat

I

THE EXHAUSTED PURPOSE

FUNDAMENTALLY, EMPIRES EXIST only in terms of power. Power to acquire them, and power to protect them. No one, at the close of the first World War, could have seen any real diminution in the apparent power of the Western empires. The defeat of a dynamic, industrial Germany only appeared to add to their strength as it added to the size of their territories. Britain particularly, now dominated the main parts of the old Ottoman Empire in the Near East. But, in fact, the redistribution of possessions stretched power rather than reinforced it. The new Arabian dependencies brought neither economic nor industrial advantage except, of course, in the control of oil-fields. The source of power in the post-war world was not so much the extent of British territory and the ubiquitousness of the Royal Navy as the industrial and financial strength behind them. Britain had emerged from the war weakened by its cost. In real strength, she had given way to the United States of America.

The United States, at the beginning of the century, having reached the limits of landward expansion, seemed about to begin her own imperialist period under the guidance of Theodore Roosevelt. But, as John Strachey has pointed out in a recent book,[1] Roosevelt's imperialism was amateur and imitative, and mainly indulged in 'in order to be "in the swim" of the great world-wide imperialist drive rather than... to make or to safeguard massive foreign investments'. The 'investment imperialism' of the late nineteenth century originated in the existence of surplus capital and nowhere at home to invest it profitably. But the United States was predominantly 'new' – great areas called out for *safe* investment, free from the risks and dubious involvements of Asia and Africa. A switch in American politics to primarily domestic issues with the election of Woodrow Wilson to the presidency in 1912, and the impact of the first World War, turned America isolationist.

[1] John Strachey, *The End of Empire*. London, 1959.

This meant a withdrawal not only from world politics but also from colonial adventure.

Because of this, the Western imperial powers still seemed to hold the colonial world in fee. Germany had been defeated, America offered no challenge and Japan had gained no territory of any importance. The imperial powers had fought a major war – and won. The world in which they emerged victorious was, however, very different from that of 1914. New strains and pressures had appeared. Though the Western empires still existed in terms of sovereignty, the old purpose seemed thin and unconvincing.

The French and Dutch, as we have seen, were little worried by the pressures of conscience, by the need to reinforce the actuality of colonial power with intellectual justification. The British, on the other hand, were preoccupied with a sense of mission and with crusading purposes which demanded rationalisation. Untroubled by intellectual considerations, the French and Dutch fought to the bitter end to retain their imperial possessions. Britain, finding her old purpose exhausted, abdicated while assuring herself that this was only the natural consequence of her imperial mission. The road Britain took to this position is one of the most fascinating in the history of man's domination of other men, and some knowledge of the milestones along it is essential to an understanding of the decline of the West in Asia and of the events to be described in the next chapter.

In India, with the collapse of the anglicisation movement that was the aftermath of the Mutiny of 1857, Macaulay's belief that English education would produce a race of mediators between the British and the Indians, had, instead, merely resulted in the provision of a corps of semi-literate clerks. Mediators, in one sense, these men certainly were, but only in the same way as a printed form is a mediator between citizen and government. As such, they were invaluable, for it left the more lucrative appointments for members of the ruling race. Macaulay's prophetic vision of a self-governing India created by a partnership between an anglicised Indian middle class and British business men and administrators had no place in post-Mutiny India. Administration was a sacred duty and responsibility to be exercised without sentiment or pandering. Mediation was unnecessary; in fact the new Indian middle class with its demands and questionings was a nuisance, and a hindrance to efficient government. The British administration sought neither the love nor respect of its subjects. They were to have good government, if necessary even over their dead bodies. The rulers knew they would only be despised and hated, but no matter, secure in their sense of duty, swerving neither to left nor right, they would carry on in their thankless task, which apparently had been forced upon them by some inexplicable Providence. British government in India felt itself to be a trustee for the mass of the Indian people; as Curzon, the last great representative of this tradition, put it, 'for the Indian poor, the Indian peasant, the patient, humble, silent millions'. Such was its duty, and no sentiment would be allowed to interfere with it.

The administration's attitude was reinforced by the general ignorance of India and its government that reigned in England. There was no question of an informed public opinion. Criticism, such as there was, came from ill-informed journalists and radical politicians, most of whom had never been in India. Indian administrators described their work as a 'noble cause', best left to experts whose efficiency would increase if they were left alone. These 'experts', soldiers and administrators, formed an exclusive club. Most had the same family background and the same education – passing, usually without distinction, through public school, and scraping a pass degree at Oxford or Cambridge. Their sole qualification lay in that background and the sound sense of superiority it gave them. Armed with a fundamental belief in their right to rule, and supported by their sense of duty, the civil servants of the empire were hardly men to make radical decisions or to believe in the possibility of abdicating their responsibility. Incorruptible, they had a vested interest in the expansion of empire, and saw it not in terms of material profit but in an extension of 'law and order' This attitude in the civil service of the empire lasted until shattered by the second World War. But by then, it had already been undermined.

In the last three decades of the nineteenth century, India had become the centre of an imperial system. British attitudes towards Russia were conditioned by that country's menace on the northern frontiers of India. Egypt and the Suez canal were outposts of Indian defence. The real foreign policy of Britain was inextricably shackled to the over-riding claims of the security of the Indian Empire. There was, in fact, nothing very new in this. But new factors had entered the equation. In the scramble for Africa, other European nations intent on empire now threatened the world power of the British. In making a deal with the French over Egypt, the British found themselves involved in strictly European rivalries, and they were forced to take sides against the rising power of Germany. For the first time in the history of their empire, the British were finding it necessary to acquire friends and had to pay for their friendship with alliances. Almost overnight, they found that the frontiers of India were upon the Rhine.

Britain's power was weakened when other nations began to play the imperial game in earnest. That great surge of industrial optimism and strength,
which had made Britain not only the workshop of the world but the most
powerful nation in it, had long since receded under the stress of competition.
The new German Empire, with modern factories and younger enthusiasms,
seemed to have taken over economic leadership. The frequency of economic
crises before 1870 had begun to shake Britain's class structure and, in particular, brought into politics the middle classes, who felt themselves threatened
on one side by a growingly demonstrative proletariat, and on the other by an
aristocratic oligarchy. The imperialism of the middle classes was of a new
and vicious character. They sought not so much territorial aggrandisement as
such, but outlets for the investment of surplus capital, and they looked for
them outside the existing imperial structure. Both China and South Africa
were to suffer the consequences of this first stage in the political rule of the
bourgeoisie. The new financiers and industrialists were quick to elevate their
desire for profit into an act of patriotism. The greatness of Britain, they
maintained, depended upon the protection that her army and navy afforded
to its nationals. The British government, which was still made up of those
who believed the British Empire had a moral purpose, was at first unwilling
to indulge in adventures in support of dubious financiers and diamond
magnates. But it was forced to do so by the activities of these very people. The
history of colonial Africa is, to a large extent, the story of blackmail. The
crudities of the South African magnates were, however, supported by emotion. The unthinking masses endorsed the belligerence of Britain, and every
music-hall had its patter of jingoistic songs.[1] Liberal critics of imperial expansion alleged that this emotional approach was deliberately fostered by
imperialist politicians and publicists – and they were right. But it was not
only the masses who were anxious to support the new imperialism.

The recurring financial crises of the late nineteenth century had helped to
weaken the small investor. The educated middle classes, threatened by
slumps, saw in the acquisition of new territory the opportunity to play a role
in administration from which they were excluded in India by the operation

---

[1] The word 'jingo' and from it 'jingoism' is derived from the words of a music-hall song supporting Disraeli's anti-Russian policy in 1878:

> We don't want to fight,
> But, by jingo, if we do,
> We've got the ships,
> We've got the men,
> We've got the money, too.

of the 'club' principle. A greater Britain meant a place for them in the sun
and a way out from between the millstones of the privileged classes and the
newly articulate workers. Many middle-class intellectuals plunged into imperialist adventures not only in person, but in literature. The poets and
novelists of empire, who proliferated in the late nineteenth century emerged
mainly from a middle-class milieu. These men built up a more stately imperial myth than the aggressive 'send a gunboat and shoot the bloody natives'
sentiment of the music-hall lyric writer. Most sought to erect new heroisms.
Their heroes displayed similar sentiments to those of the rulers of India.
Their ears were sensitively tuned to the silver calls of duty from far-flung
frontiers and coral strands. But where the music-hall view was real – the imperial adventure *did* consist of gunboats and shooting natives – the middle-
class novelists and poets were indulging in private daydreams, and in the
business of mythmaking. The music-hall imperialists had little thought for
justifications, the novelists and the poets were enmeshed in them. Their empire was a clean and wholesome thing. Blood there was, no doubt, but the
spilling of it had a sacrificial quality. The death of a British hero was a
martyrdom by which the empire, and its countless subjects, were saved.
Much of this embarrassed the active administrator. 'Anglo-Indians' thought
Kipling's imperial incantations not only odd but vulgar. Many of the
novelists and poets of empire believed in their own myths, and because of
this were often startlingly truthful. Kipling, for example, exposed far more
than the nature of the imperial sacrifice. He also condemned the essential
frivolity and emptiness of 'Anglo-Indian' life. To Kipling, imperialism was
a discipline and the mission of the British in India could only be betrayed
by the indolence and superficiality of those who could not hear the call of
duty for the explosions of champagne corks. The old sense of mission, a very
real and almost altruistic thing, was replaced by a cult of duty and a religion
of responsibility.[1]

In this unreal and theatrical atmosphere, Liberal critics of imperialism had
very little chance of being listened to. Out of office, Liberals could question
the whole basis of the imperial idea, and reiterate the old radical slogans
that no people had a right to govern other people against their will, and that

---

[1] The role of the poet and novelist in the development of the imperial theme has not received the
attention it deserves. I hope to examine it in detail in a later work. For three preliminary studies in
this field, see my 'Rudyard Kipling and the Imperial Imagination', *Twentieth Century*, June
1953; 'The Articulate Hero: Philip Meadows Taylor', *ibid.*, September 1953; and 'True to the
Old Flag' (A study of the works of G. A. Henty), *ibid.*, May 1954.

good government was no substitute for self-government. At the same time no Liberal ever envisaged giving up the empire. His main attack was on its expansion and on the belief that British rule was eternal. He saw 'duty' as a sterile thing, an instrument of preservation rather than of mission. The British as policemen, giving the right time and maintaining public order seemed to him the diminution of a great purpose. In office, however, Liberals found themselves just as much the victims of empire as their unwilling subjects. Dominion over palm and pine had a distressing habit of dictating action rather than responding to it. As we have seen, India to a large extent dominated British foreign policy whatever party was in office. Frontiers had a tendency to move forward – in the interests of defence.

The imperialists and their middle-class and mob allies had a much stronger sense of reality towards these truths than had their radical critics. As for the masses, it is easy to see why they quickly responded to the emotions of empire. The Industrial Revolution had brought blacker vistas to the working classes. Industrial slums had spread across the countryside and, in the continuing economic crises of the late nineteenth century, unemployment increased and poverty took on a new and grinding form. Imperialist adventures diverted attention to new enemies outside the class structure. In the glow of Britain's strength overseas, all could bask – free of charge. The shouts of the mob were a safety valve and Britain's politicians were not above the demagogic practice of uniting the nation at home by adventures abroad.

The same explanation to some extent fits the reaction of the middle classes. For industrialists, a greater Britain meant a new era of prosperity, just as the home markets were becoming saturated. For those of the middle class who had suffered in the financial crises, a new empire meant a new sense of dignity, a new chance to assert themselves. But, more significantly, their support for an aggressive imperialism – behind whatever mask they were prepared to conceal it – also meant an attempt to change the sources of power in Britain itself. Late nineteenth century imperialism was not the last stage of capitalism, as Lenin and other Marxist critics insist, but the first stage in the political assertion of the middle classes.

Asia, and in particular India, that brightest jewel in the British crown, played very little part in the visions of the new imperialism. India existed and was ruled by Britain. That was a fact. Its government was frequently under attack by radical reformers. But the middle classes were not only looking for the opportunity to rule; they did not wish to govern for a fixed period of exile in an uncomfortable climate, threatened by cholera and plague. Many looked for a new and permanent life away from the spreading weed of England's dark, satanic mills and mine-shafts. South Africa offered them a *home*, just as at an earlier period starving emigrants and convicts had found a new life in Canada or Australia. In the temperate areas of Africa, English settlers were attempting to build an outlying suburb of their homeland, and in doing so they demanded the protection and support of their kin. Their imperialism was a parasite upon patriotism.

It is at this time that the British Empire so obviously divides into two separate and almost conflicting parts. The British Indian Empire, stretching from Egypt to Hong Kong and into the treaty ports of China, and the empire of British colonies inhabited by emigré Britons in Canada, Australia, New Zealand, and southern Africa. It was to be the problems of the latter part which were to shake the imperial purpose to its foundations.

The Asian possessions of Great Britain, it will be remembered, had been acquired by fighting ill-equipped and badly-led native armies. Even the wars with the French in India had been a fight between 'country' powers using native troops. At sea, the British Navy had triumphed. Without her ships, the British Empire in the East could never have existed. After the Crimean War, Britain had not been involved in any military campaign against a European power. Her success in Europe and the world was based upon diplomacy reinforced by the threat of power. The apparent strength of Britain's Asian empire, and her command of the sea, were all that was necessary to back whatever hand she chose to deal. It was upon this assumption that the new imperialism was founded. But was Britain as strong as she looked? The Indian Army, no doubt, was a formidable instrument – against Afghans. Its leaders were, no doubt, fine military strategists and tacticians – against Afghans. Defeats, of course, there had been, but most were later expunged by final victory – the source, no doubt, of the adage that Britain always won the *last* battle. But what if the newly emerging power of Germany was to challenge the British? Nobody really questioned Britain's strength, though Bismarck presumably did when, in answering a question in the German parliament in 1864 as to what he would do if the British Army landed in Germany, he replied 'Send for the police'. In the changed circumstances of the last two decades of the nineteenth century, Britain's world-wide and splendidly superior isolation *was* being challenged, not yet by large-scale war but by the emergence of new imperialisms. How was Britain to combat the challenge?

The answer was simple – a revival of purpose. The old crusade whose symbol was Macaulay was not good enough for it contained within it the essential belief that self-government would inevitably come, not only as a right of maturity, but as a natural consequence of Britain's mission. Macaulay's vision, said the new imperialists, was a daydream born in widely differing conditions. Britain, under challenge, could no longer think of dividing up the British Empire but only of extending its beneficent rule and centralising the sources of power. The new imperialists were taking to their bosoms the precepts of the Services which governed India. No longer were natives to be made over into simulacra of Victorian Englishmen. Responsibility, duty, peace and reform from above – the old methods that, so it seemed, worked so well in India were to be the watchwords in Egypt and in tropical Africa. It was necessary that the British Empire be drawn together in order to withstand the challenge of the new powers of continental Europe. Britain could only achieve new strength by extending her real control, sweeping away obstacles, and doing good with an undivided purpose. At last, the code of the Services would become the rallying cry of the new empire. This 'phrasemongering', as J. A. Hobson called it, once again masked the true purpose which was an attempt to regain Britain's world mastery.

This was all very well for the coloured countries of the empire. It would work in southern Africa, too, but what of the white colonies? What was their place in the imperial system? The imperialists maintained that these colonies were nothing more than outliers of Britain – a Greater Britain inhabited by Britons – Birminghams and Glasgows, Costwolds and Glencoes, joined by sea-lanes patrolled by the British Navy. Surely they were the basis of a strong, unified empire controlled from London. A 'cooperative Commonwealth', fundamentally loyal to British ideas, would willingly accept centralised control in the interests of security and strength. Here, the imperialists stumbled over the problem of Britain herself. The British constitution and party system were a menace to positive direction and policy. Milner, perhaps the greatest of all imperial theorists, wanted to convert the empire into a single state, with an imperial parliament. 'When we, who call ourselves imperialists,' he said in a speech at Johannesburg in 1905, 'talk of the British Empire, we think of a group of states, independent of one another in their local affairs, but bound together for the defence of their common interests and the development of a common civilisation, and so banded not in alliance – for alliances can be made and unmade, and are never more than normally lasting – but in a permanent organic union.' These sentiments had a great and lasting appeal. The Commonwealth today is an indirect ex, pression of them.

Milner's ideas at last gave precision to the myths of the novelists and poets. For Liberals, they seemed to proclaim a moral purpose once again. But the obstacles to achievement were numerous and weighty. The most important was that of the British parliamentary tradition. It was completely impractic, able to change the forms of a democracy even in the interests of such higher things as empire. The military power of the British, the power necessary to sustain the empire and, if necessary, to expand it, had received a severe shak, ing in the campaigns of the Boer War. In the South African war (1899– 1902), the British army had learned the bitterness of defeat. The much, vaunted imperial power had needed over 400,000 British troops at a cost of 250 million pounds sterling, to conquer a nation whose total population numbered around 150,000. Furthermore, Britain's 'civilising mission' had been sadly tarnished by the setting up of concentration camps for Boer wo, men and children, in which the death rate of the latter for October 1901 was 344 per thousand. Concentration camps, burned farms, and scorched earth were hardly to be reconciled with the bright vision of peace and moral pur, pose. From the Boer War onwards, the slogans of imperialism had a certain shabby and unconvincing air. Public opinion no longer felt emotional about the empire, but only uncomfortably ashamed. The atrocities of the Boer War had been committed not against natives but against white women and chil, dren. The working classes, too, now had some representation in parliament and were becoming organised in the drive for better working conditions and higher rewards at home. It even seemed possible that the hopeless misery that had driven men abroad or sent them hysterically into the streets to hail the glamour of an empire on which the sun never set, might be alleviated by political action at Westminster. Because of this heartening thought, the working classes became more interested in their own material welfare than in the glory of the British Empire.

In the wider field of foreign affairs, her treatment of the Boers made Britain the best,hated nation in Europe. Britain, who had always pretended to be the protector of small nations, now turned out to be a hypocritical bully. Europe did not care very much about massacring a few natives, for this was one of the unpleasant necessities of empire, but the Boer republics were small nations of Europeans. A bad precedent had been established, and no longer could Britain exercise moral authority on the side of right and justice when her own skirts were muddy. One of the sources of Britain's world power had lain in just that moral superiority. No more could she stand in an isolation of purity. Because of this, Britain was compelled to seek alliances, to bargain rather than impose, for not only had she lost prestige but her military weak-ness had been exposed for all to see.

These deals, with France in 1904, with Japan in 1905, and with Russia in 1907, were insurance policies, and the premiums were paid for out of long-standing imperial plans. Britain, and consequently the British Empire, was forced to fit into the old and once despised pattern of strictly European pol-itics. It seemed the work of frightened men, rather than of titans who ruled the greatest empire the world had ever known.

The outbreak of the first World War revived the imperial spirit, with its rallying cry of 'the Empire in danger'. Though Britain went reluctantly to war for little Belgium, the white dominions sent a million volunteers to fight in Europe because Britain's wars were the empire's wars, and because Canada, Australia, New Zealand and South Africa, realised that their frontiers, too, were upon the Rhine, and that should Britain fall they had no defence against the imposition of a new imperium. The necessity for a global direction to the war rehabilitated those imperialists whose dreams had been rejected by the public. Milner and Curzon, after the days in the wilderness, entered the government to save the democracy they so despised. The natural activity of imperialism was war, and its experts, military men and proconsuls naturally took over the direction of an empire at war. For the first time, a major crisis in the affairs of Britain permitted all the demands of the imperial-ists to be satisfied. No longer hampered by political questionings or the aberrations of a popular assembly, the empire had become a unity almost overnight – federated in an alliance of defence.

The defeat of imperial Germany, the considerable acquisition of terri-tory by Britain, as well as the re-establishment of her prestige, seemed to herald a new period of imperialist consolidation. But arrangements forged in the heat of war often contract in the cool of peace. For the white dominions, the fact that their frontiers were still in Europe and their first line of defence Britain herself, was unchanged in victory. But these frontiers were no longer threatened and the dominions wished to turn their energies to their own domestic problems. The soldiers of the dominions had fought not as mem-bers of the British Army, but as *national* contingents. From this a new sense of nationhood, of national pride in being, say, an Australian or a Canadian, was emerging. With it came a questioning of the right of Britain to involve the white dominions in war without consulting them. There was no question that they all were willing to fight, but they had not been asked their opinion. Their attitude to the empire was becoming empirical rather than emotional, and because of this the possibility of a unified empire was destroyed for ever. Moral purposes and concepts of duty take second place to the demands of security, and there is little romance left in defence. The fact that the white dominions needed defending at all only underlined the change in the balance of power resulting from the first World War. Australia's front line in Asia was now to be off her own coastline, and the establishment of a new naval base at Singapore merely confirmed this unpleasant fact. At the same time, it also demonstrated the essential conservatism of imperial thinking. No one, except two forward-looking members of the British parliament, thought of the possibility that the Eastern possessions could be attacked by land. The Royal Navy had made the empire and it would still remain its first and best line of defence. On the other hand, the growth of American naval power in the Pacific virtually removed Canada from the protection of the British Navy, and because of this Canada was unwilling to contribute to the upkeep of a force which she no longer needed to defend her. It was as if Canada was cutting one of the ties of empire, that of joint responsibility for its first line of defence. That Canada did so was another stage in the quest of the white dominions for individual status. The attempts of imperialists to consider the empire as an indivisible unit were continually frustrated by the unwillingness of the dominions to contribute to Britain's unilateral involvements. Nevertheless, though Britain's political power over the dominions was steadily reduced and their equality and independence given legal form by the Statute of Westminster of 1931, she still retained strategic control. Though it seemed that the dominions looked more to the League of Nations as the organ of their foreign policy, British influence was still overwhelmingly important. The man who guards the doors always has privileges. Anyway, the imperial system still stood in apparently unshaken splendour. A vast dependent empire and spheres of influence still stretched from Gibraltar to the Pacific. The old imperial ideas had faded away, the old emotions were quietly deflated, yet the image of the 'British Empire' still meant something at home and abroad. But the image, however impressive and dominating, was more like a monument than an active, living thing. The empire was no longer a dynamic, crusading force. It lived off accumulated capital rather than upon investment, but it certainly kept up appearances.

Soon external threats were to appear in the form of the old-fashioned but modernly equipped imperialisms of Nazi Germany and Japan. Their challenge was a challenge of power, and Japan had unwitting allies inside the Western empires themselves. One of these was a growing sense of nationalism grossly under-rated by the imperial powers, in the colonial possessions themselves (see p. 195 ff.) Another was the emergence of a major non-capitalist and apparently anti-colonialist power in the form of the USSR (see p. 266 ff). But above all, changes in the class structure in Britain herself, and the changed attitude towards the duties and responsibilities of empire which resulted from them, produced a pessimism which left Britain – and to some extent, the other Western imperial powers – unprepared for the combination of challenges.

These changes in the class structure forced inactivity upon the empire, for they were brought about by a redistribution of the national income with the consequence that surplus capital was no longer available for imperialist adventures. Furthermore, they brought democracy to Britain herself, and democrats into positions of authority. They too had a programme, a dynamic and exciting one which called for reform, revolutionary social reform, *at home*. The process had begun with Lloyd George's 'People's Budget' of 1909, and the ensuing Liberal reforms. During the first World War, a considerable extension of the franchise was made, giving a stronger parliamentary voice to the working classes. In a very real sense, the 'native race' of the working class, who had suffered just as much as the colonial races oppressed at the hands of the imperialists, was demanding protection from exploitation and a voice in their own destiny. Why, they were beginning to ask, should they suffer from poverty and unemployment when millions were being spent on the administration of faraway and non-white countries? Having tasted of a new and happier life, the masses were unwilling to respond to the old imperial slogans, but they were prepared to fight for their own interests against their rulers. The first World War had made Britain a nation in arms and any admiration the masses had at one time felt for the shining swords and regimentals of their military men had been dissipated through close association and the revelation of their incompetence. The war had been won, to a large extent, by non-professional soldiers, civilians in uniform who returned to their ordinary lives with a profound distaste for the regular military man. The appeals of the generals for 'forward policies' and 'strategic frontiers' no longer had an aura of infallibility about them. The middle classes no longer had faith in the ability of Britain to sustain an imperial mission.

These two elements in post-1918 Britain – an increasingly articulate working class, and a pessimistic, faithless middle class who found in the post-war world only insecurity and betrayal – came together in an improbable alliance. Because, after the collapse of the Liberal party, their political representatives in the new Labour party seemed doomed to perpetual opposition, they could afford to acquire a moral purpose themselves. This they did by taking over the old radical criticisms of empire and reviving the Macaulayan belief in ultimate self government for the colonial possessions. Not that the critics, Socialist or otherwise, believed that the empire should be 'given away'; they took over Milner's idea of a Commonwealth in which non-white dominions would have equal place with the white. The younger generation was inspired by this new mission. They also reacted strongly to the weakness shown by Britain towards the newly emerging Fascist dictatorships in Europe. This seemed to them a proof of the sterility of Britian's pretensions as a great power for justice and right, as well as of a fundamental weakness of strength both moral and material. Unlike their rulers, these young men realised that the frontiers of Britain – and of her empire – were threatened in Madrid, Manchuria and Abyssinia. And was not the cynicism of the imperialists, that whole nations could be sacrificed for the safety of the British Empire and the human spirit stifled in a concentration camp, only the same cynicism as that of the Fascists? The imperial idea, in its emotionless isolation, worshipping the idols of duty and responsibility, was it not just as immoral as the philosophy of the European dictators? The bombing of Guernica was, after all, not a great deal different from the massacre at the Jallianwalla Bagh.

Under this combination of threats – of Tory governments playing the imperial game, but without either the military or naval strength to back their play, of continuous criticism, concessions to nationalism, and the growing shadows of Germany and Japan – the old public school ethos no longer supported the Services themselves. The white man's position was no longer secure. Already, the termites were at work upon the foundations of his watchtowers. Above all, bewildered by a darkening world which their education and background had not fitted them to interpret, the Services lost faith in themselves and their mission. Home governments no longer seemed to listen to the expert advice of the man on the spot, and irritation made them feel that they were being sold out to a parcel of 'bloody democrats'. 'Once we lose confidence in our mission in the East', said Winston Churchill in the House of Commons in December 1929, 'then our presence in those countries will be stripped of every moral sanction and cannot long endure'. The possibility of dominion status for India robbed its rulers of the very purpose of their ruling mission. To make it worse, it was not a government of Labour mounte banks that was undermining their position, but members of their own clubs who ought to have known better.

It was left to the novelists to reflect this feeling of bewildered sadness. Somerset Maugham's Englishmen in the East were very odd representatives of the imperial race. And Edward Thompson makes one of his characters cry the epitaph of the betrayed administrator:

> 'We neither govern nor misgovern. We're just hanging on, hoping that the Last Trump will sound "Time" and save us from the bother of making a decision.'

The Services felt that their mandate was being snatched from them. Every thing they did was wrong. All their idols were being overthrown and, worst of all, laughed at as they fell. It was not only the system that was being brought into question, but the very right of the ruling caste to rule at all. The 'Old School Tie', instead of being a symbol of privilege, had become the badge of oafish incompetence. Instead of criticism, the empire was being as sailed with laughter, with a satire both savage and searing. In this lay the clue to the immensity of the change. Liberal and radical critics of empire had never doubted the unique position of Britain as a champion of justice, higher civilisation, and hopes of a better world. The satire of the critical intelligentsia was an attack upon those very values that had never before been questioned. Patriotism itself was becoming a dirty word, and the younger generation was prepared to die in defence of Madrid rather than that of the empire.

Again, the tired and bewildered men of the empire were to be given a new lease of life. Again, a European threat was to revive the old loyalties and re polish the imperial breast plate. To the call of the mother country, an ap parently divided empire rallied almost as one, though South Africa rallied rather reluctantly. But it was to be a very different war from that of 1914. An articulate public opinion, though willing to hand over its wartime fate to those experts it had so often attacked in peace, was not prepared to take the expert at his own valuation. He had to prove himself or get out. Other forces, too, were at work. Russia, with long laid plans of her own, was suspicious that a war to 'save European civilisation' might only be a mask for a war which would revive and extend Britain's imperial mission. The United States, always critical of the maritime empires, viewed with dislike the pos sibility of an invigorated British imperialism. In Moscow and Washington, there were leaders who looked upon the disintegration of the British Empire as a not undesirable thing, yet the dying monster had suddenly received a new lease of life. The very lessons of the inter-war years were on the side of the imperialists. Her relaxing grasp of the imperial system, concessions to nationalism abroad and democracy at home, had weakened Britain's position as the guarantor of peace. In the post-war world, in competition with two new major world powers – the United States and the USSR – she would need all her strength to maintain her role. Ideas of imperial unity were again brought out and refurbished to suit the new conditions. But the white dominions, fully conscious of their debt to Britain, were more conscious of a need for stature in the world rather than status in the empire. Britain in the East had been unable to save her possessions from the Japanese. Australia had only survived by good fortune and the help of America. The enemy this time had been not only in Europe but within a few hundred miles of Australia herself. The British Navy had done little to protect her, and the great naval base at Singapore had fallen overnight to assault from the land. Would Britain, impoverished by the war, be able to do any better after it was over? Empires are a question of power, and it seemed doubtful whether Britain would ever again exercise enough of it. Canada, too, because of her position between America and Russia, was no longer inside the old imperial system. Her problems were no longer capable of solution at Westminster. Again, hopes of an imperial confederacy were shattered by the white dominions. Imperial ideas had not really changed at all, but the facts of life had. The imperialists were the Bourbons of the modern world, who learned nothing from experience until the Suez affair of 1956 brought them the realisation that they no longer had the power, or the sanction of power, to play the old game by the old rules.

In Asia, illusions of Britain's superiority had been shattered by defeat, and defeat by an Asian nation, at that. In India, Britain did not have the power to dictate even the form of the independence she was forced to grant. The initiative was with the new nationalism. In Britain, at the end of the war, the triumphant imperialists were swept away by a triumphant democracy. At last, Labour was to rule. Behind them was a war-weary people bedevilled by drabness, devastation, food-shortages, and a suspicion that the shining world they had fought for was as far away as ever. The electors were not prepared to fight in order to keep an empire. They wanted to lick their wounds and put aside for ever the nightmare of the war years. The satisfaction of giving India independence was to lie in a revival of the old radical belief that Britain's mission, in the two hundred years of her rule, had really been to achieve that end. Macaulay's name – and his prophecy – were to be given the accolade by a Labour prime minister. The purpose, he maintained, had not been exhausted, but fulfilled.

Macaulay's purpose, however, had never been that of the imperialists. Duty and responsibility were their substitutes, and they, in themselves, were merely the instruments of power. The independence of India was, to the imperialists, a betrayal rather than a satisfaction. But apart from criticism, the imperialists were unable to act. The postwar world, though hardly safe for democracy, seemed at least to be safe from imperialism, with a powerful United Nations Organisation to see that it was so. Imperialism, nevertheless, was by no means dead. The imperialists were wiser than the radicals and the Socialists who sought to wear their mantle, for they knew that the allure of power never fades. The Soviet Union was soon to become the victim of its own interpretation of history. The Western world still remained frightened of Communist intentions. Mutual suspicion led to the revival of predatory imperialism and the Korean War heralded new struggles for power. With what appeared to be the return of the bad old days, the old imperial ideas revived. From the point of view of the British imperialists, India had gone but much of the dependent empire still remained. The British electorate, tired of austerity, once again returned the Tory party to office in 1951. This was taken by the Conservatives as a mandate to raise Britain's prestige abroad. Once again, Britain's imperial pretensions, though they were not this time openly stated as such, were to re-appear in response to the problems of power and the strategical requirements of her soldiers. The 'police action' at Suez in 1956 was an attempt to re-assert the unilateral authority of Great Britain, and to ignore international bodies which sought to diminish it. Suez was in its way a repetition of the Boer War. British arms were unsuccessful because Britain was not really capable of mounting a genuine offensive operation. Her international prestige fell with a crash. Britain, for all her two wars to save democracy, was still apparently the old lion at heart. The new nations of the Commonwealth, instead of rallying to the home country, were among the first to register their protests. Even the imperialists, with a mixture of surprise and anger, were forced to realise that the old ideas of empire no longer fitted a radically changed world.

Originally, the moral mission of the British in Asia had been produced to supply justification for the exercise of power over alien peoples. This justification they had found in a crusading purpose. There being no question of any abdication of power, its nakedness was concealed by a mask of reform and evangelical 'uplift'. Britain not only required a purpose in order to re-assure her eternal puritan conscience, but, in her position of unquestioned world authority, could even afford to have one. This moral mission, which had, as we have seen, a perfectly genuine and even altruistic content, was abandoned in India in the interests of the exercise of undivided power. But the propaganda of the purpose still remained. The new, and brutal, 'invest-ment imperialism' of the years from 1870 to the outbreak of the 1914–18 war maintained the old, high tone of morality until the façade was shattered by the consequences of the Boer War. From that time onwards, the weakening of Britain's real power was to be concealed behind a revival of the old liberal purpose of ultimate self-government. The imperialists of the inter-war years, without changing their views on the nature of power, took over some of the ideas of Milner. The slow concessions of authority in India, which were forced upon successive Tory governments, were manoeuvres in a battle, strategic withdrawals in face of the opposition. The imperialists thought that even if British power was unable to re-assert itself in India and self-govern-ment had to be granted, India would become a dominion within the empire and still contribute to the world-encircling power of Britain. But this was not to be. A failure of power more shattering than ever before was to give India her freedom. The Labour government that came into office in 1945 made an appraisal of strength and was wise enough to realise that Britain was weak and unsupported. Fortunately, the propaganda of the radical purpose could be used both as a justification and a concealment. How splendid to convert a failure of power into an immense moral gesture. France and Holland had no such justification ready as a sop to the humiliation of their defeat and oc-cupation in Europe. They felt that in the interests of national pride they had no alternative but to attempt to re-assert their shattered power in Asia.

Britain's purpose had, fundamentally, never been much different from that of previous conquerors or those who came after. The exercise of power had always been the aim, and when that power was exhausted in fighting both old and new challenges Britain was compelled to retreat. Following her, and for just the same reasons, France and Holland were forced to give up their possessions. In order that Britain should prove to her own people and to the world that her strength had a higher purpose, it had been necessary for that very purpose to become an integral part of the structure of power. It is in this that the paradox of British imperialism can be found. When radicals, whether Liberal or Socialist, condemned Britain for hypo-

crisy, they misunderstood the unique nature of her strength. Her moral purpose was as much a part of it as the Royal Navy or the Indian Army. When
imperialists sneered at their critics, they, too, misunderstood the phenomenon
of the British Empire. Imperialism and radicalism, imperialism and Socialism, were not enemies but allies. The aberrations of imperialism were inevitably followed by radical solutions. As one purpose was exhausted, the other
appeared in compensation. As power declined, moral purpose came to
smooth the way for change. This is the source of Britain's continued prestige
amongst her former colonial possessions. Without knowledge of the paradox-
ical nature of Britain's imperial way, the events of the past sixty years in Asia
lack a dimension.

II

THE CHALLENGE OF MARXISM

Marxism itself was just as much a reaction to capitalism as nationalism in
Asia was a reaction to the imperialism which, according to Lenin, is the
natural extension of capitalism. The role of Marxist ideas in colonial Asia
might appear to be comparatively small, but they thrived in the climate of
revolt against the West and appeared in full flower in the one-time imperial
playground of China. The challenge of Marxism was not only to Western
lule itself, but also to the inheritors of Western ideas in Asia. As Europe re-
rreated, Communism advanced and its success is a direct consequence of co-
tonial rule. As Communism seems to be a front for Russia's own imperialist
adventures, and moves behind a mask of anti-colonialism, its appeal to
Asians is as important to an understanding of the effect of colonialism as the
ideas of imperialism and democracy which have already been examined in
some detail.

Just as the dynamic optimism born of the Industrial Revolution had allied
itself with the revealed religion of Christianity, so also the pessimism that
emerged from the consequences of this alliance sought to offer an all-in-
clusive view of life. The hardships of the technical revolution which were
thought to be only valleys of desolation leading to the high, bright hills of
prosperity and happiness, produced the reaction of Socialism – essentially a
rational, economic and social system for dealing with the problems origin-
ating in the Industrial Revolution. Marx, however, chose to elevate these
problems into a higher sphere, to show them as part of the historical process,

and to draw from his conclusions a messianic promise of a happier state for the enslaved working classes. As the 'industrial proletariat', which was to be the Chosen People of the new religion and the predestined agent of historical evolution, only existed in the industrialised West, Asia, without industry and virtually without history, was of no practical interest. Ultimately, of course, by the process of history, Asia would follow the trek of the West, but in the meanwhile it did not count at all.

The essentially parochial nature of Marxism was to be changed into a global approach by the activities of the fully-developed capitalist empires in the era of 'investment imperialism'. Into the dialectic of history, Marxists had to find a place in which to fit the combination of Western imperialist strength, anti-Western nationalism, and the expansion of industrialisation in parts of Asia itself. It was Lenin who, in his search for clues to explain the pheno- menon of Western imperialism, found in anti-colonialism a new instrument of world revolution to add to the classic one of class warfare. The awakening of Asia, and its consequent rejection of Western political domination, was to be an important weapon in the destruction of capitalism. Lenin revised Marxism to suit new demands, and it is essentially the Leninist interpretation which has ordered the activities of the Soviet Union in the East. It was, Lenin maintained in his book *Imperialism* (published in 1917), in the nature of imperialism that the have-nots should attempt to grab the possessions of the haves, that weak imperialisms be destroyed by stronger rivals. In such wars as might occur, it should be possible to combine a revolt of the colonial peoples against their masters with a rising of the workers in the metropolitan power itself. In the face of such a combination, so Lenin reasoned, capital- ism must inevitably fall. Thus the incitement of colonial peoples to assert their independence was an essential prelude to the coming revolution.

Lenin's view would have remained merely another manifesto if its public- ation had not coincided with the October Revolution in Russia. The result was to be a great revolutionary base thrusting into the heart of northern Asia. In the withdrawal of Russia from the Western community, and its severance from its own imperial past, a new, independent *Asian* nation, hating the West and proclaiming a new dignity for the colonial struggle, emerged upon the scene. Sun Yat-sen immediately recognised the importance of this mo- mentous event. 'At present', he wrote, 'Russia is attempting to separate from the white peoples in Europe. Why? Because she insists upon the rule of Right, and denounces the rule of Might. She advocates the principle of benevolence and justice... Recent Russian civilisation is similar to our ancient civilisation. Therefore she joins with the Orient and separates from the West.'

The new factor in Asia was to have odd and apparently inconsistent political consequences. The actions of the Soviet government and of its agent the Cominform were sometimes to appear as a betrayal of those Asian nationalists who were fighting against colonial domination. But an essential part of the Leninist revised version of Marxism is its notion of 'historical relativity' inherited from Hegel. All actions are viewed in the empirical climate of immediate conditions, and thus permit a philosophy of history, an all-embracing religion-like system, to adapt itself with ease to the pressure of events, to give a messianic faith practical application to contemporary demands. The new message that Communism brought to Asia had much in common with the democratic ideas exported by the Western imperialists. Both offered the support of history to the thesis that Asia could and would be free. But the institutions of democracy were stained with the imperial smear. Could anything, even democracy itself, which the West was so proud of, be divorced from the actions of so-called democrats? In India, because the British *did* concede some of their institutions to the Indians themselves, nationalists were prepared to accept them at their face value, though not without criticism and misgivings. Through the peculiar genius of a Gandhi, it seemed that democratic institutions could not only be reconciled with traditional values but, in some occult way, be purified by them. Thus the struggle for freedom itself was a faith, and inspired men to realise its prophecies. Elsewhere in Asia, however, democracy remained an exotic foreign import, another disguise for the nakedness of power. To those peoples, and in particular the Chinese, whose civilisation had disintegrated under the blows of Western aggression, democracy offered no solution. The coldness of its ideas made them basically uninspiring, and the religion of Christianity that went with those ideas was unacceptable. The destruction of the old polity of China had removed any possibility of a reconciliation between traditional patterns and democratic institutions. What was needed was a new faith. The desire for one was particularly expressed by the intellectual classes, cut away from their past by disgust at its failure and from democratic ideals by the guilt of their association. Marxism, therefore, offered both a system and a religion, an economic materialism and the assurances of an all-embracing faith. In its 'explanation', the implications of the forces of science were simply stated in the perspective of history. Democratic philosophies of history, on the other hand, offered only a slow movement towards perfectibility, interrupted by times of troubles. In their analysis, Asia might well acquire its freedom only to lose it again in the turn of the wheel. Marxism offered something much better. It showed that the West was not becoming more tolerant but dying from an internal cancer; that though at the moment the West seemed over-whelmingly powerful, it was doomed to a destruction out of which a new world system, in which all men were truly equal, would inevitably come. An inspiring prophecy, indeed, for stricken and bewildered Asia. Furthermore, there was proof of the prophecy in the collapse of Tsarist Russia and the emergence of the precursor of a new world order in the Soviet Union. In Russia, resurgent Asia would have an ally and friend. But also, if the founder of the religion was right, and surely the October Revolution proved that he was, there were other allies inside the Western nations themselves. The oppressed peasant of Asia could link hands with the oppressed worker in the capitalist countries and work for the revolution together with him. No longer was Asia alone in the battle. The struggle was not local and apparent-ly hopeless, but world-wide and full of promise. The appeal of democracy and the slow acquisition of industrial power were pretty dull in contrast. Asia needed something heroic and inspiring, and all the West had to offer was the tutelage of the schoolroom.

Lenin's new 'Marxism of the era of imperialism', as Stalin described it, had an especial appeal to the Chinese mind as well as to its anti-Western xenophobia. The very isolation of China during its history had produced a civilisation which owed little to outside influences. China saw itself as an island in a sea of barbarians, its emperors mediators between Heaven and Earth. These attitudes gave to Chinese civilisation a vivid sense of univers-alism, with China as the centre of the world. When that civilisation col-lapsed, the desire for doctrines of universal application still remained. Marxist-Leninism supplied them.

For Asians, as we have seen, the association of Western technical and scientific superiority with the West's political institutions seemed at one time indissoluble – both were integral parts of a positive culture. To acquire mastery over one it seemed also necessary to gain the other. But Communism offered a political system free from the narrow rigidity of Western-style nationalism, so alien to Asian traditions, without the necessity of sacrificing the economic advantages of Western culture. As Asians fought for their freedom in order to acquire the material status of their conquerors, to be able to do so without taking the mechanisms of their institutions as well was a real diminution of the stature of the West itself. Once Western institutions

were divorced from the magic of Western science, there was no necessity
to compromise with the West in order to achieve scientific expertise. The
struggle against the West need to longer be a betrayal of Asian civilisation.

The 'truths' of Communism spread slowly and had only comparatively
little effect in the centres of Western power in Asia. Where the West continued to rule in strength, illusions about the magical properties of the ballot
box and representative government still remained strong. But in China, the
particularism of democracy and its limited horizon held no glamour for
those in search of universal solutions for the ills of mankind. The real
tragedy lies in the inability of the West to make of democracy an inspiring
faith, for if they had done so it would have been found that on the lowest
levels of Chinese social organisation there did exist institutions that might
have been used as the basis of democratic organs of government. Marxism,
however, offered an extension of Chinese traditional thinking adapted to the
pressures of the contemporary world. As such, it had an immense appeal to
the intelligentsia as they watched anarchy spread. It is because of its univers-
alism that Communism has its major foothold in Asia amongst the Chinese,
and that the only other Communist governments in Asia today are in north
Vietnam and North Korea, two countries whose cultures are predominantly
Chinese in origin.

The Chinese saw the Marxist faith not only as an enemy of the West, but
also of those who had adopted its rigid nationalism. Sun Yat-sen was just as
much an enemy as the foreign soldier. Ch'en Tu-hsiu, one of the founders of
the Chinese Communist party, who had started political life as a 'liberal-
democrat' and who had turned to Marxism when the Versailles peace treaty
showed that President Wilson's principle of self-determination was not to
apply to China, attacked Sun for his betrayal of Chinese universalism. 'Chinese scholars in ancient times', wrote Ch'en, 'and our old-fashioned peasants
only knew of the world and the universe and did not understand what a
nation was. Now, however, we have a group of half-baked people who
preen themselves on their modern learning and who are constantly prating
about the "nation" and "patriotism". Some of our students returning from
Japan are also bringing back this shallow, selfish type of nationalism'.
Though Ch'en himself was later expelled from the party for 'right devia-
tionism' his anti-nationalism still remains at the core of Chinese Communism, and its appeal is no less beguiling today. With this belief always in
mind, the chances of a genuine rapprochement between the narrow ideals
of the Kuomintang and the universalist faith of the Communists were nil,

and any apparent reconciliation merely a manoeuvre in the struggle for power. With the triumph of Communism in China, so her urge to 'civilise the barbarian' returned. A new imperialism appeared in Asia, whose main targets were the successors of the Western empires and, in particular, those who were trying to use Western-style institutions to solve the problems of independence. Marxism offers the exhilaration that once sent the hordes of Islam upon the campaigns of a holy war against the Infidel. The West left very little behind in Asia to combat it. The challenge of Marxism revealed the essential emptiness of the imperial message. Whatever the effects of the West's 'civilising mission' in the East have been, that mission represented conflicting philosophies and strange religions. It did not bring an all-embracing world view, nor an inspiring faith. The Western empires with great reluctance handed over some of the magical apparatus of democracy, which seemed quickly to lose its power in other hands. The sterility of Asia's European Age lay in the narrowness of European purpose and in the confusion and coldness of Western ideas. Power impresses, attracts admiration, but it rarely intoxicates those who suffer its effects. Asia has taken the material things of the West – the aeroplane and the Cadillac, the radio set and the electric shaver – for that is all the West seemed to have to offer after four hundred and fifty years of rule in Asia. It is a sad comment that only in one of the former colonial possessions do the ideals of democracy still have some meaning, and even there that appeal may only be temporary.

The challenge of Marxism was a challenge not only to imperialism but to the civilisation from which it emerged. The colonial struggle has now been extended into a world struggle. The failure of the West in Asia, as in Africa today, was a failure of inspiration. The West had no clear-cut faith to offer those it ruled because it had none that it really believed in itself.

3

The War against the West

I

THE TWENTY-THREE YEARS that separated the massacre at the Jallian-walla Bagh from the 'Quit India' campaign of 1942 saw the government of India caught in almost regular cycles of repression and concession. National-ist violence would be followed by intimidation of leaders, large-scale arrests and deportations, and then, in turn, by attempts at conciliation and the slow granting of responsibility to elective institutions. The left hand of govern-ment, to intelligent Indians, still seemed cynically unaware of what the right hand was doing.

For nationalists in 1921, the coming inauguration of the Montagu-Chelmsford reforms was overshadowed by memories of martial law in the Punjab and by Muslim agitation in what was called the Khilafat[1] move-ment. Though Indian Muslims had never acknowledged the spiritual au-thority of the Sultan of Turkey as the Caliph of Islam, the war against the Turkish Empire had produced considerable ill-feeling among Muslims who had been searching for identity within the greater fold of the Islamic world as a counter-balance to Hindu extremism. Two brothers, Muhammad and Shaukat Ali, who had been interned during the war, on their release took up Turkey's cause against the British – who, in their dealings with Turkey, ap-peared to be the enemy of Islam. The movement these brothers established was riddled with corruption. Under the pressure of its propaganda, thou-sands of Muslim peasants sold their land and emigrated to Afghanistan, where neither organisation nor welcome awaited them. Finally, wiser and poorer, they were forced to return to India. In August 1921, the Moplahs, a Muslim community in Malabar, began a sort of holy war against Hindus and by doing so helped to exacerbate communal tensions. When Turkey herself abolished the Caliphate in 1924, Indian Muslims returned to their old fears of a Hindu supremacy.

[1] The Indian spelling of 'Caliphate'.

Elections under the Government of India Act of 1919 took place in November 1921. The major effect of these reforms lay in the principle of 'dyarchy', in the division of powers, encumbered rather than supported by a delicate system of checks and balances. The Central Executive remained responsible to no one but the secretary of state in London, but legislation was, in theory, to be the function of a new Central Assembly and a Council of State, each with elected majorities but containing also an 'official' or nominated bloc. The legislative authority was, however, rendered nugatory by the fact that such legislation as the new bodies might refuse to pass could be 'certified' by the viceroy and become law. The provinces were also to have their legislative councils, in which certain responsibilities would be assigned from the centre to provincial control. This devolution covered both finance and administration, and in some measure the provinces became self-governing, though real power – in revenue legislation and the control of the armed forces – remained at the centre. Administration on provincial level was divided into two groups: 'reserved' subjects, including finance, justice and police, remained under the control of the governor, and the 'transferred' subjects, such as education and public health, were entrusted to ministers responsible to the legislative council. The franchise was restricted by a sliding scale of property qualifications. The number of voters for the provincial councils was over five million, for the Central Legislative Assembly, nearly one million, and for the Council of State, a select group of some seventeen thousand. The population of India, according to the census of 1921, was 305,693,063. The Act embodied a much more dangerous element than a franchise heavily weighted towards property owners. The Morley-Minto reforms of 1909 had allowed for separate representation for Muslims. The new Act extended this principle to Sikhs, Indian Christians, Anglo-Indians (Eurasians) and Europeans. Communal representation gave yet another incentive to Muslim-Hindu conflict.

The elections under the new Act were boycotted by Congress, but this did not prevent a third of the electorate from going to the polls. The result was that moderate nationalists became ministers in the new governments. The centre, no longer protected by an 'official' majority, became rather more sensitive to public opinion, and, because of it, repealed the Rowlatt Acts and instituted certain reforms in labour legislation, as well as beginning upon Indianisation of the army. In the international field, Indian representatives signed the Versailles peace treaty, and India became a founder member of the League of Nations. Upon a restricted stage, the new institutions seemed to be working, but in fact they functioned as agencies of an irresponsible executive at the centre and were without any precise public support.

With the blessing of the Khilafat movement, Mahatma Gandhi represented for the first and last time a united nationalist opinion. He declared a
noncooperation movement and stimulated enthusiasm by, rather foolishly,
promising *swaraj* (independence) by the end of 1921. The Moplah rebellion,
however, destroyed the fragile links of HinduMuslim rapprochement. The
riots in Bombay and elsewhere – which accompanied the visit of the Prince
of Wales in the autumn of 1921 – and the murder of twenty policemen by
'national volunteers' at ChauriChaura in February 1922 showed that passive resistance could soon move into violence. The Mahatma antagonised
Congress by publicly confessing failure, and was only rescued from utter
defeat by being arrested by the government. He was sentenced to six years'
imprisonment but released after serving one.

The leadership of the nationalist movement passed for a time to a new
Swaraj Party founded by C. R. Das and Pandit Motilal Nehru, who persuaded Congress that the best policy was to fight in the new elections of
1923, capture the administration, and harass the government from inside. This
did not prove completely effective, as the new party failed to win a sufficient
majority, and in 1925 it withdrew from the legislatures. C. R. Das, before
his untimely death in October 1925, appeared to be on the verge of a new
relationship with the secretary of state, Lord Birkenhead, which might have
resulted in new reforms. The report of the Muddiman Committee, which
had investigated the workings of dyarchy, found little good to say of it. This,
coupled with the breakdown of the administration in some provinces
through the activities of the Swarajists, convinced moderates that they were
wasting their time and Congress leaders that the opportunity was ripe for
further demands.

During these years, communal tension increased and interreligious rioting
became almost commonplace. HinduMuslim conflict revived nationalist
feeling and, in 1928, Gandhi – who had been in retirement, though not inactive – returned to Congress on a wave of enthusiasm. In a climate of communal violence, nationalist revival, and moderate pessimism, the government began hastily to think of some new concession. The 1919 Act had
contained a provision for parliamentary consideration after ten years, and in
1928–9 the Simon Commission – consisting of Sir John Simon and six
members of the British parliament – toured India to collect material for a
report. The appointment of this commission antagonised Indians because it

appeared to imply that they were to have no say in the structure of new reforms and that, whatever happened in India, real authority still lay where it
had always lain – in Westminster. Once again, the most diverse elements of
Indian opinion united against the British.

In the early part of 1928, an All-Party Conference produced its own programme for self-government, but again Muslim opinion was affronted by
rejection of the principle of communal representation. In the crisis of leadership that followed, the Mahatma seemed the only person of standing who
could give a new impetus to the struggle for freedom. This he did by demanding from the new Labour government in England – which had promised a round table conference as the next step towards dominion status for
India – a statement that the conference would draw up plans for *immediate*
self-government. For this demand the Mahatma and his followers had some
justification, for shortly before taking office the Labour prime minister, Ramsay MacDonald, had declared that:

> 'I hope that within a period of months rather than years there will be a
> new dominion added to the Commonwealth of our Nations, a domin-
> ion which will find self-respect as an equal within the Commonwealth.
> I refer to India.'

The Mahatma's knowledge of the world should have saved him from the
naivety of believing that there is any connection between the rhetoric of politicians out of office and their policy when they achieve it. The same Ramsay
MacDonald refused the demand of Congress, and in 1930 a vast civil disobedience campaign began in India.

The aim of civil disobedience was to court arrest, to flood the jails and
arouse general sympathy in the resulting chaos, which would in turn bring
the administration to a standstill. The first act in the campaign was one of
considerable symbolic effect – the Mahatma ceremoniously broke the government monopoly in salt by making it himself on the seashore at Dandi.
This act received great publicity abroad, especially in America where it appeared to have overtones of the Boston Tea Party. In India, the government
ignored it. Peaceful demonstration, it seemed, was a failure. What followed
was a revival of terrorist activity and a commercial boycott. A government
armoury was raided and officials were murdered. For the first time, Indian
women entered into the fevered world of nationalist agitation, demanding
arrest and, in the case of two Bengali students, even murdering an English
official. The commercial boycott was directed against British banks as well
as against British goods and represented an attempt by Indian business men

to ruin their trade rivals. Civil disturbances were not aimed only at the British but broke out into religious violence, further inflaming Hindu-Muslim relations. The government responded by arresting 60,000 people including the Mahatma, and restoring order by martial law.

In this atmosphere of rebellion, the first Round Table Conference met in London. The Indian delegates represented every level of special interest, from the princes upwards, except for the only effective nationalist organ – the Indian Congress. The publication of the Simon Report had not helped to promote faith in the value of such a conference for, though it condemned dyarchy, its suggestions seemed to offer little further delegation of authority and just as many 'checks and balances' as before. However, the viceroy, Lord Irwin, was able to persuade delegates that the British government was not bound to accept all or any of the commission's recommendations, and in fact the report was quickly shelved. The main result of the first conference, which ended in January 1931, was the announcement by the British prime minister that the government 'would be prepared to recognise the principle of the responsibility of the executive to the legislature' – in itself, an immense step forward from the provisions of dyarchy. With this, the Indian government had an instrument to conciliate Congress while the nationalist leaders, sensitive to the public's reaction to what appeared to be substantial concessions, had gained as much as they could hope for. In February 1931, Gandhi and other leaders were released, and the viceroy took the unprecedented step of opening direct negotiations with the Mahatma. This resulted in the Gandhi-Irwin truce which provided for the ending of civil disobedience, the release of political prisoners not accused of crimes of violence, and the representation of Congress at the next session of the Round Table Conference.

Unfortunately, though the Congress meeting at Karachi in April 1931 confirmed the truce, the organisation was itself divided by extremist intransigence which had been inspired by the Mahatma's failure to obtain the reprieve from execution of a convicted terrorist, Bhagat Singh. A terrible communal riot in Cawnpore, caused by the attempt of Congress 'volunteers' to impose a *hartal* on Muslim shopkeepers, antagonised the Muslims. Congress, at this important date in India's history, no longer represented a united front.

In London, the Labour administration had been succeeded by a so-called 'National' government led by Ramsay MacDonald, but with a Conservative majority. It appeared to the Mahatma that the government's attitude had changed, and no agreement was reached on, among other things, the communal allotment of seats in the legislatures. Within three weeks of his return from the conference, Gandhi was once again in jail and Congress had been declared an illegal organisation. The second civil disobedience campaign that followed was a failure. Isolated acts of terrorism occurred in Bengal and the United Provinces, but the mass of the people were unwilling to live their lives at the centre of a whirlpool. By the middle of 1932, a sullen peace had descended upon India.

In the meanwhile, the mountain of British parliamentary method continued to gestate and, to nationalist surprise and the regret of such die-hards as Winston Churchill, the mouse it brought forth was larger than anyone had expected. The new proposals became law as the Government of India Act of 1935.

Between 1930 and the 1936–7 elections for the new institutions provided for by the Act, the Muslim minority organised itself into a new movement – not to protect a religious group, but to further the independence of a 'nation'. Some details of how this came about are essential to an understanding of the final phase of the freedom struggle in India, for it was to lead to the creation of the state of Pakistan.

Under the pressures of the Islamic invasions, from the conquest of Sind in the eighth century to the Mughal domination that ceased only in the middle of the eighteenth, nearly a quarter of the population of India had accepted the Muslim faith. Though some were descendants of invading tribes, Indian Muslims in the main were of indigenous origin, converts to the faith of their conquerors. By the middle of the eighteenth century, the social stratification of Indian Muslims consisted of an upper class of administrators and land-owners, a professional and business class – small in size, partly because of the excellent opportunities for promotion to high office for Muslims in a Muslim administration, and partly because of the commercial efficiency of Hindu traders – and a large group of peasants and craftsmen, in the main outcaste and low-caste converts. The collapse of Muslim supremacy under the attacks of the West and of the Marathas produced a cultural as well as political decline. The Muslim community turned away from the new order and, in its demoralisation, made no attempt to take advantage of the new dispensation of Western-style education in the way Hindus did. Because of this, Hindus took the lead in such levels of the administration as were open to Indians. The Mutiny of 1857, despite its essentially Hindu character, was viewed by the British as an attempt to reinstate the authority of the Mughal Empire and served only to cut Muslims further away from the sympathy of their rulers.

The Muslim community was recalled to a sense of dignity by the work of Sir Syed Ahmad (see p. 197 ff) who sought to bring the advantages of education to an oppressed people. He also brought a belief in the separateness of the Muslim community and the necessity of dynamic competition with Hindus for public appointments. Those Muslim thinkers who followed Syed Ahmad emphasised Islamic traditions while also advocating reforms. But Muslims were still prepared to think of themselves as Indians. The early years of the twentieth century, however, brought a significant change. The old Islamic world, under the threat of European aggression, evolved pan-Islamic ideas. In India, the appearance of representative institutions prophe-sied the ultimate domination of the Hindu majority. The collapse of Turkey in the Balkan War of 1912, and her treatment by Britain after the first World War, pushed these fears of Hindu domination aside in favour of the more immediate need to defend Islam against its enemies. In India this new feeling produced an alliance between Muslim and Hindu, because Britain was, in the view of the Muslims, the real enemy of Islam. When, however, Turkey herself gave up the leadership of the Islamic states, the old fear of a Hindu supremacy returned. By 1930, as we have seen, Congress appeared to Muslims to be solely an organ of Hindu domination. Indian Islam again looked outside for a new sense of identity. It found it in the writings of the poet Iqbal (1876–1938).

Iqbal, who wrote almost exclusively in Urdu, has been aptly described as a Nietzsche in an Islamic setting. From him, the Muslim community acquir-ed a sense of inalienable destiny. The Muslim League, which had been founded in 1906, became representative of the fears of Indian Islam, and in 1927 split over the terms of the Simon Commission, though it united again in 1929 at the All-India Muslim Conference. By 1931, the Muslims seemed once again to be in the political wilderness. The search for unity continued and in 1934 the League was reorganised under the leadership of Muham-mad Ali Jinnah, a lawyer who had once been a member of Congress and held a seat in the Central Legislative Assembly. Jinnah was at this time a secularist in the manner of the Turkish dictator Atatürk. He was also an organiser of genius. Jinnah, taking the ideas of Iqbal and of Chaudhri Rah-mat Ali, who in Cambridge in 1933 invented the term Pakistan, welded the Muslim League into the vanguard of a new, independent Muslim state.

It was now two nationalist movements, suspicious of each other as well as of the British, which confronted the new challenge of the 1935 Act. This Act incorporated all the stages of constitutional development to date, with the addition of two new principles: the organisation of a federal structure, and the setting up of popular, responsible government in the provinces. Under the terms of the Act, new 'provinces' were to be formed, and Burma was to be separated from India under a new constitution following the lines laid down in the Act of 1919. In India, the federal principle at the centre was designed to incorporate the Indian states into the new system of government, but the princes would not cooperate. Nationalists viewed the federal proposals as a means of perpetuating British control through the natural divisions of special interest groups. Furthermore, dyarchy, with its 'reserved' subjects, was to remain at the centre, and the overall authority of the British parliament was to be maintained. That part of the Act dealing with the federal provisions never came into force. In the provinces, dyarchy was abandoned, and an almost completely responsible parliamentary government elected upon a considerably wider franchise was established. Indian reaction to the new reform was basically unfavourable. Even moderate leaders viewed them as undesirable and nationalists were quick to describe the Act as a 'slave constitution', and 'a new charter of bondage'. The British conceived it as the last stage before dominion status. The Muslims, once again, saw it as the threat of majority rule by Hindus. All parties, however, agreed to contest the elections of 1936–7. The results were that Congress won clear majorities in five of the eleven provinces and was the largest party in another three. In July 1937, Congress ministries were formed in seven of the provinces.

Congress, however, was ill prepared for the function of political power. In the first place, it considered itself the sole expression of the people's aspirations. Secondly, it was no longer interested in the mechanics of transition. Pandit Jawaharlal Nehru, whose position in the Congress was as second-in-command and undoubted heir to Gandhi, made this quite clear in July 1937 as Congress ministries were being inaugurated.

> 'The opinion of the majority of the Congress today is in favour of acceptance of office, but it is even more strongly and unanimously in favour of the basic Congress policy of fighting the new constitution and ending it... We are not going to be partners and cooperators in the imperialist firm... We go to the assemblies or accept office... to try to prevent the federation from materialising, to stultify the constitution and prepare the ground for the constituent assembly and independence... to strengthen the masses, and, wherever possible, in the narrow sphere of the constitution, to give some relief to them.'

In its internal organisation, Congress was becoming more and more mon-

olithic and the 'High Command' more dictatorial, a state of affairs that survived independence and still continues today. Congress was in no real sense
a political party but a vast portmanteau of conflicting opinion and special
interests. At the top was the Mahatma, worshipped by the peasants and respected by intellectuals for his world prestige. Next came Pandit Nehru, representing Socialism and social reform and, because of it, the main body of
Westernised nationalists who were unable to stomach the mystic overtones
and reactionary economic ideas of the Mahatma. Big business had its spokesman in Sardar Vallabhbhai Patel, and the extreme left wing in the Bengali,
Subhas Chandra Bose, who was to break away and found a Japanese-
sponsored free Indian government at Singapore in 1943.

The Muslim League was still prepared to cooperate with Congress to the
extent of forming coalition governments, but in general the attitude of Congress, caught in the consequences of its own propaganda, sought not cooperation but absorption. Jinnah turned, for the first time, to the Muslim peasant
for support and, possibly to his surprise, found it. In doing so, this sophis-
ticated, highly Westernised Muslim lawyer converted a bourgeois nationalist
movement into a popular expression of Muslim feeling. When the Congress
ministries resigned in October 1939, Jinnah declared it 'a day of deliverance
and thanksgiving' from the yoke of the Hindu majority. In the early part of
1940, the goal of Pakistan was made the formal policy of the League.

Locked in the closed room of its struggle for freedom, India received the
news of the outbreak of war in Europe unprepared and uninterested in the
causes of the coming holocaust. Congress was not unaware of developments
in Europe during the 'thirties, but, of its leaders, only Pandit Nehru saw the
decisive effect international events might have upon India and her movement
towards independence. Congress, bent upon increasing control of India's
internal administration, was still inclined to treat external affairs as the business of the British – something that subject India had no responsibility for.
Furthermore, India found herself at war with Germany without her consent.
In return for its support, Congress demanded an immediate declaration of
independence, 'present application to be given to this status to the largest
possible extent'. The viceroy's reply was to declare dominion status the
goal – after the end of the war. As this was unacceptable, the Congress ministries resigned. The Muslim League's attitude was not quite so precise; for
obvious tactical reasons, it preferred slow development towards independence
rather than immediate Hindu rule.

The fall of France and he probability of a Nazi invasion of Britain produced a relaxation of tension as well as a growing desire amongst Indians to defend their own country. In August 1940, the British government made a new offer – that a postwar constitution would be drawn up by an Indian constituent assembly, and not by the British parliament, and decisions made there would be accepted by the British government. The Muslim League, now intoxicated by the heady vision of Pakistan, demanded that any national government should be equally divided between Muslims and Hindus. Congress, seeing a revived Britain fighting back in Europe, decided to reject the offer altogether as just another British scheme to confuse the final issue. A new civil disobedience campaign was begun in the autumn of 1940, and by the following May some 14,000 Congressmen were in jail, a significantly small figure compared with that of 1930. The viceroy's reply was to increase the number of members in his executive council to a total of fifteen, of whom eleven were Indians.

The entry of Japan and the United States into the war at the end of 1941 led to the release of the Congress leaders and the sending to India of a British cabinet mission under Sir Stafford Cripps in March 1942. Cripps brought new proposals. India would receive dominion status as soon as possible after the war. This was only a repetition of the previous offer, but this time specific steps were announced. The constituent assembly already conceded would be elected by the provincial legislatures and the new body would negotiate a treaty with the British government and promote a constitution for an Indian Union. Muslim fears, and those of the princely states, were to be soothed by the granting to each province or state of the right to secede from the union. In the meantime, for the duration of the war, an all-party national government would be set up at the centre.

The Cripps Mission failed because Congress demanded that the new government should exercise full power immediately. With the imminence of Japanese invasion, the British government did not feel able to grant it. The true reasons for Congress intransigence lay in the refusal of the Mahatma and others to accept the reality of the Muslim League's belief in Pakistan, and their dislike of the concessions to minority opinion implied in the principle of secession. They believed that in a united India, under Congress control, Muslim separatism could be suppressed. The Congress leaders, in their refusal of this chance of an independent, and possibly undivided India, laid the foundation stone of Pakistan. Congress itself was by no means unanimously behind the decision to reject the cabinet offer. C. R. Rajagopalachari, later to be the first native governor-general of the Dominion of India, was expelled from the movement because of his criticism of the decision. The majority of Congress members, however, rallied behind the Mahatma for a new civil disobedience campaign. The slogan now was 'Quit India', and Gandhi defined the new exercise in non-violence as 'open rebellion'. The resolution to begin a new campaign was passed at a meeting of the All-India Congress Committee in August 1942. The government's answer was to intern the whole committee at Poona. A serious outbreak of violence followed in which some 900 people were killed and extensive damage caused. The outbreak was, however, short and the government turned away to the business of the war with Japan. At the end of 1942, with the Japanese at the gates of India and nationalist leaders in prison, the independence that had been within India's grasp now seemed as far away as ever.

*   *   *

Elsewhere in Asia, the nature of the anti-colonial struggle was rather different from that in India. The reasons for this were partly religious and partly a result of differing colonial systems.

In 1919, Burma, then still a part of British India, was expressly excluded from the operation of the Montagu-Chelmsford reforms on the grounds that the people were of different race, and at a different level of political sophistication. The consequence was an outbreak of nationalist activity in Burma, a commercial boycott, and a demand for home rule. In 1921, the dyarchical system was applied to Burma. The 'transferred' subjects included the forestry department, of vital importance in the country's economy. The franchise was also considerably wider than in India, being extended to householders of either sex, and with a minimum age limit of eighteen, three years below that of any European country. Various reforms were also made at all levels of the administration. From the start, the new Legislative Council contained a nationalist majority.

At the time of the Simon Commission, whose report recommended the separation of Burma from India, a new leader, Dr Ba Maw, announced that he believed separation merely a trick to keep Burma behind the constitutional level planned for India. At the time of the Burma Round Table Conference held in London between November 1931 and January 1932, an Anti-Separation League had been formed in Burma, which demanded a place in the Indian federation with the right to secede from it. In the Burmese general election of 1932, the League won a complete victory. As it was obvious that Burma would ultimately leave any new Indian federation, the British government refused to give Burma the right to secede at will. The League then completely reversed its policy and accepted separation, and the terms of a Government of Burma Act of 1935 established a new constitution. This provided for a bi-cameral legislature to be elected by a wide franchise of practically all males over 21 and all females over that age who were able to pass a literacy test. Half the seats in the upper house were to be nominated by the governor, and in the lower, forty of the 132 members were to represent special groups such as minorities and the University of Rangoon. The government still retained responsibility for 'reserved' subjects, but the cabinet of Dr Ba Maw, which took office in 1937, was to all intents and purposes in complete control of the country's internal affairs.

The new government had little time to undertake much-needed reforms before the outbreak of war in Europe in 1939. Because of this, social discontent was widespread. Agricultural indebtedness, mainly to Indian money-lenders, the existence of a large Indian coolie population, and the monopolistic tendencies of European business houses, all helped to fertilise the seeds of nationalism. But the so-called political parties that emerged in Burma were, in reality, only cliques gathered around dominating personalities such as Dr Ba Maw and his *Sinyetha*, or 'Poor Man's' party, and U Saw and the *Myochit*, or 'Patriotic' party. Only in the *Dobama Asiayone*, or *Thakin* party, mainly consisting of students and workers, can be found any parallel with Western political organisations. Part of the reason for this unusual set-up was the very slow extension of Western-style education in Burma. Secondary education had been long delayed because of the difficulty of finding Burman teachers who could speak English. It was not until 1931 that a medical course could be taken in Burma, and as late as 1937 there were only twenty-five science graduates in the whole country.

In 1939, U Saw, anti-British and pro-Japanese, became prime minister, and on his return from London in 1941 after an abortive attempt to obtain a pledge of dominion status for Burma after the war, he was arrested by the British and interned in Africa for the duration. Dr Ba Maw, after leaving office in 1939, formed a Freedom Bloc with the support of the Thakin party, and demanded immediate and unconditional independence. He was imprisoned by the British but escaped from jail at the time of the Japanese invasion, and later became puppet premier during the occupation. Some members of the Thakin party avoided arrest and escaped to Formosa, from where they returned with the Japanese in 1942 to take office in the Ba Maw cabinet.

*   *   *

In the Dutch East Indies, the absence of such well-defined reforms as had taken place in India and, again, the limitations on the spread of Western education, had concentrated nationalist feeling into an expression of Islamic revivalism as seen in the Sarekat Islam (see p. 203). But the Russian Revolution of 1917 added a new and continuing dimension to Indonesian nationalism. In 1919, the *Perserikatan Kommunist Indië* (PKI) was formed and began a battle with the Sarekat Islam for leadership of the freedom movement. At the sixth national congress of the latter, held in 1921, its leader, Aminoto, was under arrest for subversive activities, and the Communists who had remained inside the movement in the hope of capturing it were expelled. In 1922, under the influence of European-educated graduates, discontented with their lack of status, Sarekat Islam established relations with the Indian National Congress and took over its policy of non-cooperation.

Between 1923 and 1926, Communist-inspired terrorism spread throughout Java. In 1923, a railway strike was organised and the government granted itself special powers to suppress labour disturbances and amended the penal code to provide heavy penalties for labour agitators. In 1925, a major strike in the metal industry was suppressed by force. Encouraged by Moscow, Communists in the following year began a well-organised revolution in west Java and Sumatra. Under severe repression by the Dutch, the revolution collapsed and the Communist party was banned. Over 1,300 of its members were sent to penal exile in New Guinea. The Communist stage of the revolutionary movement was at an end.

Left with an empty field, Sarekat Islam found itself the main centre of nationalist activity which it diverted into the comparatively innocuous fields of education and village cooperatives. This activity, however laudable in itself, could hardly satisfy the revolutionary instincts of students and nationalists. Other parties did however exist. Some were only of local influence, others followed the party divisions existing in Holland, and others again were organisations representing communal interests such as those of the Chinese minority and the Indos, or Dutch Eurasians. Under the influence of students and the leadership of Djipto Mangun Kusuma, and of a rising young demagogue, Sukarno, a new party, the *Perserikatan National Indonesia* (PNI), was formed in 1927 in an attempt to weld the various nationalist groups into a non-cooperation movement. In 1929, however, Sukarno was jailed by the Dutch and once again revolutionary activity gave place to constructive effort in the fields of education and social service.

At no time had the Dutch ever intimated that a day might come when

some form of representative institutions might be established as a step towards self-government. During the first World War, in response to nationalist demands, a scheme for a Volksraad had passed the Dutch parliament
and came into operation in 1919. Half the members of this council were
elected by local and city councils, and half nominated by the governor-
general. The Volksraad contained a European majority and had no legislative functions but merely the power to offer advice to the governor-general,
who could not accept it without the authority of the Dutch government at
The Hague.

In 1925, as part of a new constitution, the size of the Volksraad was increased from forty-eight seats to sixty-one, and it was given a majority of
elected members; but only thirty of these were to be Indonesians. The council received some legislative functions of practically no executive significance.
The new constitution also called for a system of decentralisation. In Java, the
Residency system was converted into three provinces each with a governor
and a partly elected council with an Indonesian majority. Elections for the
Volksraad were made by the members of the provincial councils and those
other councils, local and city, which had already been established. In other
parts of the country considered too backward for even these shadowy institutions, administrations without representative councils were set up. The
formation of this system was extremely slow and was in fact completed only
just before the Japanese invasion of January 1942.

The Communist-inspired rising of 1925–6 resulted in the proliferation of
racial parties, and in 1929 there was founded the European organisation,
Vaderlandsche Club, which later developed Fascist tendencies. A severe
economic depression which struck Indonesia in the 'thirties produced wide
unemployment, the lowering of wages and extensive cuts in government
welfare services. Anti-Dutch hatred grew and, though attempts were made
by the government to conciliate native opinion, the possibility of an agreed
transfer of power was never envisaged. Unlike the British in India, such a
state of affairs had never occurred to the most liberal of Dutch administrators
and statesmen. No preparation of any kind had been made for the ultimate
independence of the East Indies. Both the Indonesians and the Dutch were
to suffer cruelly for it.

*   *   *

French policy in Indo-China had, like Dutch policy in the East Indies,
never concerned itself with the possibility of colonial self-government. But

unlike the Dutch, the French colonial administration actively followed a programme of cultural assimilation. For the French, the British idea of dominion association was no substitute for the concept of France *outre mer.* Indo-China was to be as much a part of France as Brittany. The first step towards this ideal was to be upon a cultural level, and though a grandiose scheme designed to make the study of the French language universal through-out Indo-China had to be abandoned in 1924 because of the expense, the administration aimed at the widest dissemination of French culture. Once again, as in India, those who absorbed most of the culture of the foreigner became their bitterest opponents. During the 1914–18 war, in order to keep the country quiet, France made generous promises which she was not prepar-ed to keep when the emergency had passed. The administration also antag-onised the Vietnamese by conscripting nearly 100,000 of them for service in Europe. On their return, these conscripts added a new element of discontent. The postwar period saw a ferment of political activity inspired, in the main, by the heady wine of President Wilson's declaration on self-determination. Others took their inspiration from the Communists in Canton, or from the activities of the Indian National Congress. Moderate nationalists in Annam founded a new Constitutionalist party and a Tongkingese party, both ad-vocating democratic reforms. But the government rejected even their mild proposals, and the initiative fell to the extremists.

In 1925 was founded the Revolutionary Party of Young Annam, but when its Communist members left in 1929 it soon collapsed, for the Com-munists turned police informers and the party was suppressed by the gov-ernment. In Tongking, under the influence of the Chinese Kuomin-tang, a National Annamite party was formed. About half of its members were in government service and it hoped to win over Vietnamese elements in the army. In January 1929, members of the new party attempted to murder the French governor, Pasquier, and succeeded in killing the head of the labour bureau. French reaction was so prompt and efficient, that, in an en-deavour to save themselves, the party leaders launched a full-scale rebellion with an unsuccessful mutiny at Yenbay in February 1930. Despite wide-spread violence, the French suppressed outbreaks with such severity that the rebellion was crushed, its leaders arrested, and the party dissolved.

With the vicious suppression of all nationalist activity, the small Commu-nist party of some 1,500 members, led by Nguyen Ai-Quoc, later to be better known as Ho Chi Minh, was driven underground. Ho had joined the Communist party in France before 1914, and after the end of the war, had

gone to Moscow. In Canton, he had established the Association of Revolutionary Annamite Youth. His aim was Vietnamese independence along
strictly democratic lines, and his programme appealed to both intellectuals
and peasants. Though arrested by the British while on a visit to Hong Kong
– where he was imprisoned for three years – under Ho's dynamic leadership,
the party resisted all attempts by the French to suppress it. In 1939, the party
changed its name to Viet Minh, the 'League for the Independence of Vietnam', and on the surrender of the Vichy French administration to the Japanese, became the spearhead of the nationalist movement. By its attitude towards the nationalists, a colonial power, unable to accept the relationship of
equal association, was once again unwittingly preparing itself and the people
it ruled for tragedy and bloodshed.

*   *   *

In China the revolutionary movement of Sun Yat-sen emerged as a struggle
upon two fronts – against the traditional China of the Manchus, and against
the 'investment imperialism' of the West. The movement had its roots in the
south, in the middle-class China of traders and bankers who, rebelling
against the inferior position assigned to them in the Confucianist system,
turned to the West for the mechanics of a new and dynamic China freed
from the shackles of tradition. The southern Chinese had had much longer
contact with the West, and most of the traders who had emigrated to the
countries of South-east Asia had done so in order to free themselves from the
Confucian atmosphere and to satisfy their self-interest without involvement
in a highly stratified social order. In Western techniques, they saw the possibility of a return to the Chinese homeland where their old position would be
reversed. It was from these partly-Westernised merchants that Sun Yat-sen
drew most of his financial support.

The revolution of 1911 and the attempt of Yüan Shih-k'ai to direct it into
the path of the traditional 'sacred right to rebellion', followed by a change of
dynasty, was not to lead to a new stability. Sun had hoped for favourable
conditions in which to introduce reforms, but, before his eyes, the whole
structure of Chinese civilisation was disintegrating into chaos. The situation
now demanded not reform but a completely new structure. Sun began to
recognise that Western bourgeois democracy offered no solution for China,
and that only an authoritarian regime could establish a sense of national
identity. His first step was to produce an ideology, the San Min Chu I, or
'Three Principles of the People'. In it, Sun rejected all the traditional ele-

ments of Chinese civilisation and proclaimed the three stages through which the new republic must proceed. Firstly, the struggle against the remnants of the old system; secondly, a period of preparation for democratic rule; and thirdly, in some remote future, the final establishment of democracy. Unfortunately, Sun, with his middle-class Westernised background, was an *urban* agitator, unaware that the only real revolutionary element in China was the peasant. The Russian revolution of 1917 gave Sun a new sense of direction and, with the Russian example in mind, he founded the Kuomintang, or 'People's Party'. In 1921, Sun was elected head of a government at Canton which claimed to represent the whole of China.

In the meanwhile, the Peking government was rapidly losing all vestiges of authority. On 4 May 1919, immense student demonstrations took place in the city in protest against the terms of the Versailles treaty. By early June, this protest had spread to Shanghai, where between sixty and seventy thousand workers came out on strike, and unrest spread to Nanking, Tientsin, Hangchow, and Wuhan. Out of these first examples of student-labour agitation was to emerge the Chinese Communist party, the growth of which will be discussed in a later place (see p. 312 ff.) Agitation took place within a general background of administrative chaos. The north was mainly in the hands of competing warlords. Western commercial interests still dominated the coastal areas. In the south, Sun's government at Canton had been driven out by a local warlord in August 1922, and the 'Father of the Chinese Republic' fled to Shanghai. He returned to Canton in February of the following year.

In the same month, the northern warlord Wu P'ei-fu crushed, with great severity, a strike of Peking-Hankow railway workers. His action delivered a death blow to the Communist labour unions and convinced the Russians that the Chinese Communist party (CPC) was not yet a reliable revolutionary instrument. Influenced by the opinions of agents of the Communist International in China, the Russian leaders saw the Kuomintang (KMT) as having the greatest potentiality for popular appeal, despite Sun's weathercock ideology. At this stage, a Russian representative came upon the scene, haloed with the prestige of a government which had renounced the 'unequal treaties' of its Tsarist predecessors and which, furthermore, advocated the equality of peoples. An agreement was entered into between the Soviet representative, Adolf Jaffe, and Sun, for the support of the KMT by Communists *in their capacity as individuals*. There was no question of a public alliance between the two parties. The Sun-Jaffe agreement was accepted by the CPC as a means of penetrating a popular organisation and ultimately capturing it. Russian aid was solicited and received. Mikhail Borodin became political adviser to Sun, and General Galen organised the Whampoa Military Academy with the aid of a young officer who had studied in Moscow with the Red Army, Chiang Kai-shek, and, as political instructor, Chou En-lai.

The KMT, which was to a large extent a national rally rather than a political party, still contained right-wing elements whose strength Sun completely discounted. Their reaction to Communist infiltration was to foster suspicion of Communist intentions within the movement and later to use the discipline and efficiency built up by Soviet advisers against the Communists themselves. For some time, however, the alliance appeared to function smoothly, even after Sun's death in 1925, despite the fact that the right-wing elements were now successfully undermining Communist positions within the KMT.

On 30 May 1925, British troops in Shanghai opened fire upon Chinese workers who were on strike and, in doing so, released an outbreak of virulent anti-Western feeling. A very successful boycott of British goods was organised, and shortly afterwards a complete strike of workers in Japanese-owned textile mills at Tsingtao added anti-Japanese agitation to the spreading unrest. To right-wing KMT leaders this seemed further proof that the Communists were at work outside the KMT, agitating amongst the industrial proletariat as a prelude to the taking over of the leadership of the national struggle. The right-wing position, however, was still not strong enough for decisive action and, in fact, right-wing leaders were removed from office in January 1926 by the three most powerful men in the KMT, the Russian Borodin, Chiang Kai-shek, and Wang Ching-wei.

Chiang now found evidence of a plot against his life, led by the Communist captain of a KMT naval vessel in Whampoa harbour. He took action while Borodin was away from Canton. On 20 March 1926, Chiang placed the Russian military advisers under house arrest, closed trade unions and strike committees, and arrested all Communist political workers attached to army units. Wang Ching-wei, of the KMT left wing, 'retired' from office and later left the country.

Chiang, not yet in a position of overwhelming authority, was not ready for a final showdown with the Communists, as he needed their assistance and that of the Russians in his forthcoming campaign against the northern warlords. Moscow believed that this campaign would deal a decisive blow to Western influence in China and would leave a clear field for Communist propaganda in the countryside as a prelude to a seizure of power. Any Communists, therefore, who refused to cooperate with the KMT were expelled from the CPC as Trotskyite deviationists. Confused by a contradictory policy forced upon them by Russia, the Chinese Communists were swept to destruction in Chiang's drive to the north, though, as the KMT forces moved triumphantly forward, Communist agitators preceded them with anti-capitalist and anti-imperialist propaganda. In Shanghai and Hankow, Communist-led labour unions organised crippling strikes. In March 1927, Communists in Shanghai tried to prevent Chiang's National Revolutionary Army from entering the city. In April, Wang Ching-wei reached Shanghai via Moscow, with the hope of uniting the Communists and the KMT under his own leadership. Unable to agree with Chiang on the treatment of the Communists, though receiving his support as leader of the KMT, Wang left Shanghai accompanied by the leader of the CPC, Ch'en Tu-hsiu – the father of Chou En-lai – for the new Nationalist capital at Wuhan. Now, in Shanghai, *agents provocateurs* recruited by Chiang from underworld gangs were used to foment a rising by the labour unions, which was then bloodily crushed by KMT forces. The leader of the gangs was rewarded with the presidency of the Anti-Opium League, an innocuous-seeming appointment which was in fact a licence for legal drug-smuggling and its resulting profit.

Attempts by the CPC to seize control elsewhere were defeated, and by 1928 its leaders had been driven into the mountainous country between Honan and Kiangsi province or into exile. The sixth congress of the party symbolised the end of the Communist attempt to win hold of the nationalist movement, for it was held, not upon the soil of China, but in faraway Moscow. A white terror against anyone suspected of Communist sympathies spread over the new China. Chiang became a military dictator, but was still not strong enough to do without allies altogether. He found them, in the first place, by making peace with the bankers and industrialists on the one hand, and the land-owning classes on the other. Rather vague promises of land reform had been incorporated in the KMT programme by Sun Yat-sen; these still remained official policy, but Chiang made no attempt to do anything about them. In the north, Chiang's position was still precarious, for the warlords were too strong to be defeated by a revolutionary army which had not yet consolidated its position in the rest of the country. The traditional pattern of bargaining now emerged. Secret negotiations, intrigues and assassinations replaced open warfare. But Chiang was still forced to tolerate

three of the warlords – Feng Yu-hsiang, the so-called 'Christian Marshal';
Yen Hsi-shan in Shansi; and Li Tsung-jen – and to confirm them in their
areas of influence. Negotiations with these rivals for power continued until
1936 and, though Chiang outmanoeuvred them, he was unable to suppress
them completely. Manchuria, which was under the control of the warlord
Chang Tso-lin – and, after his assassination by the Japanese, of his son
Chang Hsueh-liang – was outside Chiang's sphere of operations. In 1931
the country fell to the Japanese.

Between 1927 and 1937, it seemed that the KMT represented a genuine and
stable end-product of an equally genuine struggle for freedom – a struggle
directed not only against the old regime but, indirectly, against the Western
imperial powers and Japan, who had been responsible for the breakdown of
Chinese society. To the West, Chiang's sudden and decisive shift to the
right seemed a good augury, but to Japan – the chief legatee of the Western
imperialists – it foretold a new, united China capable of resisting the Japanese drive for empire. The movement northward of KMT forces had resulted
in attacks upon foreign concessions. KMT troops occupied the British enclaves at Hankow and Kiukang and, later, the British voluntarily surrendered their holdings at Amoy and Chinkiang. The International Settlement
in Shanghai, however, was not abandoned but was defended, on the capture
of the main part of the city, by some 30,000 foreign troops. Chinese were
later admitted into the councils which administred the Settlements at Shanghai and Amoy, the French concession at Shanghai, and the British at Tientsin. In December 1929, China, convinced that extra-territoriality could be
abolished by her own unilateral action, declared it would be so on 1
January 1930; but the actual assumption of jurisdiction was not to take place
until 1 January 1932. When that date arrived, the retrocession of the Settlements was further delayed by the Japanese attack upon Manchuria. Nevertheless, to most Chinese, the KMT revolution appeared to be winning back
the dignity that had been shattered by the onslaughts of the imperial powers.

Chiang, realising that the assumption of the administration by revolutionary means could not by itself recreate the old unity of China, began the
search for a new ethical code to fill the void. Marxism offered such a creed
and, as we have seen, one remarkably well fitted to appeal to the pattern of
Chinese thought and behaviour. Chiang found his answer in his own peculiar personality – and odd combination of Protestant Christian and sincere
Confucian. The result was the dull and uninspiring idealism of the 'New
Life Movement' – a revival of the four virtues of Confucianism, those of

Etiquette, Justice, Integrity and Conscientiousness, allied with a puritan conception of 'clean living'. This static, negative ideology sat ill upon the shoulders of KMT officials, as corrupt and hedonistic as any in the old China. The new philosophy was viewed by progressive minds as an insult. It seemed both old-fashioned and shallow – a dubious morality rather than an inspiring philosophy. By encouraging the familial virtues of the Confucian-ist ethic, the New Life Movement destroyed the prestige and power of the state and, in a new form, re-erected the dual standards of the old China in which public and political behaviour was placed below the interests of the family. Though the New Life Movement collapsed of its own inertia, the regime continued in its belief that relatives were more important than the mass of the citizens. The more progessive of China's youth turned toward the universal ethic of Marxism. The KMT rapidly divorced itself from the in-tellectuals and chose to ignore the peasant. The leadership of the struggle for freedom at the moment of Japanese aggression seemed to be moving into the hands of the Communists, though for a while the KMT and the CPC were to form an uneasy alliance against the common enemy.

II

ASIA AND THE SOVIET UNION

As we have seen, the Russian Revolution of 1917 added a new and unique factor to the problems of colonial Asia. In particular, the new Russia seemed to offer an ally in revolution and, furthermore, an ally untainted with liberal-democratic associations. The nascent nationalisms of Asia had, until then, emerged not only as a reaction against the capitalist West but in the terms of Western capitalist society, and their aims were, fundamentally, to grasp the institutions of the West in order to control, and benefit from, Western science and economic structures. To most colonial Asians, Russia from 1917 onwards seemed no longer a Western imperialist power but a new, es-sentially Asian nation whose involvement in Asia's struggle for freedom was not adopted in order to replace Western colonialism with Russian colonial-ism, as the Tsars had done, but to abolish racial superiority and to recognise the Asian peoples as equals. For the first time, the great land-mass of Asiatic Russia was no longer the head of a spear whose shaft was in Europe. Now, the new Russia looked westwards to the heartlands of the imperial powers. Here was an ally whose aim was a world revolution against the oppressors, and who was prepared to fight not in the slums of Calcutta or the alleys of Peking, but in the squares and streets of Paris and London. Furthermore, the new Russian leaders insisted upon the importance of Asia in the world struggle. Had not Lenin maintained 'that the result of the struggle depends in the last resort on the fact that Russia, India and China... form a gigantic majority of the population of the world'?

Unfortunately for the Russian leaders, and for Asian Communists, the classic structures of Marxist ideas did not appear to fit the Asian scene. In Asia, apart from Japan, industrial proletariats hardly existed at all, and most of the already active nationalist movements were, from a Marxist angle, reactionary. From an ideological point of view there could be no doubt that Communists should have supported only the 'genuine' forces of social revolution however weak they might be, and helped them to destroy such nationalist movements as did not conform to Marxist criteria of worth, before going on to the struggle against colonial 'despotism'. However, the ideals of the Communist International and the policy of the Soviet government could never quite coincide, and the *realpolitik* of the Russian leaders often appeared to Communists as cynical and opportunist. The main aim of the Soviet government, as distinct from the Comintern, was to cause trouble for the Western powers and to support any nationalist organisation that appeared to have any chance of success, even if by doing so it meant betraying local Communists. The story of Soviet relations with China has already been lightly touched upon, and a further view is given in the section on 'Communism in China' (p. 312 ff). Here, we are concerned with the Soviet support of nationalist movements in the possessions of the major colonial powers, and in Japan, which the Soviet Union considered to be part of the capitalist bloc of imperialist countries, and against which Communist-inspired and dominated nationalist resistance movements were directed during the 1941–5 war in Asia.

Of all the Eastern countries, Japan seemed to offer the best chance of success for a revolution based, as in Russia, upon an industrial proletariat. The expansion of Japanese industry during the war of 1914–18 had not only resulted in a concentration of workers in urban areas, but also in the establishment of labour organisations. The leaders of the first trade unions were moderates, believing in the cooperation of worker and employer. Despite this, and the existence of anti-strike legislation, agitation *had* resulted in strikes, the most important of which were by railwaymen in Tokyo in July 1919, and by dockworkers in Kobe in September of the same year. By the early 'twenties, a small working-class movement and the growing interest of students in Marxist Socialism was producing what seemed on the surface to be a reasonable analogy with the situation in Russia at the beginning of the century. In 1922, the Communist Party of Japan was founded.

The political tolerance of the early postwar years was not to last, and in June 1923 the Japanese police arrested most of the Communist leaders. In the excitement caused by the Tokyo earthquake of September of that year, and widespread rumours that Korean nationalists assisted by Japanese Communists had plotted to set up a revolutionary government, the police made large-scale arrests of left-wing elements some of whom were murdered after their arrest. The party, in a crisis of pessimism, dissolved itself in the spring of 1924.

By a directive of the fifth Congress of the Comintern, held in June 1924, a Workers' and Peasants' Party was founded in Japan in 1925 as part of the Peasant International (*Krestintern*), by which Soviet leaders hoped to organise countries with only small industrial proletariats. These peasant movements were conspicuously unsuccessful in eastern Europe, and only in China – where conditions were favourable – did they have any effect. In Japan, the new party had little or no success with the peasants, but some with the workers, and the authorities almost immediately banned it. In March 1926, under Comintern pressure, the Japanese Communist party was re-founded. Its success as a propagandist organisation was seen in the Japanese general election of 1928, the first held under universal manhood suffrage, when the left-wing parties polled nearly half a million votes. The results of the election so alarmed the government that it took drastic police action against Communists which led to the final break-up of the party leadership in October and November 1932. From that time onwards, Communism was a negligible force in Japan, for new organisations, more in tune with the traditional structure of Japanese society, were to canalise anti-capitalist emotions. Out of the mass discontent of the 'thirties, extreme nationalist organisations, led in many cases by army officers of peasant origin, combined the hatred of urban capitalists as exploiters of the peasant with vague slogans of social reform set in an appeal to the old virtues of traditional Japan. Such a combination had more than an edge on the intellectual and alien beliefs of international Marxism.

In colonial Asia proper, the social structure in India and Java offered little ground for the Marxist seed, though in the latter country intellectuals returning from Europe brought with them Socialist ideas. The first Javanese

Socialist party was in fact established by a Dutch Socialist, Hendrik Snee-vliet, a former teacher. In 1919, it became the Communist Party of Indonesia (PKI). The main influence of the Communists in Java was in the penetra-tion of the principal nationalist movement, Sarekat Islam, an essentially Muslim organisation. Again, the conflict between Comintern ideology and Soviet policy resulted in 1921 in a breakaway by the PKI, over its unwilling-ness to accept the discipline of Islam, followed by an attempt on instructions from Moscow to form a common nationalist front – over which negotiations broke down in 1923. The PKI then attempted to found a Workers' and Peasants' Party, and finally assumed the leadership of anti-Dutch risings in Java in 1925, and Sumatra in the following year. After the suppression of these revolts the Communist party had little influence upon the course of the nationalist movement until after the end of the war in 1945.

The predominance of 'bourgeois nationalists' in India, usually middle-class liberals and small capitalists, made it difficult for Communists to direct their appeal at the leadership of the Indian National Congress, a coterie embracing representatives of practically every opinion except that of the new class of industrial workers. Congress itself had realised that the increasingly expanding urban proletariat needed organisation. This was supplied by the establishment in 1920 of the All-India Trade Union Congress, associated with the Indian National Congress and with leaders who were bourgeois Socialists on the British pattern. Nevertheless, the A-I TUC was influenced to some extent by Marxist groups. In 1924, the Communist Party of India was founded, and two years later – in common with other Communists in predominantly agrarian countries – organised a Workers' and Peasants' Party. In 1927, at the Cawnpore congress of the A-I TUC, the Communists gained control of the trade union movement and, in consequence, caught the eye of British authority. A series of special measures passed in 1929 resulted in the arrest of several Communist leaders, including three English-men who had been engaged in industrial agitation in Bombay and Calcutta. Their trial dragged on for four years. In 1929, the trade unions split, leaving only a small body of workers under direct Communist control. The peculiar nature of the Indian nationalist movement, government suppression, and lack of widespread support among intellectuals and workers kept the Com-munist party out of the main stream of nationalist activity.

In all the countries of colonial Asia, Communism had very little effect upon the struggle for freedom before the war with Japan. This was mainly due to the essentially democratic aims of the nationalist movements. The slogans of their revolution were Western in origin. Furthermore, the enemy was an alien ruler and not one who had emerged from, or was in any way part of, the indigenous structure of society. Because of this, no element of the class struggle as seen in Russia entered into colonial nationalist movements. Though nationalists were happy to use the Soviet Union and the Comintern as bogeys, they were quick to realise that their own position was threatened by Communist activity, and soon dropped both Moscow and their own Communists when they had achieved their aims.

The rise of Nazi Germany finally led to a change of policy by the Soviet Union. Initially, Hitler, despite his anti-Communist tendencies, appeared to hate the West as much as did the Soviet leaders. But by the end of 1934 it was clear that Germany was hostile to the Soviet Union. This caused an apparent reversal of Soviet relations with the Western powers. The emphasis was now put upon the menace of Fascism, and the Soviet Union entered into treaty relations with France and Czechoslovakia, and became a member of that same League of Nations which it once denounced as 'an international organisation of capitalists for the systematic exploitation of the working peoples of the earth'.

At the seventh Congress of the Comintern, held in Moscow in 1935, the tactic of the 'popular front' was announced, and with it a new period. In collaboration with anti-Fascists, whatever their political complexion of Asia, increased activity amongst intellectuals and workers resulted. The congress was told by the secretary of the Comintern, Dimitrov, that the interests of the international proletariat could now best be served by promoting national forms of the class struggle, and by adapting tactics to particular situations. The new policy appealed to young Indian intellectuals, though without much practical effect. In Japan, a Japan Masses party was formed in 1937 and received a considerable number of votes in the elections held in March of that year. In December, however, the party was suppressed by the Japanese government. In Indonesia, a legal party of the left, the Indonesian Peoples' Movement (Gerindo) was founded in April 1937, and followed a popular front line even to the extent of regarding the Dutch as allies against the greater enemies of Fascism and Japanese imperialism.

The Nazi-Soviet pact of August 1939 saw the abandonment of the popular front in favour of the supreme interests of the Soviet Union, whose leaders were fully convinced of the inevitability of war and the probable consequences to the Soviet Union of its entanglements with the West. Stalin believed that Germany might first attack Russia, whose armed forces were in no condition to mount an adequate defence. Furthermore, Russia's long-term policies would be better suited if the capitalist powers and Germany exhausted themselves in a long and indecisive war. In the colonial territories of Asia, the consequences of the new policy were merely the overt intensification of anti-imperialist agitation, though on too small a scale to have much effect.

The German attack on Russia in 1941 changed an imperialist war into the Great Patriotic War of the Soviet Union, and the aim of every Communist to that of assisting Russia and her allies. In Europe this meant that Communists joined the resistance movements. In Asia, the situation was somewhat different. For the orthodox nationalist movements of colonial Asia, the arrival of the Japanese was greeted as a liberation from Western imperialism rather than as an extension of Japanese Fascism. In Burma and Indonesia, nationalists expected that they would gain their independence at the hands of the Japanese and despite their subsequent disillusionment were only willing to cooperate with their former rulers when it became obvious that they would defeat Japan. Communists forced to help the Soviet Union when that country was attacked by Germany were also obliged to help her allies – which in Asia were Britain and Holland, the main targets of the nationalist struggle. Only in Malaya was there a genuine resistance movement against the Japanese from the very outset. There, the Communists were almost entirely Chinese and had little or no support from the Malayans themselves. After June 1941 (the date of the German attack upon Russia), they supported the British, and their leaders were released from imprisonment shortly before the Japanese invasion. On the occupation of Malaya, the Communists formed a Malayan Anti-Japanese Army and a political party, the Malayan Peoples' Anti-Japanese Union. Though never large, it had considerable nuisance value and was supplied with arms by the Allied South East Asia Command. The experience gained was later used to considerable effect against the returned colonial administration.

Elsewhere, Communists achieved much less. In the Philippines they played a leading part in the organisation of the Anti-Japanese Peoples' Army. Though their resistance effort was very small, valuable experience in guerilla organisation, propaganda, and the formation of cells, was gained. In Indonesia, most of the nationalist leaders cooperated with the Japanese, but some resistance was offered by Communist or left-wing Socialist elements. In Burma, conservative nationalists and the younger quasi-Socialists supported the Japanese and joined the puppet government of Dr Ba Maw established in August 1943. Early in 1945, as British forces poured into northern Burma, a leftish nationalist, Aung San – who was defence minister in the puppet government, and also commanded the Japanese-sponsored Burma National Army – agreed to support Communist-led resistance groups against the Japanese. Through them, contact was made with the allied command, who had been supplying the Communists with arms. A new political body, on popular front lines, was created under Communist inspiration and called the Anti-Fascist People's Freedom League. Communist influence in it, however, was comparatively small.

In Indo-China, an Annamite resistance group was established by the veteran Communist Ho Chi Minh in 1941, which in 1944 agreed, under Chinese Nationalist pressure, to cooperate with the KMT-inspired party, the Dong Minh Hoi, and the old orthodox nationalist organisation, the VNQDD, which had led the rebellion against the French in 1930. On the replacement of the Vichy French administration by the Japanese in March 1945, Free French, Viet-Minh, and Chinese action was more or less coordinated.

At the end of the war, Communist groups were still numerically small, but all had acquired organisational experience and, above all, a measure of the prestige of resistance. Their future, however, depended not so much upon themselves as upon the attitude towards nationalist movements in general that was to be held by the colonial powers once more back in control with their strength enhanced, so it seemed, by total victory.

*   *   *

The weakness of Communist movements in colonial Asia was not a matter of great immediate interest to the Soviet Union. The function of these movements was not to *make* the revolution but to fill in time in the most destructive manner. The revolution itself would inevitably come. The Western powers were doomed by the very nature of capitalism's inner contradictions, and should their successors follow the same bourgeois pattern, they too were lost by the same thesis. This belief accounts for the lack of support and the shifty attitude of Soviet leaders to the indigenous Communist leaders of Asia. The West, as we have seen, was no longer buoyant upon a wave of constructive optimism. Its policies were day-to-day postponements of the time of reckoning. Britain, in particular, caught in the propaganda of its own liberal purpose, could see her only satisfaction in the British pattern of the legatees, as an ageing father sees immortality in the physical resemblances of his sons. The Soviet Union, on the other hand, looked forward to a golden age, and its plans were consequently long-range and operated in depth. History was on their side, though not for the same reasons their historical materialism supplied.

The great depression of the 'thirties seemed to the Russian leaders the inexorable symptom of the collapse of capitalism. Any ally, even if it meant the betrayal of orthodox Communists, must be seized upon to assist it. At the same time, the heartland of the world revolution must at all costs be safeguarded. From the Japanese invasion of Manchuria in 1931, a direct consequence of the world economic crisis, Russia's primary aim was the protection of her interests in the Far East against Japanese expansion. Japanese activity in Manchuria, now renamed Manchukuo, the building up of military and air forces, and the expansion of war industries seemed to be directed against the Soviet Union. Russian policy towards Japan became a mixture of concession and belligerence, which upon at least two occasions almost led to war.

In 1935, after two years of negotiation and despite Chinese protests, Russia sold the Chinese Eastern Railway to Manchukuo – though, in reality, to the Japanese – and negotiated an alliance with Outer Mongolia. As Japan extended her control along the northern frontiers of China, border problems increased in an area where no real demarcation had ever been attempted. Border incidents proliferated and, on one occasion, beginning in May 1939, large-scale operations involving tanks, aircraft and artillery resulted according to Russian sources in Japanese-Manchukuoan casualties exceeding 50,000 in number and more than 9,000 on the Russian-Mongolian side.

Naturally, the Soviet Union favoured a deepening of Japan's involvement in China, and the outbreak of the Sino-Japanese war in 1937 was received with considerable relief in Moscow. Under Russian pressure (see p. 317 f), a popular front alliance was promoted between the Chinese Communists and the KMT. Loans were made to China and war materials supplied in ever-increasing quantities. Russia extended her economic control of Sinkiang and built new highways into China. Instructors and 'volunteer' pilots were sent to assist the KMT air force, and Russian officers were attached as advisers to Chinese army commands. In doing this, the Russians hoped to prolong the war and wreck both Japan and the KMT in the process. Japanese leaders saw the 'China Incident' as merely a step towards the final battle with Russia. As General Tojo expressed it in a letter to the general staff: 'From the point of view of our military preparations against Soviet Russia... we should deliver a blow first of all against the Nanking regime to get rid of the menace at our back'. The Japanese foreign minister, Matsuoka, boasted 'we will plant our flag in the Urals'. Russia's reply was to increase her forces in the Far East and to make them independent of supplies from western Russia. Russian colonisation of the maritime province of Siberia was stepped up, and the NKVD controlled hundreds of thousands of slave labourers spread out in camps from Khabarovsk to the Pacific on the construction of rail, roads, airfields and military installations.

The 'incident' on the Mongolian-Manchukuo border in May 1939 already mentioned, coupled with continuous irritation over fishery rights and Japanese oil concessions in Sakhalin, seemed to be leading towards an outbreak of war between Japan and the Soviet Union. Until this time, border incidents had been declared by both sides to be nominally between Manchukuo and Outer Mongolia, with Japan and Russia only involved because of treaty obligations with the conflicting parties. But in September 1939, this fiction was dropped and the Japanese general who had suffered defeat while commanding the Manchukuoan forces against the Russian-led Outer Mongolian army issued a proclamation declaring that the Japanese army must avenge the defeat. On this occasion, the bellicosity of the local commander was not supported by the government in Tokyo. This was mainly due to the fall of the Hiranuma cabinet in August 1939 because of a popular revulsion against Germany, Japan's ally under the Anti-Comintern Pact, who had, without informing her, concluded a non-aggression pact with the Soviet Union. The new cabinet of General Abe was averse to any unassisted action against the Russians. In its turn, the Soviet government, impressed by the German reduction of Poland and intent upon claiming its promised share of the loot, was also anxious to avoid conflict on a wider scale. An armistice agreement was signed between the Japanese ambassador in Moscow and the Russian foreign minister, which came into effect on 16 September 1939. The agreement called for a standstill of their respective armies and the appointment of a boundary commission representing the four interested parties. Though some progress was made in the settling of existing problems, no real settlement of the many points of conflict between the two countries seemed within reasonable sight of conclusion. The reason for the genuine though not openly expressed unwillingness of the Japanese to approach a final agreement with the Russians lay outside the immediate area of conflict. Ever since the German-Soviet non-aggression pact, the German government had been putting increasing pressure upon the Japanese to conclude a similar agreement themselves. The result of such a rapprochement would be to release Japanese forces for an attack upon British and Dutch possessions in south Asia. Against such an agreement was ranged the traditional Japanese fear of Russia, hatred of Communism, and feelings of resentment against the German betrayal of the spirit of the anti-Comintern alliance.

The spectacular German advance through the Low Countries, the defeat of France, and the possibility that Britain might be induced to surrender, opened up exciting vistas to the Japanese. A new cabinet took office and signed a new agreement with Germany and Italy in September 1940. On Japanese insistence, a special clause was inserted providing that 'the existing political relations between each of the three treaty powers and the Soviet Union should not be affected by the treaty'.

After the signing of the treaty, Germany approached the Soviet Union with a suggestion that she should join in and help to divide up the world between the four powers. Ribbentrop, the Nazi foreign minister, in discussion with Molotov, the Soviet foreign minister, at Berlin in November 1940, urged the conclusion of a non-aggression pact with Japan. This suggestion came to nothing, as Soviet counter-proposals over spheres of influence in eastern Europe and the Baltic convinced Hitler that there would be no purpose in extending the treaty to Russia. In the meanwhile, direct negotiations with the Japanese in Moscow had continued rather fitfully, but had been bogged down by the perennial question of Japanese concessions in northern Sakhalin.

The new Japanese foreign minister, Matsuoka, unaware that Hitler was almost ready to give the word for the attack upon Russia, left for Berlin in March 1941 to find out why the Tri-Partite Pact had not been extended to the Soviet Union. On his way, he passed through Moscow and had an interview with Stalin. During his stay in Berlin, Matsuoka received a number of hints that Germany intended to attack Russia and that Japan would get what she wanted from her when Russia had been defeated by Germany, for, as Ribbentrop remarked, 'should Russia one day take up an attitude which could be interpreted as a threat against Germany, the Fuehrer would dash Russia to pieces'. Ribbentrop, however, did not reveal to Matsuoka that the decision to attack Russia had already been made.

Matsuoka returned to Moscow in the early part of April and re-opened negotiations for a non-aggression pact and for the sale of northern Sakhalin to Japan — a proposal which had been regularly made and as regularly spurned. Matsuoka then dropped the non-aggression pact and asked for a simple pact of neutrality. On 13 April 1941, this pact was signed. In it, each power pledged neutrality should the other 'become the object of hostilities on the part of one or several third powers'. The duration of the pact was to be five years, and it was accompanied by a Frontier Declaration in which mutual guarantees of territorial integrity were exchanged on behalf of Man-chukuo and the Mongolian Peoples' Republic. The signing of the pact was followed by the conclusion of a trade agreement on 11 June.

On the outbreak of war between Russia and Germany in June 1941, pressure was put upon Japan to attack the Soviet Union in the rear. But German-Japanese relations had never been close. Japan distrusted German intentions in Asia, and Hitler's theories of Nordic racial superiority hardly included the Japanese amongst the Herrenvolk.[1] Furthermore, Japan was intoxicated with her role as liberator of Asia, and her hate was almost en-tirely concentrated upon the Western powers. South-east Asia was seething with discontent and the way to a new Japanese empire was open. The main-tenance of the pact of neutrality was to the advantage of both sides. It left Japan free for her drive to the south and, anyway, she was assured of a Ger-man victory in the West. For the Soviet Union, the advantages were rather more of a long-term nature, for when the war ended Japanese imperialism had been destroyed and the Soviet Union had merely to move into the vacuum left by its collapse. The pact of neutrality can now be seen, in the light of later events, to have been the foundation stone of the Communist power in the new Asia that was to follow the end of the war in 1945.

III

THE EXPANSION OF JAPAN

From her hopes of the first World War as an opportunity to achieve her manifest destiny in China, Japan had emerged disillusioned, fobbed off, so it seemed, with some ex-German possessions in the northern Pacific. Furthermore, the peace treaty and the Covenant of the League of Nations had made it quite clear that whatever her standing as a great power (she was given a permanent seat on the council of the League) the West was still not prepared to consider Japan an equal. To the racial prejudice of the colo-

---

[1] Hitler's reactions to the Japanese victories over the white men in Asia were a mixture of sat-isfaction and grief. According to an entry dated 30 January 1942 in *Goebbels' Diaries* (London, 1948): 'The Fuehrer profoundly regrets the heavy losses by the white race in east Asia, but that isn't our fault'.

nial powers was now added an element of fear – the sorcerer's apprentice seemed to have learned all the tricks.

In 1921, Japan took part in the Washington Conference which resulted in a naval treaty fixing a ratio of 5 : 5 : 3 for the tonnage respectively of Great Britain, the United States and Japan. In return for Japan's acceptance of this, she received an assurance that no major naval installations would be built in the Philippines or at Hong Kong. The conference also resulted in the ending of the Anglo-Japanese alliance and its replacement by a worthless Four Power Treaty between the British Empire, France, the United States and Japan. The new treaty was devised as a suitable excuse for Britain to rid herself of what was now an embarrassing entanglement with Japan, for the United States, emerging as a major world power, considered the Anglo-Japanese alliance a threat to her own foreign policy in the Far East. For Japan, the abrogation of the treaty removed one of the permanent strains in Japanese policy, and terminated any possibility of British influence in Tokyo. The new treaty seriously weakened the security of British possessions in the Far East, as well as that of Australia and New Zealand. In London, it was thought that the new naval base to be built at Singapore would offset any loss at Hong Kong. Two decades later, these sanguine hopes were to be irretrievably shattered.

Japanese agreement at the Washington Conference to the return of Shantung to China, and the addition of Japan's signature to a nine-power guarantee of China's territorial integrity, seemed to be ushering in a new era in Sino-Japanese relations. In Japan itself, it appeared that liberal elements were smoothing away the bellicosities of the past. In 1924, military expenditure was cut and the army's strength reduced to four divisions. The great business cartels (the Zaibatsu) that had grown up inside the structure of Japanese industry approved of both a reduction in armaments and a policy of good relations with China. But though the army had been reduced in size, a new scheme of compulsory military training had been inaugurated. A widening of the franchise to include all males over the age of twenty-one seemed to be offset by the extension of police powers to control 'dangerous thoughts'. In foreign affairs, a settlement was reached with Soviet Russia and, in 1925, Japan evacuated the northern part of the island of Sakhalin which she had occupied at the time of the Russian Revolution. In the United States, Japan had received in 1924 further proof of her racial inequality, in the passage of legislation prohibiting the immigration of orientals, including Japanese. In order to ensure the passing of the Bill, anti-Asian agitation had reached virulent levels, particularly in California. Similar legislation was passed in Australia and New Zealand, though the prohibition was disguised behind a reading test which effectively excluded the Japanese. Once again, in her hatred of Westerners for their racial arrogance, Japan could add to her stature as the 'friend of Asia', and rally to her cause those who suffered the rule of the white man. Passion and prejudice on all sides assisted the revival of militarism in Japan.

The success of the Kuomintang in China seemed to be the portent of a new united country, threatening Japanese interests in south Manchuria and, possibly, taking a leaf out of Japan's book, going through a Westernising revolution which would make of China a serious commercial rival. In 1927, as the KMT forces surged northwards, an economic crisis struck Japan. A number of banks failed and many small businesses were ruined. The collapse, however, of the 'little man' brought new profit to the Zaibatsu whose interests dominated the two principal parties. In the minds of the people, parliamentary government became disastrously associated with big business, and when the great wave of world economic depression struck Japan in 1930 immense numbers of Japanese were ready to turn away from tarnished democracy and respond to the heady appeal of a forceful nationalism which seemed to offer to ordinary people some participation in the future of the country, even if only upon the most emotional of levels.

During the period 1927–30, under the pressures of dissatisfaction, extreme political and economic tendencies had grown up amongst junior officers in the army. Initially, these took the form of the organisation of a secret society dedicated to the planning of a coup d'état. The authority of the government in Tokyo now became of little consequence to junior officers stationed in Manchuria, a hot-bed of nationalist extremism in the army. In 1928, the Chinese warlord of Manchuria, Chang Tso-lin, was killed by a bomb which exploded in the railway carriage in which he was travelling. His murder was believed in China to have been instigated by the Japanese. After the end of the Pacific war it became known from Japanese archives that Chang had in fact been murdered by officers of the Japanese Kwangtung army – the garrison in south Manchuria – and that his death was to be the signal for a military coup in which the Japanese army was to seize the city of Mukden and, later, probably the southern half of Manchuria. The conspiracy failed because it lacked the support of the commanding generals. The desire of the government and the emperor for the punishment of those concerned was frustrated by the chief of the general staff and other senior officers, who refused to take any action which might harm the prestige of the army. This freedom from punishment assured extremist elements that they had little to fear from either parliament or the monarchy.

The year 1930, however, showed this confidence to be somewhat premature. The terms of the London Naval Treaty of that year, fixing the ratio of Japanese vessels to those of the United States, was forced upon a rebellious general staff by the government. The army feared that a similar challenge to its authority might soon be made. Bitter protests by right-wing elements, supported by the army, led to the attempted assassination of the prime minister. A military conspiracy to overthrow the government was only abandoned because the minister of war, General Ugaki, refused to be a party to it. Though the plot became known to the government, no attempt was made to punish any of those involved, and the whole affair was hushed up. Again, extremists in the Kwangtung army were to take the initiative. On 18 September 1931, a little less than six months after the abandonment of the *coup* in Tokyo, the Kwangtung army took upon itself the authority to occupy Mukden. The cabinet in Tokyo was not informed until after the city had been occupied, and was thus presented with a *fait accompli*.

At the League of Nations, Japanese representatives referred to the affair as an 'incident', a phrase which was to dominate Sino-Japanese conflicts during the 'thirties, and on 30 September 1931, Japan accepted a resolution that her forces should withdraw to their previously-held positions in northern Manchuria. Ignoring the government in Tokyo, the Kwangtung army, instead of retiring, continued its advance until almost all of Manchuria came under its control. In 1932, the state of Manchukuo was established as an allegedly independent country, and as its head of state the Japanese appointed Pu Yi, the last emperor of the Manchu dynasty in China – who, after being driven from Peking in 1924, had taken refuge in the Japanese concession in Tientsin. Chinese reaction to the 'Manchurian incident' was at first limited to a commercial boycott of Japanese goods, but early in 1932 fighting broke out in Shanghai between Chinese troops and Japanese marines, who finally occupied part of the city. Nanking, the Chinese capital, was also attacked by Japanese gunboats, and it was not until May that peace was restored. All the 'incidents' had taken place without the breaking off of diplomatic relations or any declaration of war.

These incidents produced little positive reaction from the Western powers. Britain, angered by anti-British agitation in China, was not disposed to do much about her troubles. Britain was unwilling to involve herself in peripheral interests when, at the centre of her empire, in India, she was entangled in her own problems. Japan did not seem at that stage a threat to the heart-land of Britain's overseas empire. Long before these incidents, Britain had already *emotionally* withdrawn from China; physically, her presence there was not big enough to warrant a war with Japan. Once again, it was left to the United States to take up China's cause, though with little immediate success. Nevertheless, in March 1932, under American initiative, the League of Nations appointed neutral negotiators to attempt a settlement of the Shanghai affair, and Japanese forces evacuated the city in May of the same year. Manchuria, however, was a different matter altogether, and after the adoption of the report of a League committee of enquiry in February 1933, Japan withdrew from membership of the League in the following month. The League, for all its vaunted promise as a peace-maker, did nothing about it, its authority blown away on the hot air of empty rhetoric. Japan flouted the League and remained unpunished. Italy and Germany learned the lesson. The occupation of Mukden was the beginning of a road that led through Abyssinia, Munich and Poland, to Pearl Harbour.

Despite the consolidation of Manchukuo and its very considerable eco-nomic expansion, a threat to Japanese domination remained in the prepon-derantly Chinese origin of the population. When Pu Yi was raised from head of the state to the rank of emperor in 1934, under the reign-title of Kang Tê, the Chinese majority in the population was instructed to consider itself as Manchu. This administrative measure hardly affected the Chinese attitude, and the Japanese became more and more concerned with hostile elements on both sides of the Manchukuoan frontier. In 1933, Jehol, the capital of Inner Mongolia, had been absorbed into Manchukuo. In 1934, with Japanese support, Mongol princes to the west of Jehol had set up an autonomous government in Inner Mongolia. Their authority to do this had been extracted from the reluctant Chinese, who were still nominally their suzerain, under the threat of Japanese expansion, though the new government retained Chinese advisers. KMT army units, however, still remained in the area, and border incidents were common. In 1935, Japan demanded the removal of these forces, and Japanese advisers were appointed in the place of the Chinese.

At the same time, Japan was moving troops into the north-east of China proper in areas where the hold of the Nanking government was still feeble. In May 1933, after Japanese insistence that the government of the province of Hopei should be less hostile to them, their forces had advanced to within a few miles of Tientsin and Peking. By the terms of a truce, the northern parts of Hopei became virtually a demilitarised zone and, in 1935, the Japanese forced the Nanking government to withdraw its troops from the whole province. Later in the year, it became clear that the Japanese intended to sever a large part of northern China from any sort of control by the Nanking government. It was also obvious that the Japanese intended to use the extension of their power in the northern areas as a step towards the establishment of her control over the whole of China.

In China itself, the Kuomintang government, convinced of the inevitable outbreak of full-scale conflict, sought for time to unify the country and to prepare for its defence. To achieve this, it even attempted to suppress patriotic organisations whose activities it believed might incite the Japanese to take reprisals. These attempts to hold off the inevitable had little effect, for 'incidents' were spreading as Japanese bellicosity increased. Early in July 1937 a minor clash took place at the Marco Polo Bridge near Peking, between Chinese troops and a Japanese force out on manoeuvres in an area where it had no right to be. This comparatively trivial incident appeared to be on the point of settlement – by the withdrawal of Chinese troops – when the Japanese Kwangtung army sent reinforcements to the area and demanded the punishment of Chinese officers, who, it alleged, were responsible for the incident, and the suppression of anti-Japanese organisations. The government in Tokyo tried to resist the slide into war, failed, and resigned. Japan was now involved so deeply in northern China that she could not withdraw. The younger army officers felt that the time had come for a final showdown. The Chinese, too, realised that the days of appeasement were over.

It is possible that the Japanese army hoped to confine the struggle to northern China and to establish their rule there before moving on against the rest of the country, but later in July Chinese militia in Tungchow, between Peking and Tientsin, formerly under Japanese control, killed their Japanese officers and murdered over two hundred Japanese and Korean civilians. On 27 July, the Japanese captured Peking, and throughout China infuriated mobs attacked Japanese consulates and citizens. A wave of patriotic fervour made the Chinese more determined than ever in their belief that the time for concessions was over.

In August 1937, fighting broke out in Shanghai and three months later Chinese forces were compelled to evacuate the city. Officially, China and Japan were still at peace and an attempt by the helpless League of Nations to do something constructive by condemning Japan for violating the Nine-

Power Treaty was ignored by the Japanese. In December, Japanese forces moving up the valley of the Yangtse captured Nanking and celebrated it with an orgy of looting, butchery and rape. Though no news of this was allowed to leak into Japanese newspapers, the commander-in-chief of the forces in central China and two divisional commanders were recalled, as well as the reservists who were mainly responsible for the excesses. Just before the fall of Nanking, Japanese aircraft sank the *USS Panay* in the Yangtze, and Japanese artillery shelled the British gunboat, *Ladybird*. The British government, well launched by Neville Chamberlain upon its notorious policy of appeasement in Europe, offered its other cheek in the Far East and did not protest. An instant apology and offer of compensation by the Japanese avoided a clash with the United States.

The Japanese continued their advance and the KMT government retired westwards, first to Hankow, and then to Chungking. The Japanese now controlled most of the railways and the main ports, for, in October 1938, they had seized Canton. Attempts had been made, through the mediation of the German ambassador to China, to negotiate with Chiang Kai-shek, but the Japanese terms were too severe. After the capture of Canton, the Japanese prime minister, Prince Konoye, had declared that it was Japan's policy to establish a New Order in east Asia – a political, economic and cultural union between Japan, Manchukuo, and China. He also announced the terms of the Japanese peace offer. Chiang, publicly rejecting them, reiterated his determination to continue the struggle. The Japanese who had, in December 1937, organised a Provisional Government of the Republic of China in Peking, with the aid of anti-Kuomintang Chinese, now looked about for a national figure to head the administration. They found him in Wang Ching-wei, who, believing that the war could end only in a Japanese victory, fled, in 1939, from Chungking through Indo-China to Shanghai after his failure to convince Chiang that he should accept the Japanese peace offer. On 30 March 1940, a National government, headed by Wang, was established at Nanking and was claimed, by the Japanese, to be the only official government of China. By this time, the struggle seemed to have bogged down into a stalemate. The Japanese occupied those regions easily supplied from the Japanese mainland, and where modern weapons, particularly tanks and motorised artillery, could operate. The Chinese had withdrawn into more difficult terrain. Japan had in fact grossly underestimated the length of time the war would last, and now decided not to press forward with further conquests but to consolidate her positions, organise them economically as part of her New Order by direct expropriation and other methods, and wait for the Chungking government to collapse of exhaustion. Furthermore, other glittering prizes seemed to be waiting for her to take, as war had broken out in Europe.

Since the abrogation of the Anglo-Japanese alliance, the Japanese had looked upon Britain as a friend who, after sweet words, has suddenly become an enemy. During their activities in China, the Japanese had been very willing to obstruct Britain's representatives and economic interests, and took every opportunity to humiliate her nationals. If Japan was to launch her New Order on the pretence of 'Asia for the Asiatics', the principal object in the way of its achievement would certainly be Britain, who held the biggest stake in colonial Asia. By 1940, France and the Netherlands had fallen to a victorious Germany and Japan had entered into an agreement with the Vichy French authorities in Indo-China for the stationing there of Japanese troops, in order to blockade the southern frontier of Nationalist China. By the middle of 1940, it seemed that Germany would win the war. There would be no obstacle, except the United States, to prevent Japan from establishing her New Order over the whole of colonial Asia. In September 1940, the Anti-Comintern Pact between Japan and Germany which had been signed in 1936 – mainly, from the Japanese point of view, as an alliance against Russia – was extended into the Tri-Partite Axis Pact between Germany, Japan and Italy. In 1941 on the eve of the German attack upon Russia, the Japanese foreign minister concluded a neutrality pact with Stalin.

After the attack upon Russia, Japan's future policy became the subject of much intrigue and agitation in Tokyo. Some Japanese believed that the time was ideal for Japan to declare war on the Soviet Union and extend her territories to the north. But the whole tendency of Japanese expansion was now towards the south, towards the petroleum of the Dutch East Indies and the rice-bowl of Malaya and Burma. Japan was now completely intoxicated with the idea of her destiny as the liberator of Asia. Against the fulfilment of this dream, the only opposition lay in the United States of America, still uncommitted to the war in Europe. Negotiations for a settlement of outstanding disagreements between the two countries continued. In them, neither side would concede anything that seemed of value to the other. Finally, the Japanese broke negotiations by an attack upon the American fleet anchored at Pearl Harbour, Hawaii, on 7 December 1941. The same day, Japanese aircraft bombed the American-held island of Guam, American military installations in the Philippines, and the British naval base at

Singapore. The International Settlement at Shanghai was occupied and Japanese troops entered northern Malaya. Within six months, apart from the tolerated enclaves of French Indo-China and Portuguese Timor and Macao, colonial rule in South-east Asia was at an end and the victorious Japanese at the gates of India. The Philippines, Malaya, the Dutch East Indies, and Burma had rapidly fallen to the invader, in a disaster unparalleled in the history of Western domination in Asia.

IV

'CO-PROSPERITY' IN ASIA

As the Japanese commander accepted the surrender of British forces at Singapore in February 1942, he boasted with justifiable conviction that 'one hundred years from now, when Japanese children read in their history text-books about the War of Greater East Asia, they will not read of eventual victory or defeat – they will read only of the glorious march of an outnum-bered army through supposedly impassable jungles, rubber plantations and rice-fields, to defeat the cream of the Western imperialists'. At last it seemed that Asia had been freed from the grip of the colonial empires. Asia, as the Japanese slogan had it, was for the Asiatics. But was it?

The nature of Japanese hatred for the West was complex. Dislike of the colonial powers as oppressors of the Asian peoples played very little part in it. Japan, by its own exertions and by the astounding metamorphosis she had forced herself to go through from the Meiji restoration onwards, had avoided occupation by one or more of the imperialists. Her leaders never forgot her narrow escapes. When Japan felt the impetus of imperial expan-sion herself – the natural consequences, Marxists would maintain, of her Western capitalist structure – she was continually frustrated by the old co-lonial powers unless it suited the immediate advantage of imperial rivalries. Japan's position was that of an uninvited guest arriving late at the banquet, only to find that the choicest food was reserved for others. Her hatred of the West emerged from the unwillingness of the old colonial powers to accept Japan as an associate in their aggressions. This was not unreasonable, as the West was in fact already moving out of its imperialist period when Japan began her major attempts at overseas expansion. Japan's realisation of this and of the fact that, however monolithic and immovable the Western colo-nial structure appeared to be, it was actually in decay, made the situation even worse. In China, the West seemed no longer willing to engage in imperialist interventions yet was prepared to frustrate Japan in what she believed to be her legitimate destiny. To this was added the peculiar policy of the United States, whose emotional anti-colonialism seemed to the Japanese to be only a cloak for sinister designs. Japanese leaders, quite understand-ably and with some justification, could not consider American policy to-wards China as altruistic. The colonial powers and the United States seemed to represent two levels of imperialism: the old territorial expansion and the post-1870 investment imperialism.[1] As the postwar years went by, and petroleum products began to play a larger and larger role in industry and war, Japan began to realise that though she had escaped actual colonial oc-cupation she was rapidly becoming an economic dependency of the Western powers and of the United States, who, by the employment of oil sanctions, might bring the Japanese Empire to ruin.

When the Japanese moved into South-east Asia, they were extending the Japanese Empire so that it would include the oil-fields of the Dutch East Indies, which Japan had failed to obtain by negotiation after the fall of Hol-land. Nevertheless, the image of Japan as the liberator of colonial Asia was not entirely the invention of propaganda, for though her special position as the one non-occidental great power had buttressed her traditional belief in her superiority over other Asians, the attitude of the West in such matters as anti-Asian immigration restrictions and the abrogation of the Anglo-Jap-anese alliance stimulated her sense of kinship with the rest of oppressed Asia. At the same time, the immense goodwill that Japan had gained with colonial nationalists after her victories over Russia in the war of 1904–5, had been al-most completely dissipated by her imperialist adventures in China. There is no doubt that, had the Western powers acquiesced in the Japanese occupation of China, nothing would have been heard of the ideals of pan-Asia. These ideals, however, really did exist in Japan and there were a number of polit-icians and statesmen who genuinely saw Japan as a liberating power – a senior partner in a new group of nations rather than another colonial oppres-sor.

When it became clear, as early as 1928, that the Western powers had every intention of hindering Japan in her 'manifest destiny', the propaganda of 'Asia for the Asiatics' began to emerge. The appeal of such a slogan was

[1] Though, from the Japanese point of view, and probably from that of the Filipinos as well, the American presence in the Philippines was as much a colonial occupation as, say, that of the British in India.

obvious but it was the corollary that Japan had a divine mission as the leader
of Asia that was taken up by the military as the excuse for aggression. It was
all very well for Japanese statesmen to announce a New Order in Asia
'where there will be no conquest, no oppression, and no exploitation'. Behind this front, the military could get on with the serious business of extending the Japanese Empire. Even with the drive to the south against the
territories of the Western empires, when anti-colonialist propaganda was a
weapon of considerable power, the Japanese army saw it merely as a weapon
and treated colonial nationalists with contempt and abuse. The idea of a
Greater East Asia Co-Prosperity Sphere might well have worked.[1] The
peoples of South-east Asia did greet the Japanese as liberators and the political and economic cooperation envisaged by Japanese civilian ministers
and administrators had immense appeal for the newly freed nations. The
Japanese military saw to it that these ideas were given no chance of fulfilment.

By the end of May 1942, the Western powers had been swept from the
Eastern seas and the Japanese stood victorious upon the frontiers of India.
All her immediate objectives had been obtained in the short period of six
months. Plans for administering the miscellany of races in varied stages of
political and economic development, now under Japanese control, had already been laid down in broad outline at a Liaison Conference held in
Tokyo on 20 November 1941. The newly acquired territories were to have
an initial period of military administration in which local customs were to be
respected and existing administrative machinery used wherever possible.
Naturally, the armed forces were to have priority in the matter of food and
other supplies, and raw materials 'vital for national defence' were reserved
for Japan. Significantly, the conference was explicitly opposed to the encouragement of 'premature independence movements'. After the outbreak
of war, Japanese propaganda began to refer to the concept of the Greater
East Asia Co-Prosperity Sphere as a self-sufficient economic zone in which
all the peoples of liberated Asia would cooperate to their mutual advantage.
In a speech to the Japanese Diet on 22 January 1942, the then prime minister,
General Tojo, promised independence to Burma and the Philippines if they
were prepared to cooperate whole-heartedly in the new dispensation.

After the end of the war, a draft scheme for the organisation of the occu-

---

[1] And might still do so, for some form of 'Co-Prosperity Sphere' excluding Communist China
is today the only possible source of security and progress for the nations of the rimlands of Asia.
For a discussion of this, see my *The Problems of Asia*. London and New York, 1961.

pied territories was discovered and exhibited at the International Military Tribunal, Far East (Exhibit 1333a). This document gives some idea of Japan's ultimate intentions. From it, we see that Singapore, the Straits Settlements, British North Borneo, and Sarawak, were to be Japanese territory under a government-general established at Singapore. Apart from the four northern Malay States, the remainder of Malaya was to be a Japanese protectorate. The northern states were possibly to be restored to Siam. The Dutch East Indies were to form an Indonesian Federation, but the one-time Dutch parts of New Guinea, Borneo and Timor were to remain under direct Japanese control. The Philippines, though independent, were to grant special military and commercial privileges to Japan, and Hong Kong was to be Japanese, though with the possibility of its return to China after the final establishment of peace.

Fundamentally, the Greater East Asia area was to consist of a group of satellites under various degrees of Japanese control. To establish this relationship upon a firm footing, a Greater East Asia Deliberative Council was formed in March 1942 to advise the Japanese prime minister. In November of the same year, a Greater East Asia Ministry was established to handle all the overseas areas of the Japanese Empire except Korea, Formosa, and the Japanese part of Sakhalin. Because of the continuance of the military regimes in the occupied territories, the new ministry did little more than advise the military governors, and its main activities were concerned with propaganda and education. Japanese teachers were sent to the occupied areas in a sadly misconceived attempt to substitute Japanese as a second language instead of English or Dutch, and to spread the knowledge that Japanese culture and achievements were infinitely superior to those of the West. Youth organisations were formed, looking to Japan for inspiration and example. Religions, too, were used to cement friendship between peoples of similar faith. In the autumn of 1943, in order to demonstrate to the 'liberated peoples' and to the world the success of Japan's Asian policy, a Greater East Asia Conference assembled at Tokyo attended by the 'independent' nations who were Japan's allies in the 'struggle against the West'.

The first of these 'allies' was Manchukuo, allegedly independent since 1932 but in fact firmly under Japanese control, for behind the façade of emperor and Manchu ministers real policy was formulated by the Japanese head of the General Affairs Board and carried out, in the main, by Japanese vice-ministers who formed an executive cabinet behind the shadow of the allegedly responsible ministers. Next came China, ostensibly at peace with

Japan by the terms of the treaty of November 1940, concluded with Wang Ching-wei, the renegade KMT leader. Here, too, the shadow was Chinese but the substance Japanese. By the terms of the treaty, Japan had promised to return foreign concessions, including her own, to China, but she did not do so until after Britain and the United States had ended the period of the 'unequal treaties' by renouncing their extra-territorial rights in China by a treaty with Chiang concluded in January 1942. This act was ridiculed by the Japanese as valueless, for most of the concessions surrendered were in those parts of China occupied by them. Despite this, Japan was forced to implement her own promises. This she did by surrendering her own rights and also those of France, by permitting negotiations to take place between the Nanking regime and Vichy French representatives. The next stage in Sino-Japanese relations was the signing of a new treaty with occupied China in which the two parties pledged cooperation upon a basis of equality in the work of establishing a Greater East Asia. The real significance of the treaty lay in a protocol to the subsidiary treaty of alliance in which Japan under-took to withdraw her troops from China at the end of hostilities and also renounced her rights to station troops there, which had been guaranteed by the Boxer Protocols and later agreements. The treaty, though an obvious sham, was actually intended as a proposal to Chiang Kai-shek, with whom the Japanese had never ceased attempts to negotiate a peace settlement. This proposals, like all the others, was rebuffed by Chiang. Nevertheless, the Nanking regime was, by treaty definition, an independent ally of Japan.

The third 'ally' was the only actually independent nation in south Asia, Siam – now called Thailand. There is little doubt that Thailand would have preferred to remain neutral, but she had little choice when, on 7 December 1941, Japan demanded right of passage for her troops through Thai terri-tory. Agreement to this led to a treaty of alliance and the declaration of war by Thailand upon Great Britain and the United States in January 1942. The Japanese stationed large garrisons in Thailand and took over the working of the railways, airfields and harbour installations. As the Siamese had an army, the Japanese were careful not to antagonise the government. In return for its cooperation, Thailand received back the four Malay States, Perlis, Kedah, Kelantan, and Trengganu, ceded to Britain in 1909 (see p. 136) and two of the Shan States, Kengtung and Mongpan as well. The acqui-sition of territory was, however, no substitute for economic wellbeing, and Thailand was soon suffering from an adverse trade balance with Japan. The latter had drawn heavily upon Thailand's rice production but had been unable to supply the manufactured articles usually provided by the West. Considerable hardship due to food hoarding and general profiteering did little to endear the Japanese connection to ordinary people. By the middle of 1944, it was obvious to the Siamese that the Western powers were returning in strength and that Thailand might lose her independence through guilt by association. In July 1944, a new cabinet took office in Bangkok which, though professing continued cooperation with Japan, was in fact pro-West. The Japanese were fully aware of this but could not risk the taking over of direct rule as it would have made quite clear the emptiness of Japan's claim to be fighting for the independence of Asian nations. Towards the end of the war, British and American agents were active in Bangkok with the approval of the government, and Siamese troops were preparing to go into action against the Japanese as soon as the Allies began their expected invasion.

In Burma, as we have seen, the Japanese had made contact with dissatisfied nationalists before the outbreak of war. A group of thirty members of the Thakin party (see p. 251), headed by Aung San, had left Burma after Pearl Harbour and were given military training by the Japanese. U Saw, the Burmese prime minister in 1940–1, had been arrested on his way back from London on a charge of treasonable relations with the Japanese. Dr Ba Maw, who had been prime minister in 1937–9, was, at the time of the Japanese invasion, in a British prison at Mogok. Escaping during the British retreat, he seems at one time to have been in contact with the Chinese but was, according to his own statement before the International Military Tribunal, found qy the Japanese military police and interviewed by the deputy chief of staff to the Japanese commander in Burma. Ba Maw was told that the Japanese had been searching for him so that he might head a new Civil Administrative Committee. This was because the returned Thakins had been using the Burma Independence Army, which they controlled, to settle old scores with former political enemies instead of helping to establish an administration. The Japanese disbanded the army and formed an administration under Ba Maw, in which the Thakins participated. On 1 August 1942, a Burmese Executive Administration was established at Rangoon headed by Ba Maw.

The Japanese military command, however, did not allow any real authority to the new administration, and despite mutual praise, nothing happened to implement Tojo's promise of independence, made in January 1942, until in January 1943 the Japanese prime minister promised it would be granted within one year. In May 1943, a Burmese Independence Preparatory Committee with Ba Maw as chairman was set up, but – again according to

Ba Maw – the local Japanese military did all the work and, in July 1943, on his return from visiting Tojo at Singapore, Ba Maw was presented with a draft declaration of independence and the outline of a treaty between Burma and Japan. A secret agreement gave to the Japanese commander-in-chief in Burma the right to over-rule decisions of the Burmese government if he did not approve of them.

On 1 August 1943, Burma was declared independent and the Japanese military administration formally at an end. Ba Maw was appointed head of state (Nainggandaw Adipadi) and a new government established. A treaty of alliance was signed with Japan providing for complete cooperation on all levels. In fact, the Japanese army still remained in control, and army officers made no attempt to conceal their contempt for the new administration. The Japanese still continued to suck the country dry, and economic conditions went from bad to worse. Burmese labour was still conscripted for work with the Japanese army and upon the 'death railway' between Siam and Burma, where, according once again to Ba Maw, some thirty thousand of them died. During the Japanese collapse, in order to obtain his continued support, Ba Maw was threatened by local Japanese commanders that the policy of whole-sale destruction carried out by the Japanese in the Philippines would be ruthlessly applied in Burma. When, in the spring of 1945, Aung San went over to the British, Ba Maw – now virtually under Japanese detention – was forced to retire with them and was finally taken to Japan.

The last of the 'independent allies' presented an unusual aspect for an Asian country. The Philippines (see p. 160), after three centuries of Spanish rule, was a Roman Catholic country with a considerable amount of Euro-pean blood flowing through the veins of its upper class. As one commentator has put it, 'by 1900, when Spanish rule ended, the Philippines were already more akin to a Latin American country than to the neighbouring states of Asia.'[1] American occupation had increased the Westernisation of the country and, at the outbreak of war, the government of the Philippines was constructed in the image of that of the United States. Its independence was qualified by the Tydings-McDuffie Act of 1934 and by the presence of a United States high commissioner and the control of foreign affairs by Wash-ington. In the economic sphere, the Philippines was dependent on the Unit-ed States as the largest customer for its exports. When the independence scheduled for 1946 actually arrived, US tariff protection would be with-

---

[1] F. C. Jones: *Japan's New Order in East Asia*. London, 1954.

drawn, leaving the Philippines with unsaleable surpluses. Fears of an economic collapse led to the unusual situation of an Asian colonial dependency being anxious to postpone its independence in order to continue to receive preferential treatment within a tariff wall. Such postponement was, of course, impossible, not only for nationalist reasons, but because American financial interests – particularly in sugar – were anxious to free themselves from Filipino competition. Because of this, though Filipino nationalists in general found little appeal in the slogan of 'Asia for the Asiatics', they could see no alternative to the replacement of their economic dependence upon the United States with one upon Japan. A very small minority of politicians, in anticipation of this event, were already in the late 1930's in contact with the Japanese.

The weakness of American forces in the Philippines and their sudden defeat by the Japanese invaders produced a similar effect upon the Filipinos as the collapse of the Western powers did upon the peoples of their colonial dependencies. Filipino forces were badly armed and worse trained – as the American military adviser, General MacArthur, had insisted that American forces would defend the islands until 1946, and that it was a waste of money to equip the Filipino army with what would by then be obsolete equipment! Some Filipino politicians, including the president, left the country at the time of the Japanese invasion. Others became leaders of resistance movements. Most remained behind to take office under the Japanese. This they did with little enthusiasm for the conqueror, but more for what they thought were the best interests of the Philippines. One of those who collaborated, José Laurel, stated 'I believe the war will last at least six years, and we cannot tell who will win. What are we going to do in the meantime? It is our duty to do what we can to mitigate the sufferings of our people and to ensure the survival of the Filipino race'. The good sense of this is obvious. The Japanese, on their arrival, threatened dire destruction if there was the slightest resistance to their occupation and then announced that they had come as liberators from the tyranny of the United States, with 'the Philippines for the Filipinos' as their only aim. But, they insisted, this could only be achieved through sincere cooperation. Filipinos must remember that they were Asians and throw off the degenerate trappings of occidental culture. English was to be replaced by Japanese, the new *lingua franca* of Greater East Asia.

In the economic sphere, sugar plantations forced, said the Japanese, upon the Filipinos by the rascally American imperialists, were to be replaced by the production of cotton. In industry, American firms were taken over by the

Japanese and all industry was placed under military control. Politically, a Philippine Executive Committee had been established in January 1942, with Japanese advisers and ultimate control in the hands of the military administration. A new political front, the Kalibapi or 'Association for Service in the New Philippines', was organised to supersede the old political parties and, on 18 June 1943, it was instructed to arrange a preparatory commission for Philippine independence. A draft constitution was produced and, on 20 September 1943, the Kalibapi formed out of itself a national assembly which, five days later, elected José Laurel as president. On 14 October, after a visit by Laurel to Japan, a pact of alliance was signed and the independence of the Philippines proclaimed. As elsewhere in 'independent' Asia, the Japanese army remained actually in control. The Japanese distrusted the new regime, particularly because of Laurel's unwillingness to declare war on the Western powers as the other 'allies' had done. Laurel was also believed to be in contact with resistance groups, though this has never been proved. Because of their unwillingness to remove the regime they had themselves set up as representative of Philippine independence, the Japanese took the unusual step of promoting an opposition organisation, the Makapali or 'League of Patriotic Filipinos', headed by the pro-Japanese politician, Ramos. It had been left, however, too late, as the Americans were already preparing to invade the country and most of the forces raised by Ramos to cooperate with the Japanese army either deserted or were killed by resistance groups. In December, when American forces were almost at Manila, the Japanese removed the members of the Laurel cabinet to Baguio, and in the following March some of them were taken to Japan.

Elsewhere in South-east Asia, Japanese policy was not only different but emerged from entirely different motives. Essentially, the Japanese only granted the fiction of independence to those nations with either firmly established nationalist movements – as was the case in the Philippines – or existing puppet regimes, as in Manchukuo, or where memories of independence were comparatively recent, as in Burma.[1] There, pro-Japanese 'governments' could perhaps be relied upon to cooperate with Japan after the end of hostilities when the major effects of the co-prosperity plans were to come into force. Cooperative satellites would put much less strain upon Japanese resources than occupied territories. In Malaya and the Dutch East Indies, no

---

[1] Ba Maw stated in his evidence after the war that he believed the Japanese were at one time considering recreating the kingdom of Burma with a grandson of the last king, Thibaw, on the throne.

clear national pattern existed. Both areas were bound together only by the administrative frontiers of the colonial rulers. When these artificial boundaries ceased to have meaning, no sense of Malayan or Indonesian 'nationality' remained but only a collection of racial, linguistic and religious differences. Out of them, the Japanese hoped to create new patterns which would assist their continued control.

These two areas were the real prize of Japanese expansion. Elsewhere, the results of Japanese victory were comparatively trifling, but the tin, rubber and oil of Malaya and the East Indies would make Japan independent of outside sources of these essential raw materials. The Japanese, immediately after the occupation of the East Indies, set about destroying the Dutch administrative system, and replacing it with a highly centralised government approximating to that operating in Japan itself. By 1945, in Java alone, over 23,000 Japanese were employed by the military administration. Sumatra was detached from Java under a separate military government, and Dutch Borneo, the Celebes, and the Lesser Sunda islands were placed under the control of the Japanese navy with headquarters at Macassar. In all these areas, the administrative system was roughly the same. The Japanese were particularly vicious to certain minorities. The Dutch, obviously, were badly treated, and over 60,000 of them were interned. Eurasians were also cruelly oppressed until it was realised that the administration could not function efficiently without them. The large Chinese minority was forced into pro-Wang Ching-wei associations, and those suspected of any inclination towards Chungking were ruthlessly dealt with by the Japanese secret police (*Kempei*). As with other countries under Japanese occupation, the educational system was reshaped to disseminate anti-Western and pro-Japanese ideas. The attempt to force the Japanese language upon the peoples of the East Indies had, naturally, only small success. That language is far too difficult for easy learning, and Behasi Indonesian, a variant of Malay, which had been taught in the nationalist schools in an attempt to weld the people together through a common language, had to be used, as it was the only available medium of communication on the widest scale. Because of this, its use became much wider. This by-product of anti-colonial nationalism was unwittingly assisted by the Japanese to become a national language and, for the first time, gave the term 'Indonesian' some real meaning.

The Japanese administrators, who came from Japan, Formosa or Korea, knew little or nothing about the East Indies, its peoples, languages, or social organisation. In consequence, it became necessary to employ Indonesians in

nominally subordinate positions, but, because of their local knowledge and
the ignorance of their superiors, they began to exercise actual executive authority. The inefficiency of Japanese administrators endeared them to the
Indonesians as little as did the brutality of the Kempei. In the economic field,
the usual Japanese methods of expropriation and control were put into effect,
and the same hardships emerged because of the inability of the Japanese to
supply manufactured consumer goods. The army of occupation devoured
food supplies, and by 1945 famine was very near.

At the time of the Japanese conquest, the nationalist leaders exiled by the
Dutch to New Guinea were brought back to Java. Sukarno and Hatta
were willing to collaborate with the Japanese, but two others, Sjahrir and
Amir Sjarifuddin, were not and went underground. Sukarno and Hatta
soon found out that any belief they might have had that the Japanese would
be willing to assist Indonesian aspirations for independence was sadly mistaken. The Indonesian flag and anthem were banned. The Japanese en-
courged divisive tendencies, Muslim against Hindu and Christian, minority
against minority. They intended to keep control of the East Indian archipelago for their own use and were unlikely to encourage any form of unity.

While 'independent' governments were being established elsewhere in
Greater East Asia, the Japanese felt compelled, if only for propaganda purposes, to make some gesture towards the peoples of the East Indies. They
permitted them, as a reward for their cooperation, to have some say in the
administration. On 1 August 1943, it was announced that a central advisory council and regional councils would be established in Java and that
Indonesians would be appointed as advisors in some of the departments of
the military administration. The first meeting of the central advisory council
was held in the middle of October 1943.

In November 1943 Sukarno went to Tokyo and, when there, appealed to
General Tojo to grant independence to Indonesia as had been done in
Burma and the Philippines. This the Japanese prime minister refused to do.
In Java, the military authorities began to act less harshly towards the Chinese
and Eurasians, possibly in an endeavour to counteract Indonesian nationalism. They also dissolved the Poetera, an organisation similar to the Kalibapi
in the Philippines, which they had set up in November 1942 with Sukarno
as director, membership of which was not open to Chinese or Eurasians.
The Poetera was replaced by a 'Corporation for Communal Services in
Java', a new all-community front designed to mobilise all sectors of the
population behind the Japanese.

As the Western allies advanced in Burma and the Pacific, various concessions were made to Indonesian nationalists and, finally, in April and May
1945, discussions took place at Singapore which led to the formation of a
preparatory committee to draft a constitution – but only for Java. On 17
July, when the whole of the Japanese defences were crumbling, it was decided that the independence of the East Indies should be recognised as soon
as possible. This time, the whole archipelago was to be included in the new
state which was to be proclaimed in September 1945. On 14 August, an
Independence Preparatory Committee was set up. Its first meeting was
scheduled for 19 August, but on 15 August members were secretly told of
Japan's surrender to the Allies. On 17 August, despite Japanese reluctance,
the independence of Indonesia was proclaimed by Sukarno. Though by the
terms of the surrender the Japanese military authorities should have prevented
this, they did not do so, and in fact handed over the administration to the
new state and supplied it with arms. When the Allies arrived in Java, they
found a republic in occupation which could not be dismissed as a Japanese
creation as it had been proclaimed two days *after* their capitulation.

In Malaya, the usual Japanese military administration was established and
apart from Singapore, which was made a separate municipality under the
new name of Shonan ('Light of the South'), the rest of Malaya was divided
into eight regions each under a Japanese administrator. The former British
divisions of Straits Settlements, Federated, and Unfederated Malay States
were abolished, and it was stated that Malaya, now rechristened Malai, was
to be a part of the Japanese Empire. As elsewhere in Greater East Asia, the
education system was reorganised with emphasis on the Japanese language
and culture and, except in official documents, the use of English was forbidden. As the tide turned against the Japanese they found themselves forced
to make some concessions to the Malay people and, from the autumn of
1943, the proposition that Malaya was part of the Japanese Empire was
quietly dropped and replaced with vague references to a 'New Malai'. In
October 1943, Consultative Councils were established at Singapore and in the
eight regions, and in February 1944 it was announced that Malaya was to be
'a self-contained, self-respecting member of the Toa [East Asian] family of nations', though when this was to be was still wrapped in the mists of the future.
When, in August 1945, it was announced that Indonesia was to become
independent, it was suggested that if the Malay people increased their cooperation with the Japanese army they could expect similar treatment. Events,
however, overwhelmed the Japanese before these promises could be fulfilled.

Anti-Western propaganda was particularly virulent in Malaya, and every means was used to humiliate white prisoners before the Malays. Eurasians, always suspect, were instructed to forget their privileged position between the two races and become Asiatics. The Chinese community, as usual, was bullied – and butchered – by the Japanese, not only for their alleged pro-Chiang sympathies but also for their relations with Communist guerillas. The dislike of the Malay population for the Chinese shopkeeper and money-lender was also pandered to in the Japanese treatment of the Chinese. Economically, Malaya suffered from the standard abuses of expropriation and inefficiency, and the inability of the Japanese to supply consumer goods. By 1945, under the pressure of military demands, food was scarce.

When capitulation came, the Japanese, as elsewhere in Greater East Asia, concealed the fact until 20 August, five days after the actual surrender. Their army command in Singapore announced that they were giving in in order to spare their fellow Asians from the horrors of the atomic bomb which had been dropped upon Hiroshima. The Japanese were quick to point out that the bomb had not been used against white men in Europe, so giving the act an anti-racial colour which has never quite been disposed of in Asia.

The French possessions in Indo-China remained, until the Japanese *coup d'état* of March 1945, an odd enclave of white rule in an ostensibly all-Asian co-prosperity sphere. The Vichy French administration was left in control and French troops remained armed and active, particularly in the suppression of anti-French nationalist movements. Japanese troops were stationed in Indo-China by agreements concluded in September 1940 and July 1941, and by a further agreement made in December of the same year, by which the continuance of French rule was guaranteed by the Japanese. The arrangement was purely one of common sense. The Japanese had not the resources to run the country if they had wanted to, and it was unlikely that the Vichy French would oppose their demands as long as there appeared to be no possibility of an Allied offensive. The Japanese, however, were quite prepared to discredit the French regime up to a point, and gave some clandestine encouragement to nationalist movements, in particular to the Cao Dai, a strange, religious organisation whose beliefs were an engaging mixture of East and West and whose leader was in exile in Japan. In December 1941, the Nationalist Chinese threatened to send troops into northern Indo-China, but were persuaded that it would only lead to the Japanese occupation of the country. Instead, the Chinese sponsored an Annamite nationalist movement, headed by Ho Chi Minh.

The French governor-general, Admiral Decoux, was threatened on all sides by Chinese intrigue, Annamite nationalism, Gaullist intrigue, and American plans to remove Indo-China from French authority after the war and place it under an international trusteeship. Decoux's aim therefore was to preserve the French presence in Indo-China, and when the Japanese army demanded that French forces should assist them in repelling a possible American invasion, he refused, and attempted to compromise. This, however, was March 1945, when the Japanese were hardly in a position to do so, and their troops stormed Decoux's residence in Saigon and took him prisoner. French forces throughout the country were disarmed and French soldiers and civilians massacred. The Japanese prime minister denounced the French administration as treacherous. 'It has been', he said in a speech to the Japanese Diet on 10 March 1945, 'Governor Decoux's policy to perform to a minimum the obligations under the pact of joint defence, doing enough only to give Nippon no good excuse for independent action, and on the other hand tolerating indiscriminate bombing by the United States forces without making serious protest.'

On 11 March 1945, the emperor of Annam, Bao Dai, was persuaded to denounce the Franco-Annamite treaty of 1884 and to declare his independence and support for Japan. This was followed two days later by a similar proclamation by the king of Cambodia. In Cochin China a Japanese official was appointed governor, and the French Residents in Tongking and Laos were replaced by Japanese. The leaders in newly independent Annam had little in common with the nationalists of the Viet Minh, and that organisation refused to cooperate with them. After the Japanese capitulation, Decoux tried to persuade the local Japanese commander to release him so that he could attempt to regain control of the country before the arrival of the Allies. This was refused and the Japanese began to supply arms to the Viet Minh. On 22 August, Bao Dai abdicated and a provisional government was set up under Ho Chi Minh which, on 2 September, issued a declaration of independence at Hanoi. Again, the Japanese had left behind a legacy of trouble for the returning colonial power.

Though the Japanese do not appear to have had the slightest intention of mounting a full-scale invasion of India, despite extensive propaganda that they were about to do so, they did hope to stir up a revolt against the British. In June 1943 the Japanese organised an Indian Independence League conference in Bangkok, which called for the 'absolute independence of India after liberation'. By the end of August 1942, 40,000 Indian prisoners of war in Japanese hands had signed a pledge 'to join the Indian National Army'. Many of them had been coerced by threats and terror but others genuinely believed that they might be pioneers of India's freedom – a by no means unworthy aim. Nevertheless the Japanese, as always, were divided in their attitude. Civilian ministers and officials recognised the value of the League and wished to treat it as an ally. The Japanese military, on the other hand, sneered at the Indian National Army and despised all talk of independence. The first commander of the INA, Mohan Singh, refusing to be browbeaten by Japanese officers, was arrested and interned, but not before he had told the Japanese commander that if Japan attempted to replace Britain in India, India would fight her too. Later, the INA was reorganised by Rash Behari Bose, who had been a German agent in 1915 and had founded an Indian independence movement in Japan as early as 1916. In February 1943, his namesake, Subhas Chandra Bose, arrived in Tokyo from Germany where he had attempted to organise an independence movement without much success. Bose (see p. 248) had in 1938 been president of the Indian National Congress but, impatient with what he had believed to be Gandhi's flaccid policy, he had fled from a sedition charge in 1941 to Afghanistan and, after failing to interest the Russians in his plans, on to Berlin.

Subhas Bose was received in Tokyo by the Japanese prime minister Tojo, and assured that the Japanese meant India to be independent. In October 1943, a Provisional Government of Free India was established at Singapore, with Bose as head of state (Netaji), prime minister, and minister for war and foreign affairs. In January 1944, the government was transferred to Burma so as to be ready to follow the Japanese into India, and the Indian National Army took part in the Japanese campaign in Assam. But the offensive failed and the INA was shattered. In Rangoon, unaware of the catastrophe that had struck the Japanese forces, Bose prepared himself for the march into India. The celebration of 'Netaji Week' included a parade at the tomb of the last Mughal Emperor, Bahadur Shah, who had died in exile at Rangoon in 1862. At the end of October 1944, Bose went to Tokyo with Dr Ba Maw. While there, he made a number of speeches. In the course of one, given at Tokyo University, he made a direct appeal to the United States. This was a defence of himself but also of the new Asian nationalism which the Japanese had helped to release. Bose at this time spoke for all those nationalists who had hoped that Japan would assist them to freedom; above all, for those intelligent enough to see it, he gave a warning that whatever happened the old order in Asia could never return.

'I want to tell my American friends that Asia is now surging with revo-lutionary fervour from one end to the other... We are men as much as you are. We want our freedom and we shall have it by any means. You had an opportunity of helping us but you did not do so. Now Japan is offering us help and we have reason to trust her sincerity. That is why we have plunged into the struggle alongside of her. It is not Japan that we are helping by waging war on you and on our mortal enemy – England. We are helping ourselves – we are helping Asia...'[1]

When Burma was reoccupied by the British, Bose left for Malaya where on 13 August 1945 he was informed of the Japanese decision to surrender. Three days later he left for Tokyo. The plane he was travelling in crashed in Formosa and Bose received injuries from which he died.

Though the gap between Japanese protestations of belief in Asia's in-dependence and the actual state of affairs in the territories occupied by Japan was wide, the obvious answer that they were only propaganda does not quite fit the facts. There is no doubt that as an instrument of war, the slogan 'Asia for the Asiatics' was a weapon of incalculable effect, though it was not used with particular efficiency. But the granting of independence in the East Indies, and the overthrow of the Vichy French regime in Indo-China were neither just propaganda, nor attempts to bribe nationalists into supporting Japan in her hour of need. Why the Japanese should have gone ahead with the preparation of Asians for independence when it was only a matter of time before their old colonial rulers returned, can only be answered when seen as an attempt – a successful one, as it turned out – to achieve at least one of Japan's major aims in east Asia. That aim was to ensure that, whatever happened to the Japanese Empire, Western domination in Asia would be seriously weakened. Already, before the end of the war, the announcement of the granting of independence to Burma and the Philippines had forced the Allies to adopt new policies for their former colonial possessions. Such concessions as they were prepared to make would necessarily be less than the full independence offered by the Japanese. Japan had not only destroyed the myth of Western military superiority once and for all, but had also discredited the very foundation of Western rule – its belief in progress and democracy and all the rest of its invisible exports. At the same time, the Japanese had been unable to offer anything in their place, except the totalitarian incli-nations of their military leaders, and the empty ethic of the Samurai. The

[1] Quoted in Hugh Toye's excellent study of Bose, *The Springing Tiger*. London, 1959.

Japanese left behind a feeling of unease, a dissatisfaction with old nationalist aspirations of freedom along Western lines. When freedom finally came in that form, the men who were to work it had an incomplete faith in the machine. The partial vacuum caused by the Japanese impact on east Asia was to be filled by a new and virile philosophy which, because of its essential anti-colonial and therefore anti-Western nature, seemed to offer a new and dynamic alternative – that of Communism.

v

THE END OF EMPIRE

The collapse of Japan, and with it the grandiose structure of a Greater East Asia, seemed to herald the return of the old colonial powers, their purpose revived in the fire of a hard-won victory. But the decline of the West which an inspired journalist, Oswald Spengler, had foretold in the climate of pessimism that followed the first World War, had now come true. The war of 1914–18 had seriously weakened the imperial purpose and the inter-war years can now be seen as a rearguard action. The second World War dealt a final blow to the superior standing of Western Europe. The world scene was no longer dominated by Great Britain, and the British themselves were aware of it. The Dutch and the French, weakened by invasion and division of loyalties, sought to soothe their wounds by trying to put back the clock in Asia. The British, convincing themselves that it was their destiny to be the only empire ever voluntarily to dissolve itself, accepted the fact of Asian nationalism as proof of it. Wisely, they decided to play the fond father, sending his sons out into the world trained to stand on their own two feet. To solace themselves for the loss of an empire, the British erected the mysterious symbol of the Commonwealth, a loose get-together of former imperial territories which defies definition.

When the colonial powers returned to their old possessions, they did so with a declared purpose that some form of self-government would certainly be granted. The Dutch had promised that the East Indies would have a new relationship with the Netherlands. Burma, the British declared, was to have dominion status. The United States made it quite clear that the Philippines would be independent. The French offered Indo-China a federal union with France. Unfortunately, the Western powers did not understand – or were perhaps unwilling to understand – the explosive conditions prevailing in colonial Asia. No longer would the cautious granting of degrees of self-government be enough. Asia had tasted freedom and authority, however circumscribed they may have been. Patience was no longer possible.

In India the British moved rapidly towards a final solution. By the summer of 1945, British fears of a revolt behind their backs had been disposed of. Victory over Japan had raised her prestige. Congress leaders were released from detention, and the progress of India towards self-government could continue. But the India of 1945 was not the India of 1939. Great changes had taken place in industry and commerce. In the building up of India as a base against Japan, industry had found itself expanding to unprecedented levels. At one time Indian industries were supplying nine-tenths of the military equipment for the Indian and Near-Eastern armies. Large numbers of white men, British and American, without either the prejudices or the preoccupations of administrators, passed through the country. The Indian Army, the largest volunteer force in the world, totalling over two million men, was recruited from all classes and areas and brought together people of widely differing ethnic and caste backgrounds. These and many other factors, including the pressures of food and other shortages during and immediately after the war, produced a new though not easily definable sense of urgency in the field of politics. In India, too, Japan's promotion of Asian independence had had its moral effect. Subhas Chandra Bose was hailed as the patriot he undoubtedly was. The British themselves unwisely sent three officers of the Indian National Army to trial in the Red Fort at Delhi. The agitation that surrounded the trials turned the issue of Indian independence into an area of popular emotion. As Jawaharlal Nehru put it: 'These three officers and the INA became symbols of India fighting for its independence. All minor issues faded away... The trial dramatised... the old contest: England versus India... It became... rather a trial of strength between the will of the Indian people and the will of those who hold power in India'.[1]

Once again, the nationalist movement was to be given a popular slogan in the frustrated cry of Subhas Bose. But once again, too, the shadow of Hindu majority rule frightened the Muslims. Communal disturbances spread throughout India. Most sinister of all, a mutiny occurred in February 1946 in the Indian Navy. Since the Mutiny of 1857, the armed services had been particularly free from unrest. In Britain, a new administration had come into power at the general election of July 1945. Then, the Labour party had been

[1] Foreword to the published proceedings of the INA Court Martial.

swept into office with a large majority. Labour politicians in the wilderness of their opposition had always been favourable to India's demands for self-government; now they were to be given the opportunity to show that this sympathy was more than rhetoric.

On 19 February 1945, the new prime minister, Clement Attlee, announced that a cabinet mission was to be sent to India. The mission arrived in Delhi in March 1946. After a series of separate discussions with leaders of the Indian National Congress and of the Muslim League, in which no area of agreement between the desires of the two parties could be found, the mission made took it upon itself to make its own recommendations. These were announced on 16 May 1946.

The main proposals were that (1) a federal government should be set up at the centre, which would include all the states, (2) India should be divided into three provincial groups consisting of the North-west Frontier province, Sind, Baluchistan and the Punjab; Bengal and Assam; and the rest of India, (3) a constitution should be framed by a constituent assembly elected on a communal basis by the provincial legislative assemblies, (4) the provinces should have the right of secession from the federation after the election of the constituent assembly, and (5) a provisional national government should be set up immediately whose members would be the leaders of the different nationalist parties.

These proposals were accepted by the Muslim League on 6 June but they were rejected by Congress, who did, however, state that they were prepared to join a constituent assembly for the purpose of framing a constitution. The cabinet mission left India on 29 June and the Muslim League demanded that the viceroy should immediately constitute a provisional government, if necessary without the participation of Congress. Naturally, this was not possible, as any national administration must consist of representatives of all the interested parties. The League's response was to withdraw its previous acceptance of the mission's proposals. The viceroy reconstituted his executive council with Congress members only. The Muslim League then declared 16 August as a day of 'direct action'. On that day, though most of the demonstrations were orderly, a number of Hindus were murdered and property was looted and destroyed in Calcutta. The Hindus now retaliated, and Calcutta became the scene of the most brutal communal riots in the city's history. The government of Bengal at that time was a Muslim League administration and it took no decisive action to stop the rioting. Their weakness was encouraged by the British governor of Bengal and the central government, who took no action either, despite the responsibility of the governor for the maintenance of public order. The swearing-in of Pandit Nehru and other Congress nominees to the viceroy's executive council was followed by other outbreaks of communal rioting.

The viceroy now attempted to persuade the Muslim League leaders to accept portfolios in his executive council, and in fact succeeded in doing so. The viceroy informed the Congress leaders that the League had once again revised its attitude towards a constituent assembly, and had now agreed to join it. Unfortunately, communal divisions in the streets had their parallel in the executive council, and agreement upon policy could not be achieved. This unhappy situation was further exacerbated by the discovery that the Muslim League had in fact no intention of joining a constituent assembly at all, but had merely said it would in order to be able to join the executive council. In spite of this, and without the participation of the Muslim League the assembly actually met on 9 December 1946 and appointed committees to draft the provisions of the new constitution.

On 20 February 1947, the British government announced its intention of leaving India by June 1948 and appointed the former supreme commander of the Allied forces in South-east Asia during the war, Lord Mountbatten, as the new viceroy. Mountbatten's task was to carry out the transfer of power as expeditiously as possible. The Muslim League, with conspicuous irresponsibility, once again indulged in 'direct action' in spite of the bloody lessons of 1946. Murder, arson and general violence convulsed the Punjab and the North-west Frontier province. Reluctantly, Congress was forced to accept the premise that in order to achieve independence, India would have to be divided.

On 3 June, the new viceroy broadcast the declaration of the British government's policy, the substance of which can be summarised as follows:

(1) If the areas with a majority of Muslims in the population so desired, they should be allowed to form a separate dominion and a new constituent assembly would be set up for that purpose. In that case, there would be a partition of Bengal and the Punjab if the representatives of the Hindu majority districts in the legislatures of those provinces so desired.

(2) A referendum would take place in the North-west Frontier province to ascertain whether it should join the Muslim Dominion of Pakistan or not.

(3) The district of Sylhet would be joined to the Muslim area in Bengal after the views of the people had been ascertained through a referendum.

(4) Boundary commissions would be set up to define the frontiers of the Hindu and Muslim provinces in Bengal and the Punjab.

(5) Legislation would be introduced in the current session of the British parliament to enable the immediate granting of dominion status to India (or to India and Pakistan if partition was decided upon) without any prejudice to the final decision of the constituent assembly (or assemblies) in this respect.

This scheme was finally accepted by both the Congress and the Muslim League, and the India Independence Act was passed through the British parliament on 1 July 1947. The Act fixed the date for the transfer of power to India and Pakistan as 15 August 1947. On that day the Constituent Assembly in Delhi declared India a dominion within the British Commonwealth, with the last viceroy, Lord Mountbatten, as its first governor-general. In Karachi, Mr Jinnah, leader of the Muslim League, was chosen as the first governor-general of Pakistan. The British-Indian Empire was at an end.

In the weeks preceding independence, the Punjab, which was about to be divided between the successor states, rapidly degenerated into anarchy. Well-armed bands of Sikhs and others roamed the countryside burning villages and massacring their inhabitants. By 17 August, communications between the Punjab and Delhi were cut except by air, and long processions of miserable refugees, Muslims fleeing westwards and Hindus and Sikhs eastwards, numbered hundreds of thousands. Trains were attacked by gangs of well-armed men, and travellers belonging to communities other than those of the gangs were murdered. No one knows how many people were killed in the Punjab, but the total number of refugees involved in the upheavals has been estimated at more than eight and a half million. The resettlement of these refugees is still a problem in both India and Pakistan, and memories of the violence in the Punjab have continued to embitter Indo-Pakistan relations.

On 26 January 1950, India severed all legal ties with Great Britain by becoming a republic. She still, however, remained within the Commonwealth.

*   *   *

The orderly transition from British rule to independence was achieved without the shedding of blood – the blood, that is, of the former rulers – though the communal massacres in the Punjab, perhaps even the very existence of Pakistan itself, had their indirect cause in the principle of separate electorates enshrined in the Morley-Minto reforms of 1909 and extended in later con-

cessions. We are too near the events themselves to weigh the evidence satisfactorily, but there is some tiny justification for the bitter remark made to the
author in August 1947 in Delhi, that the British, when they came, found a
divided India, and a divided India remained when they left. In Burma too,
freedom was not to come easily.

During the Japanese conquest and occupation and the British invasion
that followed, Burma suffered considerable destruction of life and property.
The structure of government had collapsed and dacoity (armed banditry), a
favourite occupation of Burmese criminals at all times, was on the increase as
communications were disrupted and law and order only feebly enforced. On
the collapse of the Japanese, the Burma governor and government, who had
happily spent the war in the quiet backwater of Simla, returned to take over
from the military administration set up by the British after their return. The
new administration, which was only the old one, had been insulated from
the effects of the Japanese domination of Asia by the rarefied air of the Hi-
malayan foothills, and now set about reconstructing Burma's economy – or
at least that part of it dominated by British interests. A promise of ultimate
dominion status for Burma was made, but it was announced that this could
not be implemented before December 1948. The freedom front of the Anti-
Fascist Peoples' League was ignored by the government and when the organisation replied with the formation of the armed Peoples' Volunteer Organisation, the threat of civil war was imminent. In December 1946, the
Labour government in London offered to grant independence to Burma on
the same terms as India, and negotiations were opened with the leader of the
AFPFL, Aung San. These negotiations caused a split in the AFPFL, and one
Communist group (The Red Flag) was hostile to *any* negotiations with the
British. The Burma Communist party (known as The White Flag) did not
oppose negotiations, but rejected the conditions accepted by Aung San and
was expelled from the AFPFL.

In January 1947, Aung San signed an agreement in London giving Burma independence and a choice of whether to remain in the Commonwealth
or not. On Aung San's return to Burma, and the holding of an election,
AFPFL candidates won a large majority against strong Communist opposition. On 19 July 1947, a gang of gunmen employed by the former prime
minister, U Saw, entered the secretariat in Rangoon and murdered Aung
San and six other ministers of the transition government. Thakin Nu – later
known as U Nu – concluded the final treaty with the British in October
1947. On 4 January 1948, at a propitious time determined by Buddhist

astrologers, the independent Union of Burma came into being. The new state did not join the Commonwealth, the only one of Britain's former colonial possessions which did not do so.

*   *   *

In Indonesia, after the fall of the Japanese and the establishment of a republic in August 1945, the road to freedom was pitted with shellholes. The Dutch, their homeland only recently freed from Nazi occupation, were unable to provide troops to reimpose their administration in the East Indies. The Allied South-east Asia Command, because of a shortage of transport, could not despatch forces to Indonesia until late in September. During the interim period, the Japanese military command was instructed to maintain order. The Japanese, for various reasons, made no attempt to prevent the establishment of a nationalist government, and handed over administrative functions and arms to the new regime. British troops landed at Batavia (renamed by the Japanese Jakarta) on 29 September, and were followed over the next twelve months by detachments of Dutch troops. The British finally left on 30 November 1946. The main ports of Java and Sumatra were reoccupied and the Dutch assumed control once again in Borneo, the Celebes, the Moluccas, and most of the smaller islands. This was not achieved without some fighting, as the Republicans were not prepared to accept the return of the Dutch or their plan to implement the offer of 1942, 'for a complete partnership of the Netherlands Indies in the kingdom, and complete freedom in its internal affairs'. Having achieved some measure of independence, the nationalist leaders quite rightly were prepared to fight for it. By October 1946, the Republicans held most of central Java, but the rest of the country outside the immediate control of the Dutch was in a state of anarchy. In the same month, the Dutch and the Indonesians agreed to a truce, though it was not completely effective and desultory fighting continued. Due in part to British efforts at mediation, an agreement was concluded on 15 November between the Dutch and the Republicans for the establishment of a United States of Indonesia. The agreement was signed at Linggadjati, and is known by that name.

The new accord provided for the association of three autonomous states – the Republic of Indonesia, consisting of Java, Sumatra, Madura, and the adjacent islands; the Dutch part of Borneo; and the 'Great East' which included the Moluccas, the Celebes and the Lesser Sunda Islands. The United States of Indonesia was to be a part of a Netherlands-Indonesian Union composed of the Netherlands, the Dutch West Indies, Surinam and Cura-çao, and the United States of Indonesia. All the partners were to be of equal rank, and the tie between them, the ruler of the Netherlands. The new Union would cooperate in foreign affairs and in the financial, economic and cultural fields. The agreement was ratified on 25 March 1947, but fighting was re-sumed, for though the arrangements satisfied moderate opinion, the Repub-licans were divided by internal conflict between moderates and extremists.

During October 1945, four main political parties had appeared in the Republican-held areas. The first to emerge was the Nationalist Party (PNI), mainly recruited from the Javanese intelligentsia and from Javanese officials in the pre-war civil service. The second became the largest party of all, the Masjumi, with considerable influence amongst the peasants, and a program-me distinctly Islamic in character. The Masjumi, though it contained some progressive and even socialist elements, was dominated by traditionalists and conservatives. The two other parties were the Socialist and the Communist. The official Communist party (PKI), because of weak and indecisive leader-ship, was without much influence. A Trotskyite group, led by the veteran Indonesia Communist, Tan Malaka, played a leading part in the formation of a rabidly anti-Dutch movement, known as the Fighting Front. The Front collapsed because of the refusal of the Socialists and Masjumi to join it. In July 1946, the Tan Malaka group made an unsuccessful attempt to seize power. During 1946, the Republican government consisted of a coalition between the PNI, the Masjumi, and the Socialists, with one of the latter, Sjahrir, as prime minister. The signing of the Linggadjati Agreement was denounced by the Masjumi and the PNI, but supported by the Socialists and the PKI. The Communists, who had been given a new lease of life under the direction of two experienced leaders who had returned from exile, gained control of the new trades union organisation, Sobsi. In June 1947, the pro-Communist Socialist leader, Amir Sjarifuddin, became prime minister.

In the meanwhile, a revolt had broken out against the Republican regime in west Java, and an independent state had been established there. The Dutch were asked by the rebels for military protection and they began a 'police action' allegedly to restore order in Republican territory, but in reality in an attempt to destroy the Republic. The Dutch also went ahead with the setting up of the United States of Indonesia, without reference to the Republican government. In December 1946, they proclaimed the state of East Indonesia, consisting of all the former Dutch possessions east of Java, but excluding Borneo which was later (in May 1947) declared self-governing. These acts were considered by the Republic to be in violation of the Linggadjati Agreement. The continuing anarchy in the East Indies and the obvious attempts by the Dutch to impose their own neo-colonial solutions, inspired India and Australia to bring the matter before the newly-formed United Nations. On 1 August 1947, the UN Security Council ordered the combatants to cease fire and appointed a Good Offices Committee consisting of an Australian, a Belgian and an American to negotiate a settlement. The Dutch, though furious at the interference of the outside world in what they held to be their own domestic affairs, yielded and a truce was signed aboard the battleship, *USS Renville*, on 18 January 1948. The new agreement undoubtedly favoured the Dutch in that they were allowed to retain territory occupied by them in 1947, subject to a plebiscite in Java, Madura, and Sumatra, and Dutch authority was to continue until the establishment of the United States of Indonesia. On the signing of the agreement, the Republican administration of Sjarifuddin fell, and in February the ex-prime minister founded a Peoples' Democratic Front (PDF) consisting of left-wing elements including the PKI.

The PDF, with Russian assistance and under the leadership of the old director of the underground Communist party during Dutch rule, Muso, who had returned from Prague, declared that what was needed was a peaceful seizure of power. In September, pro-Communist troops in the Madiun area revolted against the Republican government but were suppressed by loyal forces. The Communist leaders were arrested after an attempt to kidnap Sukarno had failed, and Muso and Sjarifuddin were amongst those executed. While this internal struggle had been going on, the Dutch continued their work of setting up the United States of Indonesia, and in October 1948 formed an interim federal government without the consent or participation of the Republicans. The Republic then accused the Dutch of never having any intention of giving up their East Indian possessions. The Dutch countered with accusations of bad faith and Republican attempts to infiltrate into their zones, as well as denouncing the Republic as Communist-dominated. On 19 December 1948, after announcing that negotiations had failed and that they had no further use for the Good Offices Committee, the Dutch began a second 'police action' against the Republic, allegedly to 'eliminate Republican terrorist activities', but actually to force the Republic to enter the new federal system. From the outset, the Dutch were successful and the Republican leaders, Sukarno and Hatta, were captured and imprisoned.

The Dutch victory was of short duration. It was no longer possible for an imperialist power to 'go it alone' and ignore the opinions of everyone else. Most of the nations of the world had realised that cooperation was a better proposition than domination. The Dutch, like stubborn old men in a changed world, found themselves isolated. Furthermore, their initial suc-cesses against the Republic did not lead to a surrender by the nationalists, and fighting continued. The UN Security Council passed a new resolution order-ing an immediate cease-fire. The United States of America suspended economic aid to the Dutch in Indonesia, and Asian nations sent represent-atives to a conference in Delhi in order to decide on support for the Indo-nesians against the Dutch. Under this combination of pressures, the Dutch released the nationalist leaders and announced their willingness to discuss the transfer of sovereignty to an all-Indonesian administration. After long negotiations, an agreement was signed in November 1949, and on 27 De-cember, the United States of Indonesia became a fully sovereign state. The new country was to be a federal republic of sixteen states, in equal partner-ship with the Netherlands. The Dutch portion of New Guinea, now known as West Irian, was not to be a part of the federal republic, but negotiations upon its status were to be continued. Sukarno became first president of the republic and Hatta its first prime minister.

The new state was almost immediately threatened by rebellions. Some were led by Dutch army officers who resented the transfer of the army to Indo-nesian control. Others were Communist or represented extreme Muslim fanaticism. The general trend was against the federal structure, for it was believed that only a strong central government could solve the growing prob-lems of security, stability and economic recovery. In protest against the move to centralisation, the South Moluccas declared themselves independent in April 1950. Nevertheless, on 15 August, the United States of Indonesia became the unitary Republic of Indonesia. National elections were held and a new constituent assembly set about producing a constitution. In August 1954, the proposed union between the Netherlands and Indonesia was finally and irrevocably abandoned. From that date onwards Dutch-In-donesian friction has continued as the new state, torn unnecessarily by Dutch unwillingness to make friends rather than subjects, has tried to construct a new and independent life for itself.

*   *   *

As with the Dutch, the humiliation of defeat in Europe brought the French back to Asia with a consuming desire to reinstate their presence and to slap down the people who had taken advantage of their temporary eclipse to declare themselves free.

Before the expulsion of the Japanese from the former French possessions in Indo-China, the Free French leader, General de Gaulle, had announced a plan for a federal union of France and the French colonial possessions. Within the union, Indo-China was to have a federal structure and a state council made up of Indo-Chinese and Frenchmen. Events, however, moved too fast for such an outmoded division of authority to have any possibility of acceptance.

In July 1945 Chinese troops, bringing with them the Viet Minh leaders, crossed the Indo-Chinese border and occupied an area down to the 16th parallel. British and French troops occupied the southern part of the country and proceeded to suppress nationalist forces, even using Japanese soldiers for the purpose. In September 1945, a Vietnamese republic was established in the Chinese-occupied sector and the independence of the whole of Indo-China announced. The Chinese disarmed French troops and refused to allow French administrators into their zone. The nationalists, under Ho Chi Minh, rapidly consolidated their power and, in January 1946, elections were held in which Ho was returned as the first president of Vietnam. The new administration consisted of Communists, Socialists, Democrats, Independents, Catholics, and former members of the imperial court of Annam. By the time the Chinese withdrew in the spring of 1946, the French found it necessary to come to an agreement with Ho, by which the Republic of Vietnam was recognised as a 'free state with its own government, parliament, army and finances, forming a part of the Indo-Chinese federation and the French Union'.

Friction continued over the question of Cochin China, but it was proposed that a plebiscite should be held there. French troops would be allowed to return to Tongking and northern Annam but their numbers were to be restricted to 15,000 French and 10,000 Vietnamese under French command. These troops were to be withdrawn in 1952. France had already come to separate agreement with Cambodia and Laos, by which they received autonomy except for French control of foreign affairs and defence. Despite French lip-service to the principle of a plebiscite in Cochin China by which the people could decide whether or not to join the Republic of Vietnam, every attempt was made to keep it under French control. Ho Chi Minh, anxious for a real and lasting settlement, went to Paris for negotiations. Unfortunately, liberal sentiments in Paris were not echoed in

Saigon, where the French tradition of initiating colonial acts without reference to the home government continued, reviving the old belief that statements made in the capitals of the colonial powers were merely for home consumption. In Saigon, the French high commissioner, Admiral d'Argenlieu, rabid Gaullist and ex-Carmelite monk, proclaimed an autonomous Republic of Cochin China and convened a 'federal conference' which excluded the Republic of Vietnam. In Paris, Ho and the French minister for overseas terittories concluded a *modus vivendi* providing for the protection of French economic and cultural interests in Vietnam, for a customs union within Indo-China, a unified currency, and called for an end to violence.

Meanwhile, in the Vietnamese republic itself, French police and army units were assisting the Viet Minh to destroy the Chinese-supported Vietnam National Party and the Vietnam Revolutionary League. But the relations between the republic and the French were uneasy as a consequence of the actions and statements of Admiral d'Argenlieu. On 23 November 1946, after a dispute over whether the French or the republic should control the customs at Haiphong, the French bombarded the city with artillery, killing thousands of Vietnamese. On 19 December, as a reprisal, French subjects were attacked in Hanoi, though on this occasion the casualties included only forty dead.[1] French forces, however, were unable to win a decisive victory and despite every effort by 1949 controlled only the major cities and heavily armed posts. The Viet Minh dominated the countryside and, after dark, even the streets of the cities.

In the political field, the French sought to oppose Viet Minh with a new political front consisting of the two parties they had helped to suppress in north Vietnam, two nationalist religious organisations, the Cao Dai and the Hoa Hao, and the Anti-Communist Catholic League. The French sought to rally this ill-assorted collection behind the figure of Bao Dai, the former emperor of Annam, who had, for a time, acted as an adviser to Ho Chi Minh. The choice of the ex-emperor was particularly inept. Before the war, he had been a colonial puppet, during the war, a Japanese puppet, and was

[1] The delay between the French massacre at Haiphong and Viet Minh reprisals at Hanoi was due to attempts to settle the dispute peacefully. Extremists on both sides, however, were determined upon a showdown. P. Devillers, in his *Histoire du Vietnam de 1940 à 1952* (Paris 1952), records that a conciliatory telegram from Ho Chi Minh to the French prime minister, Léon Blum, written on 15 December, was deliberately held up by the French censors in Saigon and did not reach Paris until a week after the Hanoi incident. Devillers's book makes instructive reading, especially in the light of French colonial activities in Algeria during the last few years.

altogether a colourless personality representing long-dead traditions. For the French, the main problem was that though the nationalist organisations were anti-Ho, they were first and foremost anti-French. Nevertheless, Bao Dai became head of the state of Vietnam in December 1949. Henceforward, Ho's Democratic Republic of Vietnam was referred to as Viet Minh. Bao Dai's government was recognised in February 1950 by the United States, Great Britain, Thailand, and the rest of the 'free world', while Ho was re-cognised by the USSR, Communist China, the Iron Curtain countries, and most of his Asian neighbours. The problem of Vietnam was no longer strictly French, though with considerable stupidity France continued her policy – if it can be described as such – with results only in blood and the waste of millions in money that might have been spent on more worthy things. The problem of Indo-China had now little to do with the happiness of its peoples. The country had become a pawn on the chessboard of the struggle between the United States – with the demoralised West hanging on to her pocketbook – and the Soviet Union. But even with economic and military aid, the French had no hope of defeating the Viet Minh or of re-gaining her old hegemony in Indo-China. French unwillingness to yield to nationalist sentiment forced Ho Chi Minh, a genuine Vietnamese nationalist, into full and probably reluctant cooperation with Communist China and the Soviet Union. When the other parts of Indo-China achieved their free-dom, French intransigence ensured that they should do so in a climate of threat and counter-threat.

At the beginning of 1950, Indo-China consisted of Laos and Cambodia, Bao Dai's Vietnam – all nominally independent within the French Union – and Viet Minh. The French authorities, refusing to believe that they could be beaten by the people they had once dominated, attempted to win the civil war by orthodox military tactics. Viet Minh, on the other hand, had learned its lesson in a tougher and more realist school. The Viet Minh forces, or-ganised upon guerilla patterns, infiltrated rather than attacked and easily cut off French forces into small groups for destruction. This technique had al-ready been revealed to the world in a book by the Communist Chinese leader, Mao Tse Tung, but this was a work that had not been read by French military leaders educated in the antique classrooms of Saint Cyr. Unexpectedly, for the French and the United States, Viet Minh forces won a decisive victory in the spring of 1954, by capturing the 'impregnable' fortress of Dien Bien Phu, which almost directly led to an international con-ference at which an agreement for the cessation of hostilities was reached.

As a result, Vietnam was divided along the 17th parallel and an inter-national commission composed of representatives of Poland, India and Canada was appointed to supervise elections by which it was hoped to determine the government of the future. These elections have never taken place. The demarcation line, intended only as a cease-fire frontier, has become a political boundary. In south Vietnam, Bao Dai, who had become more and more an absentee ruler, preferred the fleshpots of the French Riviera to the bitter realities of Indo-China. In 1955, Ngo Dinh Diem, who had been appointed prime minister by Bao Dai in 1954, removed the latter from office and became himself president of the Republic of Vietnam, freed from French domination but more and more dependent on the economic aid of the United States.

*   *   *

In the Philippines, the government of President Quezon, which had fled to the United States at the time of the Japanese invasion, returned with the American army in June of 1945. Quezon himself had died in 1944, and the vice-president, Osmena, now headed the administration. Until the end of the war with Japan the American army remained responsible for civil government, but with the advice and assistance of a Filipino Rehabilitation Commission. Also, in June 1945, the Philippine Congress elected in 1941 held its first meeting for four years. Special US agencies were organised to assist in the reconstruction of the country, but it was made quite clear that the provisions of the Tydings-McDuffie Act of 1934 – calling for independence in 1946 – would be realised on time.

The Philippines, consequently, prepared for new national elections, and in April 1946 these took place. They were won by the Liberal party, headed by Manuel Roxas, a wartime adviser of the puppet president, José Laurel. Roxas himself was elected president. The Liberal party represented the old vested interests, the landlords, business men, the press and civil service, as well as having the sympathy of General MacArthur, the American supreme commander. On 4 July 1946, after four hundred years of Spanish rule and nearly fifty of American, the Philippines became an independent republic.

The situation in the country was enough to frighten more experienced governments. The new president hardly exaggerated when he said:

'There is hunger among us... Plagues of rats and locusts gnaw at our food. Public health and sanitation have been set back a quarter of a century. Housing... is shocking in its inadequacy and squalor. Our communications are destroyed, stolen or disrupted... Schools have been burned and teachers have been killed.'

Banditry was rife. Discontented resistance elements, particularly the Communist-inspired Hukbalahap who had fought the Japanese with great vigour, now directed their attention against the reactionary conservatism of the new regime and its friends the Americans. In doing so, the Huks, as they were called, represented the land-hungry peasant who saw his old-time enemy, the landlord, first collaborate with the Japanese, and then gain the support of the United States. American aid, lavishly given to the tune of many hundreds of millions of dollars, though it rebuilt the cities and industry, brought no relief to the peasant. On the way, large sums stuck to the fingers of Filipino politicians. By the Bell Act of 1946, the Philippines remained directly tied to the United States economically and in questions of defence, and the Act extended the protection of the American tariff wall for another twenty-eight years, though US duties on Filipino imports would rise by five per cent per year for the last twenty years.

In 1948, after the refusal of an amnesty by the Huk leaders, their organisation was outlawed and attempts were made to suppress it by force. These failed, as all orthodox military campaigns against guerilla tactics are bound to do, and it was not until 1953, under the reforming administration of Ramon Magsaysay, that the peasants found someone in power who was interested in their problems. The Huk leader, Luis Taruc, surrendered, saying 'I must admit that our nation is now ushered into the right path and it is the duty of every citizen to support Magsaysay.' The old oligarchy, however, found Magsaysay too much of a reformer and frustrated his policies by every possible means. When he died in an air crash in 1957, it seemed to the peasant that they had lost their only friend and that the old guard were to have it all their own way once again. The Philippines remained an American satellite, to some extent an economic dependency by legal treaty, her foreign policy firmly in line with that of the United States.

*   *   *

When the Soviet Union at last declared war upon Japan, on 8 August 1945, she moved her armed forces rapidly into Manchukuo and occupied Korea north of the 38th parallel. The American army took over in the south. In February 1945, it had been agreed between Russia, Britain, the United States and China, at the Yalta Conference, that there should be a period of trusteeship before the setting up of an independent regime in Korea.

This was followed in December 1945 by an agreement concluded in Moscow between Britain, the US and the Soviet Union, for the establishment of a provisional Korean government under four-power trusteeship for a period of five years. Negotiations between the Russian and American commands in Korea to implement this programme through a joint Soviet-American commission failed, and in the summer of 1947 the Russian representatives on the commission were withdrawn.

Meanwhile, in their respective zones, the occupying powers had encouraged the establishment of 'independent' governments. In the Soviet zone, a North Korean Peoples' Government pledged to a revolutionary land policy was given office. In the south, despite economic chaos and the inability of politicians to cooperate, a South Korean Legislative Assembly was sponsored late in 1946. Again, the United States flooded money into the country, much of which was diverted from projects which might have relieved distress. In November 1947, the United Nations Organisation, at the suggestion of the United States and in the face of Russian opposition, formed a commission of nine states to go to Korea and help in the setting up of an all-Korean government. The North Korean administration refusing to cooperate, the commission went ahead with elections in South Korea. In May 1948 a constituent assembly had its first meeting, and in June elected a conservative, Synghman Rhee, who had been in exile since 1919, as president of the Republic of South Korea. In December 1948, the new state was officially recognised by UNO as the only legitimate government of Korea. In September 1948, the Russians had established the Korean Democratic Peoples' Republic, also claiming jurisdiction over the whole of the country. This regime was recognised by the Soviet Union and its satellites. The Russians and the Americans both removed their troops in 1949, but neither withdrew its influence nor its economic support. It seemed that Korea had merely replaced one occupation with two.

*   *   *

In many ways the future of Malaya at the end of the war presented problems differing from those of the rest of colonial Asia. Before the Japanese occupation, there had been little nationalist sentiment amongst the Malays, but the Japanese had succeeded in rousing them against the large Chinese minority by the use of such slogans as 'Malaya for the Malays'. The returning British found themselves faced with considerable disorder and violence, not, surprisingly enough, directed against themselves, but against the Chinese.

The climate of unease also produced an outbreak of violent crime with which at first the police forces were unable to cope.

An immense effort was put by the British into economic and social reconstruction, and when these activities were well on the way to some considerable success, the British put forward new plans for the progress of Malaya towards self-government. Unfortunately, the awareness shown in the British treatment of India did not extend to an understanding of the changes brought about by the Japanese occupation of Malaya. The pre-war system of virtually independent sultanates with British Residents as advisers seemed to offer no possibility of a viable existence for Malaya if the British withdrew. It seemed common sense to the British planners that, in the interests of security, a free Malaya must be a united Malaya. Consequently, in October 1945, the British negotiated with the sultans the transfer of their sovereign rights to the British government. This was successfully completed because the British representative was empowered to investigate the sultan's behaviour under Japanese occupation and decide whether a ruler should be allowed to retain his throne. Under the threat of removal, the sultans were only too happy to appease the avenging British. With these new treaties safely in hand, the British were prepared to form a new union of the nine Malay States together with Penang and Malacca. The new state would be a British protectorate. The sultans were to be left little more than their titles, all authority being invested in a central government at Kuala Lumpur. The proposals also included a provision concerning citizenship. This was to be granted to all persons born in the territory of the union or in Singapore, and to immigrants who had lived there for ten out of the preceding fifteen years.

The publication of these proposals in January 1946 produced an immediate uproar amongst the Malays, incensed at the thought of equal treatment being given to the hated Chinese and to Indians. One of the results was the formation by the prime minister of the state of Johore, Dato Onn Bin Jaafar, of the United Malay National Organisation (UMNO), pledged, as its founder put it, to 'warding off the devastating ignominy of race extinction'. Under this unexpected attack and pressure from pro-Malay British ex-civil servants, the British government dropped the proposals and after consultations with a wide range of 'representative opinion' ranging from the sultans to the minority groups, returned legal sovereignty to the states and set up a federation. By the new constitution which came into force on 1 February 1948, a Federal Executive and a Legislative Council were established under a British high commissioner. The Legislative Council could still be overruled by the high commissioner, and Britain retained control over foreign affairs and finance. Federal citizenship was to be granted to all Malays and those Indian and Chinese British subjects of the second generation born in federal territory. Other immigrants could acquire citizenship after fifteen years' residence in the new federation, provided they intended to make it their permanent place of residence. The new constitution favoured the Malays, and the minorities felt themselves deliberately discriminated against.

The new federation was greeted with the outbreak of a Communist revolt. The Communists had attempted to form 'mass organisations' and in partic' ular had sought to dominate the labour unions. They were successful mainly amongst the Chinese, and with that community's opposition to federation they increased their influence. However, the Communists were prevented from taking control of the labour organisations because of the work of British trade union officials who reorganised the Malayan unions.

In June 1948, widespread terrorist acts against Europeans and pro-KMT Chinese took place as a preliminary to piecemeal seizure of power by the Communists. But the measures taken by the British drove the Communists into the jungle. There, well-organised and supplied with arms, they began an outright war against the British. Again, orthodox strategy was unsuccess' ful against guerilla activity, and it took nearly five years of bitter and expen' sive fighting before any sign of victory appeared As the 'emergency', as the British preferred to call this civil war, dragged on, Malaya moved slowly to' wards an independence which finally came in 1957. Singapore had to wait two more years.

*   *   *

In April 1955, a meeting of Asian and African states took place at the mountain resort of Bandung in Java. Twenty-nine countries were repre' sented but the conference was dominated by the newly-freed nations of South Asia, and Communist China. The conference had very little real meaning and its effects have been negligible. The delegates had come not so much to negotiate or to create a new world; they were there, in fact, to bury Caesar – for the European Age was over.

The ghosts of imperialism still lurked about the fringes of the conference. Enclaves of the European still remained in Asia. Malaya was not yet free. Dutch Borneo, British Borneo, Sarawak, and New Guinea remained as continuing reminders of former domination. The first of the empires, the Portuguese, still held on to the first of the imperial capitals, Goa, as well as to

Timor and Macao. Hong Kong, a memory of wars for drugs and railways and concessions, still glittered tantalisingly at the mouth of the Canton river. But to the nations of Asia gathered at Bandung it appeared that they had emerged from the dark night of colonial oppression. Unfortunately, the glare of the daylight was as frightening as the dark. Asia had demanded a place in the world, but the world it found itself in had not done with the struggle for Asia. Two great forces appeared to dominate the coming battle – the United States and Russia. On the horizon loomed another and perhaps more frightening figure – that of Communist China. For the first time in the modern world, a united China, reinvigorated and dynamic, cast a lengthening shadow over South Asia.

VI

COMMUNISM IN CHINA

In order to display the full sequence of the rise of Communism in China it is necessary to return to the early months of 1927 when, after the conquest of Shanghai by Kuomintang forces, their leader Chiang Kai-shek turned against the Communists and slowly established himself as a military dic-tator (see p. 257 ff.).

In December 1926, as the KMT assault on the northern warlords gained momentum, the Russian adviser, Borodin, persuaded the KMT left wing to prevail upon the party's Central Executive Committee (CEC) to have the capital moved from Canton to Wuhan where Communist influence was strong. This was done against the wishes of Chiang, who would have pre-ferred the new capital to be at Nanchang where he had his headquarters. In March 1927, at the next meeting of the CEC, a new system of party admin-istration was adopted which made Chiang, who was then chairman of both the political and military councils, subordinate to a collective leadership dominated by the Communist and left-wing elements. The Communists, who were also in control of the arsenals at Canton and Wuhan, began to sabotage war material despatched to those KMT forces under Chiang's com-mand. Chiang's response was to capture Shanghai and Nanking (see p. 258). Two days after the capture of the latter, Chiang's supporters on the KMT's cen-tral supervisory committee declared that Communist activities were a prelude to an insurrection and authorised Chiang to arrest the party leaders. Despite attempts by Wang Ching-wei to re-unite the contending parties, Chiang moved against the Communists in his own area, and in particular against the General Labour Union in Shanghai. The 'April 12 Massacre', as the Communists called it, was soon followed by anti-Communist butchery and terror in Hangchow, Nanking, and Canton. [1]

Chiang's actions alarmed the KMT government at Wuhan, surrounded as it was by Communist forces, and at a session held under the chairmanship of Wang Ching-wei the party executive expelled Chiang and, on 17 April 1927, offered a reward of 250,000 dollars for his head. In reply, Chiang established a rival government at Nanking on the following day.

Before the news of Chiang's drive against the Communists had reached Moscow, the Comintern was still pressing for KMT-Communist cooperation as the only solution to China's problems. According to one source, as late as 5 April Stalin was saying of Chiang and the right wing of the KMT that 'they have to be utilised to the end, squeezed out like a lemon and then flung away'. Because of Comintern pressure, the congress of the Chinese Communist Party (CPC) held at Wuhan on 1 May officially adopted a policy of cooperation with the left wing of the KMT, headed by Wang. In order to do this, the CPC was prepared to make considerable revision in its declared aims. In the first case, it decided to modify its expropriationist land policy in deference to the predominantly landholding interests of the KMT. The party also endeavoured to restrict peasant-worker 'direct action', and after KMT forces from Wuhan had slaughtered Communists and their supporters in Changsha, even attempted to restrain peasant forces from taking reprisals.

These efforts at conciliation were brought to a head in June 1927 by an Indian Comintern representative, M. N. Roy, then in Wuhan. On 1 June, Roy showed Wang Ching-wei a document containing instructions to the CPC from the Comintern, in which the party was instructed to tone down its land policy even further, but at the same time to raise a new army of workers and peasants outside the control of the KMT. Roy, who apparently had hoped that the latter threat would inspire Wang to further cooperation, only succeeded in convincing him that any such association could only lead to his, and his friends', removal from power. Wang's response was to convene a meeting of loyal KMT leaders, and on 13 July, the Central Executive Committee ordered the CPC to withdraw from the KMT and the nationalist government.

In their demoralisation at the collapse of their plans, subjected to contra-

[1] The feel of these vicious times and, in particular, of the 'white' terror in Shanghai, can be found in that great novel of André Malraux, *La Condition Humaine*.

dictory pressures from the Comintern, and the growing strength of Chiang Kai-shek, the CPC declared its leaders to be 'right opportunists' and sabo-teurs of the revolution. In failure, there had to be scapegoats, and as Moscow could do no wrong these would have to be found amongst the Chinese. Ch'en Tu-hsiu, the secretary-general of the party, was singled out to carry the responsibility of failure, and removed from office. Ch'en was made of sterner stuff than many Communist leaders, and was not prepared to admit that he had made mistakes; he was finally expelled from the party in 1929.

Apart from the public fixing of blame, the Communists were forced to initiate a new policy, in order to 'save the revolution'. To hand were three possible instruments: the peasants, the workers, and the army. The first two had at one time rushed to join the mass movements organised by the Communists and had displayed their strength on more than one occasion. An armed uprising based upon such movements in alliance with an army revolt seemed the answer. On 1 August 1927, about 25,000 troops of Chiang's National Revolutionary Army broke out in revolt at Nanchang, but by 8 August had been driven from the city and defeated. A peasant rising in Hunan under the leadership of Mao Tse-tung was crushed in early September and the remnants were forced to flee into Kiangsi province, where they established a rural soviet. In Canton, an attempt on 11 December at a workers' rising was defeated by apathy and the foreknowledge of the local KMT commander. Several important CPC leaders and a number of Rus-sians were killed. The Communists had left 'direct action' until too late. The KMT was now strong enough to crush opposition within its own territories

The sixth congress of the CPC, as we have seen, was held in July 1928, no. on Chinese soil but in Moscow; its very presence in the Russian capital wat a symbol of the party's failure. The lack of success at 'direct action' resulted in yet another change of leadership. To the post of secretary-general, the con-gress elected an illiterate ex-boatman, Hsiang Chung-fa, and the new Central Committee included Li Li-san, Chou En-lai and Mao Tse-tung. The latter was not present in Moscow but in retreat in the mountainous area between Hunan and Kiangsi. The new headquarters of the CPC in China was, ironically enough, safe in the International Concession at Shanghai.

The actual direction of the party, because of the incompetence of the new secretary-general, was now in the hands of Li Li-san. Li's policy was to continue armed uprisings, but on a greater scale than before, in an attempt to capture urban centres. These campaigns, which had some small initial success, merely antagonised the Chinese people who had to suffer them *and* the KMT counter-attacks that followed. In March 1931, Li was summoned to Moscow and remained there in exile until the close of World War II.

A new leader, Ch'en Shao-yu, a theorist rather than a revolutionary, still continued the policy of military revolts, all of which failed. Insulated in the foreign settlement at Shanghai, the party leadership had little real power, especially as the centre of Communist strength in China was undoubtedly in the Kiangsi soviet and its chairman, Mao Tse-tung. In 1932, Ch'en left for Moscow as the CPC representative on the Comintern and in 1933 the Shanghai Party Central Committee agreed to transfer itself to Juichin, the capital of Mao's 'Chinese Soviet Republic' in Kiangsi. This triumph for Mao was finalised in January 1935 when the leadership, both in name and in fact, was invested in him. Policy, henceforward, was to turn away from military uprisings and attempts to establish urban footholds. The revolution was now to have its source in the rural areas, and its armies were to consist of the peasant in arms. Once the countryside was in their hands, the Communists reasoned that the cities would fall of their own accord.

When Mao and the remnants of his peasant army had fled into the Hunan-Kiangsi border areas in September 1927, he had added to his men those of two local bandits. Out of these he had formed the First Division of the Chinese Workers' and Peasants' Red Army. In April 1928, survivors of the abortive rising in Nanchang also joined, under their commander Chu Teh. Mao's forces now numbered some ten thousand men armed with two thousand rifles. These forces later became the Fourth Chinese Workers' and Peasants' Red Army under the command of Chu Teh, with Mao as political commissar. Between 1927 and 1931, twenty-six such Red Armies were organised in various parts of China. By 1930, according to official CPC histories, they totalled some 60,000 men, half of whom were in the areas controlled by Mao.

These forces were not left unmolested by the KMT, and from July 1928 onwards larger and larger Nationalist forces were sent against them until, beginning November 1930, KMT troops engaged in five 'extermination drives' against Mao's Chinese Soviet Area. Increasing numbers of KMT troops were employed in these 'drives' until, in 1932, a total of over half a million men, under the personal command of Chiang Kai-shek, drove the Red Army out of the Soviet Area and into Szechuan. A final drive, in October 1933, allegedly by over a million men and two hundred aircraft, set the Red Army off on the now famous 'Long March'. On 15 October 1934, nearly 130,000 soldiers accompanied by party officials set out from Juichin to march over almost impassable mountains, rivers and empty grasslands, six thousand miles to Northern Shensi where they finally arrived in October 1935.[1] In December they made their headquarters at Yenan.

The new area had certain strategical advantages. It removed the Com, munists from the centres of KMT strength. Northern Shensi was also close to the Soviet Union and its satellite Outer Mongolia. It was also nearer to the advancing Japanese, and it is reasonably sure that the CPC hoped to provoke the Japanese into a general war which would raise Communist prestige with the Japanese-hating Chinese people, as well as relieving the Communists from KMT military pressure. Their weak military position convinced the CPC leaders that without the diversion of an external enemy, KMT forces would eventually destroy them. Furthermore, a new alliance with Chiang Kai-shek would undoubtedly lead to opportunities which next time would not be allowed to slip from their grasp.

While the 'Long March' was still in progress, a conference was held at Maoerhkai near the Szechuan-Sinkiang border, where the final decision to move to Shensi was made. Apart from this major decision which was taken against opposition from Chang Kuo-t'ao – who commanded the First Red Army – a new general policy was also decided upon. On 1 August 1935, a proclamation was issued appealing to all Chinese of whatever political colour to join an Anti-Japanese National United Front. The CPC leaders made a special appeal to Chiang Kai-shek to stop the fight 'against his own people' and to organise a new army of national salvation against the Japan, ese invader.

This appeal coincided with an announcement made at the seventh world conference of the Comintern on 2 August, by Georgi Dimitrov, of the policy of a world united front against Fascist aggression. From Shensi, the CPC intensified its anti-Japanese united front propaganda, but, in the ab, sence of any positive response from Chiang, still remained anti-KMT in practice. When, however, Japanese operations on the borders of Outer Mongolia and the USSR were extended, and Japan became a signatory of the Anti-Comintern Pact of 25 November 1936, the Soviet Union in her own interests began to promote the idea of a united Chinese front against the Japanese. The CPC shifted its activities from propaganda to agitation amongst the Manchurian troops of the 'Young Marshal', Chang Hsüeh-liang, in an

---

[1] According to an official party history, the Red Army totalled 300,000 men before the 'Long March', but only 30,000 actually arrived in Shensi. Ho Kan-shih: *A History of the Modern Chinese Revolution*, Peking, 1960.

endeavour to raise anti-Japanese feelings. One of the results of these activities was the famous 'Sian Incident'.

The 'Young Marshal', son of the anti-Communist warlord, Chang Tso-lin, who had been murdered by the Japanese (see p. 272), was in 1936 one of Chiang's deputies and commander-in-chief of the Bandit [i.e. Communist] Suppression Campaign in the north-west. However, as Japanese pressure upon him increased, his attitude towards Chiang changed, and he charged his leader with ignoring the Japanese menace and fighting the Communists against the true interests of the country. On 12 December 1936, Chiang Kai-shek, while on a visit to Sian, was kidnapped by the 'Young Marshal' and held for a fortnight. During this period, the CPC intervened to save Chiang's life. This they did under direct instructions from Moscow. Chiang was released but only on the condition that the civil war be terminated and a new anti-Japanese alliance between the CPC and the KMT concluded. The terms of this new association were made by the Communists and accepted by the KMT in February 1937.

In consequence of the alliance, the Communists agreed that the Red Army should be reorganised under Chiang's authority, land reform would be stopped, and the former Chinese Soviet Republic converted into a special area within the Republic of China. The CPC undertook to cease agitation and paid public deference to the 'Three People's Principles' of Sun Yat-sen, as 'an urgent necessity for modern China', and promised to put all their effort into the fight for their achievement. After ten years of fighting, the civil war was temporarily submerged in the greater war against Japanese imperialism.

After the incident on the Marco Polo Bridge on 7 July 1937 (see p. 000) began the war against Japan, the terms of the new alliance were quickly put into practice. In August the Red Army officially became the Eighth Route Army of the Nationalist forces. Though it remained under its old commanders, the Nationalist war department paid the troops as well as dictating the area and scope of their activities. By this method, Chiang hoped to exercise some measure of control over the size of the Communist forces.

As the tide of Japanese advance overwhelmed China and drove back the lines of orthodox military defence, both Communist and Nationalist guerilla groups remained behind in the thinly-held Japanese areas. The Communists, with a decade of partisan experience behind them, not only harassed the Japanese but absorbed the Nationalists into their own organisation and even displaced such Nationalist administration as continued to function behind the Japanese advance. These clashes of interest continued, despite the Nationalist government's attempt to define spheres of operation and responsibility. Negotiations reached a deadlock in October 1940, and the Nationalist government ordered Communist forces to move north of the Yellow River. Alleging that the Communist New Fourth Army had disobeyed these orders, a Nationalist force in Southern Anhwei attacked and killed the Fourth Army's commander in January 1941, captured his deputy, and destroyed the headquarters units. Clashes continued and resulted in the slowing down of the campaign against the Japanese. The Communists alleged, and there seems no reason to doubt their figures, that by late 1940 the Nationalists were using over 200,000 well-armed men in an attempt to establish a military and economic blockade of the Communist-held areas. The Nationalists, in defence, quoted Mao as saying that *his* policy was 'seventy per cent self-development [i.e. expansion of Communist control], twenty per cent compromise, and ten per cent fighting the Japanese'. Whatever the truth of this, there is no doubt that the Communists were concentrating their efforts on expanding and consolidating their own positions.

The Southern Anhwei incident naturally had serious repercussions upon the 'alliance' between the CPC and the KMT. In March 1941, the Communists refused to send delegates to the meeting of the People's Political Council (PPC) at the Nationalist capital Chungking. Normally, Communist representatives had attended the meetings of the PPC, but this time they were unwilling to do so unless recognition was given to the Communist-sponsored regimes behind the Japanese lines. To these demands, Chiang Kai-shek replied: 'There can only be one regime – there cannot be two regimes – within a country'. He was wrong, for whatever he might say, two regimes actually existed. The political stalemate continued, but for the most part, military clashes no longer took place until, in May 1944, negotiations were again opened for a settlement of differences. No progress was made, and in September of the same year Communist demands had increased to a call for a 'coalition government of all anti-Japanese parties and groups'. This demand for participation in the central government of China was an index of the expansion of Communist strength. By the end of 1943, the Communist-held 'liberated areas' had a population of over eighty million people. These enclaves in nominally Japanese-held and puppet-controlled China consisted of five large 'anti-Japanese bases' in northern China, with a population of about fifty million people; about thirty million people in central China, organised into eight bases; and in areas on Hainan island

and along the Canton-Kowloon railway (see map p. 336). By the time of the Japanese surrender, the Communists controlled nineteen 'liberated areas' with a population of one hundred million.

Communist armed forces had also increased formidably from (according to Communist figures) 80,000 in 1937 to 570,000 regulars and 2,200,000 militia by the end of 1944. At the same time, the party organisation had been tightened and streamlined by a 'Party Rectification Movement' which ensured the unchallenged authority of Mao Tse-tung. With a new, well-disciplined party machine, a large well-indoctrinated army, and the revived slogans of land redistribution and agrarian reform, the CPC was ready for the challenge of the Japanese collapse.

In the meantime, the KMT, locked in the rural fastness of Chungking, moved further and further into the quicksand of reaction. Cut off from the connection with coastal capitalism which had given it birth, the party found itself inevitably drifting into the hands of landlord pressure groups. The 'liberal' urban capitalists and Westernised bourgeois who still thought in terms of democracy, even if at some vaguely distant date, were replaced by the very class against which the peasant would be willing and anxious to fight. Communism had failed in the industrial areas to rally proletarian opinion to its side, but the land-hunger of the peasant, primitive and instinctive, could be used by a trained elite to gain power. The KMT, with its new land-owning leadership, could, without difficulty, be turned into the living symbol of oppression and exploitation.

As Nationalist troops moved back to the coastal areas after the defeat of Japan, the disaster in KMT leadership became apparent. Returning to the industrial cities, the KMT brought with it urban-hating landowners in positions of power. The Nationalist government became anti-capitalist, not in a Marxist but in a pre-industrial sense, and antagonised the very middle classes whose support it needed so badly. The government, with its reactionary, small-minded rural landlord leadership, proliferated inefficiency and corruption. Uncontrolled inflation ruined the small business man and brought poverty to the professional classes. Capitalists and industrialists, in fine contradiction, turned in their despair to the Communists, as did most of the intelligentsia, horrified by the dead face of atavistic reaction represented by the KMT. In contrast, the CPC seemed to offer something dynamic, forward-looking, and above all inspiring. Furthermore, it was backed by real power exercised in the 'liberated areas'. The KMT, at the greatest crisis in its existence, had moved backwards into the old China. In between it and the new China of Communism, the liberal, Westernised nationalist would inevitably be crushed and with him the hope of a free and democratic China.

Two days after the Soviet declaration of war on Japan (8 August 1945), the Communist general, Chu Teh, ordered his troops to take over the areas of former Japanese occupation. The next day, Chiang Kai-shek instructed Chu to cancel these orders and await further ones from him. This Chu ignored and clashes between Nationalist and Communist troops in the former Japanese-held areas were the beginning of the final struggle which was to destroy the KMT and drive it, a refugee, into the island of Formosa.

Initially, the Communists once again called for their admittance into a coalition government as a natural extension of the wartime 'united' front. The United States, believing that she had spent billions of dollars and many thousands of lives in order to save China from disintegration and aggression, felt herself involved in that country's destiny. Under pressure from Washington, the Nationalist government invited Mao Tse-tung to Chungking, and talks began on 28 August 1945. An agreement was finally concluded on 10 October, in which it was decided to call a Political Consultative Conference with eight delegates from the KMT, seven from the CPC, and eleven from other minor political groups.

While these negotiations were going on in Chungking, clashes between Communist and Nationalist forces were increasing in scale until at the end of 1945 the Nationalist government decided to mount a full-scale offensive against the Communists. At this stage, the United States once more entered the arena. On 15 December, President Truman announced that he was sending General Marshall, former chief of staff of the US Army, to mediate between the opposing parties. As a result of Marshall's efforts a cease-fire agreement was signed on 10 January 1946. The carrying-out of this agreement was to be supervised by an Executive Headquarters at Peking, consisting of Nationalist, Communist, and American representatives. In these happier circumstances, the Political Consultative Conference held its first meeting.

As its name implies, the PCC was without power, but it proceeded to adopt resolutions calling for considerable reform, including an expansion of political activity, the holding of popular elections, agrarian and educational reforms, and the demobilisation and reorganisation of the armed forces. There is little doubt that either side held the slightest belief in the possibility of their implementation. The KMT leadership hated and feared the Communists as well as disliking the idea of democratic reform in principle. The CPC leaders must have been fully aware of this. The chances of compromise were remote but the Communists had everything to gain from protracted nego, tiations. Both sides intended a showdown, and time was on the side of the Communists. American interference, however well meant, only deprived the KMT of a chance to defeat the Communists while it was still in a position to do so.

Negotiations continued, while each side prepared for war. In Manchuria, still under Russian occupation, the Communist forces continued their training with the approval and technical assistance of the Soviet army. Fighting between the Nationalists and the Communists broke out in June 1946, and in August General Marshall admitted that mediation had failed.

In the beginning it seemed that the numerically superior and better armed nationalist troops would defeat the Communists, and they made considerable advances in the north, even, in March 1947, capturing the Communist capital at Yenan. But by July the tide had turned and the Communists, well supplied with arms from Japanese dumps in Soviet-occupied Manchuria, began an offensive. The People's Liberation Army, as the Red forces now called themselves, appealed to the Chinese people to overthrow Chiang and help build a new China. More pertinently, it announced that landlords would be liquidated in the liberated areas, and the unfulfilled promise of the 'Father of the Nation', Sun Yat-sen, that land would be given to the tillers of the land, would at last be realised. The appeal of this was not restricted only to the peasant actually upon the land and awaiting liberation in Nationalist territory, who, in exchange for land, would assist the Com, munists. It was also to the soldier in the Nationalist armies, himself more often than not a landless peasant.

By October 1948, the whole of north-east China including the valuable industrial area of Manchuria (Manchukuo) was in Communist hands. The collapse of KMT forces in this area meant the surrender of over 470,000 men armed with the most modern American equipment, most of whom joined the Communist forces. The Communists now mounted a force of over three million men, while the numbers in the Nationalist armies had de, creased to less than two and a half million. KMT losses by surrender contin, ued, though some units fought with determination and even heroism. In January 1949, Tientsin and Peking surrendered, and in April the People's Liberation Army crossed the Yangtze and occupied Nanking. Shanghai fell to the Communists in February and Hankow, Wuchang, and Hanyang soon followed. In October, Canton – to which the Nationalist capital had been moved – went over to the PLA. With mainland China almost under their complete control, the Communists on 1 October 1949 announced the establishment of the People's Republic of China.

KMT forces still held out in parts of the west and south-west, and the Nationalist capital was once again removed, to Chungking. But the final victory of the Communists was inevitable, for the people of China were at last in a position to make their opinion felt against a corrupt and reactionary regime which had started with great promise of progress but had bogged down into a narrow dictatorship of self-seeking and self-interest. The Chinese people withdrew their support from the Nationalist government, believing that nothing could be worse than a continuance of KMT rule. Chiang retired to the island of Formosa which, with some of the offshore islands, remain the final enclave of Nationalist rule and a continual threat to world peace.

As the Red armies spread over China, bringing with them disciplined and incorruptible officials, something without precedent in the history of modern China had appeared. The Communists established a truly Chinese government in a China free from foreign concessions, business men, 'advisers', customs officials, engineers, missionaries, and gunboats. To ordinary people it meant a new sense of dignity and security. The West, whose coming had disintegrated the old standards, which had glared arrogantly at China from the skyscrapers of the Bund at Shanghai, had been driven out. But instead of a step forward, China had taken a leap backwards into an orthodoxy as rigid as that of the most powerful of the Chinese emperors. To a new sense of superiority over the foreign 'barbarians' have been added the old universalist pretensions in a Marxist guise. When the old colonial dependencies achieved freedom, it seemed that the war against the West had been won, but the Communist victory in China brought frightening proof that it had only begun and that a new and dynamic China was about to embark upon its own 'civilising mission' with the possibility of disintegrating *Western* civilisation as some ironic retaliation for the destruction of its own.

4

The New World of Asia

THOUGH THE YEAR 1955 saw the end of Asia's 'European Age', and is the terminal point of this book, the revolution in Asia was only beginning. The process of history does not pause for the historian to analyse it, and such convenient divisions as he makes – however logical they may appear – are essentially arbitrary. The process of history cannot be interrupted. One of the problems of historical interpretation is the extent to which subsequent events can be allowed to colour the historian's appreciation of those that preceded them.

The effects of Western domination in Asia are still implicit in present events and will continue to be so in the future. Apart from the division of India, the old strategic frontiers established by the imperial powers – often without geographic, and never with ethnic, justification – still remain. These frontiers are often, as in the case of the borderlands where India and China meet, the source of continuing incidents with all their attendant problems. The industrial techniques and scientific know-how brought by the West are being adopted on an ever-widening scale. Educational systems are still, basically, Western in concept. Public services – transportation, medicine and social welfare – are all patterned to Western standards even in China. The indigenous religions, though often reinforced in their orthodox rigidity as a weapon against the West, are becoming more and more the target of that secularist spirit which is essentially Western in its origin. In the one-time colonial possessions, genuine or quasi-democratic institutions still persist, though how long they will continue to do so is quite another matter.

Apart from the threat of Communist dictatorship – a very real but not yet overwhelming danger – the future of democracy in Asia lies in its efficiency in getting things done. Democracy and its institutions suffer in Asia from what is in fact their greatest virtue. The slow adaptation of institutions and the questioning caution of the evolutionary approach to political and social problems are organic in the democratic idea. Asia fought for the right to operate those institutions in which the West's superiority was supposed to lie. In Asia, power had magical sources and society is a reflection of some divine order. The European, from the Asian point of view, had magical weapons in the steamship, the railway, and the electric telegraph. Because he possessed them he must also, quite logically, possess superior occult powers. At first it was assumed that his religion might give a clue to the European's mastery of the forces of nature but this was proved not to be true. Perhaps, then, the key lay in democracy and those institutions which the European was so reluctant to grant to his colonial subjects.

Among the colonial nationalists, very few considered the possibility that democracy might not function outside the civilisation from which it had emerged. To them it was a total thing, as precise, functional and all-embracing as a religion. The radical statesmen and writers, and the Labour politicians who were the inheritors of the radical tradition, only confirmed the nationalist – not just in British possessions but in those of the other colonial powers – in their belief that this was so. Furthermore, the struggle for equality was just as much a struggle for the right to acquire Western-style freedom, as it was for the possession of the machine and the manufactured products of high-level economies. Democracy was a symbol of national maturity.

Ironically enough, it was the imperialists – of whatever political colour – who questioned the suitability of democratic institutions for the government of alien societies. In this they were right, for such institutions had emerged in the West from a social complex radically different from any existing in the East. Democracy was an expression of strictly Western idealism, and throughout the history of Europe people had fought and died in order to achieve its benefits. Above all, in the twentieth century, 'freedom' – which is the essence of democracy – was a special type of freedom. In the West, a man feels himself free when his utilitarian services pass into his own keeping, when within the structure of society he can exercise the right of choice. In the East, freedom has quite a different meaning. There, it is quite simply release from the limitations of objective existence – not a material thing but a religious one.

When the British Conservative leader and former prime minister, A. J. Balfour, answered criticisms of British administration in Egypt in the House of Commons in 1910, he outlined his views on the unsuitability of Western institutions for alien societies:

> 'You cannot treat the problems with which we have to deal in Egypt and elsewhere as if they were problems affecting the Isle of Wight or the

West Riding of Yorkshire. They belong to a wholly different character...

Look at the facts in the case. Western nations as soon as they emerge
into history show the beginnings of those capacities for self-government,
not always associated, I grant, with all the virtues or all the merits, but
still having merits of their own. Nations of the West have shown these
virtues from the beginning... You may look through the whole history
of the Orientals in what is called, broadly speaking, the East, and you
never find traces of self-government. All their great centuries – and they
have been great – have been passed under despotisms. All their great
contributions to civilisation – and they have been great – have been made
under that form of government. Conqueror has succeeded conqueror;
one domination has followed another; but never in all the revolutions of
fate and fortune have you seen one of those nations of its own notion
establish what we, from a Western point of view, call self-government.
That is a fact. It is not a question of superiority or inferiority.'

Balfour was right, however much radicals and colonial nationalists might
brush history aside as irrelevant. When the West retreated from Asia, it left
behind the ready-made institutions of democracy as it did the roads and the
railways, and Asians quite impartially expected them all to work with
equal efficiency. When they did not, faith in the institutions declined. In India,
under the dynamic genius of Nehru, the great experiment of adaptation is
taking place, an experiment to produce a wholly Asian brand of democracy.
Elsewhere the structure has crumbled into various forms of absolutism,
though all pay lip-service to the still magical word 'democracy' and maintain the façade of its institutions. In time, there is no doubt that the newly
independent nations can work out their own forms of democracy to suit the
cultural heritage of their peoples. But if there is one thing Asia – and the
world of which it forms so catalytic a part – does not have, it is time.

The people of Asia are demanding more than freedom. They are demanding not so much a better life, as life itself. The struggle of Asia against
Western domination was a struggle of infinitesimal minorities, and partly-
Westernised minorities at that. They led, in whichever direction they
pleased, a vast amorphous peasantry, who listened to their prophecies and
believed in the imminence of a Golden Age. Now the masses are calling
for the benefits of freedom which they were so glibly promised. The men
who fought for democracy throughout the history of the Western world
knew that it could not be bought in the bargain basement, but achieved

only through major sacrifice and apparent set-backs. But the down-trodden peasant of Asia is beginning to raise his head – and his hand – against the inheritors of the colonial powers. In China he sees a new faith which apparently brings the material gifts that freedom and democracy once promised. Those intellectuals who have witnessed the failure of Western institutions, and to whom the example of China represents a speedier and surer way to happiness *in their own life-time*, have in the peasant a new force for revolutionary change.

The struggle for Asia did not end with the passing of the European Age. The battle now is between those who hope to synthesise a new and peculiarly Asian form of democracy, and those who represent the old absolutism refurbished in a Communist disguise. The offensive is still – as the foregoing pages have shown – against the West, and the prize is no longer the freedom of colonial dependencies, but the freedom of the world. Asia still needs the West, to fight the consequences of Western imperialism. The West, more than at any time during the colonial period, needs Asia. Free Asia does not want only money and expertise; it needs sympathy and understanding for the revolution that is still in progress. To a large extent, Asians still look to the West for something greater and more inspiring than 'foreign aid'. If the West cannot supply it – and it can only do so by looking forward with a positive faith of its own – Asia will choose Communism; and it will be that forgotten figure, the peasant, who, in the final analysis, will make the choice.

THE MAPS

ASIA IN 1961

S O V

BLACK SEA

Ankara

KAZAKHST

Poti

CASPIAN SEA

ARAL
SEA

Erivan

TURKEY

LEBANON

Beirut

Baku

Tashk

OXUS R.

SYRIA

Tel-Aviv

Damascus

Tigris

Samar

ISRAEL

Amman

JORDAN

IRAQ

Baghdad

Teheran

Euphrates R.

I R A N

(PERSIA)

AFGHANISTAN

Kabul

Kuwait

SAUDI

PERSIAN GULF

WEST

RED SEA

ARABIA

TRUCIAL OMAN

PAKISTAN

INDUS R.

La

Karachi

YEMEN

O M A N

ADEN

A R A B I A N

Bombay

S E A

Goa (Port.)

Cali

I N D I A N

1800

1860

1942: Maximum extent of Japanese conquests in World War II
is shown by a broken line

1955

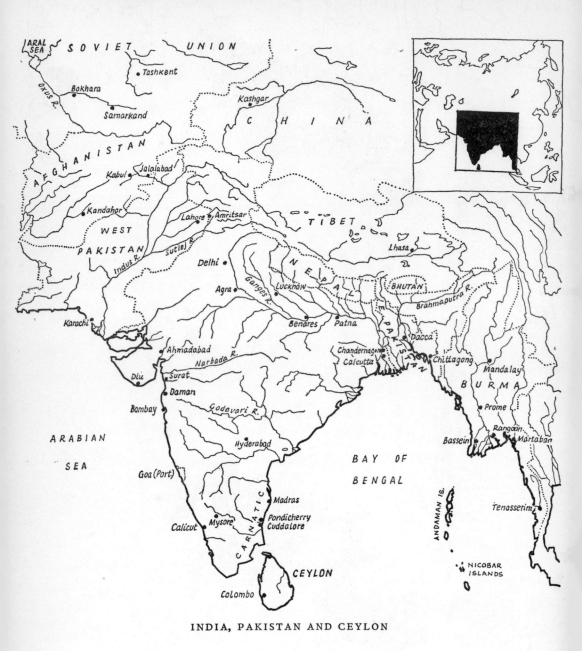

INDIA, PAKISTAN AND CEYLON

MAINLAND SOUTH-EAST ASIA

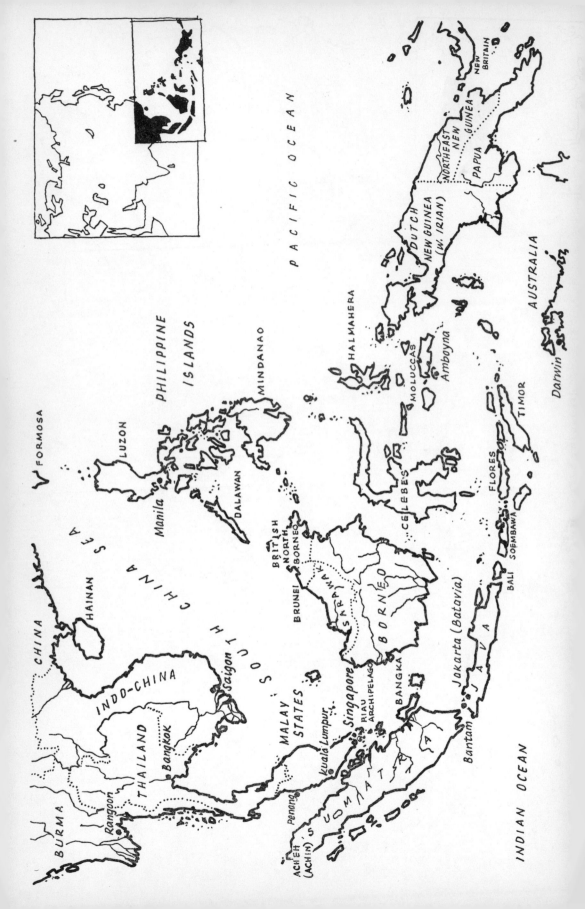

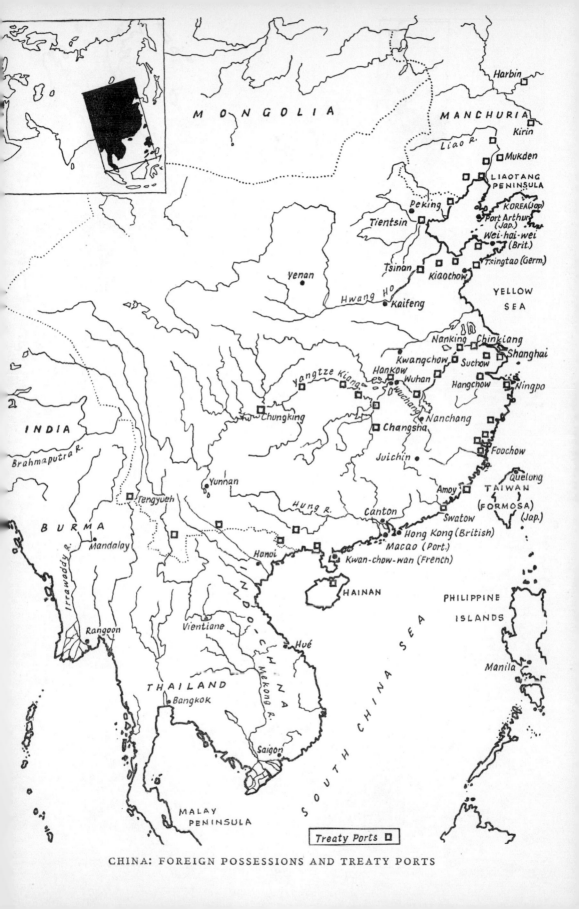

CHINA: FOREIGN POSSESSIONS AND TREATY PORTS

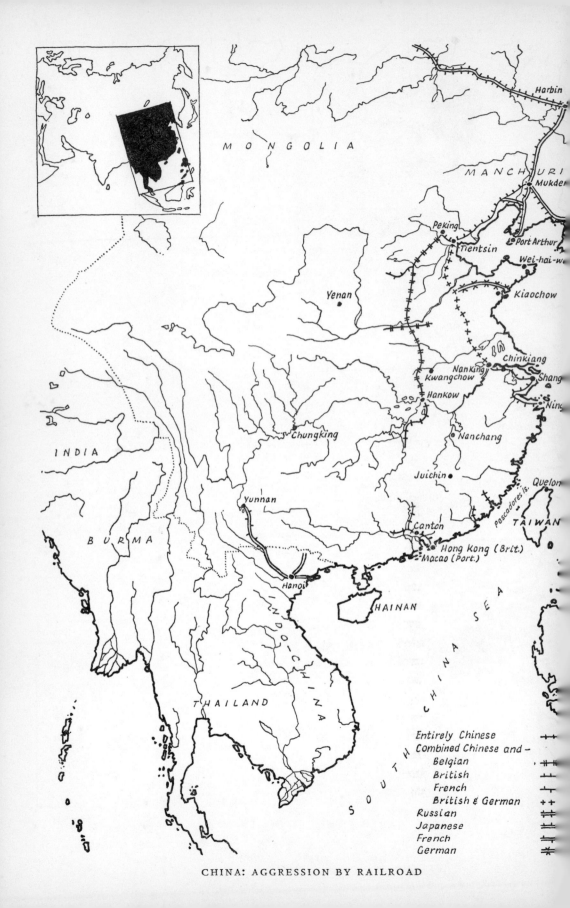

CHINA: AGGRESSION BY RAILROAD

JAPAN AND MARITIME CHINA

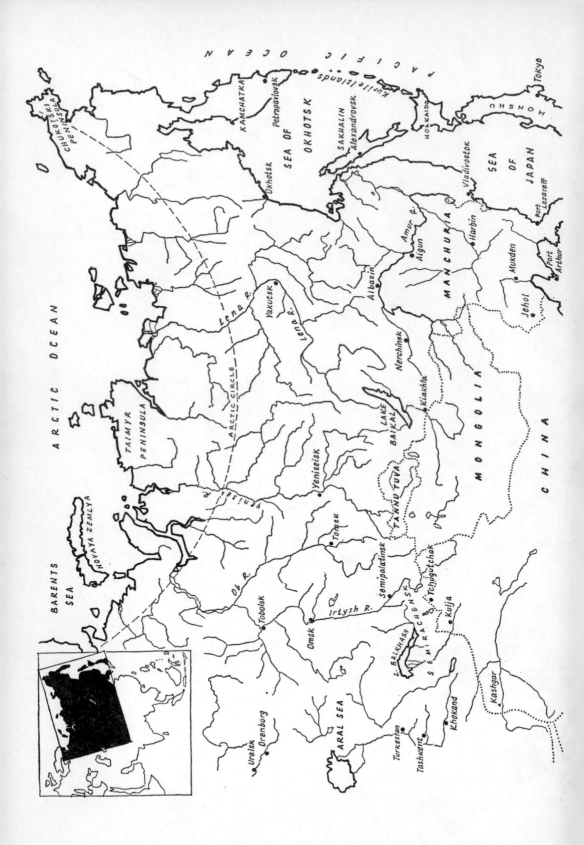

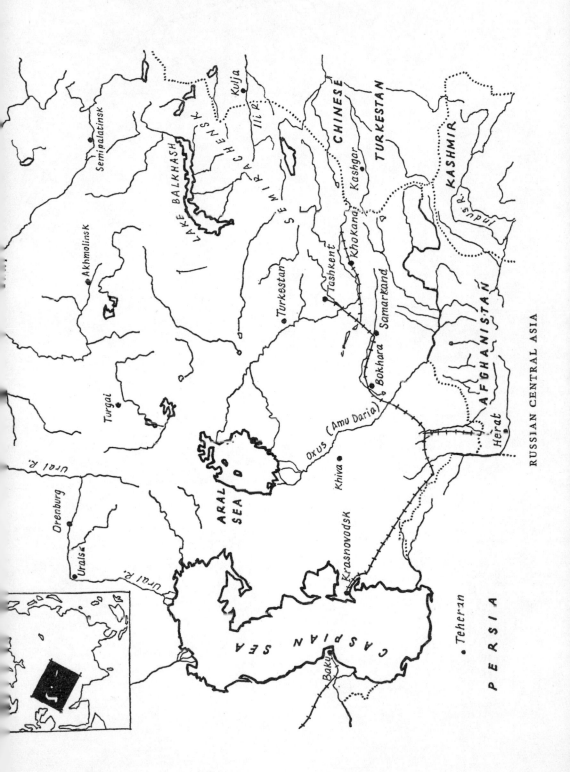

Semipalatinsk

Kulja

Ili R.

CHINESE

TURKESTAN

KASHMIR

Akhmolinsk

LAKE BALKHASH

SEMIRECHENSK

S E M I R E C H E N S K

Kashgar

Indus R.

Khokand

Turkestan

Tashkent

Samarkand

Turgai

Bokhara

AFGHANISTAN

Oxus (Amu Daria)

Herat

A R A L S E A

Khiva

Orenburg

Ural R.

Uralsk

Krasnovodsk

Teheran

C A S P I A N   S E A

P E R S I A

Baku

RUSSIAN CENTRAL ASIA

A NOTE ON BIBLIOGRAPHICAL SOURCES

INSTEAD of supplying the more usual bibliography – which tends to consist of a selection of titles designed to bolster the author's thesis and which, representing a very small percentage of the works available, is generally inadequate – I give here a list of bibliographies covering the various areas with which the present work is concerned. All include works outside the purely historical field, and form an admirable foundation on which to base wider reading. Most, it will be observed, are published in the USA—an indication of the importance attached to Asian studies there.

India
> Selected bibliography in EDWARDES, MICHAEL: *A History of India.* London and New York 1961
> WILSON, P.: *Government and Politics of India and Pakistan 1885–1955.* Berkeley California 1956

Mainland South-East Asia
> EMBREE, J. F. and DODSON, L. O.: *Bibliography of the Peoples and Cultures of Mainland South-East Asia.* New Haven 1950
> HOBBS, CECIL C.: *South-East Asia: an annotated bibliography of selected reference sources.* Washington 1952

Burma
> *Annotated Bibliography of Burma.* New Haven 1956

Siam/Thailand
> TOSHIO KAWABE: *Bibliography of Thai Studies (in Western languages).* Tokyo 1957

Indo-China
> HOBBS, CECIL C. (and associates): *Indochina: a bibliography of land and peoples.* Washington 1950

Indonesia
> KENNEDY, R.: *Bibliography of Indonesian Peoples and Cultures.* Revised edition, New Haven 1955

Philippines
  Selected Bibliography of the Philippines. New Haven 1956
Far East
  The best general bibliography is KERNER, R. J.: *North-eastern Asia:
  A Selected Bibliography.* Berkeley California 1939
China
  CORDIER, H.: *Bibliotheca Sinica.* Paris 1904–8, supplement 1922–24
  YUAN T'UNG-LI: *China in Western Literature.* (Continuation of
  CORDIER, above). New Haven 1958
Japan
  BORTON, ELISÉEFF (and others): *A Selected List of Books and
  Articles on Japan in English, French and German.* Cambridge Mass. 1954
Russia in Asia
  MORLEY, C.: *Guide to Research in Russian History.* Syracuse NY 1951

The reader is also referred to the bibliographies contained in works listed
in the footnotes throughout the text.

INDEX